WAS 1 ESDRAS FIRST?

Society of Biblical Literature

Ancient Israel and Its Literature

Steven L. McKenzie, General Editor

Editorial Board

Suzanne Boorer
Victor H. Matthews
Thomas C. Römer
Benjamin D. Sommer
Nili Wazana

Number 7

WAS 1 ESDRAS FIRST?
An Investigation into the Priority and Nature of 1 Esdras

Volume Editor
Lisbeth S. Fried

WAS 1 ESDRAS FIRST?

An Investigation into the Priority
and Nature of 1 Esdras

edited by

Lisbeth S. Fried

Society of Biblical Literature
Atlanta

WAS 1 ESDRAS FIRST?
An Investigation into the Priority and Nature of 1 Esdras

Copyright © 2011 by the Society of Biblical Literature

All rights reserved. No part of this work may be reproduced or transmitted in any form or by any means, electronic or mechanical, including photocopying and recording, or by means of any information storage or retrieval system, except as may be expressly permitted by the 1976 Copyright Act or in writing from the publisher. Requests for permission should be addressed in writing to the Rights and Permissions Office, Society of Biblical Literature, 825 Houston Mill Road, Atlanta, GA 30329 USA.

Library of Congress Cataloging-in-Publication Data

Was 1 Esdras first? : an investigation into the priority and nature of 1 Esdras / edited by Lisbeth S. Fried.
    p. cm. — (Society of Biblical Literature : ancient Israel and its literature ; no. 7)
    Includes bibliographical references and index.
    ISBN 978-1-58983-544-3 (paper binding : alk. paper) — ISBN 978-1-58983-545-0 (electronic format)
    1. Bible. O.T. Apocrypha. Esdras, 1st—Criticism, interpretation, etc.—Congresses. I. Fried, Lisbeth S. II. Society of Biblical Literature. III. Title: Was 1 Esdras first?
BS1715.52.W37 2011
229'.106—dc22
2011008515

Typeset by Forthcoming Publications Ltd
www.forthpub.com

Printed on acid-free, recycled paper conforming to
ANSI/NISO Z39.48-1992 (R1997) and ISO 9706:1994
standards for paper permanence.

For Michael

Contents

Acknowledgments ix
Abbreviations xi

INTRODUCTION
    Lisbeth S. Fried 1

ARTICLES ARGUING AGAINST THE PRIORITY OF EZRA–NEHEMIAH

LOWER CRITICISM AND HIGHER CRITICISM:
THE CASE OF 1 ESDRAS
    Deirdre N. Fulton and Gary N. Knoppers 11

CHICKEN OR EGG? WHICH CAME FIRST, 1 ESDRAS OR EZRA–NEHEMIAH?
    Lester L. Grabbe 31

THE RELATIONSHIP BETWEEN EZRA–NEHEMIAH AND 1 ESDRAS
    Adrian Schenker 45

ARTICLES ARGUING AGAINST THE PRIORITY OF 1 ESDRAS

THE STORY OF THE THREE YOUTHS AND THE COMPOSITION OF 1 ESDRAS
    Bob Becking 61

THE SECOND YEAR OF DARIUS
    Kristin De Troyer 73

WHY THE STORY OF THE THREE YOUTHS IN 1 ESDRAS?
    Lisbeth S. Fried 83

WHY 1 ESDRAS IS PROBABLY NOT AN EARLY VERSION
OF THE EZRA–NEHEMIAH TRADITION
   Juha Pakkala 93

ANCIENT COMPOSITION PATTERNS MIRRORED IN 1 ESDRAS
AND THE PRIORITY OF THE CANONICAL COMPOSITION TYPE
   Zipora Talshir 109

LITERARY QUESTIONS BETWEEN EZRA, NEHEMIAH, AND 1 ESDRAS
   James C. VanderKam 131

REMEMBER NEHEMIAH:
1 ESDRAS AND THE *DAMNATIO MEMORIAE NEHEMIAE*
   Jacob L. Wright 145

ARTICLES INVESTIGATING THE NATURE OF 1 ESDRAS

THE IMAGE OF THE KING(S) IN 1 ESDRAS
   Sebastian Grätz 167

DARIUS' COURT AND THE GUARDSMEN'S DEBATE:
HELLENISTIC GREEK ELEMENTS IN 1 ESDRAS
   Paul B. Harvey, Jr. 179

CYCLICAL TIME AND CATALOGUES:
THE CONSTRUCTION OF MEANING IN 1 ESDRAS
   Sylvie Honigman 191

1 ESDRAS: ITS GENRE, LITERARY FORM, AND GOALS
   Sara Japhet 209

THE RENDERING OF 2 CHRONICLES 35–36 IN 1 ESDRAS
   Ralph W. Klein 225

1 ESDRAS AS REWRITTEN BIBLE?
   H. G. M. Williamson 237

Bibliography 251

Index of Authors 267
Index of Ancient Sources 271
List of Contributors 285

Acknowledgments

I want to express my appreciation to all the contributors who devoted their time, their energy, and their considerable expertise to this project. They discussed the textual history and the literary goals of 1 Esdras first in a conference paper and then prepared an essay for this book. To them I offer a sincere thank you. A big thank you too goes to the folks at SBL for accepting this project into their Ancient Israel and Its Literature series, to Steve McKenzie who read and edited the first draft, and to Leigh Andersen and Duncan Burns whose tireless efforts and skills turned the manuscript into a book. I also want to express my appreciation to my doctor-father, Baruch A. Levine, for his ready willingness to engage in scholarly discussion and advice, and to my daughter, Carolyn F. Thorpe, who was always available to tell me how a proper English sentence should be constructed. It is with unbounded gratitude and love, however, that I dedicate this book to my husband, Michael Fried, for relieving me of creating the author index, and for being there for me through all the ins and outs of married life. Thank you.

ABBREVIATIONS

AB	Anchor Bible
AJSL	*American Journal of Semitic Languages and Literature*
AOAT	Alter Orient und Altes Testament
ATD	Das Alte Testament Deutsch
BASOR	*Bulletin of the American Schools of Oriental Research*
BBB	Bonner biblische Beiträge
BEATAJ	Beiträge zur Erforschung des Alten Testaments und des antiken Judentum
BETL	Bibliotheca ephemeridum theologicarum lovaniensium
Bib	*Biblica*
BibInt	Biblical Interpretation Series
BibS(F)	Biblische Studien (Freiburg, 1895–)
BJPES	*Bulletin of the Jewish Palestine Exploration Society*
BJSUCSD	Biblical and Judaic Studies from the University of California, San Diego
BK	Bibel und Kirche
BN	*Biblische Notizen*
BZAW	Beihefte zur Zeitschrift für die alttestamentliche Wissenschaft
CBC	Cambridge Bible Commentary
CBQ	*Catholic Biblical Quarterly*
DSD	*Dead Sea Discoveries*
ErIsr	Eretz-Israel
FAT	Forschungen zum Alten Testament
FRLANT	Forschungen zur Religion und Literatur des Alten und Neuen Testaments
GTA	Göttinger theologischer Arbeiten
HAT	Handbuch zum Alten Testament
HSM	Harvard Semitic Monographs
HTKAT	Herders theologischer Kommentar zum Alten Testament
ICC	International Critical Commentary
IEJ	*Israel Exploration Journal*
JAOS	*Journal of the American Oriental Society*
JBL	*Journal of Biblical Literature*

JHS	*Journal of Hebrew Scriptures*
JJS	*Journal of Jewish Studies*
JSHRZ	*Jüdische Schriften aus hellenistisch-römischer Zeit*
JSJSup	Journal for the Study of Judaism in the Persian, Hellenistic, and Roman Periods: Supplement Series
JSOT	*Journal for the Study of the Old Testament*
JSOTSup	Journal for the Study of the Old Testament: Supplement Series
JSP	*Journal for the Study of the Pseudepigrapha*
JSPSup	Journal for the Study of the Pseudepigrapha: Supplement Series
JSS	*Journal of Semitic Studies*
KAT	Kommentar zum Alten Testament
LCL	Loeb Classical Library
LSTS	Library of Second Temple Studies
LXX	Septuagint
MSU	Mitteilungen des Septuaginta-Unternehmens
MT	Masoretic text
NCB	New Century Bible
NICOT	New International Commentary on the Old Testament
NTT	*Nieuw Theologisch Tijdschrift*
OBO	Orbis biblicus et orientalis
OCT	Oxford Classical Texts/Scriptorum classicorum bibliotheca oxoniensi
OTL	Old Testament Library
OTR	Old Testament Readings
OTS	Old Testament Studies
RevQ	*Revue de Qumran*
SBLDS	Society of Biblical Literature Dissertation Series
SBLMS	Society of Biblical Literature Monograph Series
SBLSCS	Society of Biblical Literature Septuagint and Cognate Studies
SBLSymS	Society of Biblical Literature Symposium Series
SCSt	Septuagint and Cognate Studies
SEThV	Salzburger Exegetische Theologische Vorträge
SIG	*Sylloge inscriptionum graecarum*. Edited by W. Dittenberger. 4 vols. 3d ed. Leipzig, 1915–24
SR	*Studies in Religion*
SSN	Studia semitica neerlandica
STDJ	Studies on the Texts of the Desert of Judah
Transeu	*Transeuphratène*
TSAJ	Texte und Studien zum antiken Judentum
UTB	Uni-Tachenbücher
VT	*Vetus Testamentum*
VTSup	Supplements to Vetus Testamentum
WBC	Word Biblical Commentary
WMANT	Wissenschaftliche Monographien zum Alten und Neuen Testament
ZAW	*Zeitschrift für die alttestamentliche Wissenschaft*
ZTK	*Zeitschrift für Theologie und Kirche*

INTRODUCTION

Lisbeth S. Fried

This volume of essays began as a question that I once asked of David Noel Freedman. I was deep in the throes of writing a commentary on Ezra–Nehemiah for his newly created Eerdmans Critical Commentary Series (now unfortunately discontinued), when I asked Noel if I had to worry about 1 Esdras. Was Ezra–Nehemiah a revision of the apocryphal 1 Esdras, or was it the other way, with 1 Esdras a revision of Ezra–Nehemiah? In typical fashion he answered that I'd have to work through the matter for myself. After much pondering, I eventually concluded that the issue was quite beyond me and that I would have to ask someone. So I asked someone; in fact, I asked eighteen of the most expert people on the planet, and they agreed to try to answer my question. First they answered it in a series of sessions at the November meetings of the Society of Biblical Literature (2007–2009) plus a session at the International SBL Meeting in Rome in the summer of 2009. Then they answered it in the articles you have before you, for the most part revisions of their talks.

In addition to the authors represented here, two others spoke at the meetings—Tessa Rajak and Arnaud Sérandour, but other responsibilities and family illnesses unfortunately kept them from contributing to this book. Sadder is Noel's death in April of 2008. Noel presided over our first meeting in November of 2007 in San Diego and had agreed to write a response to the articles, but this was not to be.

The book consists of three parts: articles arguing against the priority of Ezra–Nehemiah, articles arguing against the priority of 1 Esdras, and articles investigating the nature of 1 Esdras. To begin with, in "Lower Criticism and Higher Criticism: The Case of 1 Esdras," Deirdre Fulton and Gary Knoppers argue that textual criticism, or "lower criticism," can shed light on source-critical and redaction-critical issues, in particular whether or not 1 Esdras' Hebrew *Vorlage* was drawn from Ezra–Nehemiah. The authors focus on 1 Esd 2:15 and Ezra 4:6–11a, of which the Ezra text is by far the longer. They conclude that 1 Esdras is to be preferred. If the writer of 1 Esdras deliberately condensed a much-longer *Vorlage* of several letters—a letter to Xerxes and two more to Artaxerxes—one would expect the work to speak summarily of a plurality of letters written during the reigns of these kings. This is not the case. In contrast, the author of Ezra could easily have wanted to show a sustained opposition to the Jews over many years and so embellished his text by adding more letters and more kings.

In "Chicken or Egg: Which Came First, 1 Esdras or Ezra–Nehemiah?" Lester Grabbe argues that 1 Esdras and Ezra–Nehemiah were composed in stages. The earliest stage is represented by chapters 2 and 5–9 of 1 Esdras (= Ezra 1:1–4:5; 5–10; Neh 8). This is the Ezra source (see graph, p. 43). The compiler of Ezra–Nehemiah split off a portion of the original Ezra tradition to form Neh 8 when he combined the chapters with the Nehemiah tradition. The author of 1 Esdras instead added the story of the three guardsmen.

Adrian Schenker elaborates on his own previous work and on that of his student, Dieter Böhler, to argue that 1 Esdras is the original version of the Ezra story. He demonstrates, first, that the narrative of the three youths is a late addition to 1 Esdras and, second, shows that 1 Esdras presents one and the same narrative twice, in two parallel stories. In contrast to the simple narrative structure of Ezra (ignoring the historicity of the order of the kings), 1 Esdras begins with a return under Cyrus and Sanabassaros (Sheshbazzar) and an authorization to rebuild the temple. Because of an intrigue, the Persian king Artaxerxes halts the repair of the city walls and market places as well as the work on the temple's foundations. Work is stopped until the second year of Darius. The story begins again in 1 Esd 5:4 with a new return, but the name of the king is not mentioned. These returnees build the altar, lay the foundations of the temple, and commence building the temple itself. Again, enemies halt the construction until the second year of Darius. Thus, the two parallel versions of the same story were smoothed into one narrative by the author of the canonical Ezra.

Besides these articles arguing for the priority of 1 Esdras, several argue that Ezra–Nehemiah was first. In considering "The Story of the Three Youths and the Composition of 1 Esdras," Bob Becking concludes that this story (the primary difference between the versions) provides a key as to which version was first. If 1 Esdras was first, then the story was willfully removed when Ezra–Nehemiah was compiled. If 1 Esdras was not first, then the story was added to existing material. Many commentators view the story as a late interpolation and assume that a version of 1 Esdras existed without the story. Becking takes issue with this assumption since the character of the Greek language is the same in both the story and the main body of the text. Basically the two versions differ on what allowed temple construction to begin again after it had been halted. In Ezra, it is Haggai and Zechariah's prophesying; in 1 Esdras, in contrast, it is Zerubbabel's winning a competition in which, for his victory prize, he reminds Darius of his vow to return the temple vessels. This competition belongs to Greek storytelling style, not Persian, and the reference to the Idumeans (4:45, 50) further demonstrates authorship in the Hasmonean period. Since the author of canonical Ezra–Nehemiah must be situated in the Persian period, it must have been written first.

In her essay, "The Second Year of Darius," Kristin De Troyer argues that the indication of that year, "the second year of Darius," provides a clue to the history and the relationship of MT Ezra–Nehemiah and 1 Esdras. According to MT Ezra, the temple-building project is stopped only once and is resumed only once, in the second year of Darius, by the prophetic activity of Haggai and Zechariah. The specific date on which the temple building resumes does not need to be mentioned in Ezra because it is already noted that building is halted until the second year of Darius. In contrast, building activities are stopped twice in 1 Esdras. They are started in the reign of Cyrus and stopped in the reign of Artaxerxes; they are started again in the reign of Darius and stopped once again during that king's reign. To place the prophets in their correct year, the author of 1 Esdras needs to add (in 6:1) that it is the second year of Darius, a phrase not necessary in the canonical book. In 1 Esdras, the date acts as a resumptive clause connecting the reader back to 1 Esd 2:30 after the long insertion of the story of the three youths, the altar building, and the appearance and the rejection of the enemies.

Lisbeth Fried argues that the original story was a typical ancient Near Eastern temple-building story, but in both versions of the story, the elements were displaced to conform to the author's ideology. Both versions displace the construction of the altar to the time before the temple is built. In Ezra the altar is built immediately upon the return of the exiles, apparently during the reign of Cyrus, whereas in 1 Esdras, it is built after the return of Zerubbabel, apparently during the reign of Darius. Both versions add the story of the stoppage of work on the temple, perhaps to explain the eighteen-year delay in temple building, from the first year of Cyrus to the second year of Darius. In Ezra, the accusing letter to Artaxerxes that stops the work is placed after Zerubbabel begins the temple-building project, whereas in 1 Esdras the letter is sent by satrapal officials, apparently of their own volition. In Ezra, Zerubbabel's rejection of the "enemies of the Jews" is what causes the work on the temple to be stopped, whereas in 1 Esdras, the letter to Artaxerxes is written and work on the temple is stopped well before Zerubbabel even arrives in Jerusalem. Fried concludes that the components of the building story were rearranged in 1 Esdras and the story of the three youths added all in order to alleviate Zerubbabel's responsibility for stopping the work on the temple and to provide him with an alibi. It is easier to assume that a guilty Zerubbabel was rendered innocent than it is to assume that the stoppage of temple building was moved to a point under Zerubbabel's watch and that Zerubbabel was made the cause of the stoppage.

In "Why 1 Esdras Is Probably Not an Early Version of the Ezra–Nehemiah Tradition," Juha Pakkala argues that Ezra–Nehemiah results from a long history of growth and revisions that have often left the text inconsistent and incoherent. First Esdras, on the other hand, is an attempt to smooth over the rough passages and clear up the inconsistencies. Among the many passages that Pakkala discusses is Ezra 4:6–11, which he suggests is rewritten in 1 Esd 2:15. The single letter that 1 Esdras reports exhibits traces of the three letters that are present in Ezra, revealing knowledge of the Ezra text and suggesting that the 1 Esdras text is a smoothed-out version of the earlier text in Ezra. In other passages, slight pluses and slight rewordings in the Greek have the effect of giving the figure of Ezra more prestige in 1 Esdras than he receives in the Masoretic version. One may only compare Ezra 7:6 and 1 Esd 8:4, as well as the many times that Ezra is referred to as high priest, a title absent in the canonical text. It is difficult to imagine that a later version would revise a text to render Ezra less prestigious and to take away his high-priestly title.

Zipora Talshir argues again for her view that the compiler of 1 Esdras rearranged the text of Ezra–Nehemiah in order to insert the tale of the three youths. The tale was added to provide a background to the appearance of Zerubbabel and to give him more prestige than he has in the canonical book. To explain her view, Talshir shows that the process of adding stories and rearranging biblical texts is a common feature of ancient writing. The LXX of Samuel–Kings shows additions and rearrangements that fill out the canonical text, as do the Greek Daniel and Esther. Talshir demonstrates that all the features of 1 Esdras can be found in contemporary Greek versions of the biblical texts. Even the ending and beginning, which look odd to us, are similar to features in Chronicles. Chronicles, too, starts in the middle of the story of Saul's reign and similarly ends with a verb midsentence—a sentence that is finished only in Ezra!

James VanderKam considers "Literary Questions between Ezra, Nehemiah, and 1 Esdras," primarily the question of the role of Zerubbabel in the two texts. To VanderKam, 1 Esdras is the most ancient interpretation of the book of Ezra and the earliest attempt to cope with puzzles in it. The main puzzle the book addresses is the short shrift that Zerubbabel receives in the canonical text. Primary among the attempts to increase Zerubbabel's presence is the addition of the story of the three youths and his inclusion in the story as the third youth. Outside the story of the youths, the author of 1 Esdras gives Zerubbabel credit along with Sheshbazzar (1 Esd 6:18) for bringing the holy temple vessels up to Jerusalem. Indeed, the fact that the passage, in both 1 Esdras and Ezra, continues with singular forms, as if Cyrus gave the vessels to just one person, and identifies this person as Sheshbazzar, betrays the secondary character of Zerubbabel's name in 1 Esd 6:18. VanderKam adds further that the name Zerubbabel is not present here in a number of manuscript copies of 1 Esdras and is not found at this point in Josephus, *Ant.* 11.93. In comparing 1 Esd 6:27 to Ezra 6:7, and 1 Esd 6:29 to Ezra 6:8, VanderKam concludes that in both cases 1 Esdras has been expanded to include Zerubbabel. This is consistent with the idea that 1 Esdras is a revision of an older text, not a reflection of the original text itself. It is also clear that Zerubbabel is enhanced further by absorbing some of the characteristics given to Nehemiah in the older text. Quoting Talshir, VanderKam points out that the two specific requests made by Nehemiah—a letter of safe passage and a permit to procure timber—are precisely the first two things granted Zerubbabel in the letters Darius writes for him (1 Esd 4:47–48).

In "Remember Nehemiah: 1 Esdras and the *Damnatio memoriae Nehemiae*," Jacob Wright argues that the author of 1 Esdras knew Ezra–Nehemiah as one book and that he purposely rewrote the story of Ezra to blot out Nehemiah's memory. Nehemiah's memoir had offended the priestly writers who composed 1 Esdras because of its insinuation that the priesthood was corrupt and had made alliances with, and had even married into, non-Israelite families. Ezra–Nehemiah also presents the city of Jerusalem in ruins until Nehemiah, a non-priest and non-Davidide, came and rebuilt it, rather than showing it built by the priests immediately upon their return. All this was rectified by a new and perfected version of the story of the return with an exalted Zerubbabel replacing Nehemiah.

Besides the question of the priority of either Ezra or 1 Esdras, several scholars investigate the nature of the book of 1 Esdras itself. In "The Image of the Kings(s) in 1 Esdras," Sebastian Grätz shows that the portrayals of the kings, starting with Josiah and ending with Artaxerxes, are the focus of the entire book of 1 Esdras. Grätz points out that the depictions of the Persian kings in 1 Esdras mimic its portrayal of Josiah in the way that they enable the celebration of Passover and provide the temple cult with its needs. Nothing like this occurs in the canonical book of Ezra–Nehemiah. The book thus ends with Jewish autonomy under the religious and political leadership of Ezra, just as it starts with the political (and partly religious) leadership of Josiah.

In his article, 'Darius' Court and the Guardsmen's Debate: Hellenistic Greek Elements in 1 Esdras," Paul Harvey Jr. shows that the debates offered by the bodyguards before the great king and his court have their origin within the contexts of Greek history, historiography, and rhetoric. In particular, the title "kinsman of the king," συγγενής Βασιλέως (3:7), is peculiar to Ptolemaic Egypt of the third century B.C.E., being introduced by Ptolemy II Philadelphus, who ruled 283–246 B.C.E. The term is not attested for other Hellenistic Greek monarchies, so that we have a *terminus post quem* for the story as well as a locale in Ptolemaic Egypt. Indeed, the list of officials in 1 Esd 3:7, 14 is a list of Ptolemaic honorific titles (given in order of rank) mixed with Ptolemaic administrative officers. The debate itself is a combination of two Greek literary genres: the "speeches" are in the form of deliberative/persuasive formal *logoi*, familiar from Herodotus' debate over the best form of government (Herodotus, *Hist*. 3.80–82). This form had its home in fifth-century Athens but continued in the Hellenistic world into the Roman period. The second form is the *progymnasmata*, the student compositions on topics assigned by the classical rhetorician schoolmaster. School texts on just those subjects debated in 1 Esdras can be found in second-century papyri. These school texts and the *gymnasia* that produced them were common in all the major cities, including Ptolemaic Alexandria.

In "Cyclical Time and Catalogues: The Construction of Meaning in 1 Esdras," Sylvie Honigman argues that in their stories of rebuilding Jerusalem and the temple after the return from destruction, both Ezra–Nehemiah and 1 Esdras display a Judean search for collective identity. The major question addressed by these texts is: why is Darius' name associated with the temple when Cyrus, the founder of the Achaemenid Empire and of a new dynasty, should have been the one who restored the temple? The two texts address the problem differently, according to their different conceptions of time. Whereas in Ezra–Nehemiah there is a linear conception of time, in 1 Esdras time is cyclical. The many repetitions in 1 Esdras are not simply due to the arbitrary juxtaposition of parallel stories but are rather to be explained by the cyclical understanding of time. In 1 Esdras there are in each of its three stages a king; prophets; a leader of the returnees; the holy vessels; the returnees themselves; the return; a disruption; and a successful restoration of the cosmic order embodied in altar, temple, and law. Each is followed by a celebration. Of these three cycles, only the one in which Darius is king is complete. The Cyrus cycle lacks a founding ceremony and festival. The cycle of the law reading lacks a prophetic voice to initiate it. The repeated reference to Darius' second year adds cohesion to the narrative. Honigman sees the cyclical structure of the narrative as a perfect means to root the author's present firmly into the founding events of the past.

In her essay, "1 Esdras: Its Genre, Literary Form, and Goals," Sara Japhet addresses the question of the purpose of 1 Esdras, asking why it was composed. She answers by affirming that its goal was "to create a new historical picture of a certain period in the history of Israel." The period is that of the restoration, which it presents in three different phases: 1) the end of the Judean period (1 Esd 1); 2) the return from exile and the rebuilding of temple and city (1 Esd 2–7); and 3) the establishment of religious norms and practices (1 Esd 8–9). The three phases are depicted as a historical continuum, a continuum that expresses the view that the turn about of Israel's fortunes has actually been achieved; the reality of the restoration period is the wished-for salvation of Israel. The period in which the temple lay in ruins was merely a short *intermezzo*, during which the people of Israel suffered a deserved punishment for their transgressions but after which the temple was quickly rebuilt and restored to its former glory. To emphasize the continuity, 1 Esdras transfers Jerusalem's rebuilding to the beginning of the restoration period and the time of Zerubbabel. Thus, at the beginning of the restoration period the effects of exile are fully reversed, both temple and city are rebuilt and the vessels returned. The climax of the historical process is reached in the third period with the firm establishment of religious affairs under the leadership of Ezra (now labeled "high priest" [9:39]). With the leadership in the hands of a high priest, the historical development reaches the author's own time. The story thus legitimizes the political reality then current and sanctions the ideology that supported this reality.

Ralph Klein concludes in his article "The Rendering of 2 Chronicles 35–36 in 1 Esdras" that we have the original beginning to 1 Esdras and that 1 Esdras is not a fragment from the larger history of the Chronicler. The Chronicler says that Josiah had transformed the sinners of his time into people with perfect obedience, but

1 Esd 1:22 states that the people of Josiah's time persisted in sinning and acting impiously. The Chronicler says that Pharaoh Neco's archers killed Josiah (2 Chr 35:23), but according to 1 Esdras he dies of a sickness. Both of these disagreements prohibit any edition of 1 Esdras that included 2 Chr 34. Moreover, vv. 21–22 of 1 Esd 1 would not have fit in the context of 2 Chr 35, and thus there was never a corresponding Hebrew text there that later fell out. In fact, the pun that exists in the Greek—but not in the Hebrew—suggests these verses were originally written in Greek and are not a translation: that is, Josiah's piety, εὐσεβείας in v. 21, and the impiety of the people in v. 22, rendered by ἠσεβηκότων (root = ἀσεβέω). Talshir's retroversion of these words into Hebrew shows no punning at all. The first word is retroverted by her as יראה (fear) and the second by a participial form of פשׁע.

In "1 Esdras as Rewritten Bible?" Hugh Williamson asks why anyone would have written this work in the first place and why he would have done it in this particular form. Williamson suggests by way of an answer that 1 Esdras is an example of "rewritten Bible." He cites Geza Vermes' definition: rewritten Bible is a term that can be applied to a seemingly diverse group of texts having in common that they work through a section of the Bible, embedding that text within their presentation and simultaneously offering additional material and interpretative comments. One example is the book of Chronicles, and another is Josephus' *Antiquities*. In examining P. S. Alexander's criteria for the label "rewritten Bible," Williamson concludes that the criteria are met by 1 Esdras. Among other things, 1 Esdras is a free-standing composition that replicates, but does not supersede or replace, the canonical book on which it is based. In 1 Esdras the city is rebuilt at the time of Zerubbabel and the returnees immediately settle in it, which Williamson sees as an attempt to minimize the effects of the exile. Understanding the text as rewritten Bible, Williamson concludes, allows the reader better to appreciate what the author was trying to achieve by his selection, reordering, and re-presentation of the text.

Although a definitive resolution to the issue of the priority of 1 Esdras has not been achieved, the essays clarify the issues and increase our understanding of the goals and historical context of that book. These studies have wider ramifications, for they also elucidate the process by which the ancient authors wrote and rewrote the biblical books. Whether or not 1 Esdras was first, however, perhaps will only be resolved when Elijah returns to answer all our questions.

Articles Arguing against the Priority of Ezra–Nehemiah

LOWER CRITICISM AND HIGHER CRITICISM: THE CASE OF 1 ESDRAS

Deirdre N. Fulton and Gary N. Knoppers

INTRODUCTION

Over the past decades, the study of 1 Esdras has assumed a variety of different forms. The careful studies of Ralph Klein and Zipora Talshir have focused on textual questions, examining minute differences between the Greek text and the Hebrew/Aramaic texts.[1] Other studies, such as the insightful treatment of Tamara Eskenazi, have focused on the literary structure and themes of 1 Esdras.[2] To understand the origins of particular stories, scholars have utilized source-critical analyses, principally in relation to the tale of the three youths (1 Esd 3:1– 5:6).[3] To elucidate the interrelationships of 1 Esdras–Ezra; 1 Esdras–Chronicles; and 1 Esdras–Chronicles, Ezra, and Nehemiah, Adrian Schenker, Dieter Böhler, and Juha Pakkala have employed the tools of textual criticism, source criticism, and redaction criticism.[4] Finally, some scholars have employed historical-critical

---

1. Ralph W. Klein, "Studies in the Greek Texts of the Chronicler" (Ph.D. diss., Harvard University, 1966); Zipora Talshir, *1 Esdras: From Origin to Translation* (SBLSCS 47; Atlanta: Society of Biblical Literature, 1999); idem, *1 Esdras: A Text Critical Commentary* (SBLSCS 50; Atlanta: Society of Biblical Literature, 2001).

2. Tamara C. Eskenazi, "The Chronicler and the Composition of 1 Esdras," *CBQ* 48 (1986): 39–61.

3. For a discussion of the origins of this story, see Talshir, *1 Esdras: From Origin to Translation*, 42–109; idem, *1 Esdras: A Text Critical Commentary*, 225–43; Jacob M. Myers, *I and II Esdras: A New Translation with Introduction and Commentary* (AB 42; Garden City, N.Y.: Doubleday, 1974). For a different view on this matter, see Paul B. Harvey's work in the present volume, "Darius' Court and the Guardsmen's Debate: Hellenistic Greek Elements in *1 Esdras*."

4. Adrian Schenker, "La relation d'Esdras A' au texte massorétique d'Esdras-Néhémia," in *Tradition of the Text: Studies Offered to Dominique Barthélemy in Celebration of His 70th Birthday* (ed. Gerard J. Norton and Stephen Pisano; OBO 109; Freiburg: Universitätsverlag; Göttingen: Vandenhoeck & Ruprecht, 1991), 218–49; Dieter Böhler, *Die heilige Stadt in Esdras α und Esra-Nehemia: Zwei Konzeptionen der Wiederherstellung Israels* (OBO 158; Freiburg: Universitätsverlag; Göttingen: Vandenhoeck & Ruprecht, 1997); idem, "On the Relationship

approaches to gain a better grasp of the significance of specific stories. An example is the manner in which scholars have interpreted the tale of the three youths, namely, investigating how this story might bear witness to life in the Diaspora.

I. Textual Criticism in the Wake of the Discoveries at Qumran

In traditional scholarship, the variety of biblical criticisms outlined above is divided chiefly into two categories: lower criticism and higher criticism. The former is thought to engage the work of scribes, while the latter is thought to engage the work of authors, tradents, and redactors. In the wake of many important studies of the differences among the Masoretic Text (MT), the Septuagint (LXX), and the Dead Sea Scrolls (DSS), the situation can no longer be judged to be so simple. Recent analysis of a variety of writings, such as Genesis, Exodus, Numbers, Deuteronomy, Joshua, Judges, Samuel, Kings, Jeremiah, Ezekiel, and Daniel, demonstrates that the chasm between lower criticism (principally textual criticism) and higher criticism (source criticism, tradition criticism, historical criticism, redaction criticism, form criticism) is an artificial one.[5] Higher criticism has often been judged to be more speculative than lower criticism, but

---

between Textual and Literary Criticism: The Two Recensions of the Book of Ezra; Ezra–Neh (MT) and 1 Esdras (LXX)," in *The Earliest Text of the Hebrew Bible: The Relationship between the Masoretic Text and the Hebrew Base of the Septuagint Reconsidered* (ed. Adrian Schenker; SBLSCS 52; Atlanta: Society of Biblical Literature, 2003); Juha Pakkala, *Ezra the Scribe: The Development of Ezra 7–10 and Nehemiah 8* (BZAW 347; Berlin: de Gruyter, 2004). See also the works of Schenker and Pakkala in the present collection.

5. See, e.g., Frank Moore Cross, "The Contribution of the Discoveries at Qumran to the Study of the Biblical Text," *IEJ* 16 (1966): 81–95; idem, "Problems of Method in the Textual Criticism of the Hebrew Bible," in *The Critical Study of Sacred Texts* (ed. W. D. O'Flaherty; Berkeley, Calif.: Graduate Theological Union, 1979), 31–54; Julio C. Trebolle Barrera, *Centena in libros Samuelis et Regum: Variantes textuales y composición literaria en los libros de Samuel y Reyes* (Textos y estudios "Cardenal Cisneros" 47; Madrid: Consejo Superior de Investigaciones Científicas Instituto de Filología, 1989); Eugene C. Ulrich, "Multiple Literary Editions: Reflections Toward a Theory of the History of the Biblical Text," in *Current Research and Technological Developments of the Dead Sea Scrolls: Conference on the Texts from the Judean Desert, Jerusalem, 30 April 1995* (ed. D. W. Parry and S. D. Ricks; STDJ 20; Leiden: Brill, 1996), 78–105; repr., idem, *The Dead Sea Scrolls and the Origin of the Bible: Studies in the Dead Sea Scrolls and Related Literature* (Grand Rapids, Mich.: Eerdmans, 1999), 99–120; Adrian Schenker, *Septante et texte massorétique dans l'histoire la plus ancienne du texte de 1 Rois 2–14* (CahRB 48; Paris: Gabalda, 2000); Emanuel Tov, *Textual Criticism of the Hebrew Bible* (2d rev. ed.; Assen: Van Gorcum, 2001); idem, *Scribal Practices and Approaches Reflected in the Texts Found in the Judean Desert* (STDJ 54; Leiden: Brill, 2004); idem, *Hebrew Bible, Greek Bible, and Qumran* (TSAJ 121; Tübingen: Mohr Siebeck, 2008).

analysis of the biblical texts among the Dead Sea Scrolls has demonstrated that the results of textual criticism shed new light on source-critical and redaction-critical issues.

The variations in length (shorter and longer texts), order, and content among different witnesses to biblical writings are highly significant. In the case of the book of Samuel, the multiple witnesses attested for this work—most notably the MT, LXX, 4QSam^a, 4QSam^b, 4QSam^c, and Josephus—testify to complicated stages in the growth of the text.[6] With respect to the MT and LXX texts of 1 Samuel, a few cases exist in which the MT and LXX present strikingly variant texts.[7] Such differences suggest intentional changes to specific narratives, which may have occurred for specific exegetical or theological reasons. For instance, in 1 Sam 1–2 (the story of Hannah), the MT likely represents an earlier edition, whereas the LXX represents a secondary or reshaped version. Of 1 Sam 1–2, Eugene Ulrich comments, "My strong suspicion is that a number of the variants coalesce to constitute a pattern indicating that the Hebrew text which lay behind the Old Greek may well have been a variant edition from that which has been transmitted through the Masoretic *textus receptus*."[8] But in the example of 1 Sam 17–18 (the story of David and Goliath), the LXX seems to represent the earlier edition, while the MT represents the later or composite version.[9] Such examples from the textual history of Samuel are important, because they demonstrate that the difficult, but necessary, enterprise of textual criticism serves as one key to gaining a better grasp of the literary history of particular biblical writings.

Like the book of Samuel, the book of Jeremiah presents variant textual traditions. These are seen most notably in the MT, 2QJer, 4QJer^a, and 4QJer^c, on the one hand, and the LXX and 4QJer^b, on the other hand. In this case, one is also confronted with a different order in the two major witnesses, principally in the location of the oracles against the nations. This evidence is significant, because the difference between the MT and the LXX may sometimes include variant orders of whole sections of the text. In their studies, Ulrich and Emanuel Tov have convincingly argued for two successive editions in the textual history of

---

6. The work of Josephus sometimes agrees with the LXX, 4QSam^a, and 4QSam^c texts against the MT; Eugene C. Ulrich, *The Qumran Text of Samuel and Josephus* (HSM 19; Missoula, Mont.: Scholars Press, 1978), 39–41, 48–49. See also Frank Moore Cross, "A New Qumran Biblical Fragment Related to the Original Hebrew Underlying the Septuagint," *BASOR* 132 (1953): 15–26; P. Kyle McCarter, *I Samuel* (AB 8; Garden City, N.Y.: Doubleday, 1980).

7. Discussion of the version of Samuel employed by the Chronicler is relevant in this context. The text of Samuel shares a number of important traits with the OG of Samuel, 4QSam^a, and the version of Samuel cited by Josephus. See further Gary N. Knoppers, *I Chronicles 1–9: A New Translation with Introduction and Commentary* (AB 12; New York: Doubleday, 2004), 69–71.

8. Ulrich, *Dead Sea Scrolls*, 66.

9. Ibid., 67–68. See also the comments of Tov, *Textual Criticism*, 334–36.

Jeremiah.¹⁰ Tov categorizes the LXX and 4QJer^b as "edition I" and the MT, 2QJer, 4QJer^a, and 4QJer^c as a later and expanded edition that he refers to as "edition II."¹¹ The differences among the witnesses to Jeremiah suggest a fascinating process of textual growth, involving the supplementation and editing of earlier text.

A final example of textual variety is the book of Daniel. Here, one finds significant differences between the MT and the LXX as well as important variants in the fragmentary witnesses in the Dead Sea Scrolls (1QDan^b, 4QDan^a, 4QDan^c, 4QDan^d, 4QDan^e, pap6QDan). Interestingly, in the case of Daniel, comparative analysis of the available textual witnesses suggests secondary expansions to an earlier text in both the LXX and the MT. In other words, scholars are not faced with a simple case in which the MT represents the older text, while the LXX represents the younger text (or vice versa). In some cases, the *Vorlage* of the MT version underwent secondary expansion, while in other cases the *Vorlage* of the LXX underwent secondary expansion.¹² As a result, neither the MT nor the LXX can be reduced simply to the other.¹³ Whereas in Jeremiah scholars are confronted with two successive editions of a (basically) single textual tradition, in Daniel scholars are confronted with the phenomenon of separate textual growth in the editions represented by the MT and the LXX.

In 1 Esdras the situation is also complex. As commentators have long recognized, 1 Esdras has at least some overlap with material in Chronicles, Ezra, and Nehemiah. Yet, 1 Esdras also possesses its own unique material.¹⁴ Each work

---

10. Ulrich, *Dead Sea Scrolls*, 69. On the shorter Greek text of Jeremiah, see the foundational treatment of Gerald Janzen, *Studies in the Greek Text of Jeremiah* (HSM 6; Cambridge, Mass.: Harvard University Press, 1973). For a reconstruction of the Hebrew text used for the Greek prose sections of Jeremiah, see Louis Stulman, *The Other Text of Jeremiah* (Lanham, Md.: University Press of America, 1985).

11. Emanuel Tov, *The Septuagint Translation of Jeremiah and Baruch: A Discussion of an Early Revision of Jeremiah 29–52 and Baruch 1:1–3:8* (HSM 8; Missoula, Mont.: Scholars Press, 1976); idem, "Some Aspects of the Textual and Literary History of the Book of Jeremiah," in *Le livre de Jérémie: Le prophète et son milieu, les oracles et leur transmission* (ed. P.-M. Bogaert; BETL 54; Leuven: University of Leuven Press, 1981), 145–67; idem, "The Literary History of the Book of Jeremiah in the Light of Its Textual History," in *Empirical Models for Biblical Criticism* (ed. Jeffrey H. Tigay; Philadelphia: University of Pennsylvania Press, 1985), 213–37; idem, *Textual Criticism*, 319–27; Konrad Schmid, *Buchgestalten des Jeremiabuches: Untersuchungen zur Redaktions- und Rezeptionsgeschichte von Jer 30–33 im Kontext des Buches* (WMANT 72; Neukirchen-Vluyn: Neukirchener Verlag, 1996).

12. Ulrich, *Dead Sea Scrolls*, 72.

13. John J. Collins aptly comments that "both the MT and the OG seem to have undergone secondary developments"; *Daniel* (Hermeneia; Minneapolis: Fortress, 1993), 6.

14. 1 Esdras contains a version of the material in 2 Chr 35–36, much of Ezra, and ch. 8 of Nehemiah in succession. The most noteworthy difference between Ezra and 1 Esdras is the tale of the three guardsmen, present only in 1 Esdras. It must be underscored that most of Nehemiah (chs. 1–7 and 9–13) is lacking in 1 Esdras.

shows signs of secondary reworking and expansion. Given that the texts are only partially parallel, one is dealing inevitably with both textual and literary issues. To complicate matters further, scholars have long debated the compositional history of Ezra–Nehemiah and, if you will, Chronicles–Ezra–Nehemiah. Most now consider the linkage between Chronicles and Ezra–Nehemiah to be secondary, that is, a later development within antiquity.[15] Interestingly, this linkage seems to be already presupposed, at least in some ancient scribal circles, in the translation of 1 Esdras.[16] But in any case, the debate rages on about the compositional history of Ezra–Nehemiah. Is Ezra–Nehemiah a carefully arranged and carefully edited single work, which draws on disparate older sources?[17] Or is Ezra–Nehemiah a loosely edited conflation of two or more different sets of Ezra and Nehemiah stories?[18] Or does the composition of Ezra–Nehemiah reflect

---

15. Sara Japhet, "The Supposed Common Authorship of Chronicles and Ezra–Nehemiah Investigated Anew," *VT* 18 (1968): 330–71; idem, "People and Land in the Restoration Period," in *Das Land Israel in biblischer Zeit* (ed. G. Strecker; GTA 25; Göttingen: Vandenhoeck & Ruprecht, 1983), 103–25; idem, *The Ideology of the Book of Chronicles and Its Place in Biblical Thought* (BEATAJ 9; Frankfurt am Main: Lang, 1989); idem, *I and II Chronicles* (OTL; Louisville: Westminster John Knox, 1993); H. G. M. Williamson, *Israel in the Books of Chronicles* (Cambridge: Cambridge University Press, 1977); idem, *1 and 2 Chronicles* (NCB; Grand Rapids, Mich.: Eerdmans, 1982); T. Willi, *Juda – Jehud – Israel: Studien zum Selbstverständnis des Judentums in persischer Zeit* (FAT 12; Tübingen: Mohr Siebeck, 1995); Knoppers, *I Chronicles 1–9*; Ralph W. Klein, *1 Chronicles* (Hermeneia; Minneapolis: Augsburg Fortress, 2006).

16. Knoppers, *I Chronicles 1–9*, 75–80. On the use of catch-lines to separate works, see further the following works by Menahem Haran: "Book Scrolls at the Beginning of the Second Temple Period," *ErIsr* 16 (1982): 86–92; "Book Scrolls in Israel in Pre-Exilic Times," *IJS* 32 (1982): 161–73; "Book Size and the Device of Catch-Lines in the Biblical Canon," *JJS* 36 (1985): 1–11.

17. H. G. M. Williamson, *Ezra, Nehemiah* (WBC 16; Waco, Tex.: Word, 1985); Joseph Blenkinsopp, *Ezra–Nehemiah* (OTL; London: SCM, 1988). Note that Blenkinsopp defends the unity of Chronicles–Ezra–Nehemiah. The compositional history of Ezra and Nehemiah is the subject of a recent collection of essays edited by Mark J. Boda and Paul L. Redditt, *Unity and Disunity in Ezra–Nehemiah: Redaction, Rhetoric and Reader* (Hebrew Bible Monographs 17; Sheffield: Sheffield Phoenix, 2008).

18. James C. VanderKam, "Ezra–Nehemiah or Ezra and Nehemiah?" in *Priests, Prophets, and Scribes: Essays on the Formation and Heritage of Second Temple Judaism in Honour of Joseph Blenkinsopp* (ed. Eugene C. Ulrich, John W. Wright, Robert P. Carroll, and Philip R. Davies; JSOTSup 149; Sheffield: JSOT Press, 1992), 55–75; idem, *From Joshua to Caiaphas: High Priests after the Exile* (Minneapolis: Fortress, 2004); Bob Becking, "Ezra on the Move: Trends and Perspectives on the Character and His Book," in *Perspectives in the Study of the Old Testament and Early Judaism: A Symposium in Honour of Adam S. van der Woude on the Occasion of His 70th Birthday* (ed. F. García Martínez and E. Noort; VTSup 73; Leiden: Brill, 1998), 154–79; idem, "Continuity and Community: The Belief System of the Book of Ezra," in *The Crisis of Israelite Religion: Transformation of Religious Tradition in Exilic and Post-Exilic Times* (ed. Bob Becking and M. C. A. Korpel; OTS 42; Leiden: Brill, 1999), 256–75; Margaret

several layers of editing and later reworking?[19] The larger issue of the composition of Ezra–Nehemiah is relevant, because it may bear on how one understands the origins of 1 Esdras. Some have contended that the *Vorlage* of 1 Esdras represents the original text of Ezra or, at least, the earliest version of Ezra that we have.[20] Others have claimed that 1 Esdras is but a fragment of an originally longer work.[21] Yet others have argued that 1 Esdras is a secondary work, a (presumably) second-century translation of sections of Hebrew and Aramaic Ezra–Nehemiah.[22] In this reconstruction, 1 Esdras is a compilation of materials based upon a selection of passages from Chronicles and Ezra–Nehemiah. As such, 1 Esdras provides insight into how Ezra was interpreted and reused in a Diaspora setting, but it does not provide modern scholars with access to an older form of Ezra (or of Ezra–Nehemiah).

Each of the aforementioned major approaches has its merits. The treatment of 1 Esdras as a distinct literary work, for example, is a welcome development, because it recognizes that the work has its own structural integrity and contains material (the story of the three youths) that has no direct parallels anywhere else in the Scriptures. The exploration of how various sections of 1 Esdras may rework and reinterpret an older textual tradition is also a welcome development, because it shows how the Ezra material was understood and reapplied in a new setting. But is it possible that some past studies have put matters too starkly?

Cohen, "Leave Nehemiah Alone: Nehemiah's 'Tales' and Fifth-Century BCE Historiography," in Boda and Redditt, *Unity and Disunity in Ezra–Nehemiah*, 55–74. It is interesting, as many have noted, that Ben Sira's praise of the ancestors, which commemorates the accomplishments of important figures, includes Nehemiah (Sir 49:13) but lacks any mention of Ezra. Whether this fact sheds any light on the (un)availability of a work comprising Ezra–Nehemiah in the author's time is not entirely clear.

19. The treatments of Pakkala (*Ezra the Scribe*) and Jacob L. Wright (*Rebuilding Identity: The Nehemiah Memoir and Its Earliest Readers* [BZAW 348; Berlin: de Gruyter, 2004]) differ in many respects, but they agree that Ezra–Nehemiah bears witness to a complex, multi-layered compositional and editorial process.

20. On these possibilities, see the essay by Adrian Schenker in the present volume (and the further references contained therein).

21. A review of the Fragment Hypothesis may be found in Knoppers, *I Chronicles 1–9*, 55–58.

22. See, e.g., H. G. M. Williamson, "The Problem with First Esdras," in *After the Exile: Essays in Honour of Rex Mason* (ed. John Barton and David J. Reimer; Macon, Ga.: Mercer University Press, 1996), 201–16. Talshir's work adds another complication in that she contends that the translation of 1 Esdras was based on a Hebrew-Aramaic original. This includes an Aramaic original of the story of the three youths; *1 Esdras: From Origin to Translation*, 102–6. Talshir argues, in fact, that "the book was created in order to incorporate this story, originally written in Aramaic, in the narrative of the Return" (*1 Esdras: A Text Critical Commentary*, ix).

There is no doubt that 1 Esdras draws upon older material in Ezra, but was the *Vorlage* employed by 1 Esdras virtually identical to MT Ezra?[23] Is it possible that those who argue that 1 Esdras reflects the original Ezra may have some justification for what they assert insofar as the underlying text reflected in 1 Esdras may not be a direct equivalent to MT Ezra? Given the textual pluriformity evident within the MT, the LXX, and the DSS for a number of biblical books, such a finding for Ezra and 1 Esdras would not be unprecedented. It may be that there are many telltale signs of the indebtedness of 1 Esdras to a text resembling sections found within MT Ezra, but there may be other cases in which the text of 1 Esdras bears witness to an older, less elaborate form of Ezra. In the latter case, the text of 1 Esdras may be employed cautiously to reconstruct older readings in the textual development of Ezra.

In this essay, we will pursue a single case study that involves significant textual differences between 1 Esdras and Ezra.[24] Although there are many more examples of textual divergences in the two works, the following case study has been selected to provide examples of the merit to be gained by close comparative analysis: 1 Esd 2:15 // Ezra 4:6–11a.[25] In some respects, this case study is admittedly unusual in the number of small-scale and large-scale variants that exist between the two major witnesses. Some examples may elucidate issues of translation and transmission, but others may shed light on larger issues of composition and textual growth. Although it is impossible in the context of this short essay to tackle all of the substantial issues raised by the proponents of the major theories sketched above, a focused exercise in lower criticism may prove helpful in informing higher-critical questions.

---

23. Böhler provides a helpful survey (*Die heilige Stadt*, 18–32). The cautions of Talshir (*1 Esdras: A Text Critical Commentary*, ix) about the complex process of textual transmission should also be kept in mind. She writes that the *Vorlage* of 1 Esdras differed from the MT "to a certain extent" (*1 Esdras: From Origin to Translation*, 113) and that, although the MT and 1 Esdras have "a large common basis," they also have "a long and substantial separate history of transmission" (*1 Esdras: From Origin to Translation*, 115).

24. In more detail, see the insightful but different approaches of Talshir (*1 Esdras: From Origin to Translation*; idem, *1 Esdras: A Text Critical Commentary*) and Böhler (*Die heilige Stadt*). The important work of Klein ("Studies in the Greek Text") discusses the textual differences between MT and LXX of 2 Chr 35–36 and the corresponding material in 1 Esdras.

25. There were a number of other case studies briefly presented in our SBL paper of 2010 (1 Esd 2:16–18 // Ezra 4:11b–13; 1 Esd 2:21–24 // Ezra 4:17–22; 1 Esd 6:1–4, 17 // Ezra 5:1–4, 14; 1 Esd 8:43–44 // Ezra 8:16; and 1 Esd 9:37–38 // Neh 7:72–8 1). These may become the subject of another essay by Deirdre Fulton. Space limitations do not permit us to discuss these case studies here.

II. The Letter(s) of Complaint Sent to the Persian King(s): 1 Esdras 2:15 // Ezra 4:6-11a

In the case study that follows, reference will be made regularly to the testimony of the *Antiquities* of Josephus. The text of Josephus seems to be dependent on a version of 1 Esdras but in some cases diverges from 1 Esdras. The question has therefore been raised whether Josephus also had access to a version of the book of Ezra.[26] Alternatively, some commentators have argued that the version of 1 Esdras employed by Josephus was an earlier (and variant) form of the text.[27] To be sure, the work of Josephus must be used with some caution, because of his tendency to paraphrase, add commentary, and press his own agenda about the course of early Judean history. The textual comparisons chiefly focus on 1 Esdras and Ezra–Nehemiah, but the work of Josephus may also occasionally shed some light on the development (and reception) of the text.

Within the overlapping material found in 1 Esdras and Chronicles, Ezra, and Nehemiah, 1 Esd 2:15 // Ezra 4:6-11a illustrate a major textual divergence in both content and sequence.[28] In the broader literary context of 1 Esdras, chapter 2 introduces the decree of Cyrus, commending the return of the exiles to Judah and the rebuilding of the temple in Jerusalem. The efforts of the returnees meet local resistance, and the text proceeds to mention a letter sent to Artaxerxes protesting the rebuilding efforts, as well as the king's return letter commanding the termination of the current building project.[29] In the context of Ezra–Nehemiah, the text of Ezra 4 begins with comments on the opposition to the rebuilding of the Jerusalem temple under Zerubbabel and Jeshua by the "adversaries of Judah and Benjamin" (Ezra 4:1). The text then goes on to mention achronologically other cases of local resistance to rebuilding initiatives in Judah.[30] In so doing, Ezra 4:5-10 mentions three other Achaemenid kings: Darius, Ahasuerus (Xerxes), and Artaxerxes.[31] For the convenience of readers, the texts may be presented in parallel fashion.

---

26. So, e.g., Myers, *I and II Esdras*, 42.

27. In the view of Loring W. Batten, for instance, the version of 1 Esdras used by Josephus was, from the vantage point of textual criticism, superior to the version of 1 Esdras preserved in later tradition; *A Critical and Exegetical Commentary on the Books of Ezra and Nehemiah* (ICC; Edinburgh: T&T Clark, 1913), 6-13. Batten contends that the text of 1 Esdras was partially revised, at some point, toward the developing MT.

28. Böhler (*Die heilige Stadt*, 222) offers a succinct chart of the parallel texts of this section of Ezra and 1 Esdras.

29. 1 Esd 2 is parallel to Ezra 1 and 4.

30. In most detail, David Glatt-Gilad, *Chronological Displacement in Biblical and Related Literatures* (SBLDS 139; Atlanta: Scholars Press, 1993), 113-42.

31. Artaxerxes is actually mentioned four times (Ezra 4:6, 7[*bis*], 8).

1 Esdras 2:15[32]	Ezra 4:6–11a[33]
15: Ἐν δὲ τοῖς ἐπὶ Ἀρταξέρξου τοῦ Περσῶν Βασιλέως χρόνοις κατέγραψεν αὐτῷ κατὰ τῶν κατοικούντων ἐν τῇ Ἰουδαίᾳ καὶ Ἱερουσαλὴμ Βέσλεμος καὶ Μιθριδάτης καὶ Ταβέλλιος καὶ Ῥαοῦμος καὶ βεελτέεμος καὶ Σαμσαῖος ὁ γραμματεὺς καὶ οἱ λοιποὶ οἱ τούτοις συντασσόμενοι, οἰκοῦντες δὲ ἐν Σαμαρείᾳ καὶ τοῖς ἄλλοις τόποις, τὴν ὑπογεγραμμένην ἐπιστολήν.	6: ובמלכות אחשורוש בתחלת מלכותו כתבו שטנה על־ישבי יהודה וירושלם: 7: ובימי ארתחששתא כתב בשלם מתרדת טבאל ושאר כנותו[34] על־ארתחששתא[35] מלך פרס וכתב הנשתון כתוב[36] ארמית ומתרגם ארמית: 8: רחום בעל־טעם ושמשי ספרא כתבו אגרה חדה על־ירושלם לארתחששתא מלכא כנמא: 9: אדין רחום בעל־טעם ושמשי ספרא ושאר כנותהון דיניא ואפרסתכיא טרפליא אפרסיא ארכויא[37] בבליא שושנכיא דהוא[38] עלמיא: 10: ושאר אמיא די הגלי אסנפר רבא ויקירא והותב המו בקריה די שמרין ושאר עבר־נהרה וכענת: 11: דנה פרשגן אגרתא די שלחו יהועל

Granted that the book begins with the decree of Cyrus (Ezra 1:1–4), it is not surprising that he is mentioned in the context of the long struggle to rebuild the Jerusalem temple (Ezra 4:5). But, interestingly, Ezra 4:6 mentions an unspecified letter of accusation against the inhabitants of Judah and Jerusalem written to

---

32. The Greek text is taken from Robert Hanhart, *Esdrae liber I* (Septuaginta Vetus Testamentum Graecum 8,1; Göttingen: Vandenhoeck & Ruprecht, 1991). Critical comments will also take into consideration the edition of A. E. Brooke, N. McLean, and H. J. Thackeray, *The Old Testament in Greek According to the Text of Codex Vaticanus, IV.1: I Esdras, Ezra-Nehemiah* (London: Cambridge University Press, 1935).

33. On the Hebrew text, see the recent edition of David Marcus, ed., עז־רא ונחמיה; *Ezra and Nehemiah* (Biblia Hebraica Quinta 20 Stuttgart: German Bible Society, 2006).

34. Qere כנותיו.

35. Qere ארתחששת.

36. The term נשתון (which appears in Ezra 4:7, 18, 23; 5:5) is an Old Persian loanword from ni-štā-van; "נשתון," *HALOT* 2:732a. Cf. A. Cowley, *Aramaic Papyri of the Fifth Century B.C.* (Oxford: Clarendon, 1923), 53 [17.3]. Although it could be argued that the phrase וכתב הנשתון כתוב, "the writing of the document was written," is redundant, it may clarify that the communication was indeed a written one (Williamson, *Ezra, Nehemiah*, 64) or allude to the use of a particular script. On the use of נשתון, see also the comments of Blenkinsopp, *Ezra-Nehemiah*, 110; Richard Steiner, "Bishlam's Archival Search Report in Nehemiah's Archive: Multiple Introductions and Reverse Chronological Order as Clues to the Origin of the Aramaic Letters in Ezra 4–5," *JBL* 125 (2006): 655–61.

37. Qere ארכויא.

38. Qere דהיא. As Marcus (*Ezra and Nehemiah*, 42*) observes, the Qere refers to an otherwise unknown group, the Dehavites.

Ahasuerus (Xerxes) within the context of his accession year (בתחלת מלכותו).[39] Nothing more is said about this letter or its reception at the beginning of Xerxes' tenure (ca. 485 B.C.E.).[40] Ezra 4:7-11a speak (apparently) of two complaints sent during the reign of Artaxerxes (I; ca. 465-424 B.C.E.). The text of Ezra 4:7-8 is certainly difficult to interpret.[41] Nevertheless, it is possible that the letter in Aramaic sent by Bishlam, Mithredath, Tabeel, and their colleagues to Artaxerxes is to be distinguished from the missive sent to Artaxerxes by Rehum, Shimshai, and their colleagues (Ezra 4:8-11a).[42] Only the latter (and the imperial response) is elaborated upon in the following text.[43] In support of such a distinction, it may be observed that the reply by King Artaxerxes is addressed "to Rehum the

---

39. Josephus (*Ant.* 11.19-30) relates a different context for the letter-writing campaign, mentioning the reigns of Cyrus and Cambyses. The letter to halt the building of the temple is set during the time of Cambyses. Josephus may be attempting to solve what he views as a chronological problem, thus changing Artaxerxes to Cambyses. For a discussion of this issue, see Lester L. Grabbe, "Josephus and the Reconstruction of the Judean Restoration," *JBL* 106 (1987): 233. In the alternative view of Batten (*Ezra and Nehemiah*, 11-12), the text of Josephus reflects a variant (and older) form of 1 Esdras.

40. Nothing more about this missive (Ezra 4:6), its senders, or its content is provided to readers. Presumably, in literary context, the general antecedent of "they wrote" is "the adversaries (צרי) of Judah and Benjamin" in Ezra 4:1 and, more immediately, "the people of the land" (עם-הארץ) in Ezra 4:4. For discussions, see Wilhelm Rudolph, *Esra und Nehemia samt 3 Esra* (HAT 20; Tübingen: Mohr Siebeck, 1949), 34-35; Shemaryahu Talmon, "The Judaean ʿam haʾareṣ in Historical Perspective," in *The Fourth World Congress of Jewish Studies, 1: Papers* (Jerusalem: World Union of Jewish Studies, 1967), 71-76; Williamson, *Ezra, Nehemiah*, 54-61; Willi, *Juda - Jehud - Israel*, 11-17. For a somewhat different point of view, see Lisbeth Fried, "The ʿam-hāʾāreṣ in Ezra 4:4 and Persian Imperial Administration," in *Judah and the Judeans in the Persian Period* (ed. Oded Lipschits and Manfred Oeming; Winona Lake, Ind.: Eisenbrauns, 2006), 123-45.

41. Batten comments that "it is difficult to find a more corrupt text than vv. 7-11"; *Ezra and Nehemiah*, 166. Recently, Steiner has argued that the inconsistencies in Ezra 4:7-11, specifically the problematic nature of what appear to be multiple introductions, are due to the preservation of four different "documentary strata"; "Bishlam's Archival Search," 642. While Steiner admirably addresses the textual inconsistencies present within Ezra 4-6, he does not address the relevant 1 Esdras material and how this may affect the reconstruction of the composition of Ezra.

42. Whether Bishlam (בשלם) is a proper name or represents part of an original greeting ("with the agreement of") need not concern us in this particular context, because בשלם was construed as a name by the translator of 1 Esdras. For a discussion, see Richard Steiner, "Why Bishlam (Ezra 4:7) Cannot Rest 'in Peace': On the Aramaic and Hebrew Sound Changes That Conspired to Blot out the Remembrance of Bel-Shalam the Archivist," *JBL* 126 (2007): 392-401.

43. For the view that Ezra 4:7-11a refers basically to one letter of complaint sent to the imperial crown, see Blenkinsopp, *Ezra-Nehemiah*, 110-13. In such a reconstruction, the text of Ezra 4:8-10 could be construed as a series of elaborations upon the letter initially referred to in Ezra 4:7.

commissioner (בעל-טעם),⁴⁴ Shimshai the scribe (ספרא), and the rest of their colleagues," who reside in Samaria and the rest of Transeuphrates (Ezra 4:17).⁴⁵ Moreover, when the Persian king's response is received, Rehum, Shimshai, and their colleagues rush to Jerusalem and put a stop to the rebuilding activity (Ezra 4:23). By contrast, the complaint of Bishlam, Mithredath, Tabeel, and their colleagues (Ezra 4:7) is not referred to again in the text.

When comparing 1 Esd 2:15 with Ezra 4:6–11a, it is quite striking that the Ezra account represents by far the longer text, supplying many details that are not present in 1 Esdras. The letter of accusation written to Ahasuerus (Xerxes) against the inhabitants of Jerusalem and Judah (Ezra 4:6) is mentioned neither in 1 Esd 2 nor in Josephus. Whereas Ezra 4:6–11a may imply two (possibly three) complaints sent to two different Persian monarchs (Xerxes and Artaxerxes), 1 Esdras only mentions one letter sent to one Persian monarch (Artaxerxes). Ezra 4:7 discloses that the communication sent to Artaxerxes was written in Aramaic and translated.⁴⁶ No such claim is made in the parallel text of 1 Esdras, but the statement does not seem to be an accident.⁴⁷ Ezra 4:8 records that other dignitaries wrote a letter to Artaxerxes, including Rehum, the "commissioner." Ezra 4:11a opens with the statement: "This is a copy of the letter that they sent to him." The precise phrase, "that they sent to him" (די שלחו עלוהי), in reference to the copy of the letter sent to Artaxerxes, is not present in 1 Esd 2:15.⁴⁸

In what appears to be a continuation or, more likely, an elaboration of the listing of the letter's authors, initially said to be Rehum and Shimshai (Ezra 4:8), Ezra 4:9–10 reiterates the names and titles of Rehum and Shimshai and then mentions colleagues connected to sending the missive—judges, officials, officers, overseers, the men of Erech, Babylon, and Susa (further identified as Elamites),

---

44. The term בעל-טעם only appears in Ezra 4:8, 9, and 17 in connection to Rehum. As commentators have observed, בעל-טעם is not a military title but rather a strictly administrative position; Williamson, *Ezra, Nehemiah*, 54; Blenkinsopp, *Ezra-Nehemiah*, 112–13. The term בעל-טעם appears in the late fifth-century B.C.E. Elephantine papyri. Richard Steiner observes that *bēl ṭēmu* occurs once in a Babylonian tablet from the time of Cyrus or Cambyses and another from the era of Darius, but does not appear to be used later than the fifth century B.C.E. ("Bishlam's Archival Search," 546).
45. Kurt Galling explains the discrepancy by postulating that Rehum was the successor to Mithredath; *Studien zur Geschichte Israels im persischer Zeitalter* (Tübingen: Mohr, 1964), 210.
46. Presumably into Persian. The material in Ezra 4:8–6:18 is written in Aramaic.
47. The response from the Achaemenid king mentions that the missive sent to him was read to him word for word (מפרש; Ezra 4:18). The text does not necessarily imply a translation (*pace* NJPS). Cf. מתרגם in Ezra 4:7.
48. In this instance, Josephus mentions a letter "whose contents were as follows" (*Ant.* 11.21). Cf. 1 Esd 2:15, τὴν ὑπογεγραμμένην ἐπιστολήν.

as well as others whom "the great and glorious Osnappar deported and settled in the city of Samaria and the rest of the province Beyond the River."[49]

By contrast, the several people involved in writing the letter to Artaxerxes in 1 Esd 2:15 are "Beslemos, Mithradates, Tabellios, Raoumos, Beelteemos, Samsaios the scribe, and the rest of their colleagues, residing in Samaria and in the other places."[50] At first glance, Beelteemos (Βεελτέεμος) appears to be a name not present in the list of Ezra, but his appearance in the LXX reflects the translator's misunderstanding of the position of Rehum, who was the בעל־טעם or "commissioner" of the community.[51] The work of Josephus (*Ant*. 11.26) also reflects the (mis)understanding manifest in 1 Esdras of בעל־טעם as a proper name.[52] Given this fact, one may generalize that the names, which seem to be associated with two letters to Artaxerxes in Ezra 4:7–11a, appear as the authors of one letter to Artaxerxes in 1 Esdras. But it must be pointed out that 1 Esdras does not list the judges, officials, officers, overseers, and so forth in Ezra 4:9. Nor does 1 Esd 2:15 include any mention of Osnappar's forced dislocation and resettlement of various foreign peoples in Samaria and the rest of the province of Beyond the River (Ezra 4:10). Given the fact that Ezra 4:8 and Ezra 4:10 both end with the similar transition markers (כנמא in v. 8; וכענת in v. 10), one is inclined to view the intervening material in vv. 9–10 as an interpolation.[53]

In any case, there is a basic congruence in proper names between the two texts. Of special note is Josephus' mention of Rathymos and Semelios, as well as the judges of the council in Syria and Phoenicia, sending a letter to Cambyses.[54]

---

49. Some textual witnesses read the expected plural ("cities"). For a discussion of the identification of Osnappar with Ashurbanipal, see Alan R. Millard, "Assyrian Royal Names in Biblical Hebrew," *JSS* 21 (1976): 11–12. Other have suggested Esarhaddon (cf. Ezra 4:2), but this seems less likely; see Lester L. Grabbe, *A History of the Jews and Judaism in the Second Temple Period, 1: Yehud; A History of the Persian Province of Judah* (LSTS 47; London: T&T Clark, 2004), 288–89.

50. Although these colleagues are often thought to stem from Samaria, this is only partially true. The text presents a wide array of transplanted foreigners in the province of Beyond the River in league together against the returnees in Judah. More on this below.

51. See, further, Myers, *I and II Esdras*, 39; Talshir, *1 Esdras: From Origin to Translation*, 238–47; idem, *1 Esdras: A Text Critical Commentary*, 106–7.

52. In the official response (Ezra 4:17), King Artaxerxes writes "to Rehum the commissioner," על־רחום בעל־טעם, but in 1 Esd 2:21 the king writes to "Rehum the recorder of events and to Beelteemos" ('Ραούμῳ τῷ γράφοντι τὰ προσπίπτοντα καὶ Βεελτέεμῳ). In this latter case, 1 Esdras both transliterates the name and explains the position. Josephus basically follows suit, listing Rathymos as the recorder of events (τῷ γράφοντι τὰ προσπίπτοντα) and providing a transliteration of his name (Βεελζέμῳ; *Ant*. 11.26).

53. In the latter case (Ezra 4:10), the writers of *HALOT* (5:1901a–b) state that the transition marker should be deleted. But if the material in 4:9–10 has been inserted into the text as an addition, the appearance of וכענת as a link to what follows is deliberate.

54. Josephus (*Ant*. 11.21) specifically situates the letter in the context of the beginning of Cambyses' reign, "When Cambyses, the son of Cyrus, had taken the kingdom" (Καμβύσου δὲ τοῦ Κύρου παιδὸς τὴν βασιλείαν παραλαβόντος).

In the context of the letter (*Ant.* 11.21), these officials are acting on behalf of Judah's neighbors (the residents of Syria, Phoenicia, Amman, Moab, and Samaria). Hence, in this case the text of Josephus seems to diverge somewhat from both Ezra and 1 Esdras.[55]

Without being exhaustive, the pluses in the MT (over against 1 Esdras) may be summarized as follows:

1. Reference to a letter sent to King Ahasuerus (Ezra 4:6).
2. Specific reference to the sending of an Aramaic letter (Ezra 4:7).
3. Reference to the translation of the Aramaic letter (Ezra 4:7).
4. An introduction to the following letter as Aramaic (Ezra 4:7).
5. References to (possibly) two letters during the reign of Artaxerxes (Ezra 4:7–10).
6. Reference to a variety of officials (Ezra 4:9–10), amplifying the initial listing of Ezra 4:8: Rehum the commissioner (בעל-טעם) and Shimshai the scribe (ספרא).
7. Reference to the foreign ethnicities of the letter senders as deportees resettled in Samaria and the rest of Beyond the River by Osnappar (Ezra 4:9–10).
8. Repetition of names. Artaxerxes' name is mentioned four times in Ezra 4:7–10 and only once in 1 Esdras. Rehum and Shimshai are mentioned twice in Ezra 4:6–10 but only once in 1 Esdras.

Thus, the MT is by far the longer text, including significantly more information and mentioning multiple letters written to the Persian monarchs. By comparison, 1 Esdras seems to presuppose a drastically shorter text than that which appears in Ezra. But what about the text of 1 Esdras itself? It will be useful to examine the account in 1 Esdras to see if it has any other significant variants or additional material in comparison with the account in Ezra.

We have seen that there are several pluses in the MT, but 1 Esd 2:15 includes unique material, most of which is of a minor nature. One of the minor

---

55. Earlier, Josephus (*Ant.* 11.19) mentions that the "neighboring nations, especially the Cutheans, whom Shalmaneser (V), king of Assyria, brought out of Persia and Media, and had settled in Samaria, when he carried the people of Israel into captivity, sought out the governors" to frustrate the building of the town and temple during the time of Cyrus. In this case, Josephus alludes to narrative of 2 Kgs 17:24–33 to amplify his understanding of the early postexilic period as presented in Ezra 4:1–5 and 1 Esd 5:63–70. That Josephus has access not only to 1 Esdras but also to some version of Ezra (or to an alternate version of 1 Esdras that included some elements found in Ezra) seems to be evident in his reference to the successful bribes (χρήμασι), which stymied the building campaign during the remainder of Cyrus' reign (*Ant.* 11.20; cf. סכרים in Ezra 4:5). The account of 1 Esdras (5:69–70), by comparison, does not mention bribes, although it does aver that the peoples of the land successfully thwarted the building campaign.

differences between the two texts is the addition of the conjunction καί before several names, including Mithradates and Tabellios, Raoumos, and Beelteemos. Although the additional instances of καί could be viewed as reflecting minute additions to the text or as reflecting a slightly longer *Vorlage*, the reality may be slightly more complicated. The repeated appearance of the conjunction καί is a hallmark of colloquial Koine Greek, when compared to Classical Greek.[56] Thus, καί need not be construed as evidence for a longer, more elaborate *Vorlage* but may reflect a stylistic technique in translating a Semitic text into typical (colloquial) Koine.

Another variant in the LXX of 1 Esdras is the reference to the letter senders as "living in Samaria and the other places" (Σαμαρείᾳ καὶ τοῖς ἄλλοις τόποις). As we have seen, the letter senders in Ezra 4:9–10 stem from "the city of Samaria and the rest of Beyond the River." Interestingly, the text of the letter itself in 1 Esdras refers to the letter senders as residing in Κοίλῃ Συρίᾳ καὶ Φοινίκῃ (1 Esd 2:16).[57] The latter ("Coele Syria and Phoenicia") is the common rendering of the Persian province עבר־נהרה ("Across the River") in 1 Esdras and 1 and 2 Maccabees.[58] Given that such a variant reflects the terminology employed by the translator to render his *Vorlage*, it should not necessarily be considered as a plus to the material found in the MT. The king's later response is sent to "Samaria and Syria and Phoenicia" (Σαμαρείᾳ καὶ Συρίᾳ καὶ Φοινίκῃ; 1 Esd 2:21).[59] Thus, it must be said that the text of 1 Esdras does not speak precisely with one voice as to the geographic locales of the letter writers.[60]

To summarize, within this particular case study, the MT preserves the longer text, while the LXX preserves the shorter text. Inasmuch as 1 Esd 2:15 presents a much briefer text, does it also represent, for the most part, the older text (*Brevior lectio praeferenda est*)? Such a determination would not lead necessarily to the

---

56. The frequent tendency to use the conjunction καί can also be seen in the Gospel of Mark. An examination of Mark (e.g., 1:15–45; 2:1–12) reveals the common usage of καί as one means to tie together narrative statements and frame a larger plot.

57. By contrast, the letter writers in the missive of Ezra 4:11b–16 identify themselves simply as "your servants, men of Beyond the River" (עבדיך אנש עבר־נהרה; 4:11b).

58. On the translation of the name of the Persian province, "Across the River," see further Myers (*I and II Esdras*, 41) and Talshir (*1 Esdras: A Text Critical Commentary*, 119). The use of "Coele Syria and Phoenicia" is in contrast to Ezra B (e.g., 4:10, 11, 16, 17, 20), in which the Greek renders "Across the River" more literally as περάν τοῦ ποταμοῦ.

59. In his reference to the return letter, Josephus (*Ant.* 11.26) writes, "Cambyses, the king, to Rathymos, the recorder of events, to Beelzemos, and to Semelios the scribe, and the rest that are arraigned together, and residing in Samaria and Phoenicia" (βασιλεὺς Καμβύσης Ῥαθύμῳ τῷ γράφοντι τὰ προσπίπτοντα καὶ Βεελζέμῳ καὶ Σεμελίῳ γραμματεῖ καὶ τοῖς λοποῖς τοῖς συντασσομένοις καὶ οἰκοῦσιν ἐν Σαμαρείᾳ καὶ Φοινίκῃ). Syria is missing (cf. καὶ Συρίᾳ in 1 Esd 2:21), perhaps because of haplography (*homoioarkton*).

60. The relevant variations in the MT (Ezra 4:7, 8, 9–10, 11, 17) have already been noted (see above).

conclusion that 1 Esdras represents the original text of Ezra, because 1 Esdras may itself incorporate secondary material. But it might mean that in this case, 1 Esdras bears witness to an older version of the text than that found in the MT.

It will be useful to consider some possible counterarguments to following the *lectio brevior* rule in this instance. Theoretically, 1 Esd 2:15 could be a vastly pared-down and abbreviated version of the longer text Ezra 4:6–11a. Perhaps the translator of 1 Esdras (or the writer of the *Vorlage* employed by the translator of 1 Esdras) thought that the text of Ezra 4:6–11a was overly complicated and decided to simplify matters drastically. Alternatively, it could be argued that 1 Esdras has suffered severe textual corruption.[61] Such possibilities need to be taken into account. The text of 1 Esdras is uneven, but the abridgment argument largely fails to convince. If the writer of 1 Esdras deliberately condensed his much-longer *Vorlage*, one would expect the work to speak summarily of a plurality of letters written during the reigns of Xerxes and Artaxerxes.[62] But 1 Esdras only mentions one letter. There is no reference to a letter to Ahasuerus in 1 Esdras (cf. Ezra 4:6), whereas the impetus for a scribe to add such a reference in the development of the text of Ezra may be readily apparent. The summary statement of Ezra 4:5 speaks of sustained opposition to the community's rebuilding efforts from the time of Cyrus to the reign of Darius, whereas the letter exchange in Ezra 4:11b–22 pertains to the later reign of Artaxerxes. The addition of a reference to an epistle in the time of Ahasuerus (Ezra 4:6) thus fills a perceived lacuna in the larger presentation.[63]

We have seen that the text of 1 Esdras lacks any reference to the letter sent to Artaxerxes as having been written in Aramaic and translated (presumably into Persian). Hypothetically, it could be that the writer of 1 Esdras omitted these details both in the initial description of the letter (Ezra 4:7) and in the king's response (Ezra 4:18). The translator of 1 Esdras was, after all, writing in Greek and not in Hebrew and Aramaic, hence such details could be easily skipped over. But upon careful consideration, the situation does not seem to be so simple. To begin with, there are cases in the Hebrew Scriptures in which the transition from Hebrew to Aramaic is not formally marked (Gen 31:47; Jer 10:11) as it is in Ezra 4:7. Such comparative evidence includes the book of Ezra itself. The transition from Aramaic to Hebrew in Ezra 6:18 is not explicitly designated. Similarly, the transition from Hebrew to Aramaic pertaining to the Rescript of Artaxerxes is not formally marked (Ezra 7:12 // 1 Esd 8:9). Nor is the transition back from

---

61. So Batten, *Ezra and Nehemiah*, 159–73.

62. Moreover, one would want to see unmistakable examples of other cases in which the LXX translators deliberately truncated the Hebrew (or Aramaic) text before them. Accidental haplographies are, of course, a different matter, because such mistakes are quite common in textual transmission; P. Kyle McCarter, *Textual Criticism* (Philadelphia: Fortress, 1986), 38–42.

63. On this matter, see also the useful comments of Böhler, *Die heilige Stadt*, 233–35.

Aramaic to Hebrew (Ezra 7:26 // 1 Esd 8:24).[64] This evidence indicates that the original transition from Hebrew to Aramaic in Ezra 4 need not have been explicitly marked either.

Second, there is the case of the Assyrian envoys sent by King Sennacherib speaking in "Judahite" (יהודית) to the inhabitants of Jerusalem. There, both the MT and the LXX mention the request that they speak in "Aramaic" (MT and LXX 2 Kgs 18:26 // Isa 36:11). The fact that the LXX is a translation does not lead the translators to omit this important detail found in their *Vorlage*. Third, in another case in which the transition from Hebrew to Aramaic is explicitly marked (ארמית; Dan 2:4), the LXX to Dan 2:4 follows suit. There is no discrepancy between the MT and the LXX in this instance. The same is true for the transition back from Aramaic to Hebrew (Dan 7:28). In sum, the comparative textual evidence cautions against assuming that the writers of 1 Esdras deliberately omitted this detail from their *Vorlage*. Rather, it stands to reason that the detail was lacking in their source.

Finally, one could contend that because 1 Esdras contains the proper names of the letter senders in Ezra 4:7–10 ("Beslemos, Mithradates, Tabellios, Raoumos, Beelteemos, and Samsaios"), the writers of 1 Esdras must have had the full text of Ezra before them. In such a reconstruction, the writers of 1 Esdras reproduced all the names found in their *Vorlage* but reduced the communications sent by these dignitaries to the central Achaemenid court to one. But such a scenario seems unlikely. In most, albeit not all, cases of textual transmission, a text tends to become longer and more complex over time, rather than shorter and simpler over time.[65] Given the likelihood that Ezra 4:6–11a contains one or more expansions in its literary development, it will be beneficial to explore, however briefly, the force of such additions.

III. The Foreign Opponents of the Judean Returnees in Ezra 4:6–11a

It is surely interesting that the MT version speaks of multiple letters written during the reigns of a succession of Achaemenid monarchs. Assuming that this

---

64. The much-debated compositional history of the firman need not deter us here. See, e.g., Sebastian Grätz, *Das Edikt des Artaxerxes: Eine Untersuchung zum religionspolitischen und historischen Umfeld von Esra 7,12–26* (BZAW 337; Berlin: de Gruyter, 2004); Gary N. Knoppers, "Beyond Jerusalem and Judah: The Commission of Artaxerxes to Ezra in the Province Beyond the River," in *Ephraim Stern Volume* (ed. J. Aviram, A. Ben Tor, I. Eph'al, S. Gitin, and R. Reich; ErIsr 29; Jerusalem: Israel Exploration Society, 2009), 78–87.

65. In this context, Blenkinsopp (*Ezra–Nehemiah*, 115) contends that the reference to the "rest of the province Beyond the River" (Ezra 4:10, 17), as well as the allusion to the Davidic-Solomonic kingdom (v. 20), are later editorial expansions, because it is unlikely that the king would address the entire satrapy with his letter.

phenomenon represents a development within the text of Ezra, what was the impetus to creating such an expansion (or set of expansions)? The scribes responsible for Ezra 4:6-11a document a history of sustained opposition to the rebuilding efforts of the Judean returnees. In so doing, the writers elaborate upon a common theme found elsewhere in Ezra-Nehemiah, namely, the active resistance of Judah's neighbors to allowing the returned exiles to rebuild the major institutions of their community.[66] To be sure, this element is also found within 1 Esdras. There, as we have seen, one finds opposition from those "in Samaria and the other places" to the returned exiles.

But there is an additional element in Ezra 4:6-11a that is quite fascinating. The writers of Ezra 4:9-10 depict an assortment of peoples, including foreigners whom Osnappar dislocated and resettled in Samaria and the rest of Beyond the River, as allied together against the Judeans. There are partial parallels to such a phenomenon elsewhere in Ezra-Nehemiah that are worth discussing. In Nehemiah, one reads of local potentates—Sanballat of Samaria, Tobiah of Ammon, and (sometimes) Geshem the Arab—arrayed against the cupbearer to the king's efforts to rebuild the walls of Jerusalem (e.g., Neh 2:19; 3:33; 4:1-2; 6:1, 6).[67] But one does not find associated officials in locales across the entire province of Beyond the River arrayed against Nehemiah.

The assertion of a conspiracy involving a range of bureaucrats in Trans-euphrates against the returnees in Ezra 4 // 1 Esd 2 finds a closer parallel elsewhere within the initial section of Ezra (chs. 1-6). In the time of Darius I, Tattenai, the governor of Beyond the River; Shethar-bozenai; and their colleagues question the temple-building project of Zerubbabel and Jeshua (Ezra 5:3). This resistance includes the dispatch of a letter from "Tattenai, the governor of Beyond the River; Shethar-bozenai; and his colleagues, the officials of

---

66. Japhet, "People and Land," 103-25; H. G. M. Williamson, "The Composition of Ezra i-vi," *JTS* 34 (1983): 1-30; Baruch Halpern, "A Historiographic Commentary on Ezra 1-6: Achronological Narrative and Dual Chronology in Israelite Historiography," in *The Hebrew Bible and Its Interpreters* (ed. William H. Propp, Baruch Halpern, and David Noel Freedman; Biblical and Judaic Studies 1; Winona Lake, Ind.: Eisenbrauns, 1990), 81-141; Daniel L. Smith-Christopher, "Between Ezra and Isaiah: Exclusion, Transformation, and Inclusion in Post-Exilic Biblical Theology," in *Ethnicity and the Bible* (ed. M. G. Brett; BibInt 19; Leiden: Brill, 1996); 116-42; Wright, *Rebuilding Identity*, 39-43.

67. Nehemiah's reforms also occur during the reign of Artaxerxes. The incident(s) mentioned in Ezra 4:7-23 is not referred to in Nehemiah, unless one takes the report of Neh 1:3 as an oblique allusion; Rudolph, *Esra und Nehemia*, 103; Williamson, *Ezra, Nehemiah*, 172; Antonius H. J. Gunneweg, *Nehemia* (KAT 19/2; Gütersloh: Gütersloher Verlagshaus, 1987), 45-47. But see the lengthy objections of Wright, *Rebuilding Identity*, 31-44. [See also the discussion by Lisbeth S. Fried, "The Artaxerxes Correspondence of Ezra 4, Nehemiah's Wall, and Persian Provincial Administration," in *'Go Out and Study the Land' (Judges 18:2): Archaeological, Historical and Textual Studies in Honor of Hanan Eshel* (ed. A. M. Maeir, J. Magness, and L. H. Schiffman; JSJSup; Leiden: Brill, in press)—Ed.]

Beyond the River" to King Darius (Ezra 5:6). Darius' response (Ezra 6:6–12) acknowledges that the antagonism is more than local, mentioning not only Tattenai and Shethar-bozenai but also "their associates, the officials in Beyond the River." Insofar as the hostility stems from officials across the satrapy, the opposition shown toward Zerubbabel and Jeshua forms a closer parallel to the situation described in Ezra 4 than does the local antagonism toward Nehemiah shown by Sanballat, Tobiah, and Geshem.

But what should one make of the alien origins of the opponents in Ezra 4:7–11a? The authors make no claim that Tattenai, Shethar-bozenai, and their colleagues in Beyond the River were the seed of foreign transplants in Neo-Assyrian times. A clue to what may have propelled the writers of vv. 9–10 to add this material may be found earlier in the chapter. There, we read that the "adversaries of Judah and Benjamin" approached Zerubbabel, Jeshua, and the heads of the ancestral houses, volunteering to help in the temple reconstruction program (Ezra 4:1). Claiming to worship the same deity as the children of the exile, these persons identify themselves as descendants of foreigners whom King Esarhaddon imported into the land (Ezra 4:2). After the offer is rebuffed by Zerubbabel and Jeshua, the "people of the land" successfully foil the rebuilding campaign during the rest of Cyrus' reign (Ezra 4:5).

In the context of narrating the struggles of the postexilic Judean community, the declaration in Ezra 4:9–10 that the letter writers in the time of Artaxerxes were, in fact, foreign settlers imported into the land by the "great and glorious Osnappar" vindicates the decision made generations earlier by Zerubbabel and Jeshua. The early Judean leaders were not being xenophobic in rejecting an offer of assistance from outsiders. What may have seemed on the surface to be a good-faith gesture by foreign transplants in the satrapy was disingenuous. The scribes responsible for the additions in Ezra 4:7–11a expanded upon the notion of resistance shown by the "people of the land" (Ezra 4:4) to include a range of enemies within the larger satrapy at work during the reign of Artaxerxes.[68] The opponents of Judean returnees included, in fact, a range of officials descended from foreign settlers, who joined together in an anti-Judean coalition in the reign of Artaxerxes. In this respect, the authors of the additions in Ezra 4:7–11a elaborated upon and extended motifs found elsewhere within Ezra 1–6.

Conclusions

In his discussion of the compositional history of Ezra–Nehemiah, Wright speaks of *creatio continua*, a long process of reinterpreting, rewriting, and embellishing older texts.[69] The creation of new texts sets the older material into which such

---

68. As we have seen (section II), the desire to document such alien opposition also helps to explain the addition of most of Ezra 4:6.
69. Wright, *Rebuilding Identity*, 3.

texts are inserted in a new context.[70] In this essay, we have found text-critical evidence for such a process in the development of Ezra–Nehemiah. Although our study has focused on one particular passage in Ezra and its parallel in 1 Esdras, it suggests the promise of such detailed explorations of textual variants in illuminating the compositional histories of both literary works. To be sure, there are many more cases in which the text of Ezra may be profitably used to explain the development of 1 Esdras than vice versa. Nevertheless, critical examination of the textual variants among the overlapping sections of Chronicles, Ezra–Nehemiah, and 1 Esdras may shed welcome light on the compositional and editorial histories of all these neglected writings. In the last centuries before the Common Era, most biblical texts were not absolutely fixed in all details. A certain amount of fluidity in the development of biblical writings is apparent when one compares the multiple textual witnesses available for such writings. As Talmon comments, scribes working within different textual traditions acted as "minor partner[s] in the creative literary process."[71] In the wake of the discoveries at Qumran, scholars have come to recognize that exercises in lower criticism have ramifications for higher criticism.

---

70. As applied to many other biblical texts, see, for instance, the insightful studies of Michael Fishbane, *Biblical Interpretation in Ancient Israel* (Oxford: Clarendon, 1985); Bernard M. Levinson, *Deuteronomy and the Hermeneutics of Legal Innovation* (New York: Oxford University Press, 1997); idem, *Legal Revision and Religious Renewal in Ancient Israel* (New York: Cambridge University Press, 2008).

71. Shemaryahu Talmon, "The Textual Study of the Bible: A New Outlook," in *Qumran and the History of the Biblical Text* (ed. Frank Moore Cross and Shemaryahu Talmon; Cambridge: Harvard University Press, 1975), 381.

CHICKEN OR EGG?
WHICH CAME FIRST, 1 ESDRAS OR EZRA–NEHEMIAH?

Lester L. Grabbe

If we went back a generation or two, we would find a considerable consensus that 1 Esdras preceded Ezra–Nehemiah. Granted, this tended to be tied up with a theory (the so-called Fragment Hypothesis) about the Chronicler, who was assumed to have written, or at least compiled, 1 and 2 Chronicles and Ezra–Nehemiah as a more-or-less continuous narrative of Israel's history.[1] More recently, an increasing number of scholars have assumed—and a few have argued—that 1 Esdras was simply an extract from the canonical Ezra–Nehemiah.[2]

My aim in this article is to argue that 1 Esdras represents a stage in the development toward the final composition that is found in the MT Ezra–Nehemiah and the LXX Esdras β, that is, that the original base text of 1 Esdras was earlier than MT Ezra–Nehemiah and was drawn on by it as a major source.[3]

---

1. Sigmund Mowinckel, *Studien zu dem Buche Ezra–Nehemiah I* (Skrifter utgitt av Det Norske Videnskaps-Akademi i Oslo II; Historisk-Filosofisk Klasse, Ny Serie 3; Oslo: Universitetsforlaget, 1964); Karl-Friedrich Pohlmann, *Studien zum dritten Esra: Ein Beitrag zur Frage nach dem ursprünglichen Schluss des chronistischen Geschichtswerkes* (FRLANT 104; Göttingen: Vandenhoeck & Ruprecht, 1970).

2. H. G. M. Williamson, *Israel in the Books of Chronicles* (Cambridge: Cambridge University Press, 1977), 12–36; idem, "The Problem with First Esdras," in *After the Exile: Essays in Honour of Rex Mason* (ed. John Barton and David J. Reimer; Macon, Ga.: Mercer University Press, 1996), 201–16; Tamara C. Eskenazi, "The Chronicler and the Composition of 1 Esdras," *CBQ* 48 (1986): 39–61; Zipora Talshir, *1 Esdras: From Origin to Translation* (SBLSCS 47; Atlanta: Scholars Press, 1999); idem, *1 Esdras: A Text Critical Commentary* (SBLSCS 50; Atlanta: Society of Biblical Literature, 2001); Kristin De Troyer, "Zerubbabel and Ezra: A Revived and Revised Solomon and Josiah? A Survey of Current 1 Esdras Research," *Currents in Biblical Research* 1 (2002): 30–60. My thanks to Professor De Troyer for sharing her article with me before publication.

3. "1 Esdras" refers to the text in the Göttingen edition, as edited by Robert Hanhart (*Esdrae liber I* [2d ed.; Septuaginta Vetus Testamentum Graecum 8/1; Göttingen: Vandenhoeck & Ruprecht, 1991]). The traditional Hebrew and Aramaic books of Ezra–Nehemiah are referred to as "MT Ezra–Nehemiah" (or "MT Ezra" and "MT Nehemiah"). The literal Greek

1. A Thesis on the Origins of 1 Esdras

The thesis that 1 Esdras is independent of Hebrew Ezra–Nehemiah has been revived in recent years in a form different from the old Fragment Hypothesis.[4] Dieter Böhler and I independently, about a decade ago, took this view, though each of us was using different arguments.

1.1. STRUCTURE OF 1 ESDRAS

The book of 1 Esdras is not just similar or parallel to the Hebrew/Aramaic Ezra and Nehemiah but, except for 1 Esd 3–4, clearly was translated from a text almost the same as 2 Chr 35–36, Ezra 1–10, and Neh 8 (though differing in many minor details). Any theory about the origins of the book and its relationship to the canonical books must take account of this fact. The parallel texts can be summarized as follows:

1 Esdras	MT	
1:1–22	2 Chr 35:1–19	Josiah's Passover
1:23–55	2 Chr 35:20–36:21	Josiah's reign to the fall of Jerusalem
2:1–14	Ezra 1	Return of exiles
2:15–25	Ezra 4:7–24	Building of temple begins, then stopped
3:1–5:6	No parallel	Story of the three bodyguards
5:7–45	Ezra 2	List of those returning from exile
5:46–70	Ezra 3:1–4:5	Altar set up; temple foundations laid
6	Ezra 5:1–6:12	Building of temple resumed
7	Ezra 6:13–22	Temple finished; dedicated at Passover
8:1–64	Ezra 7–8	Ezra's expedition to Jerusalem
8:65–9:36	Ezra 9–10	Crisis of mixed marriages
9:37–55	Neh 7:72–8:12	Ezra reads the law
[Missing	Neh 8:13–18(?)	Celebration of Feast of Tabernacles]

Some comments should be made about certain sections of 1 Esdras in relationship to 2 Chronicles, Ezra, and Nehemiah to show the complicated nature of the relationship in individual sections. First Esdras 1 generally agrees with 2 Chr 35–36 sentence for sentence and even word for word. Yet as already noted, there are

---

translation of MT Ezra–Nehemiah is referred to as "Esdras β" and is cited according to the Göttingen edition, as edited by Hanhart (*Esdrae liber II* [Septuaginta Vetus Testamentum Graecum 8/2; Göttingen: Vandenhoeck & Ruprecht, 1993]). Please note that the verse numbers below, which are given according to Hanhart's Greek text of 1991, may differ slightly from those in some English translations.

4. Dieter Böhler, *Die heilige Stadt in Esdras α und Esra-Nehemia: Zwei Konzeptionen der Wiederherstellung Israels* (OBO 158; Freiburg: Universitätsverlag; Göttingen: Vandenhoeck & Ruprecht, 1997); Lester L. Grabbe, *Ezra and Nehemiah* (OTR; London: Routledge, 1998), 69–81, 109–15.

many minor differences, usually affecting detail, but sometimes there are more important ones. For example, the summary of Josiah's reign in 1 Esd 1:21–22 has no parallel in the MT. Second Chronicles 36:22–23 and Ezra 1:1–3a are virtually the same, word for word. First Esdras 1 (which had been parallel up to 2 Chr 36:21) has nothing corresponding to this. It is, rather, 1 Esd 2:1–5, which parallels Ezra 1:1–3, that has this passage. In other words, the end of 2 Chr 36 and the beginning of Ezra 1 have the same passage twice; 1 Esdras has it only once.

First Esdras 3–4 have no counterpart in the Hebrew Bible. The banquet of the king (3:1–3) resembles Ahasuerus' banquet in Esth 1, but only the general theme is the same, not the details. Both mention 127 satrapies or provinces in the Persian empire from India to Ethiopia, but the content of the banquet account is otherwise somewhat different. Rather than borrowing from Esther, it seems more likely that 1 Esdras has used the common motif of the sumptuous banquet of the oriental king (cf. also Dan 5). Darius' solicitude for the Jerusalem temple also resembles the letter of Darius in Ezra 6:6–10 as far as making provision for the expenses of the temple to be defrayed at government expense (cf. also the vast quantity of resources Ezra has in Ezra 7:21–24). Again, though, this is a motif of general Persian care for the Jerusalem temple and is not necessarily a direct borrowing.

As has long been recognized, Zerubbabel's choice of topic indicates that an original story has been embellished by a pious redactor. The account of the three arguments as to which is stronger fits well the topics of wine, the king, and women, but the subject of the truth is clearly added on and goes against the ground rules, which are to find which one thing is strongest. The author of 1 Esdras has taken over a traditional story but either has a version already expanded by the addition of the element of truth or has done the expansion himself. First Esdras still has the problem that Artaxerxes precedes Darius, but Ezra's problem of Zerubbabel coming in the time of Cyrus does not exist in the 1 Esdras account because Zerubbabel is not associated with the first wave of immigrants.

In an extremely long chapter of more than ninety verses, 1 Esd 8 covers the same ground as is found in Ezra 7:1–10:5. Most of the time, 1 Esdras is very similar to the text of Ezra, evidently the same, word for word, much of the time when allowance is made for the fact that one text is in Greek and the other in Hebrew and Aramaic. Differences include some small discrepancies in names and numbers of the list in 1 Esd 8:28–40 (// Ezra 8:1–14), the number of temple vessels in 8:56 (// Ezra 8:27), the name of one of the Levites in 8:62 (// Ezra 8:33), and the number of lambs sacrificed in 8:63 (// Ezra 8:35). What appears to be a damaged text in Ezra 8:3a has an intelligible counterpart in 1 Esd 8:39. Ezra finds he has neither priests nor Levites in his company (8:42, whereas it is only Levites in Ezra 8:15). First Esdras 8:66 has "Edomites" where Ezra 9:1 has "Ammonites." First Esdras 8:89 has Jechoniah son of Jehiel speak to Ezra; the man is called Shecaniah son of Jehiel in Ezra 10:2.

There are, in addition, other small differences (apart from the main one in 1 Esd 3–4, which has no parallel). Some differences are likely to be the result of a different underlying Hebrew or Aramaic text, though it is not always possible to be sure. The text is in relatively good Greek and is less literal than the Septuagint translation of the Hebrew Ezra and Nehemiah known as Esdras β; also, the translator apparently had little in the way of other translations of the OT to use as a guide and was experimenting with finding appropriate language to express the original Semitic text.[5] All of this makes determining the Hebrew/Aramaic *Vorlage* more problematic; nevertheless, we can be sure that that text was mostly the same but occasionally slightly different from the MT. Thus, either 1 Esdras was made by editing Ezra–Nehemiah, Ezra–Nehemiah were produced by editing a text like 1 Esdras, or some other formal literary relationship pertains. The answer to the question of the relationship could be important for understanding how the Ezra tradition developed.

There are some remarkable parallels between parts of the MT Ezra–Nehemiah.[6] We also find a certain pattern of parallelism in 1 Esdras:

1: Josiah's Passover; conquest of Jerusalem	[inclusio with the presumed lost ending]
2:1–14: decree of Cyrus	8:1–27: decree of Artaxerxes
2:15–25: delivery of wealth/temple vessels	8:28–64: delivery of wealth/temple vessels
3:1–5:6: story of three guardsmen	no parallel
5:1–45: list of immigrants	no parallel [cf. 8:28–48]
5:46–62: sacrifices offered; temple begun	no parallel
5:63–70: foreigners raise opposition	8:65–87: problem because of foreigners
6:1–33: opposition overcome	8:88–9:36: problem resolved
7:1–9: temple completed	9:37–55: mission completed (law read)
7:10–15: Passover celebrated	[Lost ending: Tabernacles celebrated?]

One can debate what this parallelism means. It indicates a structure but seems less exact than that in MT Ezra–Nehemiah. Is this because the book was created by excerpting, or does it indicate that the book has been edited? The one thing that it might indicate is that 1 Esd 3:1–5:6 was a later addition to the book.

Finally, we should look at Josephus, who (most scholars agree) used a version of 1 Esdras for his story of Joshua/Zerubbabel and Ezra. As was his custom, he rewrote the text, making minor alterations and omitting what he thought would not suit his purpose. He also has the death of Ezra, but this is probably his own inference. He then has a story about Nehemiah that is unlikely to come from the canonical book of Nehemiah, suggesting that his Nehemiah tradition

---

5. Karl-Friedrich Pohlmann, *3. Esra-Buch* (JSHRZ 1/5; Gütersloh: Gütersloher Verlagshaus, 1980), 378–80.

6. Grabbe, *Ezra and Nehemiah*, 67, 107–9; idem, *A History of the Jews and Judaism in the Second Temple Period, Volume 1: Yehud; A History of the Persian Province of Judah* (LSTS 47; London: T&T Clark, 2004), 72.

was a separate one. Although it is parallel in many ways to Neh 1–6, it has some significant differences (including the omission of Neh 5), which suggests an independent tradition that perhaps developed directly from the Nehemiah Memoir. In other words, Josephus did not know our canonical Ezra–Nehemiah; instead, he had 1 Esdras plus possibly a tradition about Ezra's death (though all that he says about Ezra might be deduced from 1 Esdras) and traditions about Nehemiah (but not our present canonical book of Nehemiah).

Josephus's narrative in the *Antiquities* has 1 Esdras as the basis of its account of the return from exile. The parallels are roughly as follows:

Antiquities	1 Esdras
11.1.1–3 §§1–11	2:1–14
11.1.3 §§12–18	6:23–31
11.2.1 §§19–20	(cf. 5:63–70)
11.2.1–2 §§20–30	2:15–25
11.3.1–9 §§31–67	3–4
11.3.10 §§68–74	5:41–45
11.4.1 §§75–78	5:46–53
11.4.2–4 §§79–88	5:54–70
11.4.4 §§89–94	6:3–21
11.4.5 §§95–96	(cf. 6:1–2)
11.4.6–8 §§97–110	6:22–7:15
11.4.8–9 §§111–19	No parallel
11.5.1–5 §§120–57	8–9 (with some alterations)
11.5.5 §158	No parallel

Exact parallels are not possible because Josephus makes changes and small additions. Some of the more significant additions and changes to 1 Esdras include the following: lists tend to be omitted; the names of kings are changed to fit Persian chronology better (at least, as Josephus understands it); a number of times the "enemies" of the Jews are explicitly said to be the Samaritans (cf. 11.2.1 §§19–20); Sheshbazzar seems to be identified with Zerubbabel (cf. 11.1.3 §§11, 13; 11.4.4 §93); other minor changes to remove potential contradictions and smooth the flow of the passage.

1.2. ARGUMENTS FOR THE PRIORITY OF 1 ESDRAS

Here are the basic arguments for my own position:

1.2.1. A variety of independent traditions are incorporated into 1 Esdras and MT Ezra–Nehemiah. This is partly based on conjecture but also partly attested in a variety of sources.[7] We know of or can conjecture at least four foundation stories associated with four separate leaders: Sheshbazzar, Joshua/Zerubbabel, Ezra, and

---

7. Grabbe, *History of the Jews and Judaism*, 74–76, 276–77.

Nehemiah. These are known singly or in various combinations, of which MT Ezra–Nehemiah is only one witness. First Esdras is known only in a Greek version (and in translations of the Greek into Latin, Syriac, and some other languages); however, there seems little doubt of a Hebrew and Aramaic original, as the style of the Greek strongly suggests (even though no traces of an original Semitic text have so far been found). Because it has a separate history of transmission from Ezra–Nehemiah, 1 Esdras is a valuable textual source for the Joshua/Zerubbabel and Ezra traditions. Its main difference from MT Ezra–Nehemiah is that it lacks the Nehemiah tradition.

1.2.2. The concept of rewritten Bible has been around for a number of decades, but most examples of rewritten Bible have an interpretative function that distinguishes them from the original. If the Hebrew Ezra–Nehemiah was available and accepted as Scripture, it makes little sense that someone created a parallel, but truncated, edition by excerpting some bits from it, along with a passage from 2 Chronicles. The only cogent argument that I have seen is that of Zipora Talshir,[8] who argues that the purpose was to give a context to the story of the three youths. If the story of the three youths is seen as the center of the book, then Talshir's explanation makes sense, yet there are two problems to consider:

(a) An analysis of the tradition's development suggests that the story of the three guardsmen is a secondary addition to 1 Esdras. It is not one of the foundation legends mentioned in 1.2.1 above. It is not found in MT Ezra–Nehemiah, which otherwise has parallels to all the contents of 1 Esdras. Most scholars agree that it is a traditional tale that has somehow been turned into a Jewish morality tale (the third candidate for the most powerful is clearly "women," yet the concept of "truth" has been tacked on with no logic except for the evident desire to add a moral to the story).

(b) If the three-youths story is the focus of 1 Esdras, then why include the Ezra story? After all, the Zerubbabel story could easily stand alone, if the writer wanted to focus on it. Also, why does Zerubbabel disappear from the story and remain absent at the dedication of the temple? In other words, one can recognize how the three-youths story forms a significant addition to the story without assuming that it is the core of the book.

1.2.3. Why eliminate Nehemiah? If a combined story with Nehemiah as a main protagonist was already in circulation, why go to the trouble of removing him? The Nehemiah tradition circulated on its own, and some writers plainly accepted it without knowing of, or at least not accepting, the Ezra tradition or the Joshua/

---

8. Talshir, *1 Esdras: From Origin to Translation*; idem, *1 Esdras: A Text Critical Commentary*.

Zerubbabel tradition But if the compiler knew the MT Ezra–Nehemiah, why would he go to the trouble of omitting Nehemiah? If the combined account of Ezra–Nehemiah already existed and lay before him, it was most likely an authoritative account by this time. There is no clear reason why the compiler of 1 Esdras would then go to such trouble to excise Nehemiah.

1.2.4. If we were to proceed on the basis that someone did indeed wish to remove Nehemiah from the narrative, we would expect the ancient redactor to have simply taken away the book of Nehemiah. This would have been the easiest and most obvious way of editing out Nehemiah. Nevertheless, we find a parallel to Neh 8:1–12 in 1 Esd 9:27–55: how is it that the ancient author just happened to hit upon a literary analysis that matches that of modern critics? Ezra's name occurs in some other passages of MT Ezra–Nehemiah that are not included in 1 Esdras (e.g., Neh 12:33, 36) Source criticism has concluded that Neh 8 is indeed a part of the Ezra tradition, but would an ancient author have come to the same view?

1.2.5. The relevant section of Josephus reminds us of what is well known but often overlooked: the MT Ezra–Nehemiah was only one version of the tradition, and a variety of traditions continued to circulate, both separately and combined. Second Maccabees (1:18–36; 2:13) knew only a Nehemiah tradition, in which Nehemiah does a number of the things ascribed to Zerubbabel and Ezra elsewhere. Ben Sira knew of the Zerubbabel/Joshua tradition and the Nehemiah tradition, but nothing about Ezra. First Esdras gives a Zerubbabel/Joshua tradition in combination with an Ezra tradition. Josephus knew the Zerubbabel/Joshua tradition and the Ezra tradition, but only as mediated through 1 Esdras. He also knew a Nehemiah tradition that seems to differ from anything known to us previously and is not taken from our present MT Nehemiah. We should not take the MT Ezra–Nehemiah as normative in the early period but rather as only a late development in which originally separate traditions had eventually come together into one writing. If we do not make MT Ezra–Nehemiah our starting point, 1 Esdras looks like a standard tradition variant in the earlier period. There is no reason to make 1 Esdras derivative from MT Ezra–Nehemiah any more than the passages in Ben Sira or 2 Maccabees or, indeed, in Josephus.

1.2.6. The conclusion that naturally arises from these various considerations is that 1 Esdras is a Greek translation (and adaptation) of a Hebrew/Aramaic work that also served as a source for the later MT Ezra–Nehemiah. Please note that 1 Esdras was not the specific source used; rather, it is itself also a development of that source. The tradition picked up by the MT Ezra–Nehemiah apparently did not have the story of the youths' contest. I can see no reason why this story would have been omitted in the Hebrew Ezra if it was extant in the source, so it was probably added at a later date to 1 Esdras. Similarly, 1 Esd 1 (which parallels 2 Chr 35–36) could well have been added to give a more suitable introduction to the Ezra tradition.[9] If so, the Ezra tradition used by the compiler of the Hebrew Ezra–Nehemiah was probably close to that now found in 1 Esd 2 and 5–9. Finally, the original form of 1 Esdras evidently ended with the celebration of Sukkoth (as in the present Neh 8:13–18), but this ending was somehow lost.[10] The arguments for this are (a) the strange textual reading at the end of the present book, (b) the likelihood of portions of Neh 8:13–18 being part of the original, and (c) the inclusio formed by the first and last chapters (1 Esd 1 and 9) with regard to the celebrations of annual Jewish festivals. The book begins with a significant Passover, the one celebrated by Josiah. If the book originally included the rest of what we now find in Neh 8, the inclusio would be even more striking, because it would end with the last festival of the year, the Feast of Tabernacles, just as it began with the first festival of the year, the Passover. For a diagram illustrating the development of the traditions as I see them, see below.

2. Arguments Against the Priority of 1 Esdras

One of the main arguments used to show that 1 Esdras was simply an excerpt from MT Ezra–Nehemiah is that 1 Esdras presupposes a text in which Neh 7 and 8 were already combined. This has been most recently argued by Williamson,[11] but it has a long history.[12] If this argument is correct, it would suggest that 1 Esdras was excerpted from the combined book Ezra–Nehemiah. The reason for saying that Neh 7 and 8 were already combined lies in the fact that Neh 7:72–8:1 (// 1 Esd 9:37–38) is similar to Ezra 2:70–3:1 (// 1 Esd 5:45–46). This argues that when the list in one text was copied into the other, the final verses were also copied with the list, as if a part of it. Yet there have already been significant disagreements over this interpretation. Some argue that the original list was in Ezra 2 and was subsequently copied into Neh 8,[13] while others argue that the original list was in Neh 8 and was then copied into Ezra 2.[14] In either case, though,

---

9. It seems to have been a simple copying out of 2 Chr 35–36 with some minor changes. This, however, is only a suggestion, which requires careful study.

10. Scholars who argue this point include Wilhelm Rudolph (*Esra und Nehemia samt 3 Esra* [HAT 20; Tübingen: Mohr Siebeck, 1949], xiv–xv).

11. Williamson, *Israel in the Books of Chronicles*, 32–35; idem, "The Problem with 1 Esdras."

12. E.g., Rudolph, *Esra und Nehemia*, xiii–xiv.

13. E.g., Mowinckel, *Studien I*, 31; Pohlmann, *Studien zum dritten Esra*, 57–64; Joseph Blenkinsopp, *Ezra–Nehemiah* (OTL; London: SCM, 1988), 43–44.

14. See H. G. M. Williamson (*Ezra, Nehemiah* [WBC 16; Waco, Tex.: Word, 1985], 29–30). I believe that either the list was copied into both Ezra 2 and Neh 8 from a common source or that Ezra 2 is the original.

certain conclusions about Neh 7 and 8 would still be presupposed: that 1 Esdras originally had a text before it with the list in two places and only then dropped the one that corresponded to Neh 7, retaining the duplicated verse.

The fact is that 1 Esdras does not contain Neh 7, however; the assumption, therefore, that Neh 7 and 8 were already combined in the "original" is mere speculation. A variety of explanations have been given to account for the actual text we find in 1 Esd 9:37–38. A frequent assumption is a textual corruption or a later editor/interpolator.[15] Although it is an old assumption that the statement in question is a duplicate copied with the list,[16] this is not a necessary conclusion, as Pohlmann has pointed out.[17] On the contrary, the two verses have significant differences, indicating that 1 Esd 9:37 is not a reflex of Neh 7:72b. The two verses are indeed similar up to a point, and there may have been mutual influence in the wording, either in the original composition or as the text was transmitted by copying. But each passage still has a different wording in Greek and seems to represent a different underlying Hebrew.

MT Ezra–Nehemiah	Esdras β	1 Esdras
Neh 7:72–8:1	17:73–18:1	9:37–38
וישבו הכהנים והלוים והשוערים והמשררים ומן-העם	καὶ ἐκάθισαν οἱ ἱερεῖς καὶ οἱ Λευῖται καὶ οἱ πυλωροὶ καὶ οἱ ᾄδοντες καὶ οἱ ἀπὸ τοῦ λαοῦ	Καὶ κατῴκησαν οἱ ἱερεῖς καὶ οἱ Λευῖται καὶ οἱ ἐκ τοῦ Ἰσραὴλ ἐν Ἰερουσαλὴμ καὶ ἐν τῇ χώρᾳ
והנתינים וכל-ישראל בעריהם	καὶ οἱ ναθινιμ καὶ πᾶς Ἰσραὴλ ἐν πόλεσιν αὐτῶν.	
ויגע החדש השביעי	Καὶ ἔφθασεν ὁ μὴν ὁ ἕβδομος,	τῇ νουμηνίᾳ τοῦ ἑβδόμου μηνός—
ובני ישראל בעריהם	καὶ οἱ υἱοὶ Ἰσραὴλ ἐν πόλεσιν αὐτῶν,	καὶ οἱ υἱοὶ Ἰσραὴλ ἐν ταῖς κατοικίαις αὐτῶν—
ויאספו כל-העם כאיש אחד אל-הרחוב אשר לפני שער-המים	καὶ συνήχθησαν πᾶς ὁ λαὸς ὡς ἀνὴρ εἷς εἰς τὸ πλάτος τὸ ἔμπροσθεν πύλης τοῦ ὕδατος	καὶ συνήχθη πᾶν τὸ πλῆθος ὁμοθυμαδὸν ἐπὶ τὸ εὐρύχωρον τοῦ πρὸς ἀνατολὰς τοῦ ἱεροῦ πυλῶνος

---

15. Mowinckel, *Studien I*, 21–25; cf. Pohlmann, *Studien zum dritten Esra*, 66–71; Williamson, *Israel in the Books of Chronicles*, 32–35.

16. Cf. Mowinckel, *Studien I*, 40–45.

17. Pohlmann, *Studien zum dritten Esra*, 66–71.

And dwelled the priests and the Levites and the gatekeepers and the singers and some of the people	And dwelled the priests and the Levites and the gatekeepers and the singers and some from the people	And dwelled the priests and the Levites ——— some from *Israel in Jerusalem and the countryside,*
and the Netinim in their cities, and all Israel in their cities.	and the Netinim in their cities and all Israel in their cities.	—————— And all Israel (were) in their *villages.*
And the seventh month approached and the sons of Israel (were) in the cities and all the people gathered as one person in the plaza in front of the water gate.	And the seventh month arrived and the sons of Israel in their cities. And gathered all the people as one person in the plaza in front of the water gate.	But when the seventh month arrived— and the sons of Israel (were) in their *dwellings*— and all *the crowd* assembled *with one accord* in the plaza *of the east gate of the temple.*

Even the end of the list in 1 Esd 5:45–46 is not exactly the same as that in its parallel passage in Ezra 2:70–3:1, though the wording in the two passages appears to be closer than 1 Esd 9:37–38 is to Neh 7:72–8:1 (// Esd β 17:73–18:1). Notice:

MT Ezra–Nehemiah	Esdras β	1 Esdras
Ezra 2:70–3:1	2:70–3:1	5:45–46
וישבו הכהנים	καὶ ἐκάθισαν οἱ ἱερεῖς	καὶ κατῳκίσθησαν οἱ ἱερεῖς
והלוים ומן־העם	καὶ οἱ Λευῖται καὶ οἱ ἀπὸ τοῦ λαοῦ	καὶ οἱ Λευῖται καὶ οἱ ἐκ τοῦ λαοῦ αὐτοῦ ἐν Ἰερουσαλὴμ καὶ τῇ χώρᾳ,
והמשררים והשוערים	καὶ οἱ ᾄδοντες καὶ οἱ πυλωροί	οἵ τε ἱεροψάλται καὶ οἱ θυρωροί
והנתינים בעריהם וכל־ישראל בעריהם: ויגע החדש השביעי ובני ישראל בערים ויאספו העם כאיש אחד אל־ירושלם:	καὶ οἱ ναθινὶμ ἐν πόλεσιν αὐτῶν καὶ πᾶς Ἰσραὴλ ἐν πόλεσιν αὐτῶν. Καὶ ἔφθασεν ὁ μὴν ὁ ἕβδομος, καὶ οἱ υἱοὶ Ἰσραὴλ ἐν πόλεσιν αὐτῶν, καὶ συνήχθη ὁ λαὸς ὡς ἀνὴρ εἷς εἰς Ἰερουσαλήμ	καὶ πᾶς Ἰσραὴλ ἐν ταῖς κώμαις αὐτῶν. Ἐνστάντος δὲ τοῦ ἑβδόμου μηνὸς καὶ ὄντων τῶν υἱῶν Ἰσραὴλ ἑκάστου ἐν τοῖς ἰδίοις συνήχθησαν ὁμοθυμαδὸν εἰς τὸ εὐρύχωρον τοῦ πρώτου πυλῶνος τοῦ πρὸς τῇ ἀνατολῇ

And dwelled the priests and the Levites and some of the people	And dwelled the priests and the Levites and some from the people	And dwelled the priests and the Levites and some from *his* people *in Jerusalem and the countryside,*
and the singers and gate-keepers and the Netinim in their cities, and all Israel in their cities.	and the singers and the gatekeepers and the Netinim in their cities and all Israel in their cities.	but the temple singers and the gatekeepers, — — — — — and all Israel in their *villages*.
And the seventh month approached and the sons of Israel (were) in the cities and the people gathered as one man unto Jerusalem.	And the seventh month arrived and Israel (were) in their cities. And the people gathered as one man into Jerusalem.	But when the seventh month arrived and the sons of Israel were *each in their own* (cities), they assembled of one accord *into the plaza of the first gate toward the east.*

Finally, we should compare parallel passages in 1 Esdras itself: 1 Esd 5:45–46 (// Ezra 2:70–3:1) with 1 Esd 9:37–38 (// Neh 7:72–8:1 // Esd β 17:73–18:1). Again, there is some similarity in the wording, but it seems evident that the underlying Hebrew text of the two passages differed somewhat from each other. Nevertheless, there is the possibility that either the original translator or later copyists (or even both) have allowed the wording of the former to influence the latter.

1 Esdras 5:45–46	1 Esdras 9:37–38
45 καὶ κατῳκίσθησαν οἱ ἱερεῖς καὶ οἱ Λευῖται καὶ οἱ ἐκ τοῦ λαοῦ αὐτοῦ ἐν Ἱερουσαλὴμ καὶ τῇ χώρᾳ, οἵ τε ἱεροψάλται καὶ οἱ θυρωροὶ καὶ πᾶς Ἰσραὴλ ἐν ταῖς κώμαις αὐτῶν. 46 Ἐνστάντος δὲ τοῦ ἑβδόμου μηνὸς καὶ ὄντων τῶν υἱῶν Ἰσραὴλ ἑκάστου ἐν τοῖς ἰδίοις,	37 Καὶ κατῴκησαν οἱ ἱερεῖς καὶ οἱ Λευῖται καὶ οἱ ἐκ τοῦ Ἰσραὴλ ἐν Ἱερουσαλὴμ καὶ ἐν τῇ χώρᾳ τῇ νουμηνίᾳ τοῦ ἑβδόμου μηνός—καὶ οἱ υἱοὶ Ἰσραὴλ ἐν ταῖς κατοικίαις αὐτῶν.—
συνήχθησαν ὁμοθυμαδὸν εἰς τὸ εὐρύχωρον τοῦ πρώτου πυλῶνος τοῦ πρὸς τῇ ἀνατολῇ.	38 καὶ συνήχθη πᾶν τὸ πλῆθος ὁμοθυμαδὸν ἐπὶ τὸ εὐρύχωρον τοῦ πρὸς ἀνατολὰς τοῦ ἱεροῦ πυλῶνος
And the priests and the Levites and some of *his people* settled in Jerusalem and in the countryside; *also the temple singers and the gatekeepers and all Israel in their villages.*	And the priests and the Levites and some of *Israel* settled in Jerusalem and in the countryside.

But *when arrived* the seventh month and were the sons of Israel *each in (their) own* (cities), they assembled with one accord in the plaza in front of the *first* gate to the east.	*In the new moon* of the seventh month—and the sons of Israel (were) in their *dwellings*—and *the multitude* all assembled with one accord in the plaza in front of the east gate *of the temple*.

First Esdras 9:37–38 fits well in its context: there is no reason to think it is a verse copied accidentally and mistakenly from 1 Esd 5:45–46. Recognizing that the contents of Neh 8 are a part of the Ezra tradition suggests that some sort of linking passage had to connect its contents with the episode of the mixed marriages. We would hardly expect Ezra 10:44 (// 1 Esd 9:36) to be followed immediately by Neh 8:1 (// 1 Esd 9:38); a link is demanded. The examination relating to the mixed marriages is completed, the "sinners" are listed, and the suffering of the wives and children is generously mentioned. Then the statement is made that "the priests, the Levites, and some of the Israelites were living in Jerusalem and in the countryside" and on the first day of the seventh month—with the Israelites in their habitations—all the people gathered in Jerusalem in front of the temple.

The reference to the seventh month in both contexts is natural (especially if 1 Esd 9 originally ended with the Festival of Tabernacles, as Neh 8 does).[18] The statement in 1 Esd 9:37 fits well in the context. What we do not know is how the compiler of 1 Esdras chose that particular link, if he contributed it, or the state of the tradition on which he drew. What we do know is that despite some similarities, there are some important differences between the two verses that militate against one being a borrowing of the other (italicized above in the English translation, though many other minor differences cannot be indicated). Therefore, what we need not assume is that the author of 1 Esdras drew on a tradition that included a list of settlers preceding the episode on reading the law, as currently in Neh 7–8. It may be that some of the suggestions about how the passage developed, as it now stands in the text of 1 Esdras, are correct, but there is much we do not know about the state of the original tradition.

3. Conclusions

To summarize, my conclusions are the following:

- An Ezra tradition lies at the core of 1 Esdras, in 2 and 5–9, originally in Hebrew and Aramaic.

---

18. 1 Esd 5:45 not only serves as a conclusion to the list of returnees and their places of settlement but also introduces the episode of erecting the altar at the beginning of the seventh month, which makes possible the celebration of the Festival of Tabernacles (5:46–52).

- This tradition was picked up by the compiler of Ezra–Nehemiah, with a portion split off to form Neh 8 when it was combined with the (originally separate) Nehemiah tradition.
- But the original tradition continued to develop on its own, being translated into Greek at some point.
- It may be that the present beginning in Greek was not original and chapters from 2 Chronicles were added to 1 Esd 1; alternatively, the present 1 Esd 1 is original, but this material was borrowed from 1 Esd 1 (in its Hebrew phase) and used to form the present ending of 2 Chronicles.
- The story about the contest of the guards (1 Esd 3–4) was probably not original, because it seems unlikely that it would not have been retained when the present Ezra–Nehemiah was created. It was thus added at some point (whether at the Hebrew/Aramaic stage or only the Greek needs further study).
- Finally, it seems that the ending of 1 Esdras was lost; that ending probably included at least the celebration of Tabernacles (as known in Neh 8:13–18).

The proposed growth of the tradition can be diagrammed as follows:

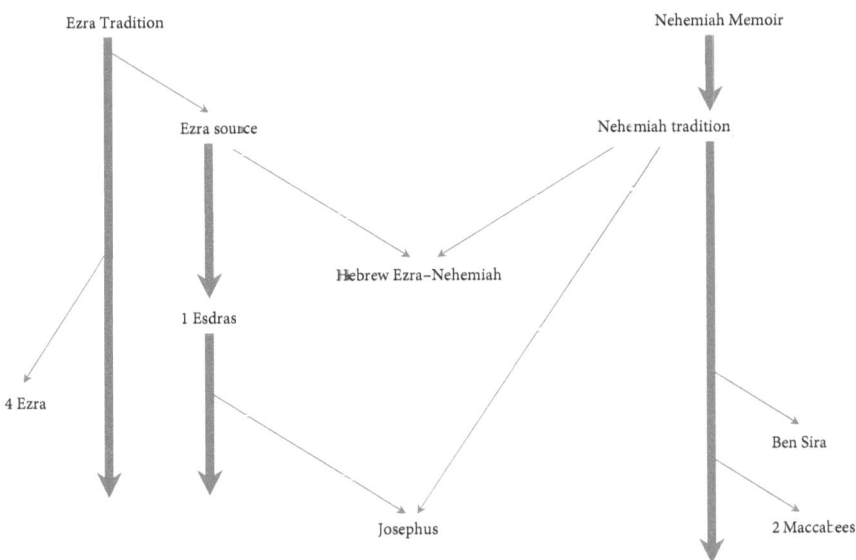

THE RELATIONSHIP BETWEEN EZRA–NEHEMIAH AND 1 ESDRAS[*]

Adrian Schenker

1. INTRODUCTORY REMARKS: THE PURPOSE OF THIS STUDY

I do not wish to repeat the reasons advanced by Dieter Böhler[1] in favor of the priority of 1 Esdras over against the Hebrew book of Ezra–Nehemiah. In my opinion, Böhler's demonstration is carefully argued and convincing. I do not know of any examination of his book in which his position has been proved by detailed arguments to be false I should like to add here one further reason in favor of the priority of the text of 1 Esdras in comparison with Ezra–Nehemiah. It seems to be a new reason, not yet proposed in the scholarly discussion.

In this study I shall presuppose that the Greek book of 1 Esdras corresponds to the translation of a Hebrew *Vorlage*.[2] Moreover, the story of the competition

---

[*] I thank Dr. Lisbeth S. Fried for her many illuminating comments and questions on a first draft of this essay. It is a privilege to have such an acute and learned reader during the preparation of an article. The responsibility for its content of course is mine.

1. Dieter Böhler, *Die heilige Stadt in Esdras α und Ezra–Nehemia: Zwei Konzeptionen der Wiederherstellung Israels* (OBO 158; Freiburg: Universitätsverlag; Göttingen: Vandenhoeck & Ruprecht, 1997); idem, "On the Relationship between Textual and Literary Criticism: The Two Recensions of the Book of Ezra; Ezra–Neh (MT) and 1 Esdras (LXX)," in *The Earliest Text of the Hebrew Bible: The Relationship between the Masoretic Text and the Hebrew Base of the Septuagint Reconsidered* (ed. Adrian Schenker; SBLSCS 52; Atlanta: Society of Biblical Literature, 2003), 35–50; cf. also P.-M. Bogaert, "La Porte Orientale, place de rassemblement du peuple, et l'extension de l oeuvre du Chroniste," *Transeu* 17 (1999): 9–16; Adrian Schenker, "La relation d'Esdras A' au texte massorétique d'Esdras-Néhémie," in *Tradition of the Text: Studies Offered to Dominique Barthélemy in Celebration of His 70th Birthday* (ed. Gerard J. Norton and Stephen Pisano; OBO 109; Freiburg: Universitätsverlag; Göttingen: Vandenhoeck & Ruprecht, 1991), 218–48. On the historical context, see Gary N. Knoppers, "Mt. Gerizim and Mt. Zion: A Study in the Early History of the Samaritans and the Jews," *SR* 34 (2005): 309–38.

2. Zipora Talshir, *1 Esdras: From Origin to Translation* (SBLSCS 47; Atlanta: Society of Biblical Literature, 1999), esp. 111–79.

of the three pages at the court of Darius with Zerubbabel's victory (1 Esd 3–4) will be considered a literary insertion into the book.³ It can indeed be shown that this story has been inserted into 1 Esdras and that it ends in 1 Esd 5:6. The reasons are the following: first and most importantly, according to 1 Esd 2:9–14, the first step made by King Cyrus in favor of the Jews in exile in Babylon was the restitution of the holy temple vessels that Nebuchadnezzar once had carried away from Jerusalem and put in his own temple in Babylon (1 Esd 2:9). As soon as some exiles, Judeans, Benjaminites, priests, Levites, and others, had resolved to go up to Jerusalem (1 Esd 2:7–8) in response to Cyrus' authorization to rebuild the temple in Jerusalem (1 Esd 2:1–6), Cyrus gave them back the holy vessels (2:9–14). This is central for 1 Esdras. The restitution of the holy vessels is reported in five verses while the permission to restore the ruined temple takes only three verses (2:4–6). On the other hand, in the story of the three youths (1 Esd 3:1–5:6), only two verses (4:44, 57) are devoted to the restitution of the holy vessels, while the authorization to rebuild the temple, to restore the political freedom of the Judeans, and to reconstruct Jerusalem is developed at great length: restoration of the city of Jerusalem in the first place (1 Esd 4:43), restoration of the temple (vv. 45–46), reconstruction of the temple, and restitution of political rights (vv. 47–56). Moreover, the two verses 4:44, 57 explicitly mention Cyrus, the first recalling that Cyrus had made a vow, when he wanted to conquer Babylon, to send the holy vessels back to Jerusalem, the second reporting that Cyrus had taken out the holy vessels from the temple in Babylon and that *Darius* sent them back to Jerusalem. In both places, 4:44 and 57, Cyrus is said to have retired or set apart (ἐξεχώρισεν) the vessels, but never is he credited with their real restitution into the hands of the Jews going up to Jerusalem. This, however, is precisely what 1 Esd 2:9–14 explicitly states, especially in 2:10–11: "he [Cyrus] handed them over (παρέδωκεν) to Mithridates, his treasurer, by whom they were handed over again (παρεδόθησαν) to Sanabassaros, the leader of Judah." Verse 14 makes it quite clear that Sanabassaros brought them to Jerusalem. This is clearly in tension and even in contradiction with the story of the pages (1 Esd 3:1–5:6).

Since 1 Esd 4:44 and 57 are the only places in the story of the youths that mention Cyrus and the holy vessels, they must allude to 1 Esd 2:9–14, because without that reference they would be an enigma in the narrative. These two verses *presuppose 1 Esd 2, but 1 Esd 2:1–14 does not presuppose 1 Esd 3:1–5:6*. Indeed, it excludes it, since it has related that Cyrus had given back the holy vessels to the Jews going up from Babylon to Jerusalem. A reader who comes

---

3. Böhler, *Die heilige Stadt*, 69–72. The Greek text of 1 Esdras will be quoted from the edition of Robert Hanhart, *Esdrae liber I* (Septuaginta Vetus Testamentum Graecum 8/1; Göttingen: Vandenhoeck & Ruprecht, 1974). The verse numbers do not always perfectly coincide in the various editions of the Greek text and in its translations. We here adopt Hanhart's division of the chapters and verses.

from 1 Esd 2:9–14 to 1 Esd 4:44, 57 finds himself obliged mentally to correct his understanding of 1 Esd 2, seeing now that, contrary to what 1 Esd 2:10–11, 14 had clearly stated (Cyrus had returned the holy vessels), in reality they were not given to the Jews *until Darius*! Cyrus had only taken them out of Nebuchadnezzar's temple! It is more than likely that such a subsequent correction, which changes the unambiguous earlier meaning, is secondary. It provides for the secondary insertion of the story of the three youths into the book of 1 Esdras. For this aim it was created.

Several subsidiary reasons confirm this result concerning the relationship between the story of the three pages and 1 Esdras. First, King Darius alone is at the origin of the return of the Jews to Jerusalem and of the restoration of the temple in 1 Esd 4:42–5:6. All firmans on this behalf are issued by him alone (4:47–49, 54–56, 61). This is not so in 1 Esd 2 and 5. For according to 2:1–14 and 5:53–54, 69–70, it was King Cyrus alone who authorized both the return of the exiles in Babylonia and the restoration of the sanctuary in Jerusalem. He wrote the firmans necessary for that (2:2 and 5:53). Here the role of Darius was only to put an end to the hostility of other peoples against the building of the temple (1 Esd 2:25; 5:69–70; 6). Therefore, 1 Esd 5:2, 6 belong to the story of the pages, which attributes the authorization to go up to Jerusalem in order to rebuild the temple exclusively to King Darius.

Second, according to 1 Esd 4:63 and 5:2–3, the authorization granted by the king to the exiles to go back to Jerusalem and to rebuild the temple was welcomed among the Jews in Babylon by playing instruments, and instruments were played during their entire trip back to Jerusalem. This feature does not appear elsewhere, either in 1 Esd 2:1–14 or in 5:7–42. Thus it is specific to the story of the pages.

Third, in 1 Esd 5:1 the *golah* that goes up to Jerusalem is composed of men and sons, women and daughters, and servants and maidservants, whereas the list of 1 Esd 5:7–42 knows only of men and sons. (The mention of the wife of an illegitimate priest in 5:38 is another matter.) This shows a difference between 3:1–5:6 and 5:7–42.

Fourth, names and ranking in the list of the leaders going up to Jerusalem differ in 5:5 and 5:7–42. This then is another difference between the story of the three youths and 1 Esdras.

Fifth, the thousand horsemen sent by Darius in order to escort those Jews who go up to Jerusalem are mentioned nowhere in 1 Esd 5:7–42. This is a further difference between the story of the pages and 1 Esdras.

These differences between the story of the youths and the narrative of 1 Esdras suggest two conclusions: first, this story does not perfectly fit into 1 Esdras but presupposes it. It was therefore inserted into it. Second, the passage 1 Esd 5:1–6 clearly shares some specific features of the story of the three pages and is therefore the concluding part of it.

2. The Overall Narrative Design of Ezra 2–6 in Comparison with That of 1 Esdras 2; 5–7

The thesis of this essay is the following: the narrative unit of Ezra 2–6 appears to be a historical report on the rebuilding of the temple. Its narrative frame is a linear chronology from Cyrus to Darius. As for 1 Esd 2; 5–7, it presents a synoptic display of one and the same narrative matter in two parallel stories. It tells the story twice in two different ways. Thus, the narrative is not arranged in chronological order. Moreover, the comparison between the two narratives, the Hebrew and Aramaic one of Ezra 2–6 in the MT and the Greek narrative of 1 Esd 2; 5–7, shows that the Semitic *Vorlage* of the latter preserves the earlier and more original form, whereas the former corresponds to a revised secondary version.

3. The Chronological and Historical Narrative of Ezra 2–7

The narrative unit Ezra 2–6 recounts one continuous succession of events in a chronological order. The exiles come back to Jerusalem and Judah (Ezra 2). At once they build a new altar on the location of the previous one and consecrate it in the seventh month (Ezra 3:1–6). They then prepare the construction of a new temple under the direction of Zerubbabel and Joshua and begin the work in the second year after the return of the *golah* (Ezra 3:7–13). They lay the foundations (Ezra 3:6, 10, 11). At that moment, the enemies of Judah and Benjamin wish to be associated with the exiles in the restoration of the temple but their claim is rejected (Ezra 4:1–3). Frustrated, they take their revenge by trying to hinder the reconstruction of the temple throughout, from the time of Cyrus until the reign of Darius (Ezra 4:4–5). They start an intrigue at the court of the Persian king against the inhabitants of Judah and Jerusalem at the beginning of the reign of Xerxes (Ezra 4:6) and during the reign of Artaxerxes (Ezra 4:7–24). They successfully obtain from King Artaxerxes the cessation of the restoration of the temple (Ezra 4:24). Others plot again and try to procure the same royal interdiction from the new Persian king, Darius. This time, however, they fail. Instead, Darius authorizes the rebuilding of the temple in the second year of his reign (Ezra 4:24; 5:1–6:24). It is achieved and consecrated in the sixth year of King Darius (Ezra 6:14–17).

This is a clear, uninterrupted chronological narrative sequence. The account presents itself as a historical report on the restoration of the temple in Jerusalem after the edict of King Cyrus. The list of Persian kings starts with Cyrus, goes on with Xerxes and Artaxerxes, and arrives at Darius. In the period of these four kings the temple was reconstructed, despite a stern opposition that caused some delay. The exiles, however, were not responsible for the delay. The historical problem of the succession of Cyrus, Xerxes, Artaxerxes, and Darius need not detain us here in the limited context of an inquiry into the textual history of Ezra-Nehemiah and 1 Esdras.[4]

4. Synoptic Display of Two Parallel Narratives in 1 Esdras 2; 5-7

The narrative of 1 Esd 2; 5-7 follows its own specific literary plan.[5] First, 1 Esd 2 starts with the edict of King Cyrus, who was inspired by the LORD, God of Israel, in conformity with the oracles of the prophet Jeremiah. He authorized the exiles to rebuild the temple in Jerusalem. By the same token he returned to them the holy vessels of the former temple, long ago carried away by the Babylonians (1 Esd 2:1-14). The leader of the exiles was Sanabassaros (Sheshbazzar; 1 Esd 2:11, 14). At the time of the Persian king Artaxerxes, however, an intrigue brought about a royal Persian intervention, prohibiting the repair of the marketplaces and walls of the city of Jerusalem and the foundation of a new temple (1 Esd 2:15-25, especially 2:17, 25). This halting of the construction lasted until the second year of King Darius (1 Esd 2:25). Thus the period of cessation of building comprised the whole reign of King Cyrus, from his first year (1 Esd 2:1) until his death, and until the second year of King Darius (1 Esd 2:25). This might be called the first account of 1 Esdras. The second one is to be found in 1 Esd 5:43-7:9.

First Esdras 5:4-42 begins with the list of names of the exiles returning home to Judah and Jerusalem under the leadership of Zorobabel and Jesus (Joshua). This list precedes a report on their vow to rebuild the temple in Jerusalem (1 Esd 5:43-45). The Persian king at the time of the restoration is not mentioned. According to 5:53 it is Cyrus. In the seventh month after their arrival, the exiles built the altar (1 Esd 5:46-48) in the midst of the hostility of the peoples of the land (1 Esd 5:49). Then they prepared materials for the construction of the temple (1 Esd 5:43, 52-53) in conformity with King Cyrus' permission. In the second year, Zorobabel and Jesus laid the foundations (1 Esd 5:54-55) and immediately proceeded to rebuild the temple itself (1 Esd 5:56). The old people who had known the previous temple destroyed by the Babylonians and who now looked at the new structure wept with disappointment (1 Esd 5:59-60), while the young people in the crowd shouted with joy (1 Esd 5:61-62).

---

4. Böhler, *Die heilige Stadt*, 17, rightly excludes corrections of the text on grounds of present-day historical knowledge.
5. Ibid., 237-39; Talshir, *1 Esdras. From Origin to Translation*, 41-43 ("duplication in the sequence of events").

Thereafter came the enemies of Judah and Benjamin who wished to have a share in the restoration of the temple. But they were driven away (1 Esd 5:63–66) because King Cyrus had only granted this privilege to Zorobabel, Jesus, and the exiles (1 Esd 5:67–69a).

It could be objected that the temple was completely restored, since the solemn music in 1 Esd 5:57–62 seems to be played for the consecration of the restored sanctuary. How then was it possible for the enemies of Judah and Benjamin to ask permission to take part in the restoration of the temple? In reality, this sound of trumpets and other instruments, of hymns and shouting, accompanied the whole work of the builders. It was itself a liturgical action. The priests attended it in their priestly garments (5:57). This solemn liturgical music drew the attention of the people to the ongoing restoration of the temple in Jerusalem (5:63). The house certainly was set up (5:59–62) so that it could be compared with the preceding one, but the restoration was not yet fully completed. This is the most natural interpretation of 5:56–69.

Rebuked, the enemies took their revenge and in their anger hindered the restoration during the remaining lifetime of the Persian king Cyrus and for two more years after, until the reign of Darius (1 Esd 5:69–70).

However, when they later sent letters to King Darius to prevent the exiles in Jerusalem and Judah from rebuilding their temple, this new king approved the reconstruction (1 Esd 6:1–33). Accordingly, the house of the LORD could be completed (1 Esd 7:1–4). The work was finished on the twenty-third of the month of Adar in the sixth year of King Darius (1 Esd 7:5). Thus, they were able to consecrate the restored temple according to the law of Moses (1 Esd 7:6–9).

It should be noted here that the first narrative section, 1 Esd 2:15–25, mentions three Persian kings, Cyrus, Artaxerxes, and Darius, while the second one, 5:43–7:9, only mentions two kings, Cyrus and Darius, perhaps with an interval of two years between them (1 Esd 5:70).[6]

5. THE TWO ACCOUNTS OF 1 ESDRAS 2:15–25 AND 5:43–6:1 ARE TWO SYNOPTIC VERSIONS OF A UNIQUE EPISODE

Five reasons lead to the conclusion that the two attempts made by the enemies of Judah against the reconstruction of the temple in Jerusalem, reported in 1 Esd 2:15–25 and 5:43–6:1, are in fact two different accounts of one and the same

---

6. One passage, 1 Esd 7:4, however, also mentions Cyrus, Darius, and Artaxerxes, the names being placed in this sequence. If this list corresponded to a chronologically arranged narrative, Artaxerxes should have figured between Cyrus and Darius. Since the Old Latin puts the name of Artaxerxes in front of Darius, the oscillation of its place in the textual witnesses (Greek, Latin) may hint at a secondary addition of Artaxerxes here.

episode. Both accounts are concerned with the royal permission to rebuild the temple, and the obstruction takes place from Cyrus' reign to Darius' second year, according to 6:1.

First, they *coincide chronologically*. Both attempts begin during the reign of Cyrus (1 Esd 2:17, 25; 5:70). The official Persian measures against the reconstruction of the temple imply in both narratives that the restoration had effectively started during the reign of Cyrus, before the reign of Artaxerxes in the first narrative and before Darius in the second. In both, the building is blocked until the second year of Darius (1 Esd 2:25; 5:70; 6:1; cf. 7:4). The two stories therefore cover exactly the same period: from Cyrus to the second year of Darius.

Second, both accounts concern the same building object, the temple (1 Esd 2:17; 5:43, 52, 55, 56, 59, 60). In the first narrative, together with the temple, the walls and marketplaces of the city of Jerusalem were restored as well.

Third, in both accounts the building of the temple had already made some progress when it was interrupted (1 Esd 2:17; 5:54–62; and 5:63–70). It is erected but not finished. This interruption, however, did not mean the demolition of what already had been restored, because such a measure is nowhere reported, either in the account of 1 Esd 2 or in that of 1 Esd 5–7. Therefore, the second account cannot be interpreted as the repair of what had been demolished as a consequence of the first interruption. Thus, if the two narratives corresponded to two successive episodes, the same temple would have been rebuilt twice from the foundation up until its completion (1 Esd 2:17; 5:43–62).

Fourth, if the first account of the cessation of building took place in the reign of Artaxerxes, it could have lasted at most two years, since this would be the time left in this case between the reigns of Cyrus and Darius, according to 1 Esd 5:70. While this is not entirely impossible, it is not likely, either in a narrative perspective or in a historical one. In both accounts the end of the obstruction is the second year of Darius (2:25; 5:70–6:1).

Fifth, the opponents of the reconstruction seem to be the same in both accounts, namely the people of Samaria (1 Esd 2:15; 5:66). While this is no strict proof of the identity of the reported opponents, since the same groups could have intervened twice, it is nevertheless remarkable that both accounts coincide with regard to the cause of the halt in building.

The major difference between the two accounts is the identity of the Persian king. In the first it was King Artaxerxes (1 Esd 2:15, 16); in the second the opposition had already arisen under Cyrus, but without the direct responsibility and involvement of this king. This is understandable enough, since it would imply a contradiction in his policy. The obstruction essentially stemmed from the people of Samaria. Another difference has been mentioned already: in the first narrative the restoration of the house of the LORD also embraced the walls and marketplaces of the city.

In conclusion, 1 Esdras most likely presents two different, but synoptic or parallel, accounts of one episode, namely the fierce opposition to the reconstruction of the house of the LORD in Jerusalem. The book contains two versions or traditions of this unique event.[7]

This is no exceptional phenomenon in Scripture. It often happens that the same event is told in two different ways that cannot be completely reconciled; for example, the first encounter between Saul and David is reported in two different stories, in 1 Sam 16:14–23 and in 1 Sam 17:55–58. These two forms cannot be brought into perfect conformity. The episode of David's sparing of Saul's life is also told twice, in 1 Sam 24 and 26, each in its own specific form. The origin of the monarchy is likewise presented twice, once negatively as a sin in 1 Sam 8; 12 and once positively as a divine choice in 1 Sam 10:22–27; 11. A close analogy is the double narrative of Jeroboam's rise in 1 Kgs 11–12; 13 and 3 Kgdms 12:24a–z. The two stories of Jesus' birth in the Gospels of Matthew and Luke would be another example. There are many more examples. It is natural that authors and readers will be inclined to understand such parallel or synoptic accounts as successive ones, although they contain some contradictory elements that resist their interpretation as successive episodes within the same narrative.

What would be the literary relationship between the two accounts of 1 Esd 2:15–25 and 5:43–70? This question is not easy to answer. There must have been a tradition or a historical recollection of an intervention against the restoration of the temple under the reign of Artaxerxes. It gave rise to one of the two accounts. Another tradition may have reported that adversaries tried to frustrate the efforts of the Jews to restore the temple during the entire time from Cyrus to Darius. These two traditions may have existed side by side until they were incorporated together into 1 Esdras. It is even conceivable that the most difficult element, the two years of opposition, 1 Esd 5:70, goes back to an old recollection or tradition. But this is mere speculation.

6. Priority of 1 Esdras

With this background, two passages seem to establish the priority of 1 Esd 2; 5–7 in comparison with Ezra 2–6. First, Ezra 3:12 reports that many old people among the priests, Levites, and leaders who had known the previous temple, long ago destroyed by the Babylonians, wept when they saw the *foundations* of the new one. In the parallel passage of 1 Esd 5:60, however, these persons saw the new temple almost completely rebuilt. This coheres with the whole account. Indeed, in 5:43 they prepared the reconstruction; in 5:56 they laid the foundations; in 5:60, "they were building the temple"; while in 5:59, "they sang hymns

---

7. This "duplication" of the narrative has been observed many times; see, for example, Talshir, *1 Esdras: From Origin to Translation*, 42–43.

to the LORD for the erection of the house of the LORD." From 5:43 to 5:60 the whole range of the successive building phases is described from the beginning nearly to the completion of the temple.

The disappointment with the new temple, so much poorer than the preceding one, is unlikely to have been caused only by the sight of the foundations (Ezra 3:12). It is much more likely that the people were disappointed when they saw the poor new temple building in its complete reality. Therefore, the narrative element of the disappointment of the old leaders implies the setting up of the temple building rather than its mere *foundation*. This must have been the original form of the narrative, and this is the form found in 1 Esd 5:60.[8]

Moreover, the difference at this point in the narrative is linked with two further textual differences between the Hebrew and Greek books. Both Ezra and 1 Esdras agree in reporting that the leaders had made vows to rebuild the temple on its location, Ezra 2:68 = 1 Esd 5:43, and that Zerubbabel and Joshua laid its foundation in the second year of Cyrus. This second year was also the second year of the return of the *golah* from the Babylonian exile (Ezra 3:8–10 = 1 Esd 5:53–54), since we must understand, according to 1 Esd 2:2 and 5:53, that the returning exiles came back immediately after Cyrus' firman in his first year. Ezra and 1 Esdras disagree, however, concerning the further progress of the construction. In 1 Esd 5:56, the next step was setting up the building, while Ezra 3:10, in the parallel passage, continues to speak only of the foundations that had been laid. Similarly, 1 Esd 5:59 mentions the erected temple, while Ezra 3:11, in the parallel verse, knows only of the foundations existing.[9] The three textual differences are coherent in their meaning. They suggest together that only the foundation and nothing else could be built. Because of their coherence in meaning, the three differences may not be explained as merely textual. They amount to a different narrative, that is, a different *literary* pattern in Ezra in comparison with 1 Esdras.

---

8. Lisbeth S. Fried, "The Land Lay Desolate: Conquest and Restoration in the Ancient Near East," in *Judah and the Judeans in the Neo-Babylonian Period* (ed. Oded Lipschits and Joseph Blenkinsopp; Winona Lake, Ind.: Eisenbrauns, 2003), 21–54, here 33–34, 42–46, explains the weeping as a ritual lamentation sung by a priest during the reconstruction of a new temple on the ruins of an old one. If this is the meaning of the weeping here too, the argument given above is still valid since this lamentation, mentioned in a ritual text from Uruk of the Seleucid period, accompanies not only the laying of the foundations but the whole work of the restoration in its full length: "It is clear from the final section of the ritual ... that the rites continue during the entire construction of the building, not just when the foundations of the new temple are laid" (Fried, "The Land Lay Desolate," 44 n. 11). An English translation of this ritual can be found in *ANET*, 340–41 (translation by A. Sachs).

9. Böhler, *Die heilige Stadt*, 284–85, and Talshir, *1 Esdras: From Origin to Translation*, 41, discuss the possibility that יסד may mean not only "to lay the foundations" but generally "to build." However, this meaning is unlikely, since there are almost no passages to prove it.

To summarize, from Ezra 2:68 to 3:11 only one step was taken in the restoration of the destroyed temple: the foundations were laid, nothing more. In 1 Esd 5:43–62, on the contrary, the building is set up. It is thus quite natural that those who had seen the previous house of the LORD were moved to tears of disappointment when they saw the new one. It is stranger, however, that they should have shed tears seeing only the *foundations* of the future building. Therefore the first account, that of 1 Esdras, is likely to be more original, while that of Ezra is secondary. Consequently, the whole section of Ezra 2:68–3:11, in which we are told three times that only the foundations of the new temple were laid, is likely to be secondary on a literary or redactional level as well.

The second reason for accepting the priority of 1 Esdras is the mention of the period of two years between the reigns of Cyrus and Darius (1 Esd 5:70).[10] First Esdras 5:70 consists of two sentences. *Sentence 1*: the opposition against the restoration of the temple lasted *the whole time of Cyrus*. *Sentence 2*: the opposition lasted two years, *until Darius*. Because of sentence 1, and because of the preposition ἕως, "until," it seems impossible to apply the two years of sentence 2 exclusively to the time of Darius. First Esdras 6:1 will add that the end of the obstruction took place in his second year. Taken together, the obstruction lasted from Cyrus to the second year of Darius, and the whole duration amounts to two years.

This double statement of 1 Esd 5:70 is missing in the parallel passages of Ezra 4:5, 23.[11] The effect of this absence is to allow time for two reigns of Persian kings. In fact, Ezra 4:6 mentions Xerxes as a first successor of King Cyrus, and 4:7–24 mentions Artaxerxes as a second one. In the parallel passages, 1 Esdras

---

10. It is also possible to interpret these two years as belonging to the reign of Cyrus. Since his edict is from the first year of his reign, 1 Esd 2:1, it would follow from this assumption that Cyrus had reigned only two years when he was succeeded by Darius. This assumption seems less likely.

11. Böhler, *Die heilige Stadt*, 251–59, 295–99, 306, limits himself to the explanation of 1 Esd 5:69–70, in comparison with Ezra 4:4–5, as to its context and narrative function. He does not discuss the difference of the "two years" mentioned in 1 Esd 5:70, with Ezra 4:5. As far as I have seen, there are no discussions on this specific point; the reason is that the text of Ezra 4:5, without mention of the duration, offers no difficulty at all. Therefore, the difficult mention of the two years in 1 Esd 5:70 is tacitly put aside as an uninteresting textual corruption. The reading "two years" is explicitly explained as an error by Bernhard Walde, *Die Esdrasbücher der Septuaginta: Ihr gegenseitiges Verhältnis untersucht* (BibS[F] 18/4; Freiburg: Herder, 1913), 117; Zipora Talshir, *1 Esdras: A Text Critical Commentary* (SBLSCS 50; Atlanta: Society of Biblical Literature, 2001), 322. In view of the many *literary* differences between Ezra and 1 Esdras, however, this specific reading of 1 Esdras should not be explained as a mere textual error without careful examination; namely, supposing that "two years," instead of another number of years, is an error still does not account for the difference, since in Ezra the whole expression "x years" is absent. This chronological indication could not come into the text of 1 Esd 5:70, according to the hypothesis of the priority of Ezra 4:5, through a textual accident but through a literary (redactional) intervention.

does not mention King Xerxes (1 Esd 2:14-15, 25). According to Ezra 4:5-24, these two kings had stopped all restoration activities in Jerusalem. The intervention of Artaxerxes, leading to the building stop, is suggested by Ezra 4:23-24. Only under Darius could the work be resumed again. Thus there was no blaming of the leaders of Judah for the long interruption of the temple construction after the restoration of the altar and the laying of the temple foundations (Ezra 3). Immediately after the arrival of the *golah*, under the leadership of Zerubbabel and Joshua, the altar is rebuilt and the sacrificial service can start (3:1-6). Then they begin to organize at once, without any delay, the rebuilding of the temple (3:7-13). They lose no time, since everything is done between the seventh month of the first year and the second year after their arrival in Jerusalem. They are stopped by the enemies in the country (4:1-3), and these plot against the Jews at the court of the Persian kings Xerxes and Artaxerxes and the latter's successor Darius (4:6-24). The Jews could not do anything else than obey the Persian power. But then came the prophets Haggai and Zechariah, and now obeying God more than men, they resume their work (5:12). They are questioned by the governor Tattenai and his colleagues, but King Darius, in unconscious accordance with the two prophets, allows them to pursue their project of reconstruction (5:3-6:12).

From the perspective of textual (and literary) criticism, there is no reason why someone should have added such a difficult chronological note, while it is easy to see why somebody would have canceled it. Therefore, it is more likely that 1 Esdras has the more original text here.

To summarize, the narrative unit of Ezra 2-6 is best explained as a redactional or recensional reshaping of the Hebrew *Vorlage* of 1 Esd 2; 5-7, that is, the narrative in its original form, not yet containing the secondary insertion of the story of the three youths. What was the purpose of the redactor or editor? It seems to have been twofold. First, he transformed the two parallel or synoptic accounts of the political opposition against the restoration of the temple into two distinct and succeeding acts of one drama. Thereby he simplified the complex literary agenda or layout of 1 Esdras into a straightforward linear chronological sequence.

Second, at the same time he considerably extended the duration of the hindrance met by the temple restoration. It embraced four reigns, from Cyrus to Darius, and included those of Xerxes and Artaxerxes. This in turn explains why the city and the walls of Jerusalem lay waste through this whole long period, since not even the first and foremost point in the restoration program, the reconstruction of the temple, had been realized. In contrast, according to the second account of 1 Esdras (1 Esd 5-7), the obstruction of the restoration lasted less than two years. Or rather, it lasted at most two years under Cyrus, until the accession to the throne of his successor Darius; or, perhaps, a few years more, namely, some years during the lifetime of Cyrus, then two more years until the second year of Darius (1 Esd 5:70-6:1). Is it more likely that an author or redactor would have diminished the duration of a serious obstruction of the temple restoration or that he would have extended it? The evidence seems to be in favor of the latter alternative.

7. Conclusions

First, the literary difference between 1 Esd 2–7 and Ezra 2; 5–7 is the *arrangement* of the narrative: in the former we read two parallel or synoptic accounts of one and the same episode, the opposition to the exiles' efforts to rebuild the temple, while in the latter these two episodes are reported as two distinct events which follow each other in chronological succession. According to 1 Esdras, the opposition during the reigns of Artaxerxes and Darius is reported in two synoptic accounts as one and the same event, while Ezra takes them as two distinct and successive events in chronological sequence.

Second, Ezra is mainly interested in rebuilding the sanctuary. Thus, it begins with the altar (Ezra 3), which is followed by the foundations of the house. But opposition during the reigns of Xerxes (4:6) and Artaxerxes (4:7–24) leads to a cessation of all building activities. These are resumed in the first year of Darius (Ezra 5–6), despite a new opposition that quickly failed. First Esdras has the exiles rebuild the walls, marketplaces, and the sanctuary of Jerusalem.

Third, the narrative of Ezra is likely to be secondary in comparison with that of 1 Esdras. There are two main reasons to favor this conclusion. First, in 1 Esd 5:60 old people weep with deep disappointment when they contemplate the fully completed new temple, so deficient in comparison to the splendor of the previous one, which the Babylonians had destroyed. In Ezra 3:12 they were in tears contemplating only the *foundations* of the new temple. The former account is likely to be more original, while the latter seems secondary. The argument is on the *narrative* level. What matters is the comparison. The new house of the LORD is compared with the old one, and the comparison disfavors the new one. In a narrative perspective, comparisons are normally between directly similar and comparable realities, for example sleek and fat cows (Gen 41:2–3); plump and thin ears (Gen 41:5); fruit trees and a bramble without fruit (Judg 9:8–15); low thorn bush and high cedar (2 Kgs 14:8); cedar, willow twig, vine (Ezek 17:2–6); the rich cattle breeder and the poor owner of one sheep (2 Sam 12:1–6), etc. The comparisons used are straightforward. The comparison between the old house and the foundation of the new one, however, is of a different kind: here an existing house is compared with a future one, since the foundations correspond to a potential building to be realized in the future. For narrative reasons, the less natural comparison between house and foundations of a house in Ezra is likely to be secondary, whereas the obvious and straightforward one of 1 Esdras seems to be original.

It might be objected that the account of Ezra, with its long dwelling on the foundations being laid without any further building progress, is nevertheless the more difficult narrative form, and as such it is more likely to be the original narrative, which then has been secondarily smoothed by 1 Esdras. However, we are not here taking a *text-critical* perspective, in which a more difficult reading is to be preferred to an easy one. The reasoning does not concern textual readings but narrative features or motifs (*Erzählmotive*), such as, for example, the youngest son being more successful than, or preferred to, the elder ones or a young boy vanquishing an old, skilled hero, etc.

A story presenting such motifs in their pure form is more likely to correspond to the original conception than a story in which such motifs are combined with others or distorted. An example would be the prophetic sign of the cloak of the prophet Ahijah the Shilonite in 1 Kgs 11:30–32, 36. He tore it into twelve pieces, obviously according to the twelve tribes of Israel, and gave Jeroboam ten pieces and Rehoboam one, of course for Judah, or perhaps for Judah and Benjamin together (1 Kgs 12:21, 23) There remains one piece without an attribution. It is likely that this piece represents Levi, because the Levites apparently did not follow King Jeroboam, as may be concluded from 1 Kgs 12:26–33. It is likely that later narrators or writers superimposed on the motif of the twelve tribes torn apart by Jeroboam's secession and represented by the prophet's cloak torn into twelve pieces, another supplementary motif—that of the special position of the tribe of Levi among the twelve. This combination of the two motifs is most likely secondary in the prophetic story of Ahijah's cloak.

Similarly, the narrative motif of the comparison between an older, ruined and a newer, restored temple, where, unexpectedly and disappointingly, the old one is more glorious than the new one, is genuine and speaks for itself. On the contrary, the comparison between a glorious old temple *building* and a miserable new temple *foundation* is a derived comparison. Therefore the first one is likely to be the original motif, while the comparison of *temple foundations* with *a temple building* hardly seems to be original.

Second, in 1 Esd 5:70 a space of only two years is left between the reign of Cyrus and the second year of Darius for the serious obstruction of the temple restoration on the part of the enemies of the exiles. This chronological element is absent from the corresponding passage in Ezra 4:5. Its secondary addition is much less likely than its suppression, since so short a time allotted to the hostility against the temple's reconstruction takes much from its weight. A short-lived obstruction is of course a less serious threat than a long and enduring attack. Here the argument is this: the tendency of scribes or editors is not to diminish the difficulty the builders had to overcome but rather to increase it.

Neither difference is an isolated retouching. Both are consistent with many other textual and literary differences in the two books. First Esdras 5 reports the several steps that lead to the complete setting up of the temple, while Ezra 3 replaces this building progression with the stereotyped and repeated information that only the foundations were laid. And the specific chronological indication in 1 Esd 5:70 of a very short period of two years for the whole obstruction contrasts with the information in Ezra 4:5–6 that in addition to the opposition during the reign of Cyrus, there was further opposition during the entire reigns of Xerxes and Artaxerxes, that is, a long space of time. These elements are no accidental themes. On the contrary, they are essential features that shape the whole story in each of the two books.

Fourth, from a historical point of view, the account of 1 Esdras, especially in 1 Esd 2, is more plausible because the exiles brought back the precious holy temple vessels to Jerusalem (Ezra 1:7–10; 1 Esd 2:10–14). Such a treasure needed a protected place to be stored in safety. First Esdras 5:44 thus mentions the holy treasure house where the money for the building of the temple was stored. There is no equivalent of this phrase in Ezra. Ancient writers certainly associated with a treasure house a fortified place, protected by walls and guards. An open city or a temple without walls was not fit for such a purpose. The very first necessity was a safe place (cf. Lam 2:7–9). Therefore, the exiles first created a walled city and temple. This is exactly what 1 Esdras reports (1 Esd 2:17). In contrast, it cannot be said that 1 Esdras would have upset the whole story of Ezra precisely for that reason. Its own specific narrative interest is not concentrated on this feature, which plays only a minor role in its narrative. But it is of central interest for Ezra–Nehemiah, since the repair of the walls of Jerusalem represents the main content of Neh 1–8. Dieter Böhler has shown that Ezra–Nehemiah is organized precisely in order to make way for Nehemiah's reconstruction of the walled city of Jerusalem.

The account of Ezra has its own specific plausibility. This is to show that the exiles aimed foremost at the reconstruction of the house of the LORD. Everything else was subordinated to this religious priority.[12] As far as they were concerned, they had done everything that depended on them. If they had not succeeded at once, this was not their fault but was due to the hostility of the conditions. The city of Jerusalem was to be rebuilt only later by Nehemiah.

Fifth, the comparison of Ezra 2–6 with 1 Esd 2; 5–6 shows the literary and textual priority of the Greek book in this section. This result confirms the results arrived at by Dieter Böhler in many other parts of the book. Thus, the case of Ezra–Nehemiah and 1 Esdras is a further example, besides Jeremiah, Ezekiel, Daniel, and many other books and sections of the Hebrew Bible, in which the old Greek translation witnesses an older Hebrew text form than the Hebrew text of the Masoretes. This observation leads to the further question of whether we have to reckon with a recension or revised edition of the Hebrew Bible realized somewhere in the second or first century B.C.E.

---

12. This is the reason why the building of the altar and the restoration of the cult were the very first works the exiles realized after their return. This narrative element was placed in front of everything else; Böhler, *Die heilige Stadt*, 309.

ARTICLES ARGUING AGAINST THE PRIORITY OF 1 ESDRAS

THE STORY OF THE THREE YOUTHS
AND THE COMPOSITION OF 1 ESDRAS

Bob Becking

1. INTRODUCTION

The focal question in this volume is whether 1 Esdras was first. The hypothesis that the present "book," 1 Esdras, was written earlier or was conceived at an earlier stage than the canonical book of Ezra has—as have all hypotheses—a set of presuppositions and some implications if true. I would like to approach them by looking at the role of the story of the three youths.[1]

2. MAIN DIFFERENCE: THE STORY OF THE THREE YOUTHS

One of the main differences between the Hebrew/Aramaic narratives in Ezra–Nehemiah and the Greek text of 1 Esdras is the presence of the story of the three youths in 1 Esd 3–4. If 1 Esdras was first, then it must be presupposed that this story has willfully been removed from the tradition to explain its absence in Ezra–Nehemiah. If 1 Esdras was not first, then this story should be seen as an addition to the existing narrative material. Since the narrative is absent in one version, a classical text-critical and text-historical comparison between two traditions is not possible. A growing consensus among scholars, therefore, construes this story as a later interpolation within 1 Esdras. This view implies that there was an older version of *1 Esdras that did not yet contain the story. This assumption solves the problem at a redaction-historical level.[2] The arguments

---

1. H. G. M. Williamson, "The Problem with First Esdras," in *After the Exile: Essays in Honour of Rex Mason* (ed. John Barton and David J. Reimer; Macon, Ga.: Mercer University Press, 1996), 201–16; Lester L. Grabbe, *Ezra–Nehemiah* (OTR; London: Routledge, 1998), 69–92; and Kristin De Troyer, "Zerubbabel and Ezra: A Revived and Revised Solomon and Josiah? A Survey of Current 1 Esdras Research," *Currents in Biblical Research* 1 (2002): 30–60, offer good introductions into the interpretative problems around 1 Esdras.

2. F. Zimmermann, 'The Story of the Three Guardsmen," *JQR* 54 (1963-1964): 179–200; Karl-Friedrich Pohlmann, *Studien zum dritten Esra: Ein Beitrag zur Frage nach dem*

for this consensus, however, are in my view not convincing, and the solution proposed is premature. I will come to that later. Other ways of investigating the plus need to be approached. I will therefore look in two directions: context and contents.

3. Context of the Story of the Three Youths

As has often been noticed, the order of the narration in 1 Esdras differs from the biblical tradition. In its present form, 1 Esdras narrates a story that starts at the Josianic celebration of the Passover. Bridging exile and return, the first narrative section ends with the celebration of the Passover in a rebuilt temple.[3] The second narrative section in 1 Esdras tells about the return of exiles under Ezra and the so-called mixed-marriage crisis. The book quite suddenly ends in a story, in the middle of a sentence even, in which Ezra is reading the Law.[4] It can be assumed that 1 Esdras originally continued after that and that this assumed continuation is lost in tradition, but in the light of absence of evidence, only speculations on its further contents can be made.

The story of the three youths, or three courtiers, is placed in 1 Esdras between two reports that describe attempts to rebuild the temple. It should be kept in mind that the majority of the content of 1 Esdras completely parallels 2 Chronicles, Ezra, and Nehemiah. It should also be kept in mind that the narrative order differs between the two traditions. The main difference can be

---

urspünglichen Schluss des chronistischen Geschichtswerkes (FRLANT 104; Göttingen: Vandenhoeck & Ruprecht, 1970); Tamara C. Eskenazi, "The Chronicler and the Composition of 1 Esdras," *CBQ* 48 (1986): 39–61; Jacob M. Myers, *I and II Esdras: A New Translation with Introduction and Commentary* (AB 42; Garden City, N.Y.: Doubleday, 1974), 1–7; Joseph Blenkinsopp, *Ezra–Nehemiah* (OTL; London: SCM, 1988), 70–71; Adrian Schenker, "La Relation d'Esdras A' au texte massorétique d'Esdras-Néhémie," in *Tradition of the Text: Studies Offered to Dominique Barthélemy in Celebration of His 70th Birthday* (ed. Gerard J. Norton and Stephen Pisano; OBO 109; Freiburg: Universitätsverlag; Göttingen: Vandenhoeck & Ruprecht, 1991), 218–49; Dieter Böhler, *Die heilige Stadt in Esdras α und Esra-Nehemia: Zwei Konzeptionen der Wiederherstellung Israels* (OBO 158; Freiburg: Universitätsverlag; Göttingen: Vandenhoeck & Ruprecht, 1997), 69–73; Lester L. Grabbe, *A History of the Jews and Judaism in the Second Temple Period, Volume 1: Yehud; A History of the Persian Province of Judah* (LSTS 47; London: T&T Clark, 2004), 83–85.

3. 1 Esd 7:10–15; see Myers, *I and II Esdras*, 75–76, 80; Grabbe, *Ezra–Nehemiah*, 96–97; Zipora Talshir, *1 Esdras: A Text Critical Commentary* (SBLSCS 50; Atlanta: Society of Biblical Literature, 2001), 380–84.

4. 1 Esd 9:37–55; see, e.g., Pohlmann, *Studien zum dritten Esra*, 34–35; Myers, *I and II Esdras*, 99–100; Böhler, *Die heilige Stadt*, 94–105, 110–15, 320–21; Grabbe, *Ezra–Nehemiah*, 98–99; Talshir, *1 Esdras: A Text Critical Commentary*, 499–500. Arie van der Kooij, "On the Ending of the Book of 1 Esdras," in *LXX: VII Congress of the International Organization for Septuagint and Cognate Studies* (ed. C. E. Cox; SCSt 31; Atlanta: Scholars Press, 1991), 37–49, however, proposed that 1 Esd 9:55 is a logical ending with the intention to close the book.

found in the middle part. In 1 Esdras there is already an attempt to rebuild the temple in the earlier parts of the story.[5] This attempt is situated in 1 Esdras after the declaration of the edict of Cyrus and after the report of the return of the temple vessels[6] but before the return of the bulk of the exiles.[7] This "pre-return" attempt of 1 Esdras is narrated in Ezra after the list of the returnees[8] and after another attempt to rebuild the temple was interrupted.[9] Not only is the order of events turned topsy-turvy, but the story of the three youths is placed between them in the 1 Esdras tradition.

There might be a historiographic reason for changing the order. In reading Ezra 3–6 there is a problem in accepting the believability of the story concerning the characters of Zerubbabel and Jeshua. They are mentioned at Ezra 3:2 among those building an altar for God in Jerusalem, which according to the text-internal chronology would have taken place in the reign of Cyrus. Zerubbabel and Jeshua are still in leading positions in Ezra 5:2, where they favor the initiative to overcome the stagnation of the rebuilding during the reign of a Persian king, Darius, who ruled—according to the text-internal chronology—*after* Cyrus, Ahasuerus, and Artaxerxes and after the exchange of letters mentioned in Ezra 4. This implies that *either* Zerubbabel and Jeshua had an extraordinarily long lifetime *or* we have to assume a pattern of quick changes on the imperial throne in Persia. The last proposition can easily be falsified by a look at the data of the reigns of the Persian kings.

The problem just mentioned has been solved by accepting that the Darius mentioned in Ezra 4:24 must be identified with Darius I Hystaspes.[10] This solution yields, however, a new problem. If this assumption were correct, then the chronology of the exchange of letters would make no sense. Accepting that Darius in Ezra 4:24 was Darius I Hystaspes would imply that the correspondence in Ezra 5 takes place in a period before the correspondence in Ezra 4. This does not make sense. The outcome of the exchange of letters with Xerxes and Artaxerxes (Ezra 4) is the interruption of the building process. The correspondence in Ezra 5 leads to the resumption and finalizing of the rebuilding. An inverted historical order would be without meaning since a finalized rebuilding process can no longer be interrupted.

---

5. 1 Esd 2:15–26; see Myers, *I and II Esdras*, 39–43; Talshir, *1 Esdras: A Text Critical Commentary*, 105–24.
6. 1 Esd 2:15; see Böhler, *Die heilige Stadt*, 221–37.
7. 1 Esd 5:7–46; see Talshir, *1 Esdras: A Text Critical Commentary*, 252–89.
8. Ezra 4:7–24.
9. Ezra 3:1–4:5.
10. See, e.g., Blenkinsopp, *Ezra-Nehemiah*, 115; H. G. M. Williamson, *Ezra, Nehemiah* (WBC 16; Waco, Tex.: Word, 1985), 56–60. Most recently, see A. P. Brown, *Hope amidst Ruin: A Literary and Theological Analysis of Ezra* (Greenville, S.C.: Bob Jones University Press, 2009), esp. 30–34.

These and other anomalies lead to the conclusion that Ezra 3–6 is not a form of objective history writing. The communication between author and reader does not take place in the dimension of verifiable history writing but in the field of the construction of a belief system. In short, Ezra 3–6 *erzählt keine Geschichte, sondern eine Geschichte*—tells not history but a story. Elements from the past are used to color the message with seemingly authentic details. The belief system of Ezra can be summarized in three points:

1. Royal and imperial backing for the appropriation of Yahwism according to the terms of the Ezra group;
2. The central role of the celebration of Passover for emerging Judaism; and
3. Abrogation of mixed marriages as important for the continuation of this community.

In the book of Ezra, the turning point from interruption to resumption can be found in Ezra 5:1–2: resumption of the building of the *house of God* after prophetic intervention by the prophets Haggai and Zechariah.[11]

In 1 Esdras the narrative order is different but not without comparable problems for accepting the believability of the story. By implication, it can be assumed that 1 Esdras, too, *erzählt keine Geschichte, sondern eine Geschichte*— tells not history but a story. In the book of Ezra the mention of the cessation of the work on the rebuilding of the temple[12] is followed by a report of the spontaneous intervention of the prophets Haggai and Zechariah. In 1 Esdras this note (2:31) is followed by the story of the three youths. As mentioned above, there is a growing consensus among scholars to construe this story as a later interpolation within 1 Esdras. In other words, there was an older version of *1 Esdras that did not yet contain this story.[13] The arguments for this view are mainly connected

---

11. See Bob Becking, "Ezra on the Move: Trends and Perspectives on the Character and His Book," in *Perspectives in the Study of the Old Testament and Early Judaism: A Symposium in Honour of Adam S. van der Woude on the Occassion of His 70th Birthday* (ed. F. García Martínez and E. Noort; VTSup 73; Leiden: Brill, 1998), 154–79; Grabbe, *Ezra-Nehemiah*, 125–53; Bob Becking, "Continuity and Community: The Belief System of the Book of Ezra," in *The Crisis of Israelite Religion: Transformation of Religious Traditions in Exilic and Post-Exilic Times* (ed. Bob Becking and M. C. A. Korpel; OTS 42; Leiden: Brill, 1999), 256–75. This view has been challenged unconvincingly by Brown, *Hope Amidst Ruin*. See also Lisbeth S. Fried, "*Deus ex Machina*: The Role of the Prophetic Voice in Ezra 5:1," in *Prophets and Prophecy in Ancient Israelite Historiography* (ed. Mark J. Boda and L. M. Wray Beal; Winona Lake, Ind.: Eisenbrauns, in press).

12. Ezra 4:24: "Then ceased the work of the house of God which is at Jerusalem. So it ceased unto the second year of the reign of Darius king of Persia."

13. Zimmermann, "Story of the Three Guardsmen," 179–200; Pohlmann, *Studien zum dritten Esra*; Wilhelm Th. in der Smitten, "Zur Pagenerzählung im 3. Esra (3 Esr. III 1–V 6),"

with the anomalies in the narrative order, for instance the ambiguity in 1 Esdras surrounding the Persian king who returned the temple vessels to Jerusalem—Cyrus or Darius. With Zipporah Talshir, I would like to challenge this view with three observations.[14]

1. The character of the Greek language. The Greek in the story of the three youths equals the Greek employed in the "main" body of 1 Esdras. The arguments of Pohlmann and Böhler on this point are not very convincing. First, they argue that in the story of the three youths, Semitisms occur that are absent in the rest of 1 Esdras. Then they state that on occasion the Greek in the story of the three youths differs in phraseology from the rest of 1 Esdras.[15] Apart from the fact that both arguments are built only on the basis of a few examples, the language variation could also be explained by the difference in *genre*: the story of the three youths is a court narrative with literary qualities, while the other parts of 1 Esdras are to be construed as "historical" narratives. Pohlmann and Böhler argue that the difference in *genre* would imply a different author, a view that I find stunningly obsolete.
2. Talshir holds a different view on the redaction history. According to her, 1 Esdras is "a section deliberately cut out from Chronicles–Ezra–Nehemiah to form a framework for the story of the youths. First Esdras never existed without the story of the youths."
3. Accepting the story of the three youths as a later addition does not solve all the problems of anomaly. In my view, the anomalies that we as modern readers detect might not have been much trouble for the ancient reader. The aim of ancient authors was not to write history in the sense of a controlled depiction of the past but to construct a story about the past that would convince its readership of a specific religious and/or moral worldview.

The story of the three youths relates a competition among three young courtiers who initiate the competition themselves. Their competition is a quest

---

VT 22 (1972): 492–95; Myers, *I and II Esdras*, 53; Böhler, *Die heilige Stadt*, 69–73; Grabbe, *Ezra-Nehemiah*, 72–73.

14. Zipora Talshir, *1 Esdras: From Origin to Translation* (SBLSCS 47; Atlanta: Society of Biblical Literature, 1999), passim. quote from p. 6; see also idem, "Ezra-Nehemiah and First Esdras: Diagnosis of a Relationship Between Two Recensions," *Bib* 81 (2000): 566–73; idem, "Synchronic Approaches with Diachronic Consequences in the Study of Parallel Redactions: First Esdras and 2 Chronicles 35–36; Ezra 1–10; Nehemiah 8," in *Yahwism after the Exile: Perspectives on Israelite Religion in the Persian Era* (ed. Rainer Albertz and Bob Becking; Studies in Theology and Religion 5; Assen: Van Gorcum, 2003), 199–218.

15. Pohlmann, *Studien zum dritten Esra*; Böhler, *Die heilige Stadt*.

for strength: "Let every one of us make a statement [about what is strongest]: he shall prevail whose statement shall seem wiser than the others, and unto him shall the king Darius give great gifts, and great things in token of victory."[16] According to the first courtier, "wine is the strongest," since it causes all men to err when they drink it. According to the second, "the king is the strongest," since a king has the power to kill and to spare. According to the third—the only one with a name—"Women are strongest: but above all things is truth which brings the victory." In fact this third courtier first follows the argument of the other two, by pointing to the fact that women have the capacity to make men do things, but then surpasses the discourse by stating that truth stands above all.[17] The king finds him the wisest of the three and offers him might, power, and well-being.[18] Zorobabel, however, avails himself of the momentum and reminds the Persian king of his vow to return the vessels to the Jerusalem temple, which then comes to pass.

Within the composition of 1 Esd 1–7, the story of the three youths functions as a subnarrative that offers a breakthrough from the stalemate at the rebuilding of the temple. King Darius takes action that leads to the return of a considerable group to Yehud with the temple vessels and a set of royal decrees. On returning to Jerusalem, they resume rebuilding the sanctuary, with its climax at the celebration of the Passover festival.[19]

This implies that Ezra 1–6 and 1 Esd 1–7 hold different views regarding the question of what eventually caused the resumption of temple building. In the book of Ezra, a focus is given to the divine intervention through the prophets Haggai and Zechariah, while in 1 Esd 1–7 the process is made dependent on a competition and especially on the piety of Zorobabel, who confronts worldly power by reminding Darius of his vow regarding the return of the temple vessels.[20]

---

16. 1 Esd 3:5; see Talshir, *1 Esdras: From Origin to Translation*, 58–80; idem, *1 Esdras: A Text Critical Commentary*, 139–42.

17. "*Homines transeunt, sed veritas manet in aeternum*"; Tomas of Kempis, *De Imitatione Christi* 1.5.2. For some scholars the element of surpassing is an argument for seeing this element as nonoriginal to the story; see in der Smitten, "Zur Pagenerzählung," 493; Grabbe, *Ezra–Nehemiah*, 73. In my view, the fourth element is necessary for the plot of both this story and the whole of 1 Esdras; see also Zimmermann, "Story of the Three Guardsmen," 179–200; A. Hilhorst, "The Speech on Truth in 1 Esdras 4,34–41," in *The Scriptures and the Scrolls: Studies in Honour of A. S. van der Woude on the Occasion of His 65th Birthday* (ed. F. García Martínez, A. Hilhorst, C. J. Labuschagne; Leiden: Brill, 1992), 135–51; T. J. Sandoval, "The Strength of Women and Truth: The Tale of the Three Bodyguards and Ezra's Prayer in First Esdras," *JJS* 58 (2007): 211–27.

18. 1 Esd 4:42; Böhler, *Die heilige Stadt*, 70; Talshir, *1 Esdras: From Origin to Translation*, 44–46; Talshir, *1 Esdras: A Text Critical Commentary*, 222–23.

19. 1 Esd 7:13–15; see Böhler, *Die heilige Stadt*, 248–59.

20. See also the discussion in Böhler, *Die heilige Stadt*, 78–142.

4. Contents of the Story of the Three Youths

The tale in 1 Esd 3–5, although narrating a "Persian story," is better understood against the background of a Hellenistic court. To give a few examples: the three youths are introduced as follows: οἱ τρεῖς νεανίσκοι οἱ σωματοφύλακες οἱ φυλάσσοντες τὸ σῶμα τοῦ βασιλέως, "the three young men, the bodyguards, the protectors of the body of the king." They very much resemble the "royal pages" as known from descriptions of Hellenistic courts.[21] The very idea of a competition as pastime is a feature that is well known in that venue.[22] It was customary for courtiers to discuss philosophical and literary topics during symposia as if they had as much time on their hands as the herdsmen of pastoral poetry.[23] In a bucolic idyll written by Bion of Phlossa, Cleodamus asks:

> Which is sweetest, to thee, Myrson, spring, or winter or the late autumn or the summer; of which dost thou most desire the coming? Summer, when all are ended, the toils whereat we labour, or the sweet autumn, when hunger weighs lightest on men, or even idle winter, for even in winter many sit warm by the fire, and are lulled in rest and indolence. Or has beautiful spring more delight for thee? Say, which does thy heart choose? For our leisure lends us time to gossip.[24]

The story in 1 Esdras can be depicted as a Hellenistic court narrative, as can be found in Esther, Dan 1–6[25], in the Ahiqar novella,[26] and in other texts.[27] A Hellenistic date of the story is reinforced by the following observations.

There are clear connections with the biblical book of Daniel:

---

21. See R. Strootman, "The Hellenistic Royal Court: Court Culture, Ceremonial and Ideology in Greece, Egypt and the Near East, 336–30 BCE" (Ph.D. diss., Utrecht University, 2007), 181–88.

22. In der Smitten, "Zur Pagenerzählung," 492–95; Strootman, "Hellenistic Royal Court," 202–16.

23. See Athenaios 6.211d.

24. Bion of Phlossa, frag. 2.1–8; see *The Greek Bucolic Poets* (trans. John M. Edmonds; LCL 28; Cambridge: Harvard University Press; London: William Heinemann, 1912). 411.

25. See Karel van der Toorn, "In the Lion's Den: The Babylonian Background of a Biblical Motif," *CBQ* 60 (1998): 626–40.

26. Recent translation and introduction by H. Niehr, *Aramäischer Aḥiqar* (JSHRZ 2/2; Gütersloh: Gütersloher Verlagshaus, 2007).

27. On Hellenistic court narratives, see also S. R. Johnson, *Historical Fictions and Hellenistic Jewish Identity: Third Maccabees in Its Cultural Context* (Hellenistic Culture and Society 43; Berkeley: University of California Press, 2004), 1–33. See especially Herodotus, *Hist.* 6.129–30; a distant parallel can be found in the story of Nachiketa in the Katha Upanishad.

1. The banquet scene in 1 Esd 3:1–3 resembles the description of the banquet scene in Dan 5. Topographically, the merism in 1 Esd 3:2 that is absent in Dan 5—καὶ τοπάρχαις τοῖς ὑπ' αὐτὸν ἀπὸ τῆς Ἰνδικῆς μέχρι τῆς Αἰθιοπίας, "and provincial officers that were under him, from India unto Ethiopia"—reflects the vastness of the Alexandrian empire.
2. Zorobabel is cast in the role of a pious Jew who is not aiming at personal profit and privileges but who cares about the future of his people. The same holds for the character of Daniel.
3. On return to Jerusalem, Zorobabel blesses and thanks the King of Heaven:

παρὰ σοῦ ἡ νίκη καὶ παρὰ σοῦ ἡ σοφία καὶ σὴ ἡ δόξα καὶ ἐγὼ σὸς οἰκέτης

From you comes victory, from you comes wisdom, and yours is the glory, and I am your servant.[28]

This phrase resembles a well-known line from Dan 7, in which the Son of Man is offered by the Ancient of Days "dominion, glory, and a kingdom."[29]

Moreover, in 1 Esd 4:45, 50 the Ἰδουμαῖοι, Idumeans, are mentioned. This ethnic indicator is used in the LXX to refer to anything connected both with the preexilic Transjordanian kingdom of Edom and with the Idumeans who occupied greater parts of southern Judah in the Persian and the Hellenistic periods.[30] In fact, the LXX translators identified the preexilic Edomites with their contemporary Idumeans. In 1 Esdras the Idumeans are mentioned twice.

---

28. 1 Esd 4:59; Talshir, *1 Esdras: A Text Critical Commentary*, 240–41.
29. Dan 7:14; see Talshir, *1 Esdras: From Origin to Translation*, 90.
30. See Ulrich Kellermann, "Psalm 137," *ZAW* 90 (1978): 43–58, esp. 57–58; B. Hartberger, *"An den Wassern von Babylon ...": Psalm 137 auf dem Hintergrund von Jeremia 51, der biblischen Edom-Traditionen und babylonischer Originalquellen* (BBB 63; Bonn: P. Hanstein, 1986), 134–39; J. R. Bartlett. *Edom and the Edomites* (JSOTSup 77; Sheffield: Sheffield Academic Press, 1989), 151–57; E. A. Knauf, "Supplementa Ismaelitica," *BN* 45 (1988): 62–81; H. M. Barstad, *The Myth of the Empty Land: A Study in the History and Archaeology of Judah during the "Exilic" Period* (Symbolae Osloenses Fasciculus Suppletorius 28; Oslo: Scandinavian University Press, 1996), 57–60; R. Albertz, *Die Exilszeit 6. Jahrhundert v. Chr.* (Biblische Enzyklopedie 7; Stuttgart: Kohlhammer, 2001), 84–85, 149–53; Oded Lipschits, *The Fall and Rise of Jerusalem: Judah under Babylonian Rule* (Winona Lake, Ind.: Eisenbrauns, 2005), 68–97; L. M. Zucconi, "From the Wilderness of Zin alongside Edom: Edomite Territory in the Eastern Negev during the Eighth–Sixth Centuries BCE," in *Milk and Honey: Essays on Ancient Israel and the Bible in Appreciation of the Judaic Studies Program at the University of California, San Diego* (ed. S. Malena, D. Miano, and Frank Moore Cross; Winona Lake, Ind.: Eisenbrauns, 2007), 241–56; Lester L. Grabbe, *A History of the Jews and Judaism in the Second Temple Period, Volume 2: The Coming of the Greeks; The Early Hellenistic Period (335–175 BCE)* (LSTS 68; London: T&T Clark, 2008), 176–80.

καὶ σὺ εὔξω οἰκοδομῆσαι τὸν ναόν ὃν ἐνεπύρισαν οἱ Ιδουμαῖοι ὅτε ἠρημώθη ἡ Ιουδαία ὑπὸ τῶν Χαλδαίων

You have also vowed to build up the temple, which the Idumeans burned when Judea was made desolate by the Chaldeans.[31]

This phrase is part of the speech by Zorobabel when he reminded Darius of his vows. In the catalogue of wishes made by Zorobabel, we read:

καὶ πᾶσαν τὴν χώραν ἣν κρατήσουσιν ἀφορολόγητον αὐτοῖς ὑπάρχειν καὶ ἵνα οἱ Ιδουμαῖοι ἀφιῶσι τὰς κώμας ἃς διακρατοῦσιν τῶν Ιουδαίων

And that all the country which they hold should be free without tribute; and that the Idumeans should surrender the villages of the Jews which they hold.

It seems obvious that the narrators of the story of the three youths here follow a biblical tradition on the vicious role that the Edomites played when Jerusalem was conquered by the Babylonians.[32] However, the historical trustworthiness of this tradition cannot be proven. It is remarkable that this tradition has no base in the "historical" books of the Hebrew Bible: the evil act of the Edomites is not referred to in either the books of Kings or Chronicles.[33] It would therefore be interesting to look in another direction. In 2 Macc 10:15–17, mention is made of a reconquest by the Maccabean forces of some Idumean strongholds. I would like to suggest that the mention of the Idumeans in 1 Esdras refers to the situation in the second century B.C.E., when Idumeans still occupied large parts of the "Judean" territory.

5. CONTENTS IN CONTEXT

It should be noted that the themes in the answers of the three youths to the question of what is strongest reappear in the rest of the story.

---

31. 1 Esd 4:45; the B text reads Ἰουδαῖοι instead of Ἰδουμαῖοι, probably an internal Greek corruption; see Talshir, *1 Esdras: A Text Critical Commentary*, 226.

32. See Obad 10–16; Ezek 25:12–14; 35:5–7; Ps 137; this tradition is continued in rabbinic writings; see S. D. Kunin, "Israel and the Nations: A Structuralist Survey," *JSOT* 82 (1999): 19–43.

33. P. C. Beentjes, "*Die Freude war gross in Jerusalem*" *(2Chr 30,26): Eine Einführung in die Chronikbücher* (SEThV 3; Münster: LIT-Verlag, 2008). See also S. L. McKenzie, "The Chronicler as Redactor," in *The Chronicler as Author: Studies in Text and Texture* (ed. M. P. Graham and S. L. McKenzie; JSOTSup 263; Sheffield: Sheffield Academic Press, 2000), 70–90 (esp. 74–77).

1. "Wine," by implication, is connected to the banquet scene. The noun occurs outside the story of the three youths in 1 Esd 6:29, where wine is listed among the commodities that will be part of the tribute to be paid out of the tribute of Coele Syria and Phoenicia to Zorobabel.[34]
2. The motif of the strength of the king plays a role throughout the story of 1 Esdras.
3. "Women" are referred to several times outside the story of the three youths. In this connection, special attention must be paid to the episode of the so-called mixed marriages. In 1 Esd 8:89 the following confession is made:

συνῳκίσαμεν γυναῖκας ἀλλογενεῖς ἐκ τῶν ἐθνῶν τῆς γῆς

we have married strange women of the nations of the land.

Here, women—and especially "foreign" women—are assumed to be of great power. Canessa has argued for a very specific connection. In his view there is a parallel between Ezra chasing away the foreign women and proving the superiority of the God of truth over women.[35]

4. ἀλήθεια, "truth," is—within 1 Esdras—only scarcely attested outside the story of the three youths. In his final argument, however, Zorobabel makes a connection between "truth" and "the God of Israel" when he finishes with εὐλογητὸς ὁ θεὸς τῆς ἀληθείας, "Blessed be the God of truth."[36] It is my conviction that this "God of truth" is the main *agens* behind all the stories in 1 Esdras. In this connection, attention needs to be given to an interesting variant in 1 Esd 5:40. In the so-called list of returnees, one reads in Ezra 2:63 // Neh 7:65:

And the governor said to them that they should not eat from the most holy things until a priest stood up with Urim and Thummim.

---

34. This has a parallel in 1 Esd 8:20.
35. A. Canessa, "De l'Originalité d'Esdras A," in *KATA TOUS O' Selon Les Septante: Hommage a Marguertie Harl* (ed. G. Dorival and O. Munnich; Paris: Cerf, 1995), 96; see also L. J. Eron, "'That Women Have Mastery over Both King and Beggar' (TJud. 15.5): The Relationship of the Fear of Sexuality to the Status of Women in Apocrypha and Pseudepigrapha: 1 Esdras (3 Ezra) 3–4, Ben Sira and the Testament of Judah," *JSP* 9 (1991): 43–66; Sandoval, "The Strength of Women and Truth," 211–27; for criticism of this view, see Talshir, "Synchronic Approaches with Diachronic Consequences," 217.
36. 1 Esd 4:40; see Zimmermann, "Story of the Three Guardsmen," 191; Talshir, *1 Esdras: From Origin to Translation*, 73–76; Hilhorst, "The Speech on Truth in 1 Esdras 4,34–41."

The LXX of Ezra 2:63—ἕως ἀναστῇ ἱερεὺς τοῖς φωτίζουσιν καὶ τοῖς τελείοις—is not a literal translation but a rendition that can be explained on the basis of the MT. In 1 Esdras this line is rendered as follows:

καὶ εἶπεν αὐτοῖς Νεεμιας καὶ Ατθαριας μὴ μετέχειν τῶν ἁγίων αὐτούς ἕως ἀναστῇ ἀρχιερεὺς ἐνδεδυμένος τὴν δήλωσιν καὶ τὴν ἀλήθειαν

And to them Nehemias and Atharias said, that they should not be partakers of the holy things, until there arose up a high priest clothed with doctrine and truth.

The oracular means of Urim and Thummim[37] have faded away and are replaced by a human figure dressed in truth. Talshir construes this variant as informed by passages from LXX.[38] In my view this variant should be construed as deliberately underscoring the importance of the theme of "truth" within the whole of 1 Esdras.[39]

6. Conclusion

The story of the three youths forms an integral part of the composition of 1 Esdras. It can best be seen as a court tale from Hellenistic times that played an integrating and structuring role in the whole of 1 Esdras. This would imply that the composition of 1 Esdras took place in the Maccabean period and that the text would have functioned as ideological and moral support for all those who wanted to cleanse the temple in Jerusalem from foreign, that is, Greek influences.[40] The book of Ezra, on the other hand, perfectly fits the situation in the Persian period, around 400 B.C.E. For all of that, I can only conclude that 1 Esdras did not come first. First Esdras should be seen as an appropriation of existing traditions in the political and religious situation of the Hellenistic Age.

---

37. On them see C. van Dam, *The Urim and Thummim: A Means of Revelation in Ancient Israel* (Winona Lake, Ind.: Eisenbrauns, 1997); Lisbeth S. Fried, "Did Second Temple High Priests Posses the Urim and Thummim?," *JHS* 7, no. 3 (2007).

38. Talshir, *1 Esdras: From Origin to Translation*, 249; idem, *1 Esdras: A Text Critical Commentary*, 281, refers to Exod 28:26 (30); Lev 8:8; Num 27:21; Deut 33:8; 1 Sam 28:6.

39. See also Blenkinsopp, *Ezra–Nehemiah*, 92–93.

40. See also Canessa, "L'Originalité d'Esdras A," 87–89.

THE SECOND YEAR OF DARIUS

Kristin De Troyer

In this contribution I will argue that the time indication "in the second year of (Darius)" can be seen as a clue to the history and the relationship between MT Ezra–Nehemiah and 1 Esdras.

The words "the second year" appear in the following expressions used in the book of Ezra–Nehemiah:

- Second year
- Second year of reign
- Second year of (their) coming
- Sometimes also the expression "two years"

"The second year of ..." also plays a role in the book of Haggai:

- Hag 1:1: in the second year of King Darius, this word came through the prophet Haggai to Zerubbabel.
- Hag 2:1: in the second year of King Darius, this word came through the prophet Haggai.
- Hag 2:10: in the second year of Darius, the word came to the prophet Haggai.

Similarly, "the second year" also plays a role in the book of Zechariah:

- Zech 1:1: in the eighth month in the second year of Darius.
- Zech 1:7: on the twenty-fourth day of the eleventh month of the second year of Darius.

Following is a list of the texts of 1 Esdras in which the expression "in the second year of Darius" can be found (the right column has been added for comparative purposes):

1 Esdras[1]	MT *Ezra*
2:25: building stopped until second year of Darius	4:24: work was stopped until second year of Darius
5:54: in second year of their coming to the temple	3:8: second year of their arrival
5:70: kept from building for two years, until Darius	4:5: bribed until Darius
6:1: in the second year of Darius, the prophets prophesied	5:1: now, the prophets prophesied

I deliberately put the text of 1 Esdras in the left column and kept the sequence of the verses as they appear in 1 Esdras. When comparing the verses with the verses in the right column, which are the verses of the MT, one immediately observes that every verse from the left column has a parallel in the right column, albeit in a different sequence. Indeed, the verse MT Ezra 3:8 does not appear up front as the first in the list of verses of the text, but as the second, after the appearance of MT Ezra 4:24. Also, there is a parallel verse to 1 Esd 6:1, namely MT 5:1. However, in this parallel verse MT 5:1, the expression "the second year of Darius" is missing, whereas it is present in 1 Esd 6:1. Similarly with 5:70//4:5.

We will now look at the narrative of Ezra. For the analysis of the expression "the second year of Darius," we will study the verses in the sequence as they appear in MT Ezra:

- 3:8 in the second year after their arrival at the house of God at Jerusalem
- 4:5 they bribed until the reign of Darius
- 4:24 work stopped until the second year of Darius
- 5:1 now[2]

These verses need to be put in the context of the first part of the book of Ezra–Nehemiah, namely Ezra 1–6. Most commentators recognize that Ezra 1–6 forms a unit:[3]

---

1. The verse numbering follows the edition by R. Hanhart. See Robert Hanhart, *Esdrae liber I* (Septuaginta. Vetus Testamentum Graecum VIII/1; Göttingen: Vandenhoeck & Ruprecht, 1991).
2. Note, again, that it is not the expression "the second year of Darius" but "now." [The author translates the νῦν at the beginning of Ezra 5:1 as "now"—Ed.]
3. See Wilhelm Rudolph, *Esra und Nehemia samt 3 Esra* (HAT 20; Tübingen: Mohr Siebeck, 1949), xxiii; Jacob M. Myers, *Ezra–Nehemiah* (AB 14; New York: Doubleday, 1965), xxxviii–xxxix; Wilhelm Th. in der Smitten, *Esra: Quellen, Ueberlieferung und Geschichte* (SSN 15; Assen: Van Gorcum, 1973), 3–6; Frank C. Fensham, *The Books of Ezra and Nehemiah* (NICOT; Grand Rapids, Mich.: Eerdmans, 1982), 27–28; David J. A. Clines, *Ezra, Nehemiah, Esther* (NCB; London: Marshall, Morgan & Scott; Grand Rapids, Mich.: Eerdmans, 1984), 14, 31; H. G. M. Williamson, *Ezra, Nehemiah* (WBC 16; Waco, Tex.: Word, 1985), xxxiv–xxxv;

1:1-11	Cyrus commands the building of the temple
2:1-70	List of the returnees to Jerusalem
3:1-13	Foundation of altar and Feast of Booths
4:1-3	"Enemies" pop up and are rejected
4:4-6	"Enemies" hinder the building project
4:7-22	"Enemies" write to King Artaxerxes
4:23-24	The building project is stopped
5:1-2	Prophesying of Haggai and Zechariah
5:3-5	Inquiry of Tattenai and Shethar-bozenai
5:6-17	Copy of letter to King Darius
6:1-12	King Darius' orders
6:13-15	The building is continued and finished
6:16-18	Dedication of the temple
6:19-22	Celebration of Passover[4]

The expression "the second year of Darius" appears in the subsection on laying the foundation of the altar and on celebrating the Festival of Booths (3:8). Ezra 3:1-3 relates that the altar is set up and burnt offerings are offered on it. Verse 4 states that after the worship has been restored, the Festival of Booths is celebrated. Verses 5-6a again emphasize that all normal worship was being restored. Verse 6b adds the important note that the foundation of the temple of the Lord was not yet laid. The worship is thus done simply on the established altar, but there is not yet a temple. Verse 7 then narrates that money is given to the masons and the carpenters and food, drink, and oil to the Sidonians and Tyrians to bring cedar trees from Lebanon to the sea, to Joppa. With v. 8, the actual temple building starts. The text literally states: "In the second year after their arrival at the house of God at Jerusalem, in the second month, Zerubbabel ... and Jeshua ... made a beginning, together with ...." In 3:8b, the Levites are appointed to have oversight of the work on the house of the Lord. The next verse, 3:9, specifies "Jeshua ... and Kadmiel ..., the sons of Henadad, the Levites together took charge of the workers in the house of the Lord."[5] In the next verses (vv. 10-13), the foundation of the temple of the Lord is laid and this event is celebrated.

Joseph Blenkinsopp, *Ezra-Nehemiah* (OTL; London: SCM, 1988), 42; G. F. Davies, *Ezra and Nehemiah* (Berit Olam; Studies in Hebrew Narrative and Poetry; Collegeville, Minn.: Michael Glazier, Liturgical Press, 1999), xx-xxi. Also indirectly—namely, by recognizing the unity of Ezra 7-10—Kurt Galling, *Die Bücher der Chronik, Esra, Nehemia* (ATD 12; Göttingen: Vandenhoeck & Ruprecht, 1954), 9; Karl-Friedrich Fohlmann, *Studien zum dritten Esra: Ein Beitrag zur Frage nach dem ursprünglichen Schluss des chronistischen Geschichtswerkes* (FRLANT 104; Göttingen: Vandenhoeck & Ruprecht, 1970), 14-15.

4. We note that the internal division of this section of Ezra is differently divided by many scholars.

5. In this contribution, we refrain from discussing the relationship between 3:8b and 3:9.

Then, the so-called adversaries of Judah and Benjamin appear on the scene. They propose to work along with the returned exiles: "Let us build with you" (4:2). The proposal for collaboration is rejected: "You shall have no part with us in building a house to our God" (4:3). The so-called adversaries then start hindering the temple-building project (4:4–5). More specifically, they write a letter of accusation to the king (4:6–16). The king responds (4:17–22). A copy of the letter of the king is read and the enemies rush to the Jews and by force make them cease with the work (4:23). The narrator adds: "At that time, the work on the house of God in Jerusalem stopped and was discontinued until the second year of the reign of King Darius of Persia" (4:24). It is precisely in the narrator's remark in 4:24 that the expression "the second year of Darius" is used.

The verse that we need to discuss next is the following one, in which the expression "the second year" does not appear but could have. Indeed, 5:1 mentions not "the second year" but "now." Then, in the next section of the text, the prophets Haggai and Zechariah are active, letters are sent to the king (Darius), and permission is given to restart the work on the temple.

An extra word is necessary here to explain why, in 5:1, the expression "now" suffices. First, after 5:1 follows a long section in which we read that the prophets Haggai and Zechariah are active (5:1), that the building of the temple is restarting (5:2), and that the legality of the building project is again questioned (5:3–5). In 5:6–17, the narrator tells how Tattenai and Shethar-bozenai speak to the Jews, ask them for an explanation as to why they started rebuilding, and write to King Darius with a proposal to have his archives searched for an edict of Cyrus, which the Jews claim exists and allows them to build their temple. Ezra 6:1 starts with "thereupon"; at the order of Darius, the archives are searched. In other words, 5:1 is truly "now"—during the time of Darius.

But can the reader know precisely in which year of Darius this last section happens? The answer is tied to 4:24: "… the work on the house of God in Jerusalem stopped and was discontinued until the second year of the reign of King Darius of Persia." Hence, the reader can only indirectly know that what happens in 5:1 is indeed the second year of King Darius. Of course, if one knew the texts of the books of Haggai and Zechariah, one could also identify the year of the restarting of the building project, as in these books the rebuilding is dated to the second year of Darius.

The four appearances of "the second year" can now be divided into two categories according to whether a specific king is named:

No named king: 3:8: in the second year after their arrival at the house of God at Jerusalem.
Darius is named: 4:5, 24; (5:1): the second year of Darius.

Moreover, the sequence of the narrative in MT Ezra is very clear:

- people return (Ezra 2);
- they start building, first the altar, then the temple (Ezra 3);
- people are hindered, the building project is stopped (Ezra 4);
- Haggai and Zechariah are active, the building project is restarted (Ezra 5); and finally,
- the archives are searched, permission to build is found (and given), and the temple-building project is finished (Ezra 6).

Now, what about the narrative of 1 Esdras and the use of the concept "the second year" in 1 Esdras? As mentioned above, the expression appears in the following verses:

- 2:25: building stopped until second year of Darius
- 5:54: in second year of their coming to the temple
- 5:70: they are kept from building for two years, until Darius
- 6:1: in the second year of Darius, the prophets prophesied

Again, we put these verses in their immediate context, namely, the first part of 1 Esdras:

2:1–14	Cyrus commands the building of the temple
2:15–24	"Enemies" write to King Artaxerxes
2:25	The building project is stopped
3:1–5:3	Darius' feast (three bodyguards)
5:4–45	List of the returnees to Jerusalem
5:46–62	Foundation of altar and Feast of Booths
5:63–68	"Enemies" pop up and are rejected
5:69–70	"Enemies" hinder the building project
6:1–2	Prophesying of Haggai and Zechariah
6:3–6	Inquiry of Sisinnes and Sathrabuzanes
6:7–21	Copy of letter to King Darius
6:22–33	King Darius' orders
7:1–5	The building is continued and finished
7:6–9	Dedication of the temple
7:10–15	Celebration of Passover

The first appearance of the expression "the second year" comes in 2:25. This verse is the verse in which the building of the house of the Lord in Jerusalem is stopped, after the enemies have written to King Artaxerxes and asked him to stop the building project (2:15–24). King Artaxerxes agrees with the enemies and requests that the Jews be stopped from building their temple (2:25). Then, in the book of 1 Esdras, comes the long and beautiful story of the three bodyguards who, at the feast of Darius, enter into a contest. Ultimately, it is Zerubbabel who wins the contest and is granted permission to go home to Jerusalem and rebuild the temple (3:1–5:3). In 5:4–45, a list is given of the people who return to Jerusalem.

In 5:46–62 the narrator relates the foundation of the altar and the Festival of Booths that is celebrated right after the establishment of worship. It is in this context that, for the second time, "in the second year" appears, namely, in 5:54.

The altar is set on its foundations, the festivities are taking place, and then the adversaries appear. Indeed, as in MT Ezra, the enemies pop up. They ask to participate in building, but after being rejected (5:63–68), they start hindering the project of building the temple (5:69–70). The section ends with the phrase, "they are kept from building for two years, until Darius" (5:70). We note that this verse does not say that they are kept from building until the second year of Darius. To the contrary, it is only said that they are kept from building for two years. In the context of the narrative, it is of course clear that Darius is already on the scene; after all, he has already given a huge party (3:1–5:3).

In MT 5:1, then, the prophets are active and the building work has restarted. Again, it is not said that the prophets prophesied in "the second year of Darius," but it is stated that "now" the prophets started to prophesy.

What are the differences between MT Ezra and 1 Esdras?[6]

First, in MT, enemies hinder the building in ch 4. In 1 Esdras, enemies hinder the work twice. In 2:15–24 the "enemies" write to King Artaxerxes and in 2:25, the building project is stopped. In 5:63–68, "enemies" pop up again and are rejected, and consequently, in 5:69–70, the "enemies" hinder the building project. Second, in MT, the prophets show up after the enemies have hindered and stopped the building. In 1 Esdras, the prophets show up after the enemies have hindered and stopped the building for the second time. Third, in MT, the enemies write to King Artaxerxes. In 1 Esdras, the first enemies write to King Artaxerxes. But the second enemies only come on the scene after King Darius has been introduced, namely, after the feast of Darius, where permission is given to build the temple.

There are thus two periods of hindering by the enemies in 1 Esdras:

PERIOD ONE
A first group of "enemies" stops the building project
2:15–24   "Enemies" write to King Artaxerxes **FIRST HINDERING**
2:25   The building project is stopped
PERIOD TWO
The building starts again
3:1–5:3   Darius' feast (three bodyguards)
5:4–45   List of the returnees to Jerusalem

---

6. See also Kristin De Troyer, *Rewriting the Sacred Text: What the Old Greek Texts Tell Us about the Literary Growth of the Bible* (Text-Critical Studies; Atlanta: Society of Biblical Literature, 2003), 91–126.

The second period of building the temple
5:46–62   Foundation of the altar and Feast of Booths
5:63–68   "Enemies" pop up and are rejected
5:69–70   "Enemies" hinder the building project **SECOND HINDERING**
Even now, problems arise, but Darius orders a decree to continue the project
6:1–2   Prophesying of Haggai and Zechariah
6:3–6   Inquiry of Sisinnes and Sathrabuzanes
6:7–21   Copy of letter to King Darius
6:22–33   King Darius' orders
7:1–5   The building is continued and finished

In other words, the author of 1 Esdras uses the concept of "the second year" to make the history line clearer: it starts with King Cyrus, then moves on to King Artaxerxes and finally to King Darius. The clarification in the history line also benefits from the reorganized text of 1 Esdras in comparison with the Ezra story.

1 Esdras	Ezra
1:1–58: Josiah and his successors	—[7]
2:1–14: Cyrus commands that the temple be built	= 1:1–11: Cyrus commands that the temple be built
	2:1–70: List of the returnees to Jerusalem
	3:1–13: Foundation of the altar and Feast of Booths
	4:1–3: "Enemies" pop up and are rejected
	4:4–6: "Enemies" hinder the building project
2:15–24: "Enemies" write to King Artaxerxes	= 4:7–22: "Enemies" write to King Artaxerxes
2:25: The building project is stopped	= 4:23–24: The building project is stopped
3:1–5:3: Darius' feast (three bodyguards)	—
5:4–45: List of the returnees to Jerusalem	
5:46–62: Foundation of the altar and Feast of Booths	
5:63–68: "Enemies" pop up and are rejected	
5:69–70: "Enemies" hinder the building project	
6:1–2: Prophesying of Haggai and Zechariah	= 5:1–2: Prophesying of Haggai and Zechariah
6:3–6: Inquiry of Sisinnes and Sathrabuzanes	= 5:3–5: Inquiry of Tattenai and Shethar-bozenai

---

7. But see 2 Chr 35–36 and 2 Kgs 22.

6:7–21: Copy of letter to King Darius	= 5:6–17: Copy of letter to King Darius
6:22–33: King Darius' orders	= 6:1–12: King Darius' orders
7:1–5: The building is continued and finished	= 6:13–15: The building is continued and finished
7:6–9: Dedication of the temple	= 6:16–18: Dedication of the temple
7:10–15: Celebration of Passover	= 6:19–22: Celebration of Passover

The comparison between 1 Esdras and Ezra shows that one section has been added and four sections have been moved: namely, the lists of the returnees to Jerusalem (Ezra 2:1–70; 1 Esd 5:4–45), the report on setting up the altar (Ezra 3:1–13; 1 Esd 5:46–62), the report on the enemies (Ezra 4:1–3; 1 Esd 5:63–68), and finally the report on how they hinder the building project (Ezra 4:4–6; 1 Esd 5:69–70). In Ezra the building project is stopped (4:24) after the enemies have appeared (4:1–3), have hindered the building (4:4–6), and have written to King Artaxerxes (4:7–22). In 1 Esdras, the theme of the hindering enemies is used twice. First, the enemies write to King Artaxerxes (1 Esd 2:15–24, which is parallel to Ezra 4:7–22) and the building project is stopped (1 Esd 2:25, parallel to Ezra 4:23–24). Note that the hindering (1 Esd 2:15–24) follows right after the report that Cyrus had commanded the temple be built (1 Esd 2:1–14 = Ezra 1:1–11). Following this section is a description of the events that happened after King Artaxerxes stopped the building process, namely, a feast of King Darius in 1 Esd 3:1–5:1. As the feast leads to the recognition of Zerubbabel, he and the Jews are permitted to go home. Immediately after this permission, the narrator offers the list of the people returning from exile (5:4–45) and the report on the laying of the foundation of the altar (5:46–62). But again enemies appear (5:63–68) and they hinder the work on the temple (5:69–70). The last section, 5:69–70, is the second use of the theme of hindering by enemies. First Esdras has thus used the theme of the hindering by enemies twice, more precisely, twice even before the actions of Haggai and Zechariah are reported. It is this double use of the hindering theme in 1 Esdras (2:15–24 and again in 5:63–68, 69–70) that allows us to see that 1 Esdras uses material found in MT Ezra.

Moreover, 1 Esdras connects the units of Zerubbabel's appointment, the lists of returnees, and the erection of the altar quite well. First, Zerubbabel receives permission to go to Jerusalem and rebuild the temple, then the list of returnees is given, and finally, a report is given about the erection of the altar. Moreover, all of this happens after the building project is stopped the first time. In other words, 1 Esdras introduces the feast of Darius to set up the next sequel of the story: Zerubbabel emerges, permission is given to return and rebuild, the list of returnees is given, and finally, a report is given about the erection of the altar. The creation of this unit, consisting of the story of the feast of Darius, the list of the returnees, and the report of the erection of the altar, not only helps clarify the historical line, it also focuses on the character of Zerubbabel. He is now directly permitted to return and build the temple, whereas in MT Ezra he was simply one of the returnees after Cyrus had given a general edict to all those who wished to go home. This unit renders explicit what was left implicit there.

Finally, the author of 1 Esdras uses the narrative of Darius' feast to introduce the second call to build the temple. First Esdras does not use Haggai and Zechariah in connection with the foundation of the altar and the first attempt to build the temple, but it does tie the second call to building the temple with these prophets' activity. Therefore, 1 Esdras needs to add the "second year" when Haggai and Zechariah are mentioned. In other words, whereas in the MT the work at the temple is only halted once, it is stopped twice in 1 Esdras. Moreover, whereas in MT the temple building is easily connected with the activities of Haggai and Zechariah in the second year of Darius, in 1 Esdras, with the commencement of the second phase of building, the link needs again to be established, hence the additional sentence, "in the second year of Darius," in 6:1. Indeed, Ezra 4:23–24 ends with the remark that the work on the temple was stopped until the second year of Darius. The next verse, 5:1, then turns precisely to the prophecies of Haggai and Zechariah, which happened in this second year—the year that was referred to a verse earlier. In 1 Esdras, however, the direct link between 4:23–24 and 5:1 is broken, first, by the story of the feast of Darius, and then by the insertion of the four sections that in Ezra are located before the report on how the building project was stopped. Whereas in MT Ezra there is not one verse between Ezra 4:23–24 and 5:1, in 1 Esdras there are the following sections between 1 Esd 2:25 (// Ezra 4:23–24) and 1 Esd 6:1–2 (// Ezra 5:1–2): 3:1–5:3 (Darius' feast); 5:44–45 (list of the returnees); 5:46–62 (foundation of the altar and festival of booths); 5:63–68 (enemies appear and are rejected); and, finally, 5:69–70 (enemies hinder), in total, 160 verses! The insertion of this material prompted the author of 1 Esdras to insert in his report on Haggai and Zechariah a clarification about the date, namely, that it happened "in the second year of Darius."

We can therefore conclude that indeed the concept of the "second year" is a clue to understanding the relationship between MT Ezra–Nehemiah and 1 Esdras.

WHY THE STORY OF THE THREE YOUTHS IN 1 ESDRAS?

Lisbeth S. Fried

As is well known to the readers of this book, work on the relationship between Ezra and 1 Esdras has been ongoing for over two hundred years. Ever since Pohlmann, however, exegetes have been divided into two main groups.[1] The first considers 1 Esdras to be a fragment of a long history that includes Chronicles, Ezra, and Nehemiah.[2] According to this group, except for the story of the three youths, a late addition, 1 Esdras reveals the original form of the text of Ezra to which Nehemiah was added secondarily. The second group of scholars sees 1 Esdras as a compilation of various passages taken from the separate books of Chronicles, Ezra, and Nehemiah, books that were already in their present form when the excerpts were taken.[3] According to this view, passages were compiled

---

1. Karl-Friedrich Pohlmann, *Studien zum dritten Esra: Ein Beitrag zur Frage nach dem ursprünglichen Schluss des chronistischen Geschichtswerkes* (FRLANT 104; Göttingen: Vandenhoeck & Ruprecht, 1970). For a history of research, see Kristin De Troyer, "Zerubbabel and Ezra: A Revived and Revised Solomon and Josiah? A Survey of Current 1 Esdras Research," *Currents in Biblical Research* 1 (2002): 30–60.

2. E.g., Charles C. Torrey, *Ezra Studies* (Chicago: University of Chicago Press, 1910; repr., New York: Ktav, 1970); Pohlmann, *Studien zum dritten Esra*; Adrian Schenker, "La relation d'Esdras A' au texte massorétique d'Esdras-Néhémie," in *Tradition of the Text: Studies Offered to Dominique Barthélemy in Celebration of His 70th Birthday* (ed. Gerard J. Norton and Stephen Pisano; OBO 109; Freiburg: Universitätsverlag; Göttingen: Vandenhoeck & Ruprecht, 1991), 218–48; Dieter Böhler, *Die heilige Stadt in Esdras a und Esra-Nehemia: Zwei Konzeptionen der Wiederherstellung Israels* (OBO 158; Freiburg: Universitätsverlag; Göttingen: Vandenhoeck & Ruprecht, 1997); idem, "On the Relationship between Textual and Literary Criticism: The Two Recensions of the Book of Ezra; Ezra–Neh (MT) and 1 Esdras (LXX)," in *The Earliest Text of the Hebrew Bible: The Relationship between the Masoretic Text and the Hebrew Base of the Septuagint Reconsidered* (ed. Adrian Schenker SBLSCS 52; Atlanta: Society of Biblical Literature, 2003), 35–50. See also Schenker's contribution to the present volume.

3. E.g., Zipora Talshir, *1 Esdras: From Origin to Translation* (SBLSCS 47; Atlanta: Society of Biblical Literature, 1999); idem, *1 Esdras: A Text Critical Commentary* (SBLSCS 50; Atlanta, Society of Biblical Literature, 2001).

and rearranged just to accommodate the story of the three youths, a story seen as integral to rewritten Ezra. Both groups recognize, however, that once the story of the three youths is removed, not only is the order of events largely the same in the initial six or seven chapters of these books, but in the majority of passages the wording is identical. Passages agree sentence for sentence. It must be concluded therefore that either 1 Esdras is a revision of Ezra–Nehemiah, or that Ezra–Nehemiah is a revision of 1 Esdras, or that they are each revisions of a third source. They cannot be independent accounts of historical events. The purpose of this paper is to attempt a decision between the first two alternatives, and hence I concentrate on the initial chapters (1–6 in Ezra, 1–7 in 1 Esdras). There are several issues:

1. THE DURATION OF THE CESSATION OF TEMPLE BUILDING

Adrian Schenker and his student Dieter Böhler advocate the priority of 1 Esdras for several reasons.[4] To begin with, both Ezra and 1 Esdras assign the recommencement of temple building after it had been stopped to the second year of Darius (Ezra 4:24; 1 Esd 6:1). However, 1 Esdras alone gives the actual duration of the interval—two years.[5]

> καὶ εἴρχθησαν τῆς οἰκοδομῆς ἔτη δύο ἕως τῆς Δαρείου βασιλείας (1 Esd 5:71)
>
> And they were barred from building two years, until the reign of Darius.

According to this passage, this period is during the life of Cyrus:

> καὶ ἐπιβουλὰς καὶ δημαγωγίας καὶ ἐπισυστάσεις ποιούμενοι ἀπεκώλυσαν τοῦ ἐπιτελεσθῆναι τὴν οἰκοδομὴν πάντα τὸν χρόνον τῆς ζωῆς τοῦ βασιλέως Κύρου (1 Esd 5:70)
>
> and by plots and demagoguery and uprisings they prevented the completion of the building the whole of the time of the life of King Cyrus.

I suspect that the text in 1 Esdras in which the length of the cessation is specified as two years is simply a misreading of that in Ezra, since it is contradicted immediately by the following verse in 1 Esdras, which makes clear that building commences again in the second year of Darius' reign, as in Ezra. In 1 Esdras we also read that the search for the building permit was made only in the second year of Darius, not in the beginning of his reign:

---

4. See n. 2 and Professor Schenker's contribution to the present volume. My comments will be organized in relation to Schenker, "La relation d'Esdras A'," since this is the foundation essay.

5. Schenker, "La relation d'Esdras A'," 224.

> ἐν δὲ τῷ δευτέρῳ ἔτει τῆς τοῦ Δαρείου βασιλείας ἐπροφήτευσεν Αγγαιος καὶ Ζαχαριας ὁ τοῦ Εδδι οἱ προφῆται ἐπὶ τοὺς Ιουδαίους ... ἐν αὐτῷ τῷ χρόνῳ παρῆν πρὸς αὐτοὺς Σισίνης ὁ ἔπαρχος Συρίας καὶ Φοινίκης καὶ Σαθραβουζάνης καὶ οἱ συνέταιροι (1 Esd 6 1, 3)
>
> Now in the second year of the reign of Darius, the prophets Haggai and Zechariah son of Iddo prophesied to the Judeans. ... At the same time Sisinnes the governor of Syria and Phoenicia and Sathrabuzanes and their associates came to them.

According to Schenker, it is totally farfetched that, after only two years, the governors of Transeuphrates would have forgotten Cyrus' decree and that it would be necessary to search the archives to recover it. Ezra avoids this problem by omitting any reference to the duration of the building stoppage.[6] Since the more difficult text is to be preferred, it must be that 1 Esdras was written before Ezra–Nehemiah.

In actuality, there is no difficulty in either text from a literary standpoint, since it is never asserted that Cyrus' decree was forgotten. Neither is there a problem from a historical perspective. Because of the revolts that attended his usurpation of power, Darius was not able to appoint satraps and governors until the second year of his reign. Nor would he have retained those appointed by Cyrus who continued in office under his sons, Cambyses and Smerdis, and against whom he had rebelled.[7] Like every usurper, Darius appointed his own people into positions of power. The governor who questions the Judeans about the temple (whether called Tattenai or Sisinnes) would have been appointed by Darius only in that king's second year and, having newly arrived in his post, would have needed to clarify the situation with his king no matter how recently the building program under Cyrus was inaugurated.

In fact, moreover, the book of Ezra does not avoid the problem of the short interval in which work on the temple was stopped. According to Ezra 4:5:

> וככרים עליהם יועצים להפר עצתם כל־ימי כורש מלך פרס ועד־מלכות דריוש מלך־פרס
>
> They bribed officials to frustrate their plan all the days of Cyrus king of Persia up to the reign of Darius king of Persia.

While the length of Cyrus' life is not specified, his reign must have been short, since Zerubbabel and Jeshua arrive apparently in Cyrus' first year (Ezra 2:2) and are still working on the temple in the second year of Darius (Ezra 5:2). This does not take into account the intervening reigns of Xerxes and Artaxerxes (Ezra 4)!

---

6. Schenker, "La relation d'Esdras A'," 225.
7. See my *The Priest and the Great King: Temple-Palace Relations in the Persian Empire* (BJSUCSD 10; Winona Lake, Ind.: Eisenbrauns, 2004).

One could argue that the problem of Zerubbabel's and Jeshua's long tenures is ameliorated in 1 Esdras by moving the Artaxerxes correspondence to a date prior to their arrival in Judah, and that 1 Esdras is the simplified text.

2. The Differences in the Number of Letters Sent to the Persian Kings, in the Names of These Kings, and in the Identity of the Senders

A second reason Schenker and Böhler suggest for preferring 1 Esdras is the several letters to the Persian kings that are included in Ezra but not in 1 Esdras.[8] In Ezra a letter is sent to Xerxes and a second letter to Artaxerxes, neither of which appears in 1 Esdras. Nor are the nations listed in Ezra as senders of what may be a second letter to Artaxerxes included in 1 Esdras. Schenker sees the extra letters and senders in Ezra as an amplification of the single letter in 1 Esdras, in an attempt to increase the number of the Judeans' enemies and emphasize the hostility. It is equally possible to see the single letter to Artaxerxes in 1 Esdras as a simplification of the confusing material in Ezra.

3. The Differing Roles for Ezra 4:24 and 1 Esdras 2:25

Thirdly, Schenker and Böhler suggest that the final verse appended to the Artaxerxes correspondence (Ezra 4:24 and 1 Esd 2:25) is not necessary in Ezra but was conceived for 1 Esdras.[9]

באדין בטלת עבידת בית־אלהא די בירושלם והות בטלא עד שנת תרתין למלכות דריוש מלך־פרס:	καὶ ἤργει ἡ οἰκοδομὴ τοῦ ἱεροῦ τοῦ ἐν Ιερουσαλημ μέχρι τοῦ δευτέρου ἔτους τῆς βασιλείας Δαρείου τοῦ Περσῶν βασιλέως
Then the work on the house of the god that was in Jerusalem stopped and remained stopped until the second year of the reign of Darius king of Persia	And the building of the temple in Jerusalem stopped until the second year of the reign of King Darius of the Persians.

First Esdras lets the reader know that only the work on the temple was stopped but that the work on the city continued. The statement is essential in Ezra as well, however, since without it the reader would suppose that only work on the city was stopped, not work on the temple. Although both temple and city are mentioned in 1 Esdras, only the city is mentioned in Ezra. The temple is never referred to in Ezra's correspondence with Artaxerxes. This concluding sentence is thus necessary in both texts.

---

8. E.g., Schenker, "La Relation d'Esdras A'," 228–31.
9. See Schenker, "La Relation d'Esdras A'," 231–34.

4. RELATION TO HAGGAI AND ZECHARIAH

A fourth reason offered for the priority of 1 Esdras is that Ezra–Nehemiah agrees far better with Haggai and Zechariah than does 1 Esdras. In Schenker and Böhler's opinion, the author of Ezra changed his *Vorlage* in 1 Esdras to conform to the writings of these prophets.[10] Commentators of Ezra have been repeatedly troubled, however, by the *lack* of agreement between Haggai and Zechariah, on the one hand, and Ezra, on the other. In the second year of Darius, Haggai asks why the Jews have not built their temple from the time they first arrived in Judah. Yet, according to Ezra, they had built the altar and laid the foundations already under Cyrus eighteen years before. Haggai appears to know nothing about this. According to Haggai (1:15), the people begin work on the temple only in the sixth month of Darius' second year. This date is never mentioned in Ezra. Haggai knows of Jeshua, the high priest, but not of any liturgy, altar, or holiday of Sukkoth. In Haggai and Zechariah, all this remains for later, when the temple is finished. Haggai quotes God as saying that from the twenty-fourth day of the ninth month of Darius' second year, "from that day I will bless you." It is likely that it was only then that the altar was finished and the headstone set in the as-yet-unpaneled temple wall by Zerubbabel, in a refoundation ceremony (Zech 4:9). This disagrees with the chronology in Ezra. The author of 1 Esdras, on the other hand, delays both altar and temple foundations until Darius' second year and Zerubbabel's arrival. First Esdras conforms to the writings of Haggai and Zechariah much more than Ezra does.

5. DIFFERENCES IN CHRONOLOGY

Schenker and Böhler's primary reason for advocating the priority of 1 Esdras, however, is the different chronology of events presupposed in the two versions. They argue that absent a reason for 1 Esdras to have rearranged Ezra–Nehemiah, it is preferable to suppose that Ezra–Nehemiah has rewritten 1 Esdras to eliminate the difficulties in the latter. That is, the more difficult text should in general be preferred. It is to this problem of the chronology of events in the two versions that I now turn.

ANCIENT NEAR EASTERN TEMPLE-BUILDING ACCOUNTS

The initial chapters of both Ezra and 1 Esdras (1–7 of 1 Esdras and 1–6 of Ezra) tell the story of the second temple's construction. It may be fruitful, therefore, to compare each version to the typical ancient Near Eastern temple-building account. Based on a comprehensive study of Mesopotamian and Northwest

---

10. E.g., Schenker, "La Relation d'Esdras A'," 224–28.

Semitic building inscriptions, Hurowitz has delineated the typology of temple-building narratives ubiquitous in the ancient Near East.[11] His work agrees with Ellis's previous effort on foundation deposits and ceremonies.[12] These scholars and others have found that building inscriptions throughout the ancient Near East follow a certain prescribed pattern.[13] The inscriptions are boilerplate, as it were, with only the details changed to accommodate the particular temple and the particular king building it. The required components of these building narratives are presented in the following table.[14] The table shows each component in its typical position and its location in the building stories of both Ezra and 1 Esdras. Because this pattern is ubiquitous, we may assume that these components represent not only how temples were built, but how they were required to be built.

Elements of Temple-Building in Ancient Near Eastern Building Inscriptions, in Ezra and in 1 Esdras

ANE	Ezra	1 Esdras
A. Brief History of the Temple—Why Was it in Ruins?	Missing.	Fall of Jerusalem (1:46–58).
B. The Decision to Build—the King Receives a Divine Command, Usually in the First Year.	In the first year of King Cyrus, YHWH stirs up the spirit of Cyrus (1:1–2).	In the first year of King Cyrus the Lord stirs up the spirit of Cyrus (2:1–2).
C. Building Materials are Brought from the Ends of the Earth.	Wood is brought from Lebanon and floated down to Jaffa (3:7).	Wood is brought from Lebanon and floated down to Jaffa (5:53).
D. Foundations are Laid and the Site is Prepared.	In the second year of their arrival, in the second month ... the builders lay the foundations of the temple of YHWH (3:10).	In the second year of their arrival, in the second month ... Zerubbabel and Jeshua lay the foundations (5:55).

---

11. Victor A. Hurowitz, *I Have Built You an Exalted House: Temple Building in the Bible in Light of Mesopotamian and Northwest Semitic Writings* (JSOTSup 115; Sheffield: Sheffield Academic Press, 1992).

12. R. S. Ellis, *Foundation Deposits* (New Haven: Yale University Press, 1968).

13. See the articles in Mark J. Boda and J. R. Novotny, eds., *From the Foundations to the Crenellations: Essays on Temple Building in the Ancient Near East and Hebrew Bible* (AOAT 366; Münster: Ugarit-Verlag, 2010).

14. After Lisbeth S. Fried, "The Land Lay Desolate: Conquest and Restoration in the Ancient Near East," in *Judah and the Judeans in the Neo-Babylonian Period* (ed. Oded Lipschits and Joseph Blenkinsopp; Winona Lake, Ind.: Eisenbrauns, 2003), 21–54.

E. A Ceremony for Later Building Stages is Held (e.g., the Dedication of the Altar).	In the seventh month, Jeshua and Zerubbabel set up the altar … and they offered burnt offerings upon it (3:1–3).	In the seventh month, Jeshua and Zerubbabel set up the altar and offer burnt offerings upon it (5:46–47).
F. The Description of the Completed Temple and Its Furnishings Plus a Statement That the Temple Has Been Built.	And this house was finished on the third day of the month of Adar in the sixth year of Darius (6:15).	So the builders built the temple of the Lord (5:57). The holy house was finished on the twenty-third day of the month of Adar, in the sixth year of Darius (7:5).
G. The Dedication Ceremony of the Finished Building.	The people celebrated the dedication with joy (6 16).	And the people of Israel … offered at the dedication … (7:6–9).
H. The God is Installed in the Temple and Takes Up Residence.	Missing.	Missing.
I. Celebration.	On the fourteenth day of the first month, the returned exiles kept the Passover (6:19).	On the fourteenth day of the first month, the returned exiles kept the Passover (7:10).
J. Presentation of Gifts and Appointment of Temple Personnel.	They appointed the Levites, from twenty years old and upward, to have oversight of the work on the house of YHWH (3:8, 6:18).	They appointed the Levites, from twenty years old and upward, to have oversight of the work on the house of the Lord (5:56 [58]).
K. Prayer or Curses	If anyone alters this edict, a beam shall be pulled out of the house of the perpetrator, who then shall be impaled on it. The house shall be made a dunghill. May the God who has established his name there overthrow any king or people that shall put forth a hand to alter this, or to destroy this house of God in Jerusalem (6:11–12).	If anyone should transgress or nullify any of the things herein written, a beam should be taken out of the house of the perpetrator, who then shall be impaled upon it, and all property forfeited to the king. Therefore may the Lord, whose name is there called upon, destroy every king and nation that shall stretch out their hands to hinder or damage that house of the Lord in Jerusalem (6:31–32 [32–33]).

As can be seen, practically every component of ancient Near Eastern temple-building stories is present in both biblical texts. Missing most notably from both is item H, in which the god enters the finished temple and takes up residence in it. Another component that is missing from Ezra but present in 1 Esdras is component A, a brief history of how the temple happened to fall into ruins. Other than these, every element is included. I have argued elsewhere that the original biblical writer based his story on the second temple's actual building inscription, an inscription that would conform to the left-hand column of the table.[15]

Knowing the typology of ancient Near Eastern building stories enables us to compare the two biblical versions not only to each other but also to the ancient Near East temple-building template. There are many differences between the two biblical accounts and the ancient template. Most notable is the inclusion of a great deal of additional material. To the typical building story, the biblical writer has added a long list of returnees, some stories of attempts by enemies to thwart the building process, a correspondence with Artaxerxes that stops temple building, a correspondence with Darius that finally permits it to go forward again, plus in 1 Esdras we have the story of the three youths and the commissioning of Zerubbabel. All of these elements are obviously extraneous to typical ancient Near Eastern temple-building narratives.

The Story of the Altar's Construction

Besides these additions, however, there is another difference between the typical building story and the biblical narratives, and that is the location in the story of the altar's construction. According to the ancient template, the altar (component E in the table) should be constructed toward the end of temple building, reserved for when the temple itself has neared completion. In both of the biblical versions, however, the altar is constructed near the beginning of the temple-building process; in Ezra it is the very first stage of temple construction. Zerubbabel sets up the altar in the seventh month of the very year he arrives in Jerusalem, apparently the first year of Cyrus (Ezra 3:1-3). The text explains that the returnees built it so early because of the dread upon them of "the peoples of the lands." The early construction of the altar also exhibits the returnees' zeal in carrying out the law of Moses and in celebrating the Festival of Booths in the seventh month, even though the temple was not yet built.

As in Ezra, in 1 Esdras a contingent of Jews also comes up to Jerusalem with Sheshbazzar in the first year of Cyrus, and Sheshbazzar begins to lay the temple's foundations. Satrapal officials immediately write a letter to King Artaxerxes, however, which stops work on the temple until the reign of Darius. Ignoring the story of the three youths, viewed by some as a late interpolation, 1 Esdras then

---

15. Fried, "Land Lay Desolate."

presents a list of what must be a second group of returnees, which returns with Zerubbabel apparently in the reign of Darius. They gather in Jerusalem in the seventh month of what must be Darius' first year, to erect the altar of the god of Israel. They offer sacrifices upon it, even though the temple is not yet built. We are then told that in the first month of the second year of their coming, presumably Darius' second year, Zerubbabel and Jeshua lay the foundations of the temple. No reason is given in this version for building the altar before the foundations are completed. It is not fear of the neighboring peoples in this version, since that is not mentioned (although it does state that some of the peoples were hostile to them). According to 1 Esdras, in fact, some from among them joined with Zerubbabel to help set up the altar (1 Esd 5:49).

Stories of Attempts to Halt the Building Process

Besides the differences in the location of the altar-building story in the two biblical versions from the ancient Near Eastern temple-building template, the biblical narratives are replete with extraneous stories of various disputes. These disputes explain the delay in finishing the temple. Historically speaking, there is a gap of some eighteen years between the decision to build in 538, the first year of Cyrus, and 520, the second year of Darius, when the historical Zerubbabel very likely entered the scene and temple rebuilding began again in earnest. This gap is so long that it is reasonable for the original biblical writer to have assumed that something untoward must have intervened to cause it. He seems to have created these disputes to fill the gap.[16] Our two texts use the disputes differently, however. In Ezra, Zerubbabel leads a contingent to Judah and Jerusalem in the first year of Cyrus, erects an altar in the seventh month of that year, and starts to lay the foundations in the first month of Cyrus' second year. The enemies of Judah and Benjamin hear the joyous clamor when the foundations are dedicated and offer to join in building the temple. Zerubbabel and Jeshua reject them, however, and in response, these spurned "people of the land" convince satrapal officials to write to King Artaxerxes to stop the building process. The process is stopped until the reign of Darius. In this version, Zerubbabel is in Jerusalem the entire time, from the first year of Cyrus to at least Darius' second year. The long delay in building the temple occurs entirely under his watch. In fact, Zerubbabel is completely responsible for it. Had he not rejected the "people of the land," there would have been no delay at all.

---

16. See P. R. Bedford, *Temple Restoration in Early Achaemenid Judah* (JSJSup 65; Leiden: Brill, 2001), and my review of it, "The House of the God Who Dwells in Jerusalem: Review article of P. Bedford's *Temple Restoration in Early Achaemenid Judah*, 2001, and of J. Schaper's *Priester und Leviten im achämenidischen Juda*, 2000," *JAOS* 126 (2006): 1–14.

In contrast, 1 Esdras uses the Artaxerxes correspondence to fill the gap between the return under Sheshbazzar in Cyrus' first year and Zerubbabel's arrival in the first year of King Darius, some seventeen years later. In this version, the delay in the temple's construction occurs right away, immediately upon the first return under Sheshbazzar, before Zerubbabel ever arrives on the scene. In 1 Esdras, the delay in temple building has nothing to do with Zerubbabel at all. It is to be assigned only to the satrapal officials and their correspondence with Artaxerxes. Even ignoring the story of the three youths, Zerubbabel is shown ending the delay, not causing it. Enemies admittedly attempt to stop Zerubbabel when he arrives; nevertheless he perseveres, spending his first two years in Jerusalem, evidently the first two years of Darius' reign, setting up the altar and laying the temple's foundations.

It seems likely, therefore, that the author of 1 Esdras moved the correspondence with Artaxerxes to the front of his narrative in order to exonerate Zerubbabel from causing the long delay in temple building. In this version, Zerubbabel is completely out of the picture. The contest among the three youths, moreover, increases belief in Zerubbabel's innocence. It provides him with the perfect alibi. He was a bodyguard at the court of King Darius, and could not have instigated the correspondence with Artaxerxes! The transfer of the Artaxerxes correspondence to the beginning of 1 Esdras from its previous position in the middle of the altercation between Zerubbabel and the people of the land is thus easily explained. The reverse is not obvious. It is not clear why an author would move the Artaxerxes correspondence to the middle of the dispute with Zerubbabel if it had originally been at the beginning of the narrative in his *Vorlage*.

In sum, it seems that even without the story of the three youths, there is ample reason to conclude that 1 Esd 1–7 is a rearrangement of Ezra 1–6 and that it was rearranged in order to absolve Zerubbabel of responsibility for the long delay in temple building.

WHY 1 ESDRAS IS PROBABLY NOT AN EARLY VERSION OF THE EZRA-NEHEMIAH TRADITION

Juha Pakkala

1. INTRODUCTION

In this paper I will analyze and present passages from different parts of 1 Esdras and Ezra-Nehemiah that indicate that the Masoretic Text (MT) generally represents an earlier textual stage than 1 Esdras.[1] My perspective is technical in the sense that I will give particular attention to the method and technical aspect of the changes. I will ask how the text may have been changed by later editors. I will try to show that in many cases a reading in 1 Esdras can be seen as an editorial change from an older text form that is preserved in the MT. In this respect, this paper also contributes to the discussion about editorial developments in the Second Temple period.[2]

Comparing the texts on the micro level, I will avoid arguments based on the probable or reconstructed general tendencies of the different versions. My examples will deal with different themes, so that the influence of one theme will not play a decisive role in the discussion. In contrast, in Dieter Böhler's theory, Jerusalem and its condition is strongly connected to the entire discussion about the relative age of the two versions.[3] Rather than thematic considerations, technical observations from the texts should be given priority.[4]

---

1. Second Esdras is a rather literal translation and is relatively close to the Masoretic one. Although there are some significant variants (for example in Neh 9:6), for the purposes of the present study it can be treated as representative of the same textual tradition as the MT. It should be added that the discussion deals with the relative age of the Hebrew/Aramaic *Vorlage* of 1 Esdras and the MT, whereas both Greek translations are very probably late.

2. That 1 Esdras contains considerable differences from the Masoretic edition is fortunate for biblical studies because the differences provide "empirical evidence" of the editorial processes and the development of biblical texts in the Second Temple period. Especially noteworthy are the radical changes that are rarely assumed to have occurred in the editing process of biblical texts.

3. See the example texts in Dieter Böhler, *Die heilige Stadt in Esdras α und Esra-Nehemia: Zwei Konzeptionen zur Wiederherstellung Israels* (OBO 158; Freiburg: Universitätsverlag; Göttingen: Vandenhoeck & Ruprecht, 1997), 143–306. Many other scholars have also argued

Moreover, I will provide evidence that 1 Esdras is dependent on a late version of the text that already contains the latest redactional layers included in the Masoretic version. Here I will draw attention to some late additions to the Masoretic version that were also known to the author of 1 Esdras. In these cases I will give examples in which 1 Esdras has developed the text even further.

In some cases 1 Esdras may preserve a reading more original than the one preserved in the MT or 2 Esdras.[5] It is clear that the development of the texts was very complicated because they were copied and transmitted in many forms and in many different contexts. After centuries of transmission, different readings emerged, so that one textual tradition may preserve a better reading in one passage, whereas another tradition is more original in another passage. In the end, each variant reading should be considered separately. The theory that is able to explain the birth of a particular reading should be given priority and one's general understanding of the primacy of the versions should not impact the evaluation of any single passage.

Since 1 Esdras differs radically from the MT, it is reasonable to discuss whether the differences are the result of a radical editing of 1 Esdras at some point in its transmission or whether this happened in the Masoretic tradition. When the differences are so extensive that one must assume the text to have been thoroughly rewritten, it is often difficult to establish which version is more original. In some cases, however, the author who rewrote the older text left traces that reveal the direction of development. These traces, which are also then parallels between the two versions, imply that the two versions are literarily dependent. Passages in which the versions differ considerably but that still contain several parallels are often very fruitful in revealing the direction of development between the versions. I proceed with examples from different parts of the composition and conclude with a discussion.

---

that 1 Esdras represents the more original text; see, for example, Gustav Hölscher, *Die Bücher Esra und Nehemia* (HAT 2; Tübingen: Mohr Siebeck, 1923), 491–502; Karl-Friedrich Pohlmann, *3. Esra-Buch* (JSHRZ 1/5; Gütersloh: Gütersloher Verlagshaus, 1980), 383–85; and Adrian Schenker, "La relation d'Esdras A' au texte massorétique d'Esdras-Néhémie," in *Tradition of the Text: Studies Offered to Dominique Barthélemy in Celebration of His 70th Birthday* (ed. Gerard J. Norton and Stephen Pisano; OBO 109; Freiburg: Universitätsverlag; Göttingen: Vandenhoeck & Ruprecht, 1991), 218–49.

4. I will not deal with other arguments or considerations in favor of the secondary nature of 1 Esdras here, but leave them for the other scholars of this volume. Perhaps the most persuasive arguments against the priority of 1 Esdras have been put forward by Zipora Talshir in her publications, for example in her review of Dieter Böhler's *Die heilige Stadt*, but there is no reason to repeat those arguments here. For details, see Zipora Talshir, "Ezra–Nehemiah and First Esdras: Diagnosis of a Relationship between Two Recensions," *Bib* 81 (2000): 566–73. See also Robert Hanhart, *Text und Textgeschichte des 2. Esrabuches* (MSU 25; Göttingen: Vandenhoeck & Ruprecht, 2003), 12.

5. For example, Ezra 10:10 refers to Ezra the priest, but 1 Esdras (9:7) omits the title. It is probable that here the MT (and 2 Esdras) is expansive and late.

2. An Omission in 1 Esdras 8:5–6 That Removed a Repetition in the Older Text

The MT contains many inconsistencies, contradictions, and disturbing repetitions, most of which are caused by earlier editorial activity.[6] It is probable that in many cases 1 Esdras tries to improve the text by leaving out some repetitions or other disturbing factors caused by earlier editing, whereas the MT seems to preserve them. There are many examples of cases where this is the key to understanding the relationship between the two versions and where it otherwise would be difficult to assume that 1 Esdras preserves an older version of the text than the Masoretic one. One example of an omission that implies that 1 Esdras is younger than the MT can be found in Ezra 7:7–9:

Ezra 7:7–9[7]	1 Esdras 8:5–6
⁷ ויעלו מבני־ישראל ומן־הכהנים	⁵ καὶ συνανέβησαν ἐκ τῶν υἱῶν Ισραηλ καὶ τῶν ἱερέων
והלוים והמשררים	καὶ Λευιτῶν καὶ ἱεροψαλτῶν
והשערים והנתינים	καὶ θυρωρῶν καὶ ἱεροδούλων
אל־ירושלם	εἰς Ιεροσόλυμα
בשנת־שבע לארתחשסתא המלך	ἔτους ἑβδόμου βασιλεύοντος Ἀρταξέρξου
⁸ *ויבא ירושלם*	
בחדש החמישי	ἐν τῷ πέμπτῳ μηνί
היא שנת השביעית למלך	οὗτος ἐνιαυτὸς ἕβδομος τῷ βασιλεῖ
⁹ כי באחד לחדש הראשון הוא יסד	⁶ ἐξελθόντες γὰρ ἐκ Βαβυλῶνος τῇ νουμηνίᾳ τοῦ πρώτου
המעלה מבבל ובאחד לחדש החמישי	μηνὸς ἐν τῇ νουμηνίᾳ τοῦ πέμπτου μηνὸς
<u>בא אל־ירושלם</u>	<u>παρεγένοντο εἰς Ιεροσόλυμα</u>
כי־אלהיו הטובה עליו	κατὰ τὴν δοθεῖσαν αὐτοῖς εὐοδίαν παρὰ τοῦ κυρίου ἐπ' αὐτῷ.

Among many other problems and repetitions in these verses, the MT contains a double reference to the arrival of the exiles[8] in Jerusalem. The repetition

---

6. Some of the problems may have been caused by textual corruption, but in most cases editorial activity can provide an explanation for the problems. Textual corruption should only be assumed if a text or parallel reading cannot be otherwise understood. That the Hebrew text contains additions from different editors has long been demonstrated by scholars; see, for example, Loring W. Batten, *A Critical and Exegetical Commentary on the Books of Ezra and Nehemiah* (ICC; Edinburgh: T&T Clark, 1913); Sigmund Mowinckel, *Studien zu dem Buche Ezra–Nehemia I–III* (Oslo: Universitätsforlaget, 1964–65); and Antonius H. J. Gunneweg, *Esra* (KAT 19/1; Gütersloh: Gütersloher Verlagshaus, 1985). For further discussion about the unity and disunity of the composition, see the contributions in Mark J. Boda and Paul L. Redditt, eds., *Unity and Disunity in Ezra–Nehemiah: Redaction, Rhetoric and Reader* (Hebrew Bible Monographs 17; Sheffield: Sheffield Phoenix Press, 2008).

7. In the present study, omissions are written in *italics* and additions in **bold**. Parallels that are being discussed are <u>underlined</u>.

of ויבא ירושלם ... בא אל־ירושלם was caused by an earlier editor who had added v. 9 to the older v. 8.[9] Similar additions that specify the dates of important events have been found in other parts of Ezra–Nehemiah and of the Hebrew Bible.

The first reference to the arrival in Jerusalem is missing in 1 Esdras. Although the original reference is the one that was eventually left out, the resulting text is less repetitive than the confusing Masoretic version. If one were to assume that 1 Esdras represents the more original text, one would have to assume the separate addition of ויבא ירושלם in the Masoretic tradition, but this is improbable, as it would be difficult to find any reason for the addition of such a sentence alone. The repetition was caused by an editor who added the whole v. 9, which also necessitated the repetition of the arrival in Jerusalem, because the date of the arrival was added. The following chart illustrates the development of this passage.

Older text		MT		Harmonization (1 Esdras)
■[10]	⇒	■	⇒	■
■	⇒	■		(omission)
■	⇒	■	⇒	■
		■ (addition)	⇒	■
■	⇒	■	⇒	■

A similar development can be found in many other parts of the composition. In this process, a section of the oldest text was omitted and a later addition included in 1 Esdras.

3. Ezra 4:6–11 Rewritten in 1 Esdras 2:15

Ezra 4:6–11 and 1 Esd 2:15[11] contain an alleged copy of a letter sent to the Persian king to warn him of the danger of allowing Jews to build Jerusalem again. The MT implies that there had been three letters from three different groups. The first letter would have been sent during the time of Xerxes by the people of the land (Ezra 4:6); the second letter during the time of Artaxerxes by Bishlam, Mithredath, and Tabel (Ezra 4:7); and the third, also during Artaxerxes' time, by Rehum and Shimshai (Ezra 4:8). The copy of one letter is included in

---

8. In the very oldest text only Ezra arrived in Jerusalem (note the singular verb), but in the later literary stages other people, especially priests and Levites, accompanied him.

9. For details, see Juha Pakkala, *Ezra the Scribe: The Development of Ezra 7–10 and Nehemiah 8* (BZAW 347; Berlin: de Gruyter, 2004), 56–63.

10. The symbol ■ represents a block of text.

11. In the present study I will refer to the verse numbers of the Göttingen edition of 1 Esdras. There are considerable differences in the verse numbers between versions, editions, and translations.

the text (in vv. 11–16), while the other two remain mere references to letters that had been sent.¹²

First Esdras refers to one letter only, corresponding with the fact that there is a copy of only one letter. Since the texts are evidently literarily dependent, there are two basic alternatives. Either the MT is younger and was later expanded by additional references to two other letters, or 1 Esdras is a shortened and thus later version of the passage. The latter alternative is suggested by the fact that 1 Esd 2:15 contains elements from all three separate references to letters of the Masoretic version, illustrated in this diagram:

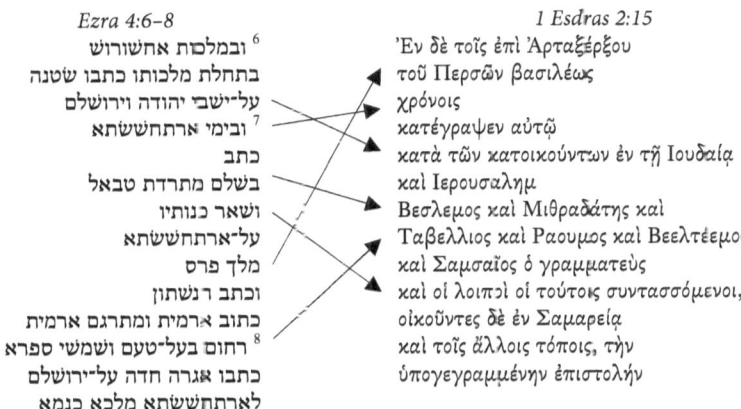

The parallels are so explicit that one has to assume that the author of 1 Esd 2:15 was familiar with all three references to letters, as represented in the MT. For example, the personal names mentioned as authors of the letters are so similar¹³ that they indisputably imply a literary connection between 1 Esd 2:15 and the last two references to letters in Ezra 4:7 and Ezra 4:8:

First letter by Bishlam, Mithredath and Tabel (Ezra 4:7)

	בשלם	Βεσλεμος
	מתרדת	Μιθραδάτης
	טבאל	Ταβελλιος

Second letter by Rehum and Shimshai (Ezra 4:8)

	רחום	Ραουμος
	(בעל־טעם)¹⁴	Βεελτέεμος
	ושמשי	Σαμσαῖος

---

12. Verses 9–10 may contain a fragment or the beginning of a second letter, but this is debatable and not imperative for the present argument.

13. Many of the differences in the personal names were caused by the translation process, but one can still recognize that we are dealing with the same names.

14. The Greek translator misunderstood the title בעל־טעם and rendered it as a proper name Βεελτέεμος.

The author of 1 Esdras was familiar with at least two references to a letter, although his own account refers to only one letter. The authors of two different letters of the MT were evidently combined as joint authors of the one letter in 1 Esdras.

Moreover, the object of complaint in 1 Esd 2:15 is identical with that of Ezra 4:6 (על־יושבי יהודה וירושלם > κατὰ τῶν κατοικούντων ἐν τῇ Ἰουδαίᾳ καὶ Ἰερουσαλήμ), which implies that the author of 1 Esd 2:15 was familiar with the third reference to a letter as well. Consequently, it is difficult to avoid the conclusion that 1 Esd 2:15 was familiar with a version of the passage similar to Ezra 4:6–8 that contained all three references to letters of complaint against the Jews. The other alternative would be to assume that an editor in the Masoretic tradition made three different references to letters from one fairly clear and consistent reference and in the process produced two unconnected references to unknown letters, creating a confusing repetition that has puzzled readers and scholars. For example, it would mean that an editor found a list of five or six (note Beelteemos above) authors of a letter but divided them into two groups and made three of them the authors of one letter and the other three (or two) the authors of another letter. It would be difficult to find any reason for such a rearrangement of the text.

In comparison, the later harmonization of a confusing and repetitive older text would be much more understandable and probable. In this process the verses were effectively rewritten so that 1 Esdras only preserved some elements from the older text. Later editing usually has logic, which, at least in this case, would be difficult to comprehend if 1 Esdras represented the older text. The original confusion in the MT was probably caused by the use of sources or earlier editing.[15] Consequently, the comparison between Ezra 4:6–8 and 1 Esd 2:15 suggests that 1 Esdras represents a later version than the MT. The older text was rewritten in 1 Esdras in order to iron out its problems and inconsistencies.

4. A Rearrangement in 1 Esdras 5:56 that Attempted to Improve the Older Text

First Esdras 5:56 (par. Ezra 3:9) is an illuminating example of a verse for which 1 Esdras probably represents a rearranged version. The MT contains a short list of persons who participated in rebuilding the temple. The list was edited, possibly by several successive editors, so that the MT has become awkward. In particular, the loose sentence at the end of the verse, בני חנדד בניהם ואחיהם הלוים, is poorly connected to the preceding text. The sentence has a parallel in 1 Esdras,

---

15. The author may have been familiar with some of the letters (authentic or inauthentic) that he refers to.

but there it is much better integrated into the main text. There are also some other differences, but they are mainly minor omissions and additions:[16]

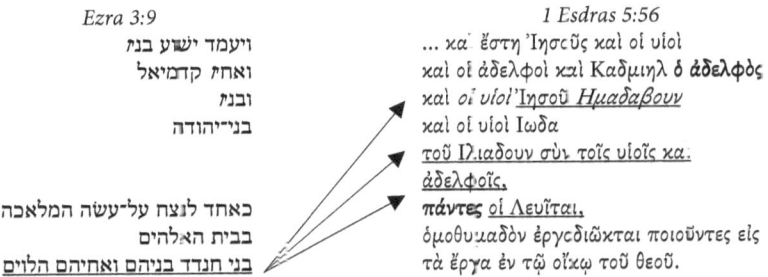

Since the last sentence is clearly awkward in the Masoretic version, and its parallel in 1 Esdras is an integral part of the main text, we are left with two alternatives: An editor in the Masoretic tradition took out pieces of information from the main text and placed parts of it as a loose sentence at the end of the verse. Or, an editor in the tradition of 1 Esdras found an awkward sentence at the end of the verse and integrated it better with the main text. The former alternative is evidently improbable, whereas the latter is understandable. Consequently, 1 Esd 5:56 is a further example of a case in which 1 Esdras provides an improved and partly rewritten text, whereas the MT represents an earlier text form that had become awkward because of an earlier addition. As in many other cases, 1 Esdras provides a more fluent text, but this also shows that it is later.

5. Ezra 4:21 Rewritten in 1 Esdras 2:24

Another example of rewriting that suggests that 1 Esdras is a later version of the text than the Masoretic one can be found in the king's reply to the letter in Ezra 4:21 and 1 Esd 2:24.

Ezra 4:21	1 Esdras 2:24
²¹ בְּעַן שִׂימוּ טְּעֵם לְבַטָּלָא גֻּבְרַיָּא	νῦν οὖν ἐπέταξα ἀποκωλῦσαι τοὺς ἀνθρώπους
אִלֵּךְ וְקִרְיְתָא דָךְ לָא תִתְבְּנֵא	ἐκείνους τοῦ οἰκοδομῆσαι τὴν πόλιν
עַד מִנִּי טַעְמָא יִתְּשָׂם	
²² וּזְהִירִין הֱווֹ שָׁלוּ	καὶ προνοηθῆναι ὅπως μηθὲν παρὰ ταῦτα
לְמֶעְבַּד עַל דְּנָה לְמָה יִשְׂגֵּא חֲבָלָא	γένηται καὶ μὴ προβῇ ἐπὶ πλεῖον
לְהַנְזָקַת מַלְכִין	τὰ τῆς κακίας εἰς τὸ βασιλεῖς ἐνοχλῆσαι.

In Ezra 4:21–22, Artaxerxes orders the building of Jerusalem to be stopped until he gives further instructions (עַד מִנִּי טַעְמָא יִתְּשָׂם), which, however, are

---

16. Some of the third-person suffixes appear to have been omitted and some words (ὁ ἀδελφὸς and πάντες) added in 1 Esdras.

never given, or the preserved text at least makes no further reference to them. These verses differ slightly in 1 Esdras, but most importantly, the reference to further instructions is omitted in 1 Esdras. The text in 1 Esdras is logical because the composition does not mention any further instructions of Artaxerxes concerning the temple. After this letter, the building of the temple was not continued until King Darius. The story in 1 Esdras is more consistent than in the MT.[17] As such it must be later, since it tries to improve an inconsistent older text, the inconsistencies possibly caused by editing earlier in the text's transmission. It is also possible that the expression in Aramaic should not be taken literally (that is to say, "continue to implement this order so long as no further orders are given") but was interpreted as an inconsistency in the tradition of 1 Esdras and therefore omitted.[18] In any case, the development in the opposite direction would be hard to explain. It would mean that a later editor intentionally added a reference to an order by Artaxerxes, but then one would certainly expect to find the order in the text. As in the previous example, 1 Esdras provides a more logical or harmonious story, but this should be seen as an indication that it is late rather than early.

6. 1 Esdras 9:49–55 Implies Late Additions

Comparison of 1 Esd 9:49–55 and Neh 8:9–12 shows that the author of 1 Esdras was familiar with priestly and Levitical additions, which represent the latest editorial stages contained in the MT. Moreover, the passage shows that 1 Esdras has developed the text even further.

In the oldest text of Neh 8, Ezra is the only person to speak to the people (note the singular verb ויאמר).[19] The following text clearly implies that Ezra was the actor and speaker. Because v. 10 does not reintroduce the speaker, which one would assume after Neh 8:9 introduces several subjects, it is probable that in the oldest text of Neh 8:9, Ezra was the sole actor. This became unclear after several additions that introduced new subjects. The text was later expanded so that in the MT Nehemiah, who is here called the governor, and the Levites are presented

---

17. Note that Böhler, *Die heilige Stadt*, 164–68, often argues on the basis of what is more logical or consistent but draws the opposite conclusion from mine and assumes that the more logical version is original. This may be the main cause of disagreement about the priority of the versions.

18. One can, for example, speculate about the possibility that the further order was omitted. However, a more probable alternative is that the request to wait for further instructions is rhetorical and only means that one should do as here ordered so long as no further instructions change the order. A later editor, understanding this reference as an inconsistency, removed the reference.

19. For further arguments that Ezra was the original actor in this passage, see Pakkala, *Ezra the Scribe*, 149–50.

alongside Ezra as additional subjects who speak to the people. The involvement of the Levites in the events was added to v. 11 as well.[20]

Nehemiah 8:9-12	1 Esdras 9:49-55[21]
⁹ ויאמר *נחמיה הוא התרשתא* ועזרא הכהן	⁴⁹καὶ εἶπεν Ατταρατης Εσδρα τῷ <u>ἀρχιερεῖ</u>
הספר *והלוים המבינים*	καὶ ἀναγνώστῃ καὶ τοῖς Λευίταις τοῖς
<u>את־העם לכל־העם</u>	διδάσκουσι τὸ πλῆθος <u>ἐπὶ πάντας</u>
היום קדש־הוא ליהוה *אלהיכם*	⁵⁰Ἡ ἡμέρα αὕτη ἐστὶν ἁγία τῷ κυρίῳ
אל־תתאבלו ואל־תבכו	
כי בוכים *כל־העם* כשמעם את־דברי התורה	καὶ πάντες ἔκλαιον ἐν τῷ ἀκοῦσαι τοῦ νόμου
¹⁰ <u>ויאמר להם</u>	
לכו אכלו משמנים	⁵¹βαδίσαντες οὖν φάγετε λιπάσματα
ושתו ממתקים	καὶ πίετε γλυκάσματα
ושלחו מנות לאין נכון לו	καὶ ἀποστείλατε ἀποστολὰς τοῖς μὴ ἔχουσιν,
כי־קדוש היום לאדנינו ואל־תעצבו	⁵²ἁγία γὰρ ἡ ἡμέρα τῷ κυρίῳ· καὶ μὴ λυπεῖσθε,
כי־חדות יהוה היא מעזכם	ὁ γὰρ κύριος δοξάσει ὑμᾶς.
¹¹ <u>והלוים מחשים לכל־העם לאמר</u>	⁵³<u>καὶ οἱ Λευῖται ἐκέλευον τῷ δήμῳ παντὶ λέγοντες</u>
<u>הסו כי היום קדש ואל־תעצבו</u>	Ἡ ἡμέρα αὕτη ἁγία, μὴ λυπεῖσθε.
¹² וילכו *כל־העם* לאכל ולשתות	⁵⁴καὶ ᾤχοντο πάντες φαγεῖν καὶ πιεῖν
ולשלח מנות	καὶ εὐφραίνεσθαι καὶ δοῦναι ἀποστολὰς **τοῖς μὴ ἔχουσιν**
ולעשות שמחה גדולה	καὶ εὐφρανθῆναι μεγάλως,
כי הבינו בדברים	⁵⁵ὅτι καὶ ἐνεφυσιώθησαν ἐν τοῖς ῥήμασιν,
אשר הודיעו להם	οἷς ἐδιδάχθησαν. καὶ ἐπισυνήχθησαν.

First Esdras is evidently familiar with these late additions to the MT. Moreover, it partly tries to improve the text that was made awkward by the earlier editors. The problem with the many subjects of Neh 8:9 is solved by making the governor (התרשתא) the sole subject and changing Ezra and the Levites from actors to addressees. In this process, לכל־העם was reused so that העם was left out and לכל received an entirely new function, from being a reference to all the people to a reference to everything that was taught (ἐπὶ πάντας).[22]

---

20. That v. 11 is a later addition is fairly evident because it competes with the preceding text. The Levites repeat nearly everything that Ezra has already said in v. 9b. Similar additions, where the activities of the priests and Levites are added, can be found throughout the composition.
21. The passages also contain many other differences (parts of the text seem to have been reformulated or rewritten; e.g., the sentence כי־חדות יהוה היא מעזכם of Neh 8:10 is rendered in 1 Esd 9:52 as γὰρ κύριος δοξάσει ὑμᾶς), but they need not be discussed here.
22. One could also suggest that the change was caused by an accidental omission (*homoioteleuton*; note את־העם לכל־העם), but then one would have to assume that ἐπὶ πάντας is unrelated to לכל. Although improbable, this possibility cannot be excluded. In any case, it would still not change the likelihood that 1 Esdras tried to improve the confusing older text

If the MT were younger than 1 Esdras, one would have to assume that the addressees were made into speakers. In this case, one would expect that the editor would have been particularly careful with the verb and changed the singular into plural, but this is not the case, as both versions use the verb in the singular. It is more probable that there was originally only one subject (Ezra), which is the reason for the singular in the first place. A later editor added new people as subjects, which resulted in incongruity between the plural subject and the singular verb. Nehemiah was added after Nehemiah's memoir was combined with the book of Ezra.[23] The Levites were added because for the Levitical editors it was important to show that the Levites had a central role in the events. A later editor in the transmission of 1 Esdras noted the incongruity caused by these earlier expansions and improved the text. An alternative solution would be to assume that, following the singular verb, he instinctively assumed that only the first in the series (the governor) was the subject and rendered the rest of the verse accordingly.[24] Nehemiah 8:9 is an example of a text in which editors with theological or other interests made additions that confused the older narrative and in which 1 Esdras later improved the text.

The passage contains another indication that 1 Esdras is later than the Masoretic version. First Esdras 9:50 does not contain a parallel to אל־תתאבלו ואל־תבכו (Neh 8:9). Either it was added in the MT or omitted in 1 Esdras. In most cases, one would tend to assume that an addition is more probable than an omission, but this does not seem to be the case here. In the MT, the people are consoled by Ezra (in Neh 8:9) *and* later also by the Levites (ואל־תעצבו in 8:11). The reason for this overlap is the earlier Levitical addition of Neh 8:11, where the role of the Levites was increased. This overlap was partly removed in 1 Esdras by omitting Ezra's words of condolence to the people in Neh 8:9. We are dealing here with something very similar to an editorial change that took place in 1 Esd 8:5–6 (par. Ezra 7:7–9). The older text contained a repetition, caused by earlier editing, which an editor in the tradition of 1 Esdras later tried to correct. That 1 Esdras omits the more original reference and includes the later addition confirms that 1 Esdras is younger.

Consequently, 1 Esd 9:49–55 shows that 1 Esdras was aware of late additions to the older text, as represented in the Masoretic version. Some of the inconsistencies, caused by earlier editing, were ironed out in 1 Esdras. In this process, parts of the oldest text were removed.

---

23. Nehemiah's involvement in the events in Neh 8 would have been a logical development after Nehemiah's memoir was added to the composition.

24. A reference to Nehemiah would have been omitted in this verse in accordance with the omission of the whole memoir in Neh 1:1–7:4. In the MT, הוא התרשתא is a clarification of Nehemiah's position and as such is possibly a later addition.

7. The Rendering of the *Golah* Expansions in 1 Esdras

There are several additions in the Ezra narrative in Ezra 7–10 and Neh 8 with a strong emphasis on the *golah*. The expansions are found in many parts of the composition, so that it is reasonable to talk about an editorial layer.[25] The leading idea of these expansions is to increase the role of the *golah* in the events to the extent that the community of the *golah* is effectively equated with Israel. Because the older text in Ezra 7–10 and Neh 8 made no reference to the *golah* or their community, in many passages the reader receives a confusing and partly contradictory picture of who is acting (for example in Ezra 10).

First Esdras has tried to harmonize the older text by removing some of the most problematic references to the *golah* (in 1 Esd 8:69 and 9:2). That not all of them were removed reveals that 1 Esdras was familiar with the *golah* additions. This excludes the possibility that the *golah* additions were added to the Masoretic tradition after 1 Esdras.

Ezra			1 Esdras
9:4	על בעל הגולה	ἐπὶ τῇ ἀνομίᾳ	8:69
10:6	על־בעל הגולה	ὑπὲρ τῶν ἀνομιῶν τῶν μεγάλων τοῦ πλήθους	9:2
10:7	לכל בני הגולה	πᾶσ. τοῖς ἐκ τῆς αἰχμαλωσίας	9:3
10:8	יבדל מקהל הגולה	ἀλλοτριωθήσεται ἀπὸ τοῦ πλήθους τῆς αἰχμαλωσίας	9:4
10:16	ויעשׂו־כן בני הגולה	καὶ ἐποίησαν κατὰ πάντα ταῦτα οἱ ἐκ τῆς αἰχμαλωσίας	9:15

The tensions inside the older text are probably the main reason for the harmonization. In particular, the idea that the sin had been committed by the *golah*, as suggested by Ezra 9:4 and 10:6, contradicted the main idea of the narrative: according to the older text, Ezra came from the exile and found out that the Jews who had remained in the land had taken foreign wives. The *golah* expansions disturbed this idea by referring to the sin of the *golah* (מעל הגולה). These references were then changed to a general sin in 1 Esd 8:69 and to a sin of the multitude in 1 Esd 9:2. A further reason for removing some of the references to the *golah* may have been the late context of the editor in the tradition of 1 Esdras. The concerns of the *golah* had receded and the emphasis of the returnees had become obsolete or even disturbing.

The assumption that 1 Esdras represents the earlier version would necessitate a much more complex development of the text. One would have to assume that some of the *golah* additions were added relatively early so that 1 Esdras

---

25. For the *golah* additions, see Pakkala, *Ezra the Scribe*, 263–65.

adopted them. After the separation of the 1 Esdras tradition from the Masoretic one, other *golah* additions were made to the Masoretic tradition but not to 1 Esdras. Although not an impossible development, one is able to assume a less complicated development if the Masoretic tradition is earlier than 1 Esdras (Occam's razor).

8. Ezra and Artaxerxes

First Esdras contains several small pluses in relation to the MT. Some of the additions have the tendency to increase the importance of a person or develop the text in a certain direction. If one assumes that the MT is later than 1 Esdras, one would also have to assume that these small pluses were omitted in the MT. Although one should not exclude the possibility that parts of the text could have been omitted—and we have already seen examples of omissions in 1 Esdras—it would be improbable in these cases. The nature of the pluses is typical of additions that were made to biblical texts. For example, in some additions Ezra is more important or has a higher status than he had in the older text. An opposite direction of development would imply that Ezra's status was systematically diminished.

First Esdras 8:4 differs from its parallel text in Ezra 7:6. The additional word δόξαν in the Greek version is central here. According to Ezra 7:6, the Persian king gave Ezra everything that he requested (ויתן־לו ... כל בקשתו). By adding a word, 1 Esdras goes further,[26] so that after the addition, which changes the object of the main verb, the Persian king even shows Ezra honor (ἔδωκεν ... δόξαν):

Ezra 7:6	1 Esdras 8:4
ויתן־לו המלך ...	καὶ ἔδωκεν αὐτῷ ὁ βασιλεὺς **δόξαν**,
כיד־יהוה אלהיו עליו	εὑρόντος χάριν ἐναντίον αὐτοῦ
כל בקשתו	ἐπὶ πάντα τὰ ἀξιώματα αὐτοῦ.

With the small addition, in 1 Esdras the roles of the two actors are effectively changed. In the MT, Ezra is presented as the one who was dependent on the Persian king, on his permission to go to Jerusalem and on receiving goods for the journey, which he had to ask for. First Esdras implies that Ezra was superior to the king.

If one were to assume that the Masoretic version preserves a secondary reading, one would have to assume that Ezra's position in relation to the Persian king was intentionally lowered by a late editor. It would be difficult to find a reason for such a change and would run counter to the general tendency in the

---

26. ויתן־לו המלך כיד־יהוה אלהיו עליו כל בקשתו > καὶ ἔδωκεν αὐτῷ ὁ βασιλεὺς δόξαν, εὑρόντος χάριν ἐναντίον αὐτοῦ ἐπὶ πάντα τὰ ἀξιώματα αὐτοῦ.

Hebrew Bible to increase the status of Jewish heroes.[27] A similar tendency to elevate Ezra by small additions or other changes is found in other passages of the composition as well.

9. Ezra the High Priest

In the MT (and in 2 Esdras), Ezra is variably called scribe, priest, or scribe and priest. However, 1 Esdras refers to him as the high priest in three verses:

Nehemiah 8:1, 2, 9	1 Esdras 9:39, 40, 49
הספר	Εσδρα τῷ ἀρχιερεῖ
הכהן	Εσδρας ὁ ἀρχιερεὺς
הכהן הספר	Εσδρα τῷ ἀρχιερεῖ

It is probable that Ezra was secondarily elevated to the status of the high priest in 1 Esdras. The development in the other direction—that Ezra would have been stripped of his high-priestly title—would be difficult to explain and would mean an intentional attempt to diminish him. One should also add that Ezra's priestly functions were gradually increased in the earlier editing process. It is probable that he was not a priest in the oldest text but was made one only later. Further editors then continued to add to his priestly functions and the culmination of this process is 1 Esdras, where he is made the high priest. The assumption that 1 Esdras represents an early literary stage would therefore contradict the general development.

10. The Sabbath Sacrifices in 1 Esdras 5:51

A rather typical expansion can be found in 1 Esd 5:51. In comparison with its parallel MT in Ezra 3:5, the verse adds the sacrifices of the Sabbaths (καὶ θυσίας σαββάτων) to an older list of sacrifices:

Ezra 3:5	1 Esdras 5:51–52
ואחריכן עלת תמיד	⁵¹ καὶ μετὰ ταῦτα προσφορὰς ἐνδελεχισμοῦ καὶ θυσίας σαββάτων
ולחדשים	καὶ νουμηνιῶν
ולכל־מועדי יהוה המקדשים	καὶ ἑορτῶν πασῶν ἡγιασμένων.
ולכל מתנדב נדבה ליהוה	⁵² καὶ ὅσοι εὔξαντο εὐχὴν τῷ θεῷ ...

The older list was evidently updated to be in line with the editor's own time, when the Sabbath had become more important. Similar expansions that updated the older text to be in line with the conventions or conceptions of the editor's

---

27. These variants are not discussed in Böhler's study *Die heilige Stadt*.

own context can be found throughout 1 Esdras and in other books of the Hebrew Bible.

The omission of a reference to the Sabbath sacrifices, which one would have to assume if 1 Esdras were older than the Masoretic version, would be difficult to explain. It is commonly accepted that the importance of the Sabbath increased in the latest stages in the development of the Hebrew Bible. For example, the commandment to keep the Sabbath was added to the Decalogue.[28] If 1 Esdras is a late version of the textual tradition, the addition would be in line with this general development, whereas the opposite order of primacy would run counter to the general development.

11. Discussion and Conclusions

The examples presented here suggest that 1 Esdras represents a younger version of the composition than the MT. In many cases 1 Esdras provides a more harmonious and consistent story than the MT, but, considering the nature of the differences in each example, this suggests that 1 Esdras is the younger text. The text was substantially edited in the earlier stages of its transmission, which resulted in contradictions, repetitions, and other problems. These problems are evident in the MT. Since 1 Esdras is familiar with the additions and repetitions, as we have seen, it is probable that it has harmonized and ironed out some of the tensions and roughness of the older text.[29] If 1 Esdras were older, one would not expect it to be familiar with the later additions that caused the tensions and contradictions in the first place.

In order to understand the relationship between the two texts, it is necessary to acknowledge that the present texts are the result of heavy and successive editing already in the earlier stages of the text's transmission. In many cases, this is the key to understanding the relationship between 1 Esdras and the MT. Without taking it into consideration, it is understandable that one could come to the conclusion that the more consistent and less repetitive 1 Esdras is older and more original than the MT.

Here lies one of the main problems of those who argue for the primacy of 1 Esdras. For example, Dieter Böhler implies that the Masoretic version of Ezra–Nehemiah is a harmonistic composition that contains a consistent view of Jerusalem and its position, which he then compares with the allegedly consistent

---

28. For example, Timo Veijola, *Das 5. Buch Moses: Deuteronomium* (ATD 8/1; Göttingen: Vandenhoeck & Ruprecht, 2004), 160–63.

29. The opposite direction of development would mean that the MT was corrupted in passages where 1 Esdras represents the more fluent reading, but this is improbable because the same kind of pattern seems to emerge in different parts of the composition. In some cases one would even have to assume that the text was intentionally made more clumsy and repetitive (for example in Ezra 3:9 and 7:7–9), but this can hardly be the case.

view of 1 Esdras on the same issue.[30] It is more probable that the Masoretic version, especially, contains many contradictory voices, even concerning the position of Jerusalem, which essentially weakens any arguments based on the comparison of perspectives between the versions.[31]

Böhler often argues on the basis of what is more logical. He usually implies that the more consistent text is more original. The MT would have become inconsistent because it attempts to avoid the impression that Jerusalem was inhabited and thriving before Nehemiah's arrival.[32] The addition of Nehemiah's memoir to the composition would have been the reason for the revision. This would be possible in principle, and here Böhler's argumentation is also coherent. However, his examples deal almost exclusively with Jerusalem or themes connected to Jerusalem (its settlement and condition). His theory stands or falls on the right assessment of what the status and condition of Jerusalem had been.

In contrast with Böhler's heavy reliance on texts dealing with the same subject, I selected passages from different parts of the composition dealing with different subjects. The passages were more-or-less randomly selected from sections in which the two versions presented a clearly differing version of events. The aim was to analyze these passages from a technical perspective in order to reconstruct the probable line of development. If one gives such technical differences priority, as I have attempted here, the evidence overwhelmingly suggests that 1 Esdras is younger than the MT.

It should finally be added that the editors of 1 Esdras were familiar with all major redaction layers that have been identified in the Masoretic version of Ezra–Nehemiah.[33] First Esdras was evidently aware of the *golah* as well as Levitical additions. The latter can be characterized as the latest large editorial phase of Ezra–Nehemiah that is included in the MT. This tradition developed even further in 1 Esdras, which can be seen as a new editorial phase of the same tradition.

---

30. This is implied by Böhler throughout his discussion of the primacy of the versions; see Böhler, *Die heilige Stadt*, 143–306.

31. If a composition contains different views, the selection of passages for comparison is crucial for the conclusion. Without distinguishing between different authors, it is doubtful that one could use Ezra–Nehemiah in such a way at all.

32. Böhler, *Die heilige Stadt*, 173–79.

33. And this is valid regardless of the redaction-critical model. 1 Esdras is evidently dependent on the latest additions of all major redaction-critical models put forward in the scholarly discussion of Ezra–Nehemiah. See, for example, Mowinckel, *Studien zu dem Buche Ezra-Nehemia*, and Gunneweg, *Esra*.

ANCIENT COMPOSITION PATTERNS MIRRORED IN 1 ESDRAS AND THE PRIORITY OF THE CANONICAL COMPOSITION TYPE

Zipora Talshir

I have not changed my views regarding the composition process of 1 Esdras and the nature of its relationship with the canonical books of Chronicles–Ezra–Nehemiah since the publication of my volumes on the book in 1999 and 2001.[1] I still believe that 1 Esdras was created on the basis of a canonical composition type, with the main purpose of incorporating the exceptional story of the three youths into the narrative of the return; in other words, there is no "1 Esdras" without the story of the youths.[2] What then is the purpose of the present study?

(1) This study seeks to revive my conclusions by viewing 1 Esdras within a somewhat larger context of composition patterns that characterize ancient literatures. I believe that this comparison supports the secondary nature of 1 Esdras and repeatedly proves that it was created on the basis of a canonical composition type of the book.

(2) It has become commonplace to suppress the diachronic dimension of philological research and concentrate instead on the work as a synchronic

---

1. Zipora Talshir, *1 Esdras: From Origin to Translation* (SBLSCS 47; Atlanta: Society of Biblical Literature, 1999); idem, *1 Esdras: A Text Critical Commentary* (SBLSCS 50; Atlanta: Society of Biblical Literature, 2001).

2. I thank Lester Grabbe for acknowledging this supposition—i.e., that the story of the youths is the *raison d'être* of 1 Esdras—as my contribution ("a new thesis") to the study of 1 Esdras, originally advanced in my 1984 dissertation (in Hebrew); Lester L. Grabbe, review of Zipora Talshir, *1 Esdras: From Origin to Translation*, JSS 47 (2002): 343. Grabbe, however, does not accept this thesis, arguing that "there was an original independent narrative already in existence which then had the youths story inserted into it" (344–45). This view is the core of the studies by Schenker and Böhler: Adrian Schenker, "La Relation d'Esdras A' au texte massorétique d'Esdras-Néhémie," in *Tradition of the Text: Studies Offered to Dominique Barthélemy in Celebration of His 70th Birthday* (ed. Gerard J. Norton and Stephen Pisano; OBO 109; Fribourg: Universitätsverlag; Göttingen: Vandenhoeck & Ruprecht, 1991), 218–49; Dieter Böhler, *Die heilige Stadt in Esdras α und Esra-Nehemia: Zwei Konzeptionen der Wiederherstellung Israels* (OBO 158; Freiburg: Universitätsverlag; Göttingen: Vandenhoeck & Ruprecht, 1997).

product.³ The scholar thus turns into "a reader" whose purpose is to discern the meaning of "the text" "as is." A fundamental difference exists, however, between (modern) self-contained works and ancient literatures that were created through compilation processes that resulted in far-from-integrative works. The art of penetrating the mind of the compiler and discerning his aims results, more than likely, in imposing on him our sophisticated impressions of his work. I would rather prefer nonconclusions of the sort: What if there is no single definable genre for 1 Esdras? What if it has no obvious structure or leading theme?⁴

(3) Another practice that increasingly gains ground in present scholarship is the confusion between textual and literary criticism. Thus, preferable textual variants in Chronicles versus Samuel–Kings are advanced as evidence against the long-established diachronic relationship between these books. It is fitting to mention Robert Hanhart's criticism—in his 2003 volume on the text history of 2 Esdras—addressed to this very method practiced by Schenker and Böhler.⁵ Allegedly preferable variants in 1 Esdras do not prove that it is preferable as a composition. We should rather aim to distinguish between the text type and the composition type.

(4) Finally, since I have been criticized, often rightly, for neglecting updated bibliography, I have made an effort in this study to react to works written during the last decade, although, I must say, the jigsaw puzzle of interreferences is quite perplexing and sometimes frustrating.⁶

1. THE SCOPE OF 1 ESDRAS: THE ABRUPT OPENING AND ENDING

The most obvious indication of 1 Esdras' secondary nature is its abrupt beginning and brusque ending.

---

3. On this development, or rather regression, in biblical studies, see Zipora Talshir, "Synchronic and Diachronic Approaches in the Study of the Hebrew Bible: Text Criticism within the Frame of Biblical Philology," *Textus* 23 (2007): 1–32.

4. See H. G. M. Williamson, "The Problem with First Esdras," in *After the Exile: Essays in Honour of Rex Mason* (ed. John Barton and David J. Reimer; Macon, Ga.: Mercer University Press, 1996), 209; repr. in idem, *Studies in Persian Period History and Historiography* (FAT 38; Tübingen: Mohr Siebeck, 2004), 294–305. In subsequent studies, however, Williamson does seek to determine the overall character of 1 Esdras. [See below and Williamson's contribution to the present volume—Ed.]

5. Robert Hanhart, *Text und Textgeschichte des 2. Esrabuches* (MSU 25; Göttingen: Vandenhoeck & Ruprecht, 2003), 11–13 n. 1.

6. Mostly, naturally, when a new commentary such as Schunck's fails to acknowledge the very existence of my work, referring solely to the "opposition"; see K.-D. Schunck, *Nehemia* (BK; Neukirchen-Vluyn: Neukirchener Verlag, 2009), xii–xiii. Much more irritating are self-indulgent surveys such as that of Garbini, whose practice is to quote only works that seemingly support his views, mainly himself (six times in ten pages); see G. Garbini, *Myth and History in the Bible* (JSOTSup 362; Sheffield: Sheffield Academic Press, 2003), 100–110.

1.1. BEGINNING IN THE MIDDLE OF JOSIAH'S REIGN

It is my view that 1 Esdras originally started at the point at which it starts today, that is, with the Passover held by Josiah. It is indeed a strange point to begin, since it takes place in the middle of Josiah's reign. However, it is quite unlikely to be accidental, given that it does begin at the very beginning of the Passover account. The quite-perplexing ending of the book also speaks against an accidental opening: if the ending is accidental it is not likely that the scroll would be damaged both at the beginning and the end, and if it is intentional, it substantiates this compiler's state of mind.

Why would the compiler of 1 Esdras begin at this point rather than at the beginning of Josiah's reign? Regardless of whether we may or may not have a possible answer to this question, it is important to note that while it may be a strange redactional decision in our eyes, to an ancient compiler this may well have been as legitimate a choice as any other. We have a wonderful example of a parallel choice made by the author of the book of Chronicles: he began his running history with the last chapter of Saul's reign (1 Chr 10 // 1 Sam 31),[7] throwing the reader into the middle of a scene that, in the book of Samuel, started long before.[8]

Not only is this a parallel pattern used by two compilers, it also teaches us a thing or two regarding the relationship between 1 Esdras and its canonical counterparts. Just as no one, hopefully (one cannot tell nowadays), suspects that Chronicles precedes Samuel regarding the setting of the war at Mount Gilboa, it should be clear that the setting of Josiah's Passover right at the opening of 1 Esdras proves it to be a secondary work in comparison with Chronicles. Characteristically, ch. 1 of 1 Esdras is totally neglected in the set of arguments of those scholars who prefer the layout of the apocryphal book.

1.2. ENDING IN MIDSENTENCE

Whether the ending of 1 Esdras is accidental or a calculated decision made by the compiler is another long-lasting question in the study of 1 Esdras. Nevertheless, one thing we may take for granted: original it is certainly not. If the compiler deliberately stopped with a reading such as ויאספו—suggested by καὶ ἐπισυνήχθησαν—he must have meant to say something technical, along the lines of "to be continued."

---

7. This comparison I first learned some twenty-five years ago from Shemaryahu Talmon, in a comment he made on my dissertation.

8. We note the subtle change at the beginning of the story: while 1 Sam 31 has the verb in a continuous present, ופלשתים נלחמים בישראל, "Now the Philistines were fighting against Israel," 1 Chr 10 begins with ופלשתים נלחמו בישראל, "Now the Philistines fought against Israel," as if beginning an independent account.

The ending of the book, like its beginning, is comparable to the case of Chronicles. In fact, the book of Chronicles similarly stops with a verb in midsentence: מי בכם מכל־עמו יהוה אלוהיו עמו ויעל, "Any one of you of all His people, the Lord his God be with him and let him go up" (2 Chr 36:23). The fitting continuation is found in Ezra: ויעל לירושלם אשר ביהודה ויבן את בית יהוה, "and let him go up to Jerusalem that is in Judah and build the House of the Lord" (Ezra 1:3). Different assumptions exist regarding the provenance of the last passage of the book (2 Chr 36:22–23), whether it is a remnant of a stage in which Chronicles–Ezra–Nehemiah formed one continuous work, or whether it was imported by the Chronicler or, rather, by a later tradent. Be that as it may, there is hardly any doubt that the passage originally belongs at the beginning of the book of Ezra–Nehemiah, where it is indispensable, and is used in Chronicles as a link or reference note, pointing to the events to come.

It is tempting to accept van der Kooij's suggestion of 1991,[9] quoted enthusiastically by Williamson in 2003,[10] that the translator's special syntactic effort in the rendition of the last verse—ὅτι **καὶ** ἐνεφυσιώθησαν ἐν τοῖς ῥήμασιν, οἷς ἐδιδάχθησαν **καὶ** ἐπισυνήχθησαν—proves that the Hebrew text in front of him indeed stopped with a verb in midsentence. We nevertheless have to consider a small text-critical problem, since the Hebrew text available does not read ויאספו but rather וביום השני נאספו, "On the second day [the heads of fathers' houses of all the people ...] gathered." The question is then whether there ever existed a Hebrew text that indeed ended with ויאספו, an ending that would initiate the subtle Greek translation.[11] This consideration, along with others, shows how fragile our work is, wavering between an assumed different *Vorlage* and the work of the translator.

Be that as it may, the fact is that the ending, like the beginning, of 1 Esdras proves that the book was created on the basis of a canonical type of composition.

2. Literary Activity around Extant Biblical Books: Interpolation of the Story of the Youths in the Narrative of the Return

I believe scholars nowadays do not consider seriously the possibility that 1 Esdras as is, the story of the youths included, could precede the canonical version of the

---

9. Arie van der Kooij, "On the Ending of the Book of 1 Esdras," in *LXX: VII Congress of the International Organization for Septuagint and Cognate Studies* (ed. C. E. Cox; SCSt 31; Atlanta: Scholars Press, 1991), 37–49.

10. H. G. M. Williamson, "1 Esdras," in *The Eerdmans Commentary on the Bible* (ed. J. D. G. Dunn and J. W. Rogerson; Grand Rapids, Mich.: Eerdmans, 2003), 851.

11. Otherwise, the translator must have decided to end with the verb, leaving out "the second day." In the case that the text was damaged in its Greek version, the words "in the second day" may have followed the verb.

history of the return.¹² Its very nature is alien to the context. It was created in order to provide a stage in the narrative that is completely missing in the canonical version, where Zerubbabel appears out of the blue as leader of the returnees. The story introduces him on the stage of history with great ado. The story itself and its interpolation in the narrative of the return is a major example of the well-known midrashic procedure of filling out gaps found in the course of events. While termed midrashic, this device is used by different authors during different times, and examples of it are found in the Hebrew Bible itself, in the apocryphal books, and in the Qumran literature, before it gains ground in rabbinic literature.

The rest of 1 Esdras runs parallel to the canonical version of 2 Chr 35–36, the entire book of Ezra, and Neh 8. The parallel chapters are not just similar to the canonical material, neither are they only a compilation of passages thereof. They neither summarize it nor elaborate on it. For the most part, they simply feature the very same material. First Esdras in its present form, with the story of the youths as its distinctive mark, is a composition based upon extant material well known from the canonical version.

The obvious example of such a composition process is naturally Chronicles versus Samuel–Kings. The author of Chronicles straightforwardly and without hesitation copied extensive parts of Samuel–Kings into his own book and, moreover, adopted the very framework of Samuel–Kings in his own composition. This is a clear-cut case, since the underlying version of Samuel–Kings has luckily survived, although there have been some recent attempts to undermine the long-established relationship between these books.¹³

There are other, even-better examples of works that were most likely created using the same patterns found in 1 Esdras: the Septuagint versions of the books of Esther and Daniel contain the canonical material but have been complemented by large additions and revised to accommodate them. Five additions are interlaced in Esther, and the prayer is added in Dan 3, together with Bel and the Dragon and the story of Susanna.¹⁴ The compiler of 1 Esdras belongs in the

---

12. Excluding scholars such as Garbini (*Myth and History in the Bible*), for whom the era of the return is first mentioned in 2 Macc 2:13 (100), Ezra first appears in 1 Esdras (101).

13. A. Graeme Auld, *Kings without Privilege* (Edinburgh: T&T Clark, 1994), and my criticism of his method, Zipora Talshir, "The Reign of Solomon in the Making: Pseudo-Connections between 3 Kingdoms and Chronicles," *VT* 50 (2000): 233–49.

14. Böhler speaks of 1 Esdras and Ezra–Nehemiah as two different recensions comparable to Proverbs, Jeremiah, and Daniel in their MT versus LXX forms. There are substantial differences between these cases. While the versions of Jeremiah and Proverbs are rightly defined as different redactions, they do not contain additional material of the sort that characterizes 1 Esdras, Daniel, and of course Esther, which he neglects to mention; see Dieter Böhler, "On the Relationship between Textual and Literary Criticism: The Two Recensions of the Book of Ezra; Ezra–Neh (MT) and 1 Esdras (LXX)," in *The Earliest Text of the Hebrew Bible: The Relationship between the Masoretic Text and the Hebrew Base of the Septuagint Reconsidered* (ed. Adrian Schenker; SBLSCS 52; Atlanta: Society of Biblical Literature, 2003), 35–50.

milieu of such literary activity around the Hebrew Bible that produced the versions of Daniel and Esther preserved in the LXX.

3. Large Interpolations Resulting in a Mixture of Genres

Despite the complicated problems that the books of Chronicles–Ezra–Nehemiah present in terms of the quality of their historical contribution, their genre would nevertheless most likely be described, with due reservation, as "historiography."[15] Should this evaluation be attributed to 1 Esdras as well? On the face of things, we could take the easy way out and define 1 Esdras as "history," as Japhet puts it in her 2001 short commentary: "a description of the history of Israel from the eighteenth year of King Josiah to the time of Ezra."[16] However, this gross definition does not do justice to the main independent contribution of this work, that is, the additional story of the youths.

The story of the youths is, clearly enough, of a different genre compared with the material that surrounds it. Unlike the Chronicles–Ezra–Nehemiah material, the story of the youths is a deipnosophistic account, a literary genre in its own right, in which a contest takes place between several participants who try to prove their skill in wisdom-oriented speeches. The three youths initiate such a contest, which revolves around the theme of "the strongest thing in the world." They advocate in lengthy and ardent speeches one out of three subjects, which turn eventually into four: wine, the king, women, and as an afterthought or peak, the truth. These speeches have nothing in common with history or historiography. The story of the youths completely blurs the genre of the work into which it was incorporated.

The problem with 1 Esdras' genre becomes even more conspicuous with Williamson's suggestion in his 2003 commentary article.[17] Since he too, like Japhet, is convinced that the book as a whole deserves a comprehensive definition of genre, he brings up the nowadays-popular category of "rewritten Bible." The preliminary question would be whether rewritten Bible is indeed a genre or rather a nongenre, since it may be applied to works of different genres. Indeed, it has been applied to a wide range of literary works, such as the book of *Jubilees*, the *Temple Scroll*, as well as a long and varied series of Qumran texts. We may say, although a contradiction in terms, that the book of Chronicles too falls

---

15. Thus Sara Japhet, "The Book of Chronicles: A History" [in Hebrew], *Shnaton* 14 (2004): 101–17. However, I would certainly disagree with Japhet's concluding assertion that the Chronicler is a historian and the book of Chronicles a "historical composition" in the full modern meaning of these terms.

16. Sara Japhet, "1 Esdras," in *The Oxford Bible Commentary* (ed. John Barton and John Muddiman; Oxford: Oxford University Press, 2001), 751.

17. Williamson, "1 Esdras," 851. [See also Williamson's contribution to the present volume—Ed.]

under the category of rewritten Bible. Williamson compares 1 Esdras to the *Genesis Apocryphon*, Pseudo-Philo, and parts of the works of Josephus. The title rewritten Bible serves these works well in the sense that rewriting the Bible is indeed their main characteristic. In 1 Esdras, however, there is hardly any rewriting at all. The compiler achieved his goal mainly by the interpolation of the story of the youths and by reordering certain units.

Compilation procedures well known within the Hebrew Bible, where poems, fables, legends, and lists were introduced into narratives that scarcely accommodate them in their midst—one example being the Elijah and Elisha cycles, which completely disrupt the Ahab-Jehoram accounts—lived on in the hands of later compilers such as those who produced the versions of the books of Esther and Daniel as preserved in the LXX. These court stories attracted additions of conspicuously different genres, one of which is the prayers. Such is the long prayer of Azariah in the midst of the fire, which has nothing much to do with his situation (LXX Dan 3:24–44), and the following praise of Hananiah, Mishael, and Azariah, who, after the intervention of an angel (vv. 45–49), "as out of one mouth, praised, glorified, and blessed God in the furnace," with a long series of Εὐλογητὸς εἶ, "blessed art thou" (vv. 52–90). Almost naturally, we find Mordechai beseeching the Lord (Esth 4:17a–i) and Esther following suit with another extensive prayer (4:17k–z), both set in a context that is careful enough not to involve or even mention God.[18] The other additions to Esther, as well as the stories of Susanna and Bel and the Dragon appended to Daniel, further confuse the genres of these books.

Such compilations were created in ancient times and 1 Esdras is one of them.

4. Juxtaposition of Alternative Narratives and Chronological Mix-Up

The incorporation of the story of the youths resulted in a quite extraordinary state of affairs: the book of 1 Esdras as a whole offers two alternative narratives regarding the events that take place at the beginning of Darius' reign. The first follows the story of the youths, the other runs parallel to the canonical version (Ezra 5–6 repeated in 1 Esd 6–7).

The story of the youths is set at the beginning of Darius' reign. First Esdras, ch. 2, begins with the first year of Cyrus, continues with Artaxerxes, and ends with the interruption of the building of the temple, said to be on hold until the second year of Darius (2:25). Chapter 3 smoothly follows, introducing the story of the youths that conveniently takes place in the reign of Darius. However, as

---

18. We mention in passing Manasseh's prayer, mentioned in 2 Chr 33:18–19, which later initiated the apocryphal Prayer of Manasseh.

we go on reading the intriguing story through chs. 3–4, and continue into ch. 5, which discloses the list of returnees and their first actions, namely, the building of the altar and the foundation of the temple, we surprisingly discover that the work at the temple site stops again and is delayed—until when? Once again, it is delayed until the second year of Darius (5:70). The account then goes on to relate the intervention of the prophets, who encouraged the people to resume the building of the temple. According to 1 Esdras, then, the building of the temple stops twice, and is delayed, both times, until the second year of Darius; and it is resumed twice, once as a result of Zerubbabel winning the wisdom contest that is introduced by the story of the youths, and the second time through the encouragement of the prophets as recounted in the canonical version. In Hanhart's words, 1 Esdras not only presupposes the chronological problems characteristic of Ezra–Nehemiah but further complicates them. This is a major factor in the argumentation in favor of the canonical version.[19]

Within the Hebrew Bible, there is a long line of celebrated duplications such as the creation stories or the introduction of David, once as a musician playing before Saul (1 Sam 16:14–23) and once, immediately following, on the battlefield challenging Goliath (ch. 17). Or, on a somewhat different level, we mention the conspicuous redactional failure to introduce the alternative conquest account of Judg 1 into the course of events, well marked by the resumption of the report of Joshua's death after the insertion (2:8), despite the beginning of the book that marks its time as "After the death of Joshua" (1:1).

Even more appealing is the clear redactional activity that results in a glaring duplication in the course of events found in the Septuagint version of the books of Kings, as an alternative story of the division of the kingdom is appended at 1 Kgs 12:24 (3 Kgdms 12:24a–z). The redactor at work on this version had at his disposal a fine story about the division of the kingdom and was eager to make use of it. He was not bothered, so it seems, by the fact that two versions of the same events happening during the same span of time are recounted side by side. The same redactor, probably, totally confuses the course of events as he adds two lengthy miscellanies in ch. 2 (at 2:35 and 2:46), which primarily mention data that reappear as the reign of Solomon goes on. Regardless of the provenance of

---

19. Hanhart, *Text und Textgeschichte des 2. Esrabuches*, 12 n. 1: "Der mir nach wie vor gleicherweise eindeutig erscheinende Befund, dass der Text von Esdr I die in Quellenverarbeitung begründete chronologische Problematik der Bücher Esra-Nehemia nicht nur voraussetzt, sondern sie noch kompliziert, bleibt für mich das bedeutsamste Kriterium für die Annahme der Priorität der masoretisch überlieferten Bücher Esra und Nehemia, der gegenüber mich neuerdings wieder vorgebrachte Argumente für die Annahme einer aus dem Text von Esdr I verifizierbaren Vorform bzw. eines über dieses Zwischenglied zur masoretisch überlieferten Textform führenden Wachstums nicht zu überzeugen vermögen." This criticism is addressed, again, at Schenker and Böhler, who assume the existence of an intermediate composition; see above, n. 2. Similarly, Williamson, "The Problem with First Esdras," 301.

the extra reports in ch. 2 or the additional narrative in ch. 12, the Septuagint version of the book of Kings in reference to these two substantial duplications must be secondary.[20]

Again, such compilations were created in ancient times; so was 1 Esdras.

5. Transposition of Large Sections

Besides the interpolation of the story of the youths, the major difference between 1 Esdras and the parallel canonical material lies in two substantial transpositions, both triggered, I believe, by the insertion of the story of the youths.

5.1. Zerubbabel's Return History (Ezra 2:1–4:5 // 1 Esd 5:7–45)

The insertion of the story of the youths required reorganization of the return narrative borrowed from the canonical composition type. Either we believe in lucky coincidences, or we realize that the main contribution of the compiler of 1 Esdras, besides the insertion of the story of the youths, is the transposition of a large-scale, continuous unit from its canonical setting to a later stage, that is, Ezra 2:1–4:5, which comprises the list of returnees (Ezra 2), the building of the altar and foundation of the temple (Ezra 3), and the interference of the local adversaries (Ezra 4:1–5). In the canonical book, Ezra 2:1–4:5 immediately follows the Cyrus account (Ezra 1), while in 1 Esdras it is postponed *en bloc* until after the story of the youths comes to an end (1 Esd 5:7–45). The reason behind this reordering of the material is the simple fact that the hero of the transferred unit (again: Ezra 2:1–4:5) is Zerubbabel, hence, it cannot take place before Zerubbabel is introduced to the stage of history through the wisdom contest in the story of the youths. On the other hand, there was no need whatsoever to move the Artaxerxes correspondence (Ezra 4:6–24 // 1 Esd 2:15–25), since Zerubbabel is not part of it and since, as it turns out, the order of the Persian kings was of no concern to the compiler. On the contrary, the Artaxerxes section ends by mentioning the second year of Darius and thus forms a perfect setting for the story of the youths. In my opinion, this is the logic behind the obvious redactional move, and this is the reason behind the reordering of the canonical material.

The compiler's move is further substantiated by a transition passage (1 Esd 5:1–6), which he provided to link the story of the youths to Zerubbabel's return narrative that follows (see below).

---

20. Regarding the secondary character of the additions in ch 2, see D. W Gooding, *Relics of Ancient Exegesis: A Study of the Miscellanies in 3 Reigns 2* (Cambridge: Cambridge University Press, 1976). As for the alternative story, it is my view that it is based on a canonical composition type of the sort of 1 Kgs 11, 12, and 14; Zipora Talshir, *The Alternative Story of the Division of the Kingdom* (Jerusalem: Simor, 1993).

As argued, the compiler of 1 Esdras moved the Zerubbabel return narrative (Ezra 2:1–4:5), leaving behind the Artaxerxes correspondence since Zerubbabel does not take part in it. It is misleading, therefore, to speak of "some rearrangement even of the biblical narrative, especially at 2:16–30" or to report that 1 Esdras "has a parallel to the letter of Ezra 4:7–24 in a different location."[21] The place of the Artaxerxes section closer to the beginning of the return narrative is only a by-product of the main move. Hence, lofty intentions can hardly be attributed to the compiler regarding the placement of this section, since he did not actually change its place but rather removed the preceding large section (2:1–4:5), leaving behind the awkward sequence of the Cyrus section (Ezra 1) and the Artaxerxes section (Ezra 4:7–24), which together form 1 Esd 2.

In a 2007 article, Japhet argues that the compiler of 1 Esdras deliberately placed the Artaxerxes section at an early stage in his book, since it served him well to depict the rehabilitation of both the temple and the city right at the beginning of the return.[22] First, as argued, the compiler of 1 Esdras did not do anything at all to improve the position of this section but rather left it untouched. Second, if he indeed had in mind such a sophisticated goal, he totally failed to achieve it. He even failed to achieve a plausible course of events. The complaint sent to Artaxerxes revolves indeed around the ongoing building of the city, but there is not one word beforehand that would even hint at any actual building activity, in reference to either the city or the temple. All that comes beforehand is the decree of Cyrus, allowing the building of the temple, and some ensuing steps that precede the actual return. It is difficult, then, to envisage a calculated plan behind this rather impossible course of events. To be sure, Japhet's argumentation is part of her attempt to define the book as a planned entity; she certainly does not think that it is original in comparison with the canonical version.

The position of the Artaxerxes section is further misused by Schenker and Böhler, who argue that this is the original setting of events. It entails a sort of confusion between "historical," so to speak, considerations and literary critical issues: the Artaxerxes section indeed presupposes the building of Jerusalem, but the literary-critical observation remains that there was no mention whatsoever of an actual building of the city beforehand. It is simply not there.[23] The argument

---

21. Respectively, Williamson, "1 Esdras," 851; Juha Pakkala, *Ezra the Scribe: The Development of Ezra 7–10 and Nehemiah 8* (BZAW 347; Berlin: de Gruyter, 2004), 17.

22. Sara Japhet, "The Portrayal of the Restoration Period in 1 Esdras" [in Hebrew], *Meghillot* 5–6 (2007): 109–28, esp. 118–19. [Now see also Japhet's contribution in the present volume.—Ed.]

23. As S. L. McKenzie ("The Chronicler as Redactor," in *The Chronicler as Author: Studies in Text and Texture* [ed. M. P. Graham and S. L. McKenzie; JSOTSup 263; Sheffield: Sheffield Academic Press, 2000], 70–90 [74]) says: "Without the explanatory foreground in Ezra this letter comes 'out of the blue'. Thus, the reader has to know the Ezra account in order to make sense of 1 Esdras."

advanced by Schenker and Böhler that the building of the city, or rather the built city, is simply presupposed does not stand to reason, since the explicit complaint against the building of the city remains pending in the air.

Regardless of its different setting, the Artaxerxes section disturbs the course of events both chronologically, since Artaxerxes interrupts the Cyrus–Darius narrative, and in terms of contents, since the building of the city disrupts the temple-oriented context. In 1 Esdras an attempt was made to bridge the gap by inserting the temple into the correspondence (see below).

5.2. THE READING OF THE TORAH (NEHEMIAH 8:1–13 // 1 ESDRAS 9:36–55)

Another section that takes its place at different points in the canonical book versus 1 Esdras is of course the reading of the Torah. While in the canonical book it is located in Neh 8, barely after Nehemiah makes his first step toward a repopulation of Jerusalem, in 1 Esdras it follows immediately upon the separation from the foreign women. The canonical sequence is notorious for two main reasons: (1) Ezra abruptly reappears on the scene after a long absence throughout Neh 1–7; (2) the reading of the Torah (Neh 8) together with the ensuing events (Neh 9–10) interrupts Nehemiah's actions, since the move he made in Neh 7 is not resumed until ch. 11. This is indeed an artificial course of events. Nevertheless, the intertwining of the Ezra narrative and the Nehemiah narrative—awkward as it may be—may in fact have been what the compiler of Ezra–Nehemiah had in mind.[24]

Does 1 Esdras offer an earlier arrangement of the material? This is the case according to Böhler's 2003 article,[25] which in the main reiterates the thesis of his 1997 book.

Böhler, resorting to text criticism at the rescue of literary criticism, conducts a text-critical analysis of a series of presumed variants—I deal with these variants in detail elsewhere[26]—that prove, in his opinion, the priority of 1 Esdras: according to his assumption, the canonical version obliterated any mention of rehabilitated Jerusalem the moment Nehemiah's memoirs were imported into the book, since the rebuilding of the city must remain Nehemiah's enterprise. Böhler consequently arrives at the peak of his conclusions, that is, the originality of the arrangement presented in 1 Esdras, with the reading of the Torah conveniently appended at the end of the Ezra material. The reading of the Torah may have originally belonged to the Ezra narrative rather than the Nehemiah narrative;

---

24. See Lisbeth S. Fried, "Who Wrote Ezra–Nehemiah and Why Did They?" in *Unity and Disunity in Ezra–Nehemiah: Redaction, Rhetoric, and Reader* (ed. Mark J. Boda and Paul L. Redditt; Hebrew Bible Monographs 17; Sheffield: Sheffield Phoenix, 2008).

25. Böhler, "On the Relationship between Textual and Literary Criticism."

26. Zipora Talshir, "Ezra–Nehemiah and First Esdras: Diagnosis of a Relationship between Two Recensions," *Bib* 81 (2000): 566–73; Grabbe, review of Talshir (see n. 2, above), in reference to Böhler; Böhler completely disregards my criticism in his later work.

nevertheless, 1 Esdras should not be quoted as independent evidence in that regard.[27] There is more than one stage in the development of this material.

We assume that the compiler of 1 Esdras used the simple redactional tool of reordering sections in order to combine the Ezra materials that belong together, while in his *Vorlage* they were intertwined with the Nehemiah memoirs. The seams of his cut-and-paste procedure remained, however, deplorably visible, most obviously in one telltale verse, that is, 9:37 (see below).

This procedure of reconstituting the course of events by moving units from one point to another is a well-known tool of redactors. We mention briefly the prophecies against the nations that occupy different positions in the two surviving editions of Jeremiah: in the canonical version they are appended at the end of the book (chs. 46–51), while in the Septuagint's layout they take their place in the middle of the book, Jer 25:14–32:14, following the structure of other prophetic books that begin with reproach, continue with prophecies against the nations, and end with consolation. The MT still features the verse that would easily accommodate the prophecies against the nations: והבאתי על הארץ ההיא את־כל דברי אשר דברתי עליה את כל־הכתוב בספר הזה אשר נבא ירמיהו על כל הגוים, "And I will bring upon that land all that I have decreed against it, all that is recorded in this book—that which Jeremiah prophesied against all the nations" (Jer 25:13), resounding in 46:1, which introduces the prophecies against the nations in the MT: אשר היה דבר יהוה אל־ירמיהו הנביא על הגוים, "The word of the Lord to the prophet Jeremiah concerning the nations." If one is not tempted to assume independent structuring of the book of Jeremiah, it must have been a redactor who moved the prophecies against the nations from the middle of the book to its end or, others would claim, vice versa.

Other examples are chs. 20–21 in 1 Kings, which are set in reverse order in 3 Kingdoms, and the intriguing shuffle of materials in the reign of Solomon, for example, the building of the palace that in the canonical version stands in between the building of the temple and its furnishing (1 Kgs 7:1–13), while in the Septuagint it is postponed until after both building and furnishing of the temple are completed (3 Kgdms 7:39–50); in Chronicles, we may note, the building of the palace disappears altogether.

Going back to Daniel again, there the changed sequence may have been created within the Greek tradition. While the canonical book is probably organized in a concentric, theme-oriented structure, reflected also in LXX MS 88, a completely different sequence emerges in the Greek version preserved in papyrus 967, clearly guided by a chronological principle. This reorganization is

---

27. Contra, e.g., Grabbe, who simply adduces 1 Esdras as evidence that Neh 8 "is a part of the Ezra tradition"; Lester L. Grabbe, "The Law of Moses in the Ezra Tradition," in *Persia and Torah* (ed. James W. Watts; SBLSymS 17; Atlanta: Society of Biblical Literature, 2001), 94.

reflected to some extent in the chronological headings. At any rate, the main redactional activity is clearly achieved through reordering of large units.[28]

Finally, we recall Josephus' treatment of the reigns of Israel and Judah. Once upon a time there must have existed separate chronicles of the kingdoms of Judah and Israel. The author of the book of Kings combined them into a synchronic account of both kingdoms but still made sure to offer strictly separate descriptions of the corresponding reigns of Judah and Israel, regardless of their overlapping periods; consequently, for example, Jehoshaphat collaborates with Jehoram king of Israel in his war against Moab (2 Kgs 3), after his own death was already officially reported (end of 1 Kgs 22). Josephus, as a historian, could not go along with this artificial, achronological setting created by the author of the book of Kings and intermingled the reigns of Israel and Judah into one continuous historical/chronological narrative, in the best of his judgment. Historically, he may have made the right considerations, but is his narrative saying anything whatsoever regarding a different, not to say original, form of the book of Kings?

Let me take the opportunity to say a word regarding the practice of using Josephus as evidence in support of 1 Esdras' structure and scope, that is, with the reading of the Torah appended at the end of the Ezra material and with the Nehemiah material excluded. The reasoning that recruits Josephus as evidence shows rather poor judgment. Says Böhler: "These memoirs had still been circulating independently from the restoration account (Zerubbabel and Ezra story) for a long time. Even Josephus still knew them in the 1st century A.D."[29] On what grounds would someone come to this exorbitant conclusion? Josephus does not testify to an original or older form of the material in any way. He simply uses 1 Esdras, the story of the youths included, and, moreover, he uses it, undoubtedly, in its Greek form. Josephus is not at his peak as historian in his treatment of this material. He embellishes his story in many ways. Not only does he incorporate the legendary story of the youths into his history, quoting at length the wisdom speeches given by the three, but he also makes sure to explain quite extensively that Cyrus' initiative was rooted in his reading of Isaiah's prophecies (*Ant.* 11.5–6) and is careful enough to provide a fine closure to the histories of both Ezra and Nehemiah, reporting the honorable death of both of them (§§158, 183)—information lacking in both the canonical and the apocryphal books. Josephus, entangled as he is in the Greek terminology regarding the foundation of the temple used in 1 Esdras, totally confuses the sequence of events and twice relates the completion of the building of the temple together with its inauguration (specifically, §§80, 106).

---

28. It is my pleasure to quote my student's dissertation on that issue; Dalia Amara, "The Old Greek Version of the Book of Daniel" [in Hebrew] (Ph.D. diss., Ben-Gurion University of the Negev, 2006), 278–94.

29. Böhler, "On the Relationship between Textual and Literary Criticism," 47; surely this evaluation is liable to turn into a "fact" later cited as evidence.

Indeed, Josephus follows 1 Esdras also in regard to Ezra's story, including the reading of the Torah appended right after the separation. However, unlike the apocryphal book that stops in the middle of things, Josephus goes on to recount the Feast of Booths, in accordance with the canonical setting in Nehemiah, making sure to end Ezra's story, as mentioned, with his death and to mark the transition between the periods by specifying the death of one high priest and his substitution by another (§158), as if the death of Ezra and the high priest are likely to coincide. He then goes on to tell Nehemiah's story in parallel to the canonical book. How is this proof of the supposition that Josephus knew the memoirs as a separate work? He simply uses the canonical book alongside the apocryphal book. And on what grounds does Böhler conclude that the memoirs as Josephus knew them were much shorter than the canonical version? Josephus goes along with Neh 1–2 (§§159–173), but the rest of Nehemiah's deeds he condenses into a short report (§§174–183), which can scarcely be considered a short version of the memoirs. Josephus cuts the extensive version short as he does on many other occasions—he seems to say so himself when he refers to many other things (πολλὰ δὲ καὶ ἄλλα ...) that Nehemiah had done before he died (§183)—rather than witness a shorter version. If we rely on Josephus regarding the original form of Nehemiah's memoirs, we can revise our entire Bible into something completely different, shaped by Josephus' priorities.

6. Telltale Passages: Where Text Criticism and Literary Criticism Might Work Hand in Hand

Unlike random variants that do not regularly provide evidence regarding the priority of the composition as a whole, there are some cases where textual criticism and literary criticism might work hand in hand. One must say that, given the image of 1 Esdras as a completely different composition compared with Chronicles–Ezra–Nehemiah and the far-reaching differences between them, it is amazing how little the compilers intervened in the text itself. We mention below several passages that might tell the story of the relationship between the parallel compositions.

6.1. The Transition Passage in 1 Esdras 5:1–6: Double Introduction of the List of Returnees

The intermediate passage at 1 Esd 5:1–6 is obviously the work of the compiler, who provided a link between the imported story of the youths and Zerubbabel's return narrative, which he located immediately afterwards (5:7–70 // Ezra 2:1–4:5). This part begins with the list of returnees that, according to the canonical version, first introduces Zerubbabel. The compilation procedure becomes clear as this passage, specifically vv. 1, 4–5, duplicates the original introduction of the list of returnees (vv. 7–8, which run parallel to Ezra 2:1–2):

> 1 Μετὰ δὲ ταῦτα ἐξελέγησαν ἀναβῆναι ἀρχηγοὶ ... 4 Καὶ ταῦτα τὰ ὀνόματα τῶν ἀνδρῶν τῶν ἀναβαινόντων κατὰ πατριὰς αὐτῶν εἰς τὰς φυλάς; ... 7 εἰσὶν δὲ οὗτοι ἐκ τῆς Ιουδαίας οἱ ἀναβάντες ἐκ τῆς αἰχμαλωσίας τῆς παροικίας ... 8 καὶ ἐπέστρεψαν εἰς Ιερουσαλημ καὶ τὴν λοιπὴν Ιουδαίαν ἕκαστος εἰς τὴν ἰδίαν πόλιν, οἱ ἐλθόντες μετὰ Ζοροβαβελ καὶ Ἰησοῦ

> 1 After this were the principal men of the families chosen according to their tribes, to go up .... 4 And these are the names of the men who went up, according to their families, among their tribes .... 7 And these are they of Judah that came up from the captivity .... 8 And they returned unto Jerusalem, and to the other parts of Judah, every man to his own city, who came with Zorobabel, and Jesus.

We mention here one similar example from the book of Chronicles. In the book of Samuel, the list of David's mighty men (2 Sam 23:8–39) is part of the appendix at the end of the book (chs. 21–24). The Chronicler makes use of this list in his introduction to David's reign (1 Chr 11:10–47). In order to accommodate the list in its new context, the author provides an opening of his own (v. 10), followed by the original opening (v. 11):

> 10 ואלה ראשי הגבורים אשר לדויד המתחזקים עמו במלכותו עם־כל־ישראל להמליכו כדבר יהוה על־ישׂראל: 11 ואלה מספר הגברים אשר לדויד ...

> 10 Now these are the chiefs of David's mighty men, who gave him strong support in his kingdom, together with all Israel, to make him king, according to the word of the Lord concerning Israel. 11 This is an account of David's mighty men ....

The duplicate introduction of the list once again shows the compiler of 1 Esdras at work, reworking the canonical composition type that was at his disposal.

6.2. WHO IS RESPONSIBLE FOR THE CHANGES IN THE ARTAXERXES CORRESPONDENCE?

The differences between the texts have little to do with their different contexts and may have happened at any stage. Be that as it may, the 1 Esdras text hardly lends itself to being preferable to the MT.

6.2.1. TELESCOPING THE INTRODUCTIONS TO THE ARTAXERXES CORRESPONDENCE.

The cluttered MT version of the introduction to the letter of complaint sent to Artaxerxes (Ezra 4:7–10) turns into a structured opening in 1 Esdras (2:15–16).
Ezra 4:7–10

> 7 ובימי ארתחששתא כתב בשלם מתרדת טבאל ושאר כנותו על ארתחששת מלך פרס וכתב הנשתון כתוב ארמית ומתרגם ארמית: 8 רחום בעל־טעם ושמשי ספרא כתבו אגרה חדה על־ירושלם לארתחששתא מלכא כנמא: 9 אדין רחום בעל טעם ושמשי ספרא ושאר כנותהון דיניא ואפרסתכיא טרפליא אפרסיא ארכויא בבליא שושנכיא דהיא עלמיא: 10 ושאר אמיא די הגלי אסנפר רבא ויקירא והותב המו בקריה די שמרין ושאר עבר־נהרה וכענת

1 Esdras reads:

> Ἐν δὲ τοῖς ἐπὶ Ἀρταξέρξου τοῦ Περσῶν βασιλέως χρόνοις κατέγραψεν αὐτῷ κατὰ τῶν κατοικούντων ἐν τῇ Ἰουδαίᾳ καὶ Ἰερουσαλημ Βεσλεμος καὶ Μιθραδάτης καὶ Ταβελλιος καὶ Ραουμος καὶ Βεελτέεμος καὶ Σαμσαῖος ὁ γραμματεὺς καὶ οἱ λοιποὶ οἱ τούτοις συντασσόμενοι, οἰκοῦντες δὲ ἐν Σαμαρείᾳ καὶ τοῖς ἄλλοις τόποις, τὴν ὑπογεγραμμένην ἐπιστολήν
> Βασιλεῖ Ἀρταξέρξῃ κυρίῳ οἱ παῖδές σου Ραουμος ὁ τὰ προσπίπτοντα καὶ Σαμσαῖος ὁ γραμματεὺς καὶ οἱ ἐπίλοιποι τῆς βουλῆς αὐτῶν κριταὶ οἱ ἐν Κοίλῃ Συρίᾳ καὶ Φοινίκῃ

> But in the time of Artaxerxes, king of the Persians, Beslemos, and Mithridates, and Tabellius, and Rathumus, and Beelteemos, and Samellius the secretary, with the rest that were in commission with them, dwelling in Samaria and other places, wrote unto him against them that dwelt in Judea and Jerusalem this letter following:
> To king Artaxerxes our lord, thy servants, Rathumus the storywriter, and Samellius the scribe, and the rest of their council, and the judges that are in Celosyria and Phenice.

Böhler sharply criticizes my analysis of the relationship between the versions, arguing mainly that I do not take into consideration scholarly opinion that the MT is a late, expansive version and that originally it was only concerned with judges rather than peoples, just as in 1 Esdras.[30] While the Ezra text may have been expanded at a certain stage, one has to remember that the MT type is probably attested also in 4QEzr,[31] before asserting an incredibly late date for this assumed expansion. First Esdras, at any rate, is not good evidence for a shorter original version.

A text such as the MT, with or without the list of nations, could have prompted intervention at any stage of transmission. We cannot even disregard the possibility that the translator is at work here, since he is renowned for his interest and skills where official correspondence is at stake. The MT is indeed awkward with its two (or three, considering v. 6) introductions, with only one letter following. First Esdras telescopes the separate openings into one, but the problems do not disappear: Why do Βεσλεμος καὶ Μιθραδάτης καὶ Ταβελλιος, mentioned in v. 15, disappear in v. 16 (as well as in the rest of the correspondence)? Where did the judges mentioned in v. 16 come from, given that they were not mentioned in v. 15, not to speak of the questionable relevance of "judges" in this context? Why are the writers first defined as living in Samaria

---

30. See his review of my commentary, Dieter Böhler, Review of Zipora Talshir, *1 Esdras: A Text Critical Commentary*, Bib 84 (2003): 281.
31. Zipora Talshir, "Synchronic Approaches with Diachronic Consequences in the Study of Parallel Redactions: First Esdras and 2 Chronicles 35–36; Ezra 1–10; Nehemiah 8," in *Yahwism after the Exile: Perspectives on Israelite Religion in the Persian Era* (ed. Rainer Albertz and Bob Becking; Studies in Theology and Religion 5; Assen: Van Gorcum, 2003), 203–7.

and other places and then related to Κοίλη Συρία καὶ Φοινίκη? Aren't those living in Samaria the people mentioned in the MT? This case, among others, shows that while the MT is problematic in many respects, 1 Esdras does not reflect an earlier text.

6.2.2. INSERTION OF THE TEMPLE INTO THE CITY-ORIENTED COMPLAINT TO ARTAXERXES. Unlike the MT, which speaks of the city throughout this section (קריתא appears eight times), in 1 Esdras the temple theme is imposed on the city-oriented correspondence on two occasions. According to the MT, the activity that prompted the complaint regards the following: קריתא מרדתא, ובאישתא בנין ושוריא שכללו ואשיא יחיטו "They are rebuilding that rebellious and wicked city; they are completing the walls and repairing the foundations" (Ezra 4:12).[32] Instead of ואשיא יחיטו, "and repairing the foundations," 1 Esd 2:17 specifies: καὶ ναὸν ὑποβάλλονται, "and do lay the foundation of the temple," which may suggest a different *Vorlage*, such as ואשי היכלא יחיטו. As the letter goes on, the local authorities recommend themselves as committed to the king, using the idiom מלח היכלא מלחנא, "Now because we eat the salt of the palace" (Ezra 4:14). First Esdras says instead: καὶ ἐπεὶ ἐνεργεῖται τὰ κατὰ τὸν ναόν, "And for as much as the things pertaining to the temple are now in hand," or rather, "and since the work at the temple is being done" (v. 18).[33] While in the first case we could imagine a different *Vorlage*, the latter is most probably the contribution of the translator, who had trouble understanding the idiomatic phrase and related היכלא to the temple rather than the palace. The translator thus intervenes in matters that affect the redaction.

All in all, the 1 Esdras text is certainly secondary in comparison with the MT, since the correspondence with Artaxerxes is clearly concerned with the building of the city and the walls, not the temple.

6.3. ONE VERSE TOO MANY: A GOLDEN KEY TO THE RELATIONSHIP BETWEEN 1 ESDRAS AND THE CANONICAL SETTING (1 ESDRAS 9:37 // NEHEMIAH 7:72)

After the conclusion of the separation unit (Ezra 10:44 // 1 Esd 9:36), 1 Esdras continues with the Torah reading, beginning with an exposition (v. 37):

Καὶ κατῴκησαν οἱ ἱερεῖς καὶ οἱ Λευῖται καὶ οἱ ἐκ τοῦ Ισραηλ ἐν τοῦ Ιερουσαλημ καὶ ἐν τῇ χώρᾳ. – τῇ νουμηνίᾳ τοῦ ἑβδόμου μηνός – καὶ οἱ υἱοὶ Ισραηλ ἐν ταῖς κατοικίαις αὐτῶν ...

---

32. Considering that the foundations are not mentioned again during the entire correspondence, one wonders whether ואשיא יחיטו is original or rather a later addition prompted by the preceding chapter.

33. מלח ... מלחנא may have reminded him of מלאכה.

And the priests and Levites, and they that were of Israel, dwelt in Jerusalem and in the country. And as the first day of the seventh month arrived, and the children of Israel were in their habitations …

This verse parallels Neh 7:72, which immediately precedes the Torah reading:

וישבו הכהנים והלוים והשוערים והמשררים ומן־העם והנתינים וכל־ישראל בעריהם: ויגע החדש השביעי ובני ישראל בעריהם

So the priests, the Levites, the gatekeepers, the singers, some of the people, the temple servants, and all Israel lived in their towns. And when the seventh month had come, the children of Israel were in their towns.

However, while in the canonical version this verse concludes—just as in Ezra 2:70—the preceding list of returnees, adduced by Nehemiah in preparation for his planned rehabilitation of Jerusalem, in 1 Esdras it is completely out of place, proving that 1 Esdras borrowed this verse, together with the section now following the Ezra narrative (1 Esd 9:37–55), from its place in the canonical version, beginning one verse earlier than he should have.[34]

Böhler criticized me severely on my analysis of this verse. He is very persistent regarding the fact that the verse concludes different matters ("Ganz anders in 1 Esdras!" he emphasizes):[35] in Nehemiah it summarizes the list of returnees, while in 1 Esdras it closes the list of those who married foreign women. Well, this is exactly the key to the problem, since this concluding verse fits only one list well, that is, the MT list of returnees, and is totally inappropriate for the other list, namely, the 1 Esdras list of intermarriages. Böhler goes on to argue that in fact the two parallel conclusions have nothing in common: 1 Esd 9:37 "hat mit Neh 7:72a nichts zu tun!"[36] Nehemiah 7:72a names the groups that are enumerated in the list of returnees, he argues, while 1 Esd 9:37 enumerates the groups that were accused of marrying foreign women. According to 1 Esd 8:92 (// Ezra 10:5), he continues, those who married foreign women are designated as priests, Levites, and Israelites, and accordingly the conclusion speaks just of priests, Levites, and Israelites, unlike the Nehemiah conclusion, which names additional groups. If we are engaged in textual criticism, let us go the whole way: (1) The evidence cited from 1 Esd 8:92 (// Ezra 10:5) should be dismissed out of hand, since it does not in fact speak of those who married foreign women but rather mentions the heads of the priests, Levites, and Israelites as being commissioned to take action against the transgressors. (2) Those who married foreign women included

---

34. Diana Edelman, *The Origins of the "Second" Temple* (London: Equinox, 2005), 152, argues that the inclusion of the reading of the Torah in 1 Esdras need not indicate a knowledge of the combined work; the inclusion of Neh 7:72 certainly does.

35. Böhler, review of Talshir, 282.

36. Böhler, review of Talshir, 283.

also singers and gatekeepers in both versions (1 Esd 9:24–25 // Ezra 10:24), meaning that the allegedly telling difference between the conclusions does not do justice to the lists themselves. (3) And how would we explain the simple verb that begins the concluding verse, καὶ κατῴκησαν, וישבו, "and the priests and Levites and those of Israel settled down in Jerusalem and in the country"? What has settling down to do with the blacklist of intermarriages? Finally, it is quite odd to assume that two very similar verses that precede the very same account (the reading of the Torah) have nothing to do with one another. Böhler forces the text to conform to his theory regarding the priority of 1 Esdras, but he has not provided an acceptable answer to the telltale passage of 1 Esd 9:37.[37] For me this verse is the golden key to the relationship between the versions regarding the location of the reading of the Torah and probably also to the omission of the Nehemiah memoirs.

7. 1 Esdras as a Whole: Title, Structure, and Concept

Nowadays, it is the prevailing quest of biblical research to understand literary works as a whole, regardless of the history of their creation. Questions regarding the literary design and the ideological purpose that guided the compiler of 1 Esdras have been asked many times and in different ways. Williamson argues that "1 Esdras represents a conscious selection and arrangement of source material in what was intended to be a book in its own right."[38] This would seem to be quite a plausible definition, were it not for its further implications. Japhet portrays 1 Esdras as "A composition in its own right with an identity of its own, written by an author," or "a literary entity of independent identity."[39] The moment a work is recognized as "a composition in its own right," it also deserves a title; indeed, on another occasion, Japhet says: "1 Esdras can rightly be called 'The Book of Destruction and Restoration.'"[40] The book must also have a clear-cut structure; in her view it is mainly divided in three

The Last Kings of Judah and the Destruction (ch. 1)
The Material Restoration (chs. 2–7)
Spiritual Restoration (chs. 8–9)

---

37. As Pakkala puts it in his 2004 volume on the emergence of the Ezra–Nehemiah narrative (*Ezra the Scribe*, 19): without a comprehensive explanation for the function of 1 Esd 9:37, it is difficult to accept that the omission of Nehemiah in 1 Esdras is original.
38. Williamson, "1 Esdras," 851.
39. Japhet, "The Portrayal of the Restoration Period," 114.
40. Japhet, "1 Esdras," 752. [See also Japhet's contribution to the present volume—Ed.]

If this is the title of the book and this is its intended, although uneven, structure, why is Josiah featured at the beginning of this work? In what way is he part of the destruction theme said to govern the first part of this book? And how do chs. 2–7 form a coherent section whose title might be "The Material Restoration," with the long contest included? Is the detailed account of Ezra's return, including the list of those who came back with him, more "spiritual" than the return of Zerubbabel? Why is Cyrus' decree less "spiritual" than the decree given to Ezra? The art of giving suitable titles is flourishing nowadays, but the attractive titles tend to misrepresent the underlying material.

Furthermore, the work is said to have a clear theological concept. Williamson states: "The significant innovation is that it would represent for the first time a narrative continuity between the fall of Jerusalem ..., the destruction of the temple and the exile on the one hand, and the account of the postexilic restoration on the other."[41] And Japhet: "The most important feature of 1 Esdras is the concept of historical continuity. First Esdras bridges the gap between the periods of the First Temple and the Second Temple by the flow of the story, with destruction, exile, and restoration fully integrated into the historical sequence."[42] This presentation presupposes that the compiler of 1 Esdras is the first to have created the continuity Chronicles–Ezra; but what if he was already working with a continuous composition? I dare to challenge the almost unanimous view that 1 Esdras is negligible as evidence regarding the existence of a continuous Chronicles–Ezra composition. Since the only outstanding contribution of 1 Esdras is the story of the youths, concerned with the return, I doubt whether the compiler would have bothered to look for a beginning other than the first year of Cyrus. More generally, the description of 1 Esdras, albeit of a different 1 Esdras from the one I know, as a carefully planned work is very appealing. I keep wondering, however, how a work can be recognized as an integrated composition, guided by such grand ideas, regardless of its abrupt beginning and ending, regardless of its mixture of genres, regardless of its unwarranted setting and jumbled chronology and course of events. The compiler of 1 Esdras is striving seriously with only one problem: how to integrate the story of the youths into the narrative of the return and set the stage for a deserving appearance of Zerubbabel in the history of his people. He may have had other ideas regarding the history of his people but his contribution to a different ideological image of the return is rather minor.

What makes 1 Esdras the work of an author rather than a compiler? I would think that the answer to this question does not emerge from his negligible contribution to the history of the return but rather from his part in the story of the youths. Did the story exist independently in its entirety, and all the compiler did was to integrate it in an extant, canonical composition type of the return

---

41. Williamson, "1 Esdras," 851–52.
42. Japhet, "1 Esdras," 753.

history? Did he write only the transition verses at the beginning of ch. 5? Or, is he also responsible for the epilogue that identifies the third youth as Zerubbabel and turns him into the redeemer of the people? Did he write the final speech about truth, or did he write the entire story? The answer to these questions would make the difference between author and compiler. If we only knew.

8. Conclusions

The above presentation of the compiler at work in 1 Esdras naturally raises the core question regarding the nature of the parallel canonical books, mainly Ezra–Nehemiah; are they also the product of compilation procedures comparable to those at work in 1 Esdras? Of course they are. The book of Ezra–Nehemiah is a cluttered book, parts of which easily fall apart, revealing the artificial fusion of materials that compose both the account of the first return in Ezra 1–6 as well as the combined narrative of Ezra and Nehemiah in the rest of the book (Ezra 7–Neh 13). However, when we return to the question of the interrelationship between these compositions, it becomes quite clear that while the compiler of Ezra–Nehemiah exercised his redactional skills on sources whose nature we can only imagine, the compiler of 1 Esdras was operating vis-à-vis sources that are well known to us, that is, a composition that ran parallel to the canonical books of Chronicles–Ezra–Nehemiah. We are not in the position to reconstruct the Ur-composition of the books under discussion, but the interrelationship between the surviving compositions is, in my opinion, very clear.

LITERARY QUESTIONS BETWEEN EZRA, NEHEMIAH, AND 1 ESDRAS

James C. VanderKam

I. INTRODUCTION: 1 ESDRAS AS REWRITTEN SCRIPTURE

Experts have taken several approaches to 1 Esdras and its relation to Chronicles, Ezra, and Nehemiah. According to advocates of the Fragment Hypothesis, it is the only surviving part of an earlier version of the Chronicler's work, with that work understood to mean Chronicles–Ezra–Nehemiah. This approach, which responds to various issues such as the curious beginning and ending of 1 Esdras, rests on the rather large assumption that there once existed an entire edition of Chronicles–Ezra–Nehemiah that we do not have other than what remains of it in 1 Esdras.[1] A competing view, the Compilation Hypothesis, holds that the book was fashioned by taking selections from Chronicles–Ezra–Nehemiah, that is, it is a secondary use of existing materials chosen and shaped to make the compiler's points.[2] Tamara Eskenazi has defended a third approach: 1 Esdras is "a distinct composition" written by the Chronicler, using Ezra–Nehemiah as a source and bringing the material in those books into conformity with the

---

1. Karl-Friedrich Pohlmann (*Studien zum dritten Esra: Ein Beitrag zur Frage nach dem ursprünglichen Schluss des chronistischen Geschichtswerkes* [FRLANT 104; Göttingen: Vandenhoeck & Ruprecht, 1970], 15-26) offers a convenient summary of the major approaches. Among the fundamental assumptions made by defenders of the fragment hypothesis he lists: 1 (3) Esdras cannot have been transmitted in its original form; both the beginning and end are broken from it. In addition, it is assumed that Josephus, who used 1 Esdras (*Ant.* 11.1-158), did not know the canonical Ezra and Nehemiah (p. 26). See also H. G. M. Williamson, "The Problem with First Esdras," in *After the Exile: Essays in Honour of Rex Mason* (ed. John Barton and David J. Reimer; Macon, Ga.: Mercer University Press, 1996), 201-16; repr. in idem, *Studies in Persian Period History and Historiography* (FAT 38; Tübingen: Mohr Siebeck, 2004), 294-305.

2. Among the assumptions underlying this approach is that the beginning and end of the book, which often strike readers as problematic, are as the compiler intended them to be (Pohlmann, *Studien zum dritten Esra*, 18-19).

thematic emphases and literary characteristics of the Chronicler.[3] Dieter Böhler maintains that 1 Esdras is prior to the canonical Ezra-Nehemiah, with Ezra being a rewriting of 1 Esdras to prepare the way for adding the Nehemiah material.[4] I prefer a version of the Compilation Hypothesis—a version that sees 1 Esdras as a rewriting of the older scriptural sections from the end of 2 Chronicles, Ezra especially, and a few lines from Nehemiah. In this essay I suggest some ways in which the Compilation Hypothesis, one that begins with the texts of Chronicles-Ezra-Nehemiah and of 1 Esdras that we have, allows one to explain certain central phenomena in 1 Esdras. One should read 1 Esdras as a literary work in its own right, but it is also helpful to compare it with what seem to me to be the older texts, to highlight differences and similarities.

If a version of the Compilation Hypothesis is correct, 1 Esdras may be classed as belonging to those works that are called rewritten Scripture (a term preferable to the anachronistic rewritten Bible).[5] In this limited sense one can agree with Eskenazi: "The former work [i.e., 1-2 Chronicles] interprets preexilic events, using Samuel-Kings as its primary source; the latter interprets postexilic events through the same lenses, using Ezra-Nehemiah as its source."[6] The authors of such works attached great importance to earlier scriptures, so much importance that they found it worthwhile to re-present them in light of contemporary circumstances. As we know from texts like the book of *Jubilees*, one interpretive concern among the several that motivated the authors of rewritten

---

3. Tamara C. Eskenazi, "The Chronicler and the Composition of 1 Esdras," *CBQ* 48 (1986): 39-61. She characterizes it as "a distinct composition" (that is, it was written as a separate exercise after the Chronicler had written 1-2 Chronicles) on p. 39.

4. Dieter Böhler, *Die heilige Stadt in Esdras α und Esra-Nehemia: Zwei Konzeptionen der Wiederherstellung Israels* (OBO 158; Freiburg: Universitätsverlag; Göttingen: Vandenhoeck & Ruprecht, 1997); idem, "On the Relationship between Textual and Literary Criticism: The Two Recensions of the Book of Ezra; Ezra-Neh (MT) and 1 Esdras (LXX)," in *The Earliest Text of the Hebrew Bible: The Relationship between the Masoretic Text and the Hebrew Base of the Septuagint Reconsidered* (ed. Adrian Schenker; SBLSCS 52; Atlanta: Society of Biblical Literature, 2003), 35-50. He bases his conclusions on a pattern of differences in textual detail between the two—a pattern related to the larger themes he finds in 1 Esdras and Ezra. Böhler develops the line of thought articulated by Adrian Schenker, "La Relation d'Esdras A' au texte massorétique d'Esdras-Néhémie," in *Tradition of the Text: Studies offered to Dominique Barthélemy in Celebration of His 70th Birthday* (ed. Gerard J. Norton and Stephen Pisano; OBO 109; Göttingen: Vandenhoeck & Ruprecht, 1991), 218-48.

5. The terminology has been the subject of numerous publications in recent decades. A helpful summary may be found in Daniel K. Falk, *The Parabiblical Texts: Strategies for Extending the Scriptures in the Dead Sea Scrolls* (Companion to the Qumran Scrolls 8; LSTS 63; Edinburgh: T&T Clark, 2007), 3-25. He does not think of rewritten Scripture as a genre so much as a technique for extending and interpreting a scriptural text. Williamson ("The Problem with First Esdras," 304-5) was, as far as I can tell, the first to categorize 1 Esdras as rewritten Bible (1996). [See now Williamson's article in the present volume.—Ed.]

6. Eskenazi, "The Chronicler and the Composition of 1 Esdras," 61. It is quite debatable whether the phrase "through the same lenses" is justified.

Scripture was solving problems encountered in the older text.[7] The writer of 1 Esdras certainly underscored some themes to a greater degree than one finds in Ezra—his primary base—but he also grappled with difficulties presented by the text of Ezra. That is, the book presents us with perhaps the most ancient interpretation of the book of Ezra and the earliest attempt to cope with puzzles in it.

II. ZERUBBABEL IN 1 ESDRAS

The theme on which I would like to focus, one often noted by the commentators and one having several subordinate points associated with it, is the larger place that Zerubbabel occupies in 1 Esdras than he commands in the book of Ezra. Eskenazi believes the stronger emphasis on Zerubbabel is one way in which the Chronicler made Ezra–Nehemiah more like his earlier work: in Chronicles he emphasized David and his dynasty; the form the theme takes in 1 Esdras is to highlight the Davidic heir Zerubbabel.[8] As a matter of fact, 1 Esdras makes very little of Zerubbabel's Davidic ancestry, with the result that it is difficult to see his role in 1 Esdras as echoing the Davidic theme in Chronicles. David as Zerubbabel's ancestor is mentioned only in 5:5, and contrary to 1 Chr 3:19, which names Pedaiah as his father, 1 Esd 5:5, 48 (// Ezra 3:2), 56 (// Ezra 3:8); 6:2 (// Ezra 5:2) list Shealtiel as his father—a clear and telling case in which 1 Esdras conforms with Ezra and not with Chronicles.[9]

Though it does not seem to be the case that the role of Zerubbabel extends the Davidic theme of Chronicles, he is transparently more prominent in 1 Esdras than he is in Ezra. In Ezra, Zerubbabel figures in four contexts: he is among the returnees enumerated in 2:1–67 (2:2 // Neh 7:7); he is involved in setting up the altar in 3:2, 8; he is the leader of the group that refuses the offer of help from "the adversaries of Judah and Benjamin" (4:2–3); and he is one of the four leaders who restart the process of building the temple in the second year of Darius (5:2; cf. also Neh 12:1, 47). Oddly enough, however, there is no mention of him in the narrative about the investigation by Tattenai and Shethar-bozenai or in the notice about completion of the temple-building project in the sixth year of Darius and the celebrations that ensued (5:3–6:22). With the suggestive importance attributed to Zerubbabel in the prophecies of Haggai (2:21, 23) and Zechariah (4:6, 7, 9, 10), his limited role in Ezra is surprising and has given rise to creative ideas about his "disappearance."

The writer of 1 Esdras pads Zerubbabel's résumé in several ways:

---

7. Among the assumptions underlying ancient exegesis, according to James Kugel, is "that Scripture is perfect and perfectly harmonious" (*Traditions of the Bible: A Guide to the Bible as It Was at the Start of the Common Era* [Cambridge, Mass.: Harvard University Press, 1998], 17).
8. Eskenazi, "The Chronicler and the Composition of 1 Esdras," 44–49.
9. Haggai (1:1, 12, 14; 2:2, 23) and Nehemiah (12:1) also identify Shealtiel as his father.

A. ZERUBBABEL IN THE STORY OF THE THREE YOUTHS (4:13; 5:5–6)

The major means is, of course, the new section about the debate among the three royal bodyguards and some surrounding material in 3:1–5:6. The section is not based on a pericope in Ezra and is thus a major innovation relative to the base text. The point stands, even if one concludes that the story originated elsewhere than in 1 Esdras.[10] The name Zerubbabel occurs at two points in the story, and naturally he is also designated by pronouns in each context.

The first passage in the story where Zerubbabel is named is 4:13, where the last of the three guards is introduced with the words: "the third, who had spoken of women and the truth (and this was Zerubbabel), began to speak ...." The commentators are agreed in characterizing the phrase ουτος εστιν Ζοροβαβελ as a gloss.[11] One can make a reasonable case that most of the story of the bodyguards is from a separate, possibly non-Jewish source and that only the identification of the third and victorious young man as Zerubbabel won it a place in 1 Esdras.[12] As we will see, some important consequences follow from the section that describes what happened after the debate—4:42–63—where there are several more references to Zerubbabel though not by name: he reminds Darius of his vow to rebuild Jerusalem and the temple and to return the sacred vessels to it; and he receives royal letters to ease his journey to the land where with royal support he is to rebuild Jerusalem, improve the lives of Jews, and support the temple cult and clergy. He also responds with grateful praise to God and rejoices with his fellow Jews "because he [Darius] had given them release and permission to go up and build Jerusalem and the temple that is called by his name; and they feasted, with music and rejoicing, for seven days" (4:62–63).

---

10. Zipora Talshir (*1 Esdras: From Origin to Translation* [SBLSCS 47; Atlanta: Society of Biblical Literature, 1999], 58) thinks that the "... Story of the Youths was the catalyst for the formation of I Esdras—its *raison d'être*. I Esdras was created in order to interpolate the Story of the Youths into the story of the Restoration, and the whole book has no real existence apart from it." The story is important, but it is difficult to see it as the main reason for forming the book. The compiler does not expend much effort to incorporate it into the book through cross-references and allusions; it is mentioned in no other passage in 1 Esdras.

11. The same words are found at 4:61 in the Lucianic MSS (see Robert Hanhart, *Esdrae Liber I* [2d ed.; Septuaginta Vetus Testamentum Graecum 8/1; Göttingen: Vandenhoeck & Ruprecht, 1991], 79; and S. A. Cook, "I Esdras," APOT 1:31, n. to v. 13). For the words as an interpolation, see H. Guthe, "Das dritte Buch Esra," APAT 1:8 n. b; Richard J. Coggins, "The First Book of Esdras," in Richard J. Coggins and Michael A. Knibb, *The First and Second Books of Esdras* (CBC; Cambridge: Cambridge University Press, 1979), 29–30; Jacob M. Myers, *I and II Esdras: A New Translation with Introduction and Commentary* (AB 42; Garden City, N.Y.: Doubleday, 1974), 53, 55; Talshir, *1 Esdras: From Origin to Translation*, 77; idem, *1 Esdras: A Text Critical Commentary* (SBLSCS 50; Atlanta: Society of Biblical Literature, 2001), 187, 249–50.

12. If so, the writer probably introduced some scriptural allusions such as the echo of Gen 2:24 in 4:40. The exclamation "Blessed be the God of truth" in 4:40 may also be less than ecumenical.

The second explicit mention of Zerubbabel in the story of the youths is at the very end of the section—5:5-6. In a list of those who migrated to the land, there is "Joakim son of Zerubbabel son of Shealtiel, of the house of David, of the lineage of Phares, of the tribe of Judah, who spoke wise words before King Darius of the Persians, in the second year of his reign, in the month of Nisan, the first month." Here too the commentators are agreed that the text is disturbed. First Esdras 5:5 lists the priests who returned to the land. They are: "the priests, the descendants of Phinehas son of Aaron: Jeshua son of Jozadak son of Seraiah and Joakim son of Zerubbabel. ...." The book of Nehemiah records a Joakim who followed his father Jeshua as the second high priest of the postexilic period; Zerubbabel, however, according to the genealogy of Chronicles (1 Chr 3:19-20), had no son named Joakim. These bits of evidence suggest that the name Joakim belongs to the priestly segment of the genealogical statement and not to the part about the family of Zerubbabel that is recorded after it. Talshir has hypothesized an original text that, through haplography, has resulted in the confused lineage of 5:5-6: Jeshua son of Jozadak son of Seraiah and Joakim *his son; and* Zerubbabel ....[13] It seems likely the text should have read something like this. It is the only passage in 1 Esdras that mentions the Davidic ancestry of Zerubbabel.

B. ADDITIONS OF THE NAME ZERUBBABEL (6:18, 27, 29)

A second way in which the compiler makes Zerubbabel more prominent in his book than he is in Ezra is by adding his name to three passages that have parallels in Ezra. The references to Zerubbabel unique to 1 Esdras (other than the ones in 4:13 and 5:5) are analyzed below.

First Esdras 6:18, though it is parallel to Ezra 5:14, which says that Cyrus gave the temple vessels to Sheshbazzar, says: "And the holy vessels of gold and silver, which Nebuchadnezzar had taken out of the house in Jerusalem and stored in his own temple, these King Cyrus took out again from the temple in Babylon, and they were delivered to Zerubbabel and Sheshbazzar the governor...." Compare v. 20 (only Sheshbazzar) and Ezra 5:16. The fact that the passage, in both 1 Esdras and Ezra, continues with singular forms, as if Cyrus gave the vessels to just one person, and identifies this individual as Sheshbazzar betrays the secondary character of Zerubbabel's name in 1 Esd 6:18. The addition seems clumsy but relates to the theme met earlier in the book (4:43-44, 57), where Zerubbabel does indeed receive temple vessels but gets them from Darius, although Cyrus was the one who had initially set them aside for delivery (see

---

13. Talshir, *1 Esdras: From Origin to Translation*, 51-52; idem, *1 Esdras: A Text Critical Commentary*, 249-50. She thinks the confusion would have been more likely in Hebrew than in Aramaic, but I think that the possessive suffix marked by the letter *he* in "his son" would more easily have led to omission before the *vav-zayin* combination at the beginning of "and Zerubbabel," that is, the mistake is easier to imagine in Aramaic.

below). Hence it was not entirely inappropriate to say that Zerubbabel had obtained the vessels from Cyrus. It is worth adding that the name Zerubbabel is not present here in a number of copies of 1 Esdras and is not found at this point in Josephus, *Ant.* 11.93.[14]

1 Esdras 6:27	Ezra 6:7
… and to permit Zerubbabel, the servant of the Lord and governor of Judea, and the elders of the Jews to build this house of the Lord on its site.	… let the governor of the Jews and the elders of the Jews rebuild this house of God on its site.

The addition is a simple one, specifying who the governor of the Jews was—an easy identification to make in the context. The title "servant of the Lord" is an interesting one. It could come from Hag 2:23; Zech 3:8, where the deity calls Zerubbabel "my servant," but the appearance of the title here may have been encouraged by or may even be a variant reading of the phrase "the *work* on this house of God," reading '*bd* in place of '*bydt*.[15]

1 Esdras 6:29	Ezra 6:8
… a portion be scrupulously given to these men, that is, to Zerubbabel the governor, …	… the cost is to be paid to these people, in full and without delay…

This reference to Zerubbabel, too, looks less than skillfully done: the text names a group ("these people"), and 1 Esdras identifies the group as Zerubbabel alone. Insertion of Zerubbabel is a transparent attempt to add detail to the less specific text of Ezra and to keep his name before the reader.[16]

---

14. See the apparatus in Hanhart, *Esdrae Liber I*, 109. Talshir thinks "Zerubbabel" was a gloss that became part of the text, perhaps intended originally to identify Sheshbazzar and Zerubbabel (*1 Esdras: A Text Critical Commentary*, 346). Coggins's explanation seems more likely: "Only at one point is an addition made which may give a significant pointer to the concern of I Esdras: the addition of the name Zerubbabel in v. 18 … is a further indication of the importance attributed to him in the whole enterprise" ("The First Book of Esdras," 50).

15. Cook, "I Esdras," 44, n. to v. 27; Talshir, *1 Esdras: A Text Critical Commentary*, 357–59 (a deliberate change); idem, *1 Esdras: From Origin to Translation*, 53.

16. Although she seemed to accept it in *1 Esdras: From Origin to Translation*, 53–54, Talshir (*1 Esdras: A Text Critical Commentary*, 362) rejects the creative attempt of J. A. Bewer to explain the addition of "Zerubbabel the governor" to the text of Ezra. Bewer related the words to the expression ומה חשׁון in Ezra 6:9a. They are not represented in our text of 1 Esdras but would have been translated into Greek as επαρκως ("sufficiently"), which was corrupted into επαρχω ("governor"). Once the title "governor" was in the text, it was a simple step to identify him as Zerubbabel. One of the problems with this solution, as Talshir indicates, is that the phrase would be transported to a different place in 1 Esdras than it occupies in Ezra. See J. A. Bewer, *Der Text des Buches Esra* (FRLANT 31; Göttingen: Vandenhoeck & Ruprecht, 1922).

Each of these unique references is problematic in some sense, and all of them have the look of notes inserted into an existing but less detailed text. Such a state of affairs is more consistent with the idea that 1 Esdras is a revision of an older text, not a reflection of the original text itself.

C. ZERUBBABEL AND NEHEMIAH

Zipora Talshir, in the course of analyzing the enhanced status of Zerubbabel in 1 Esdras, has shown that a number of traits borne by Nehemiah in the book named for him are assigned to Zerubbabel in 1 Esdras. Instances that are especially telling are the strong parallels between the subjects of the written grants given by Darius to Zerubbabel in 1 Esdras and those given by Artaxerxes to Nehemiah in the book of Nehemiah. In Neh 2:7-8 he requests letters to the governors of Beyond the River, to allow him and his band to travel through the areas on the way, and to Asaph, the keeper of the royal forest, requisitioning wood for the city construction he planned. "These are the two specific requests made by Nehemiah: a letter of safe passage and a permit to procure timber. These are precisely the two first things granted Zerubbabel in the letters Darius writes for him [1 Esd 4:47-48]."[17] Both leaders were involved in constructing the city, and both were concerned about the needs of the priests and Levites.[18] Talshir does think the failure of Nehemiah to play a role in 1 Esdras resulted from purposeful omission and relates this and the enhanced role of Zerubbabel in 1 Esdras to the "strained relations" between the leading characters (Sheshbazzar vs. Zerubbabel, Ezra vs. Nehemiah), as evidenced in later Jewish literature.[19]

Theories of this sort are, of course, hypothetical and related to larger decisions about the nature of 1 Esdras.[20] It is, nevertheless, not easy to avoid the

---

17. Talshir, *1 Esdras: From Origin to Translation*, 49.

18. Talshir, *1 Esdras: From Origin to Translation*, 49-50. The fact that Zerubbabel was involved with rebuilding Jerusalem makes it unlikely that Nehemiah's involvement in political matters was the reason he was omitted from 1 Esdras, contrary to A. E. Gardner, "The Purpose and Date of I Esdras," *JJS* 37 (1986): 25.

19. Talshir, *1 Esdras: From Origin to Translation*, 55-57. She rightly rejects Eskenazi's claim that Nehemiah was omitted because he lacked a Davidic ancestry (55).

20. Take, for instance, the theory of Charles C. Torrey (*Ezra Studies* [Chicago: University of Chicago Press, 1910; repr., New York: Ktav, 1970]) who thought the failure of the Nehemiah material to appear was an accident. He regarded 1 Esdras as "the one surviving fragment of the Old Greek version of the Chronicler's history...." (34). He added: "The extent of our First Esdras, it is hardly necessary to add, is due simply to accident Probably all the manuscripts, Semitic or Greek, which contained any other version than the official one were systematically destroyed. Just as the Old Greek version of Daniel narrowly escaped the fate which befell its Semitic original, being saved only in a single Greek codex and a secondary version, so this portion of the condemned Esdras recension was rescued by a lucky chance. There was only one such fragment, and all of our 'I Esdras' texts and translations go back to it. It probably consisted of a few quires plucked out of the middle of a codex" (34, 36).

conclusion that Zerubbabel is in some ways exalted at the expense of Nehemiah. Dieter Böhler thinks that a fundamental difference between Ezra and 1 Esdras has to do with this very subject: for him, it is no accident that the book of Nehemiah follows the book of Ezra, which prepares for it (e.g., by picturing Jerusalem as remaining in ruins so that Nehemiah can come and rebuild it), while 1 Esdras not only lacks the Nehemiah story but also in no way prepares for it, since it presents the city as rebuilt before Nehemiah's time. He also argues that the relocation of the Artaxerxes correspondence and the omission in 1 Esdras of the king's verdict "that this city not be rebuilt, *until I make a decree*" (Ezra 4:21; 1 Esd 2:28 reads: "Therefore I have now issued orders to prevent these people from building the city and to take care that nothing more be done ...") fit with the same thematic difference.[21] He finds in the two books two coherent but different stories about the restoration.

Böhler has highlighted evidence of some places in which the two books read differently, but it is inaccurate to say that Ezra pictures Jerusalem in ruins while 1 Esdras pictures it as rebuilt. In Ezra 7–10 Jerusalem does not appear to be in such a derelict state; it is mentioned a few times and assumed to be a functioning city where people live (4:6; 5:1) and where they gather for important meetings (10:7, 9; cf. 3:1). The book nowhere describes Jerusalem as Neh 1:3; 2:3, 13, 17 do. The same is the case in 1 Esdras, in which the author draws out from passages in Ezra what appear to him to be reasonable inferences. Note, for example, 1 Esd 8:81 and Ezra 9:9, part of Ezra's prayer in which he recalls what the kings of Persia have done through God's favor:

1 Esdras 8:81	Ezra 9:9
... glorified the temple of our Lord, and raised Zion from desolation, to give us a stronghold in Judea and Jerusalem.	... to set up the house of our God, to repair its ruins, and to give us a wall in Judea and Jerusalem.

The author of 1 Esdras understands the words "to repair its ruins" in Ezra 9:9 to refer to Zion, that is, Jerusalem, but it probably does so because of the following clause, which includes both Judea and Jerusalem in some sort of

---

21. Böhler, *Die heilige Stadt*, e.g. 120–22, 141–42. If the statement in Ezra 4:22 prepares for Nehemiah's rebuilding of the city walls at Artaxerxes's command, it does so in a clumsy way. The reader of Ezra, presented with the order of the letters in the MT version, would infer that work on the city *and* temple resumed in Darius' second year, not that the city project was abandoned until Nehemiah's time. Although Ezra and Nehemiah are regularly regarded as a single work, this seems unlikely to me. For the evidence, see VanderKam, "Ezra–Nehemiah or Ezra and Nehemiah?" in *Priests, Prophets, and Scribes: Essays on the Formation and Heritage of Second Temple Judaism in Honour of Joseph Blenkinsopp* (ed. Eugene C. Ulrich, John W. Wright, Robert P. Carroll, and Philip R. Davies; JSOTSup 149; Sheffield: JSOT Press, 1992), 55–75.

positive statement.[22] Whatever Nehemiah later accomplishes, the book of Ezra does little to prepare for it. The writer of Ezra seems to assume that the two rebuilding programs—city and temple—occurred during the same period, though the interest in chapters 1–6 is clearly focused on the temple more than on the city.

III. Reordering Sections of the Book of Ezra

Zerubbabel plays a role in another problem-solving exercise conducted by the writer of 1 Esdras. All historically informed readers of Ezra encounter the notorious chronological crux served up by Ezra 4 and 5. As is well known, Ezra 4:24 says that work on the temple, stopped by Artaxerxes (465–424 B.C.E.), did not resume until the second year of Darius (520 B.C.E.), some sixty or more years before the work was halted. Moreover, according to Ezra 6:14–15, the temple reached completion on Adar 3 in the sixth year of Darius, that is, in 515 B.C.E., long before Artaxerxes could have interfered with the construction project. Commentators regularly observe that the Artaxerxes section in Ezra is out of chronological order and also does not concern the temple but only the city of Jerusalem. A suggestion has been that it was added for thematic reasons: the writer grouped in one place all the Aramaic correspondence dealing with the restoration of Jerusalem and its temple.

Actually, the true solution to the impossible chronological arrangement seems now to have been found by Richard Steiner, who argues that the present sequence has arisen from copying the archive of the correspondence regarding Jerusalem; in it, the earlier letters are appended to the one that addresses the current situation, with a result that the chronological order is reversed.[23] But the writer of 1 Esdras, confronted with the sequence as it stands in Ezra 4–6 and presumably with limited knowledge about Persian history and practice, attempted to solve the problem in a different way.

One of the most familiar variations between Ezra and 1 Esdras is the revised placement of the first section relating to Artaxerxes. Ezra 4:7–24a = 1 Esd 2:16–30 is relocated to a spot following Ezra 1 = 1 Esd 2:1–15. Hence, in 1 Esdras it

---

22. See Talshir, *1 Esdras: From Origin to Translation*, 44–46; idem, *1 Esdras: A Text Critical Commentary*, 449–50. In the latter place, she considers the reference to Zion in 1 Esd 8:81 "one of the most telling differences between the canonical books and I Esdr," but, as she correctly recognizes in the former (45 n. 67), 1 Esdras may simply be interpreting the words found in Ezra 9:9. Böhler, who refers to others who hold that 1 Esdras is here interpreting Ezra 9:9, considers this improbable, since the work tends to contract a noun to a pronoun rather than the opposite (see *Die heilige Stadt*, 158–64, for his discussion of the passage).

23. Richard Steiner, "Bishlam's Archival Search Report in Nehemiah's Archive: Multiple Introductions and Reverse Chronological Order as Clues to the Origin of the Aramaic Letters in Ezra 4–6," *JBL* 125 (2006): 641–85.

figures right after the chapter about Cyrus, the temple vessels, and Sheshbazzar, and it precedes the list of returnees in Ezra 2 (a list that includes Zerubbabel). The common conclusion drawn from the dislocation is that, while the writer of 1 Esdras was trying to cope with the chronological difficulty in Ezra 4:7–24a, he actually made it worse by moving a section that deals with a much later time (the fifth century) even earlier than it is in Ezra, where it is already too early by more than sixty years.[24]

I think we should give the writer of 1 Esdras more credit than he usually receives. He not only recognized the chronological issue but others as well and tried to solve them in a comprehensive, logical way, as did other authors of the works we call rewritten Scripture.

He also noticed that three Persian monarchs were involved in the lengthy process of rebuilding the temple. Ezra 6:14–15 // 1 Esd 7:3–5 says: "So the elders of the Jews built and prospered, through the prophesying of the prophet Haggai and Zechariah son of Iddo. They finished their building by command of the God of Israel and by decree of Cyrus, Darius, and King Artaxerxes of Persia; and this house was finished on the twenty-third day of the month of Adar, in the sixth year of the reign of King Darius."[25] All three kings made decrees concerning building the temple, and the last of them must have been Darius because the project reached completion in his sixth year.[26] From the data in Ezra, one could infer that Artaxerxes must, therefore, have preceded Darius. Otherwise, how could he have issued a decree about halting the building of the temple if it was already rebuilt before his time? Josephus solved the problem by identifying this king as Cambyses (*Ant.* 11.21–30), as did some later readers of the text.[27] We need not think our author had a thorough understanding of the sequence of the Persian kings, just as the editor of the Daniel court tales puts them in an odd order.[28] The repeated names in the royal list could have caused other problems.

The writer knew, furthermore, that Cyrus was the one credited with setting the project in motion, as Ezra 1 = 1 Esd 2:1–15 made clear. That section explains that Cyrus had issued a decree to build the house of God and had given orders to return the temple vessels. The Jewish official to whom they were given was Sheshbazzar, and he brought them to Jerusalem. Other than bringing the articles to Jerusalem, Ezra 1 says nothing about any work on temple construction or use

---

24. See, for example, the summary in Emil Schürer, "The Greek Ezra (Also Called III Ezra or I Esdras)," in *The History of the Jewish People in the Age of Jesus Christ (175 B.C.–A.D. 135)* (rev. and ed. Geza Vermes, Fergus Millar, and Martin Goodman; 3 vols.; Edinburgh: T&T Clark, 1973–87), 3:709 (and see the comments on 710).

25. At 1 Esd 7:4 the Lucianic texts have the following order: Cyrus, Artaxerxes, Darius (Hanhart, *Esdrae Liber I*, 113).

26. Cf. Böhler, *Die heilige Stadt*, 137–38.

27. See Böhler, *Die heilige Stadt*, 127 n. 125.

28. See Böhler, *Die heilige Stadt*, 136–37 n. 145, for other examples in early Jewish sources.

of the vessels. Other clues in Ezra and elsewhere suggested that not much had been accomplished in this initial stage (see, e.g., Hag 1:1–11).

We should note in addition that in two places our writer adds a statement regarding Cyrus and the temple vessels: in 4:43–44, Zerubbabel reminds King Darius that he had vowed to build Jerusalem and "to send back all the vessels that were taken from Jerusalem, which Cyrus set apart [εξεχωρισεν] ...; 4:57, using the same verb, says that Darius "sent back from Babylon all the vessels that Cyrus had set apart; everything that Cyrus had ordered to be done, he also commanded to be done and to be sent to Jerusalem." Our author admits to some repetition: Darius recapitulates what Cyrus had done. It seems he is telling us that Darius may have completed the process of returning materials by repatriating ones Cyrus had not returned but merely "set aside."

I wonder—and it is only speculation—whether he is responding to the fact that Ezra consistently says of Cyrus that he returned the gold and silver vessels of the temple (1:7–11 5:14–15; cf. 7:19; 8:25–30, 33), whereas it is obvious from 1 Kgs 7:13–47 that many utensils of the sanctuary were made of bronze ("vessels" is the term for them there [see vv. 45, 47]), while others were of gold (vv. 48–50) and silver (see 2 Kgs 12:13; 14:14; 16:8 [?]; 18:15; 24:13). The summary of the items Nebuchadnezzar's officer Nebuzaradan took from the temple, after mention of the large bronze objects that he broke down for transport (25:13), reads: "They took away the pots, the shovels, the snuffers, the dishes for incense, and all the bronze vessels used in the temple service, as well as the firepans and the basins. What was made of gold the captain of the guard took away for the gold, and what was made of silver, for the silver. As for the two pillars, the one sea, and the stands, which Solomon had made for the house of the Lord, the bronze of all these vessels was beyond weighing" (25:14–16; see also 2 Chr 4; 24:14; in Ezra 7:19 Artaxerxes speaks of giving vessels for the temple to Ezra). This would suggest that Cyrus had not returned the vessels made of bronze. Our author may be implying that Cyrus had set these aside, returning only those of gold and silver. Perhaps he concluded that Darius returned the others not sent by Cyrus.

If Cyrus was the one who set in motion the sanctuary-building project and Darius was ruling when it came to an end, there was only one logical place for Artaxerxes and that was between Cyrus and Darius. I presume the author thought this was the correct sequence of the three Persian monarchs praised in Ezra 6:14.

Our writer also realized another difficulty in Ezra, this one, too, involving Zerubbabel. This Davidic prince was transparently associated with the time of Darius. The only explicit dates regarding him make the point. Ezra 4:24 mentions the second year of Darius as the time until which work on the temple stopped, and 5:1–2, the immediate sequel, then mentions that Zerubbabel, Jeshua, and the two prophets were involved in restarting it. The report about

Tattenai's investigation and correspondence with Darius follows. So, Zerubbabel was solidly associated with Darius' reign, specifically the second year. The dates in the books of Haggai and Zechariah confirm the Zerubbabel–Darius connection. As we have seen, the writer of 1 Esdras works Zerubbabel into the Darius correspondence, though Ezra does not.

Yet Zerubbabel is mentioned already in the list found in Ezra 2 and he was active in the events of altar building in Ezra 3. Indeed, Ezra 3:8 says: "In the second year after their arrival at the house of God, in the second month, Zerubbabel son of Shealtiel and Jeshua son of Jozadak made a beginning ...." For a writer who knew that Zerubbabel was tied to Darius' second year, when he was instrumental in restarting construction of the sanctuary, the second year here could only mean the second year of Darius. This entailed that the passage referred to the time of Darius and to that of the construction work that was successfully completed in just four years. The relatively short duration of the grand project may also have suggested to him that there could have been no time-consuming opposition after this point. Another implication for the writer was that the list in chapter 2, in which Zerubbabel is mentioned, must relate to the time of Darius, not to that of Cyrus, when Sheshbazzar was the governor.

Consequently, in order to restore the sections of Ezra to their proper order, our writer moved 4:7–24a before the list of returnees in chapter 2 and the story of the beginning of the temple building in Ezra 3. Both of these had to do with the time of Zerubbabel, and Zerubbabel worked during the reign of Darius, the king when the temple was completed.

By placing Ezra 4:7–24a directly after Ezra 1 and before any mention of Zerubbabel, the writer also found a logical place for the story about stopping the work of building the house of God. He, like many other readers of Ezra 4, understood the section to be talking about the temple as well as the city Jerusalem, perhaps reasoning that Jerusalem could hardly be called *rebuilt* if it lacked the temple. He revised the section so that it mentioned the temple a couple of times; his editorial work was not done in an arbitrary way.

1 Esdras 2:18	*Ezra 4:12*
Let it now be known to our lord the king that the Jews who came up from you to us have gone to Jerusalem and are building	May it be known to the king that the Jews who came up from you to us have gone to Jerusalem. They are rebuilding that rebellious and wicked city;
that rebellious and wicked city, repairing its market places and walls and laying the foundations for a temple.	they are finishing the walls and repairing the foundations.

Since Ezra 3 had credited Zerubbabel, Jeshua, and others with laying the temple foundations, it is not surprising that our writer understood *foundations* here to be those of the temple.

1 Esdras 2:20	*Ezra* 4:14
Since the building of the temple is now going on, we think it best not to neglect such a matter, but speak to our lord the king	Now because we share the salt of the palace and it is not fitting for us to witness the king's dishonor, therefore we send and inform the king.

There have been several suggestions for how one gets from "share the salt of the palace" to "the building of the temple is now going on." The word for palace (*hêkĕlā'*) could have been interpreted as "temple," and the salt terms (*mlḥ*, verb and noun) could have been confused with ones for work (*mĕlā'ka'*).[29]

IV. CONCLUSION

To sum up, it seems likely that 1 Esdras is based on an earlier text, that of Chronicles, Ezra, and Nehemiah—especially Ezra. Sections from Ezra and a few from 2 Chronicles and Nehemiah were selected and rewritten to allow the writer to present his understanding of the destruction and the waves of returnees who took part in the restoration. The book maintains that the restoration of the city and temple went hand in hand. The author chose to make Zerubbabel a more prominent character than the book of Ezra did, perhaps in order to have a more impressive political figure associated with the early phases of the restoration when the city and temple were built. To this end he also added a story (3:1–5:6), in which he inserted Zerubbabel's name and borrowed traits for him from Nehemiah. While Zerubbabel is exalted at the expense of Nehemiah, who is not mentioned, many of the changes in 1 Esdras relative to the base texts are, in the first place, exegetical in nature and meant to clarify the text and flow of the story. The writer was presumably aware of the book of Nehemiah (if he transferred traits from him to Zerubbabel, he would have known the book) and purposely omitted it from his rewriting. Experts have understandably argued that the omission was tendentious; attributing traits of Nehemiah to Zerubbabel in 1 Esdras and saying nothing about Nehemiah could point in that direction. Yet, the author may have seen no need, in his rewriting of Ezra, to add the story about rebuilding the city walls, possibly thinking it related to a later situation with which he was not dealing. In that case, the failure of the Nehemiah story to follow on the present end of 1 Esdras should not be regarded as polemical.

---

29. See Talshir, *1 Esdras: A Text Critical Commentary*, 113.

REMEMBER NEHEMIAH:
1 ESDRAS AND THE *DAMNATIO MEMORIAE NEHEMIAE*

Jacob L. Wright

To Sara Japhet

INTRODUCTION

The phrase *damnatio memoriae* in modern idiom describes a practice of the Senate of the Roman Empire officially condemning a ruler or member of the elite after his death. In pronouncing an *abolitio nominis* on an individual, the Senate sanctioned not only the seizure of his property but also the erasure of his memory—from annals, official lists (*fasti*), coins, inscriptions, and statues. Thus, after Lucius Aelius Seianus attempted to overthrow the emperor Tiberius, his statues were torn down and his name was struck from the public record and scratched off coins. In other cases, such as that of Marcus Opellius Marcrinus, books written by the condemned were confiscated and burned. As Eric Varner observes in *Mutilation and Transformation*, "The Romans themselves realized that it was possible to alter posterity's perception of the past especially as embodied in the visual and epigraphic record."[1]

The practice of (de facto) *damnatio memoriae* is not unique to the Roman Empire. Indeed, it is attested in most ancient societies and continues today in various forms. In the world of academia, for example, it is known as historical revisionism. With respect to ancient societies, we have rich evidence from both Egypt and western Asia for the alteration or defacement of epigraphic and iconographic memories. One should distinguish *damnatio memoriae* from iconoclasm and usurpation. Akhenaten's actions against Egyptian deities were, properly speaking, iconoclastic, while the attempts of Horemheb and the Ramessides to erase the memory of Akhenaten and his three immediate successsors belong to the category of *damnatio memoriae*. Similarly, one may have attempted to erase

---

1. Eric R. Varner, *Mutilation and Transformation: Damnatio memoriae and Roman Imperial Portraiture* (Monumenta Graeca et Romana; Leiden: Brill, 2004), 1.

certain aspects of history, such as Hatshepsut's full status as pharaoh.[2] To these cases we may add Egyptian attempts to suppress the memory of private, nonroyal *personae non gratae* such as the viceroys from the Eighteenth Dynasty, Usersatet and Nakhtmin, as well as Rekhmire and Menna.[3] In addition to the destruction or deportation of statues, monuments, and other symbols of an opponent's power, the archeological record from western Asia knows many examples of a victor erasing names in order either to wipe out his enemy's memory or to usurp his monument. The fear that a later generation might blot out and supplant inscribed names resonates in the imprecations engraved on a wide array of durable memory media.[4]

In ancient Israelite society, memory erasure may be studied in relation to the destruction of progeny, statues, cultic spaces and objects, monumental architecture and landscapes, municipalities ("urbicide"), place names, and not least inscriptions (e.g., the Tel Dan inscription, which appears to have been intentionally shattered at a later time),[5] libraries, and portable texts.[6] The theme of memory preservation and erasure reverberates throughout biblical literature. One encounters it, for example, in the commands to wipe out the memory of "Canaanite" cult and culture (e.g., Deut 7:24-25), in its notions of the deity keeping heavenly books from which names can be erased, and in the way its authors themselves commemorate names, events, and places from Israel's past and homeland.[7] The memory-mindedness of the biblical authors reflects a larger concern for the survival of self and society after the ravages of war. It belongs to the project of building peoplehood in response to the dangers posed by the politics of statehood. An indispensable component in this project of forming an Israelite collective identity is biblical historiography.[8] Its practitioners knew not

---

2. See Catherine Roehrig et al., eds., *Hatshepsut: From Queen to Pharaoh* (New Haven: Yale University Press, 2005).

3. See discussion in Peter James Brand, *The Monuments of Seti I: Epigraphic, Historical and Art Historical Analysis* (Probleme der Aegyptologie 16; Leiden: Brill, 2000).

4. See Karen Radner, *Die Macht des Namens: Altorientalische Strategien zur Selbsterhaltung* (Santag 8; Wiesbaden: Harrassowitz, 2005), 252–66.

5. Relevant to this topic is the conference, organized by Natalie N. May, at the University of Chicago's Oriental Institute on "Iconoclasm and Text Destruction in the Ancient Near East" (April 2011).

6. I plan to discuss this memory erasure in relationship to ancient Israel in a forthcoming study (to be published by Oxford University Press).

7. With respect to a culture of commemoration in Hellenistic-period Judah, the prologue to Ben Sira's "Praise of the Ancestors" (44:1–15) witnesses to a possible formal, ritual setting in which the names of national heroes were commemorated with the help of texts like "Praise of the Ancestors." The final lines call on the congregation collectively to join the reader in proclaiming the praise of great figures.

8. For the importance of stories to the formation of a collective identity, see most recently Rogers M. Smith, *Stories of Peoplehood: The Politics and Morals of Political Membership* (Cambridge: Cambridge University Press, 2003).

only how to remember, by collecting, combining, and composing texts, but also how to forget, by omitting, editing, and erasing memories they deemed deleterious to their visions of society and community.

Against this backdrop, we can better appreciate the anxiety that permeates Nehemiah's memoir with respect to the potential amnesia of his human and divine audience. Throughout his account, he petitions the deity to remember his own meritorious deeds as well as the transgressions of his enemies. To those who would wish upon Nehemiah ימח שמו וזכרו ("May his name and memory be wiped out!"), Ben Sira's later encomium responds יאדר זכרו ("May his memory be glorified!"). In conclusion to a passage of his memoir in which he sharply censures the Jerusalem priesthood (13:4–14), Nehemiah utters an earnest plea to his divine and human readers: ואל תמח חסדי אשר עשיתי בבית אלהי ובמשמריו, "Do not wipe out my good deeds that I performed for the house of God and for its service!" Yet, as I seek to show in this paper, the pro-priestly authors of 1 Esdras did not heed this plea.

In *Rebuilding Identity* I argue that the emergence of the book of Ezra–Nehemiah should be viewed as a history of responses to Nehemiah's first-person account by the first generations of the account's readers.[9] That this thesis bears directly upon the dating and interpretation of 1 Esdras is not coincidental. My aim was, not least, to provide a context for understanding the existence of 1 Esdras, whose most salient feature, when viewed from the perspective of Ezra–Nehemiah, is the complete absence of Nehemiah's first-person account, on the one hand, and the substantial augmentation of the account of Zerubbabel with the story of the youths, on the other.

The question of the priority of Ezra–Nehemiah—and, as I argue, the ultimate priority of the Nehemiah memoir—is by no means a peripheral one; to the contrary, it is critical to the appreciation of the social, political, and theological forces that shaped Second Temple history and that produced these two books. According to the findings of my analyses, Nehemiah's account posed many problems for early generations of readers. They responded to it by 1) contextualizing this account in a wider historical framework (Ezra–Nehemiah); 2) transforming the image of Nehemiah (the Nehemiah legend in 2 Maccabees); 3) removing the portions of it that were problematic (Josephus); or 4) removing his account entirely from the history of the restoration (1 Esdras).

Other scholars have already made a compelling case for the priority of Ezra–Nehemiah on text-critical grounds.[10] The present article presents a different

---

9. Jacob L. Wright, *Rebuilding Identity: The Nehemiah Memoir and Its Earliest Readers* (BZAW 348; Berlin: de Gruyter, 2004).

10. See Edmund Bayer, *Das dritte Buch Esdras und sein Verhältnis zu den Büchern Esra-Nehemia* (BibS[F] 16/1 Freiburg Herder, 1911); Bernhard Walde, *Die Esdrasbücher der Septuaginta, ihr gegenseitiges Verhältnis untersucht* (BibS[F] 18/4; Freiburg: Herder, 1913); Zipora Talshir, *1 Esdras: From Origin to Translation* (SBLSCS 47; Atlanta: Society of Biblical

argument against the priority of 1 Esdras and offers some suggestions as to how one might view the composition of this work. It begins with a discussion of Dieter Böhler's influential study, which represents the most elaborate recent attempt to show that 1 Esdras predates Ezra–Nehemiah.

The State of Jerusalem in 1 Esdras: A Response to Dieter Böhler

One of Dieter Böhler's leading arguments relates to the conditions of Jerusalem: 1 Esdras presents the city—its gates and plazas—as already restored and inhabited during the time of Zerubbabel and Ezra. In contrast, Ezra–Nehemiah presents the city as a whole remaining in ruins until Nehemiah's advent. Böhler concludes from these findings that the authors of Ezra–Nehemiah undertook tedious changes in order to make room for Nehemiah's building project.[11] Böhler's findings are insightful and provocative, yet his interpretation of the evidence is problematic.

First, it seems that in at least some cases the authors of 1 Esdras are adding specificity to an older text. Thus 1 Esd 6:8 seems to be motivated by the perceived need to affirm that the elders were building a temple not just somewhere "in Judah" (see Ezra 5:8) but rather at the divinely ordained location "in the city of Jerusalem." This specificity, anticipated already in the emphasis throughout Ezra 1–7 on *Jerusalem* as the location of the temple, may have been motivated by a reaction to the presence of temples elsewhere. Some of these temples were very close to Judah. For example, we know of *byt yhw* somewhere in the vicinity of Khirbet el-Kom, fourteen kilometers southwestwards from Hebron, in Idumean territory.[12] That the Idumeans were very much of concern to the authors of 1 Esdras explains why Darius decrees "that the Idumeans should give up the villages of the Jews that they held" (4:50). Hence, in this case, the authors of 1 Esdras would have had good reasons to be more specific by adding "in Jerusalem."

Literature, 1999; orig. [in Hebrew] Ph.D diss., Hebrew University of Jerusalem, 1984); H. G. M. Williamson's important study, "The Problem with First Esdras," in *After the Exile: Essays in Honour of Rex Mason* (ed. John Barton and David J. Reimer; Macon, Ga.: Mercer University Press, 1996), 201–16.

11. Dieter Böhler, *Die heilige Stadt in Esdras a und Esra-Nehemia: Zwei Konzeptionen der Wiederherstellung Israels* (OBO 158; Freiburg: Universitätsverlag; Göttingen: Vandenhoeck & Ruprecht, 1997). For a recent discussion of Böhler's findings, see David M. Carr, "A Response," in "Revisiting the Composition of Ezra–Nehemiah: In Conversation with Jacob Wright's *Rebuilding Identity*: The Nehemiah Memoir and its Earliest Readers," ed. Gary Knoppers, special issue, *JHS* 12 (2007). Carr elaborates these points in his forthcoming book on the diachronic analysis of biblical literature.

12. Andre Lemaire, *Nouvelles inscriptions araméennes d'Idumée* (Transeuphratène Supplément 9; Paris: Gabalda, 2002), 283, pl. 47.

Second, the textual differences between 1 Esdras and Ezra–Nehemiah consist most often of (sizeable) pluses in 1 Esdras, not Ezra–Nehemiah. (The major exceptions here are Ezra 4:21 and, of course, most of Neh 1–13.) Now, one cannot deny that the editors responsible for the transmission of biblical texts not only expanded but also deleted passages. Indeed, that is what this article is arguing with respect to the authors of 1 Esdras and Nehemiah's account. Yet with the exception of cases in which there are good reasons to argue for deletion (as in the case of Nehemiah's account, as I try to show below), one would expect a more expansive text to be later than a less expansive one. Thus, in the case of 1 Esd 6:8, the authors of Ezra–Nehemiah would have omitted not just the mention of Jerusalem but also other details that otherwise have nothing to do with paving the way for Nehemiah's activities, which according to Böhler is the reason that the authors of Ezra–Nehemiah modified the narrative. More importantly, in reconstructing the older precursor to the present book of 1 Esdras, which contains many readings that are clearly later than Ezra–Nehemiah (like the notice about the Idumeans in 4:50, referred to above), Böhler lacks a reliable method for distinguishing old readings from late ones. What is to say that the plus, for example, in 6:8 is not on the same compositional level as 4:50 and other passages that everyone agrees are late?

Third, it is just as plausible, if not more warranted, to conclude from Böhler's observations that the authors of 1 Esdras introduced changes into their *Vorlage* in order to obviate any need for Nehemiah's building project (instead of the authors of Ezra–Nehemiah changing the text to make room for Nehemiah, as Böhler argues).[13] By depicting the city as already rebuilt before the altar and temple were constructed, 1 Esdras would have posed major problems for the ancient readers, as it does for modern scholars. The problem is that the authors of 1 Esdras do not explain *how* and *when* the city was rebuilt.[14] Given the wide array of biblical texts in which the restoration of the city is prophesied for the future, why did they, without further ado, contradict these texts and depict the city as already restored? One would expect these authors, who were so

---

13. See my discussion in *Rebuilding Identity*, 6, 38–39, 79–80, 221–24.
14. The reader of 1 Esdras knows that in the reign of Artaxerxes the Judeans are building the city on their own, and without Nehemiah, but this reign is before that of Darius. Moreover, the reader would have to conclude that the construction was stopped at a very early point (2:10–25), which matches the notice in 4:63 that Jerusalem had yet to be built. Inexplicably, however, the city is already rebuilt in 5:47. Nowhere are we told how this city was rebuilt or why the returnees undertook this project before erecting the altar and rebuilding the temple. This attempt of 1 Esdras to present the construction of the city as being finished at an early point is anticipated in Ezra–Nehemiah, which presents Judeans, who had recently made *aliyah*, initiating the building of the walls prior to the advent of Nehemiah (Ezra 4). As I attempt to show in *Rebuilding Identity*, 31–43, the text paves the way for 1 Esdras inasmuch as it already seeks to relativize the claims of Nehemiah and "put him in his (historical) place."

thoroughly acquainted with the biblical tradition, to have seized the opportunity to report the fulfillment of these prophecies, instead of presenting the city emerging suddenly in a restored condition (5:47).

If the authors of 1 Esdras composed an account that does not report how Jerusalem was rebuilt, they must have had a very good reason.[15] That reason, I would suggest, is Nehemiah. His explicit polemics against the priesthood, his presentation of a gubernatorial jurisdiction that extended to the temple, and his advocacy of a strong, militarized Judah that threatened the alliances of the aristocratic priests—these are just a few of the things that would have undoubtedly provoked the consternation of 1 Esdras' pro-priestly authors. I argue that these authors cut Nehemiah's account out of the history of the restoration. Their historical revisionism extended beyond negative deletion to a positive reworking of the remaining narrative. According to their new and improved narrative, the absence of the Nehemiah account is compensated for by the insertion of the lengthy story of the youths (1 Esd 3–4)—which significantly augments the amount of space devoted to Zerubbabel. Moreover, the authors reworked the remaining narrative so that Jerusalem is already rebuilt during the time of Zerubbabel and Ezra. How it was rebuilt is not explained. Instead of offering an alternative to Nehemiah's account, which would have caused more problems than it solved, they shrewdly chose to pass over the problem by portraying, subtly but unmistakably, Jerusalem in a restored and repopulated state.[16]

---

15. One of the most reliable statements in Nehemiah's account is that Jerusalem was in a state of ruins. This claim is confirmed by the archeological record, which reveals that the city only began to become a place of habitation late in the mid-Persian period and especially thereafter. The authors of 1 Esdras therefore depicted the city already restored at a very early point, even though they would have likely known firsthand that the city had been rebuilt more recently.

16. In other cases, one can readily see that the reading offered in Ezra–Nehemiah is older, for example, Ezra 10:6 // 1 Esd 9:1. In Ezra 10:1, Ezra prostrates himself "before the House of God," in keeping with a conventional practice of piety; he remains there and then rises from his prostrated state "before the House of God" in 10:6 (see also 1 Esd 8:88). 1 Esdras 9:1, however, presents Ezra rising from the court. As such, the text not only is in tension with 1 Esd 8:88 // Ezra 10:1, but it also misses the point. As Böhler argues, the mention of the court probably has something to do with Neh 2:8, which refers to wood for the building of the temple gates. However, the authors of 1 Esdras most likely are responsible for the changes: after they removed Nehemiah's account, they proceeded to rework the narrative so as to leave no ruins for Nehemiah to rebuild. Similarly, Böhler fails to explain why 1 Esd 5:45 does not present the gatekeepers taking up residence in Jerusalem, in addition to the priests and Levites, if the gates are already rebuilt (see 1 Esd 5:46). Furthermore, Böhler's comments on the gatekeepers are startling: "Both versions do speak of active gate keepers. But 1 Esdras knows them already at the time of Zerubbabel. Ezra–Neh will not mention them before the accomplishment of Nehemiah's wall building..." ("On the Relationship between Textual and Literary Criticism: The Two Recensions of the Book of Ezra; Ezra–Neh [MT] and 1 Esdras [LXX]," in *The Earliest Text of the Hebrew Bible: The Relationship between the Masoretic Text*

Soldiers and Cavalry in Ezra–Nehemiah and 1 Esdras

Before discussing at greater length the motivations for the composition of 1 Esdras, I present a new argument for the priority of Ezra-Nehemiah that compares Neh 2:9b with Ezra 8:22 // 1 Esd 8:51–52 as well as with 1 Esd 5:2.[17]

The first text, Neh 2:9b, is found in the context of Nehemiah's requests first for a leave of absence in order to rebuild Jerusalem (2:1–6) and then for various letters of authorization (vv. 7–8a). We are told (vv. 8b–9a) that the king granted Nehemiah his requests "in keeping with the benevolent hand of his God that was on [him]." The narrator then adds, "The king sent with me officers of the army and cavalry" (v. 9b).[18]

Three unmistakable elements from this passage are found in Ezra 8 (as well as in the parallel 1 Esd 8:51–52). They are: "army" (חיל); "cavalry" (פרשים), and the expression "the benevolent hand of my God on me" (כיד אלהי הטובה עלי). The passage in question is found in the context of Ezra's departure for Jerusalem after Artaxerxes had just granted everything he requested "in keeping with the hand of YHWH, my God upon me" (כיד ה' אלוהי עלי, Ezra 7:27–28 // 1 Esd 8:25–27). Before his company commences their journey, Ezra proclaims a fast (Ezra 8:21–23 // 1 Esd 8:50–53). The reason he offers his readers is that he "was ashamed to ask the king for soldiers and cavalry as an escort because [they] had told the king that the hand of our God is gracious to all who seek him but his power and wrath are against all who forsake him!" (Ezra 8:22 // 1 Esd 8:52).[19]

---

and the Hebrew Base of the Septuagint Reconsidered [ed. Adrian Schenker; SBLSCS 52; Atlanta: Society of Biblical Literature; Leiden: Brill, 2003], 44). However, gatekeepers are mentioned already in Ezra 2:70 and 7:7.

17. The only scholar who draws attention to the evidence presented here is Talshir, *1 Esdras: From Origin to Translation*, 49; however, her work merely cites these two texts in passing without any discussion. Throughout *Rebuilding Identity* I present additional arguments. For example, I attempt to show that Neh 8 must have been composed ad hoc for its present context. The argument is based on various observations, not least the use of ויאספו in 8:1. If the chapter were originally written as a continuation of Ezra 10 (or for some other context in an "Ezra memoir"), then we would expect, I argue, to read ויקבצו, in keeping with consistent use of להקבץ in Ezra 7–10 (five times!). The same root is used throughout Neh 1–7. The reason for the switch to להאסף in 8:1 is easiest to explain as being directly related to the repetition of the list of Ezra 2 in Neh 7. This very same form is found in almost exactly the same statement introducing an account set in the very same month and following the same list in Ezra 2–3. See *Rebuilding Identity*, 321–30.

18. Neh 2:9b is probably older than 2:7–9a, where Nehemiah petitions the king for additional things. 2:9b is likely an original part of the first formulation of the Nehemiah memoir. For a discussion of the insertion in vv. 7–9a, see *Rebuilding Identity*, 73–81.

19. That 1 Esd 8:52 lacks a reference to "the good hand of God" does not mean that it was not in the translator's *Vorlage*. From other places where this expression occurs, one can see that the translator simply had trouble rendering it in Greek (cf., e.g., Ezra 7:6 with 1 Esd 8:4,

Comparison of Texts

Nehemiah 2:9b	Ezra 8:22	1 Esdras 8:51–52	1 Esdras 5:2
וישלח עמי המלך שרי חיל ופרשים	כי בשתי לשאול מן המלך חיל ופרשים לעזרנו מאויב בדרך כי אמרנו למלך לאמר יד אלהינו על כל מבקשיו לטובה ועזו ואפו על כל עזבו	ἐνετράπην γὰρ αἰτῆσαι τὸν βασιλέα πεζούς τε καὶ ἱππεῖς καὶ προπομπὴν ἕνεκεν ἀσφαλείας τῆς πρὸς τοὺς ἐναντιουμένους ἡμῖν εἴπαμεν γὰρ τῷ βασιλεῖ ὅτι ἰσχὺς τοῦ κυρίου ἡμῶν ἔσται μετὰ τῶν ἐπιζητούντων αὐτὸν εἰς πᾶσαν ἐπανόρθωσιν	καὶ Δαρεῖος συναπέστειλεν μετ' αὐτῶν ἱππεῖς χιλίους ἕως τοῦ ἀποκαταστῆσαι αὐτοὺς εἰς Ιερουσαλημ μετ' εἰρήνης
The king sent officers of troops and cavalry with me.	For I was ashamed to ask the king for troops and cavalry to protect us against the enemy on our way. We had told the king that the hand of our God is benevolent to all who seek him, but his power and his wrath are against all who forsake him.	For I was ashamed to ask the king for troops and cavalry and an escort to protect us from our adversaries; since we had said to the king, "[…] The power of our Lord will be with those who seek him, and will support them in every way […]."	Darius sent with them a thousand cavalry to take them back to Jerusalem in safety.

That these texts are somehow related is indisputable. The chances that two authors, completely independently of each other, just happened to employ the terms "(officers of the) army and cavalry" in the context of Artaxerxes sending someone to Jerusalem is highly unlikely.[20] The combination of these terms with the expression "in keeping with the good hand of God upon me" should dispel any uncertainty. If doubt nevertheless persists, one can point to additional overlap, such as the reference to "three days in Jerusalem" and the delivery of royal documents to the provincial officials (Ezra 8:35–36; cf. Neh 2:9–11) and an array of more subtle clues.[21] The question is therefore not *if* these accounts are related, but rather *how* they are related.

---

or Ezra 7:28 with 1 Esd 8:27). Moreover, the presence of the phrase μετὰ τῶν ἐπιζητούντων αὐτὸν in 1 Esd 8:52 renders it very likely that the whole clause was in the translator's *Vorlage*.

20. This applies even if the expression was often used in official documents. Noteworthy is that the word "officers" appears in Ezra 7:27 (ולכל שרי המלך הגיבורים, "all the king's military officers") right before the clause כיד ה' אלהי עלי. The emphasis here is on all the king's officers.

21. See discussion in *Rebuilding Identity*, 86–93. Admittedly, "three days" is a popular biblical expression. But its juxtaposition here with other common features has probative force.

Inexplicably, most commentators do not address the connections between these texts. Those who do discuss the problem often fail to appreciate its implications. Thus Frank Charles Fensham wrote:

> Ezra the priest went to Jerusalem on a religious mission. In such a case a military escort would have seemed strange, because the religious group would then have shown no faith in their God. Nehemiah went as a political official, a governor, to Jerusalem. In such a case, the king would protect his official with a military escort.[22]

Fensham's explanation does not acknowledge the *literary* dimensions of the problem posed by Ezra 8:22. In treating the account as a mere record of events, it confuses the issue by moving from the text to factors beyond the text. This same confusion of historical and literary lines of inquiry can be witnessed in several other commentaries that treat the issue.

Tamara Cohn Eskenazi's chapter on "Characters" in her book *In An Age of Prose* is a notable exception to this tendency to confuse history and literature. She compares the self-depictions of Ezra and Nehemiah from a literary perspective and notes a number of parallels that "force a comparison between Ezra and Nehemiah," creating analogies between them.[23] "As in some M. C. Escher drawings, such complementary figures delineate each other's boundaries and combine to form the full picture."[24] Eskenazi concludes: "A study of the portraits of Ezra and Nehemiah is finally a study in contrasts. But it is a contrast of a 'matched pair.' Ezra–Nehemiah deliberately pairs the two men, linking their activities and persons even at the cost of awkward phraseology and possible historical modifications."[25] Eskenazi does not attempt to situate these literary strategies in their political or literary-historical background, although she recognizes that these texts are in close genetic relationship with each other.

For those who seek a diachronic explanation of the literary commonalities between our texts, there are three basic options: 1) These commonalities reflect contemporary conventions as to how courtiers should draft travel accounts. 2) The author of Nehemiah's account knows and is playing in some way on

---

For evidence of such travel documents, see the Persepolis Fortification Tablets currently being prepared for publication by Matthew Stolper and colleagues at the Oriental Institute of the University of Chicago. Online: http://oi.uchicago.edu/research/projects/pfa/ [cited 15 March 2010].

22. Frank C. Fensham, *The Books of Ezra and Nehemiah* (NICOT; Grand Rapids, Mich.: Eerdmans, 1982), 117.

23. Tamara C. Eskenazi, *In an Age of Prose: A Literary Approach to Ezra–Nehemiah* (SBLMS 36; Atlanta: Scholars Press, 1988), 153–54.

24. Eskenazi, *In an Age of Prose*, 154.

25. Eskenazi, *In an Age of Prose*, 152–53. See also idem, "The Chronicler and the Composition of 1 Esdras," *CBQ* 48 (1986): 39–61.

Ezra's account. 3) The author of Ezra's account knows and is playing in some way on Nehemiah's account. As far as I can see, scholars who discuss the issue have never adopted the first approach. While such writing conventions may have existed, the common features in Ezra 8 and Neh 2 are distinctive. Most scholars who discuss dependency favor the third option: that the authors of Ezra are mimicking Nehemiah's account.

In support of the approach adopted by the majority of scholars, we may observe that Nehemiah remarks *in passing* that Artaxerxes sent troops and cavalry with him, whereas Ezra's account positions his statement—that he did not ask for a military escort—very prominently in his account.[26] The polemics against what the author interprets as Nehemiah's immodesty and lack of faith are palpable: "I was ashamed to *ask* (לשאול) the king for troops and cavalry to protect us against the enemy on the way. We told the king that the hand of our God is for good upon all those who *request from/seek* him (מבקשיו), but his power and wrath are against all who forsake him!" The comment encourages the reader to think that Nehemiah was granted troops and cavalry because he, lacking faith in divine assistance, *requested* them along with his many other petitions (like wood for his house; see the use of לשאול in Neh 2:1–10). The play on לשאול and לבקש is not confined to this passage; to the contrary, it extends throughout Ezra 7–8. One of the most striking differences between Nehemiah's and Ezra's accounts is that Nehemiah *must ask* for permission and is in the end granted merely a leave of absence to build Jerusalem from its wretched ruins. In contrast, Ezra *is sent at the king's own initiative* bearing extraordinary authority and material resources in order to embellish the temple that had already been rebuilt.[27] The formulation of Ezra's statement in 8:22, which is otherwise difficult to understand as a response to the king, renders it very likely that this line 1) was formulated with Neh 2:9b in view and, 2) in order to function properly (as a new context for understanding Nehemiah's comment), must have stood in a narrative sequence with Nehemiah's account (i.e., in the same book).

The present argument applies only to Ezra 8:22, not to the entire Ezra account.[28] With respect to the relationship between Ezra's and Nehemiah's

---

26. Lisbeth S. Fried, "The Political Struggle of Fifth-Century Judah," *Transeu* 24 (2002): 61–73, argues that one did not travel with armed guards in the Achaemenid Empire since the roads were safe.

27. The same also applies to the first project of building the temple in Ezra 1–6. On the motif of "request," see *Rebuilding Identity*, 55, 70–73, 84–89. In Ezra 7:6 the king grants Ezra everything he requested according to the good hand of God on him. The line is strikingly similar to the texts in question. However, it contradicts the narrative, inasmuch as in Ezra 1–6 and 7 the Persian kings act on their own accord and do not wait to be asked, in stark contrast to Neh 2. All this supports the contention that the authors of Ezra 1–6, 7–8 and 1 Esdras are responding to Nehemiah's account.

28. The oldest Ezra narrative may be isolated minimally to Ezra 7:1–6a [to: "from Babylon"], 6b, 11a, 12–28; 8:15a, 21, 23, 31–34. The intervening material in 8:1–14, and 15b–20

accounts, many scholars, such as Robert Fruin, Martin Noth, A. S Kapelrud, Ulrich Kellermann, Wilhelm Th. in der Smitten, Antonius Gunneweg, and Reinhard G. Kratz, argue that the number and character of cross-references render it very likely that Ezra's narrative was written as a response to Nehemiah's.[29] Although much of the evidence speaks in favor of this conclusion, Ezra 8:22 should probably not be adduced in support of it, since it appears to have been secondarily inserted between 8:21 and 23. Not only can it be removed without disrupting its context, but its presence also creates a problem inasmuch as it severs "for this" (עַל זֹאת) from its antecedent in v. 21. One has to reread the passage in order to locate the referent (viz., "a safe journey for ourselves, our children and all our possessions").[30] If Ezra 8:22 does not constitute an integral part of the text in which it is embedded, it should be excluded from the

and 24–30 can be easily eliminated without rendering structural damage to the narrative; of these three passages, the first and third seem to be older than the second one. In vv. 15b–20 we have a pro-Levitical insertion similar to what we find throughout Ezra–Nehemiah and Chronicles. The third-person narrative in vv. 35–36 likely stems from a different hand and is strikingly similar to the third-person narrative concluding the previous section of the book (Ezra 6:16–18 [19–22]). The evidence of this third-person conclusion renders it likely that chs. 9–10 constitute a continuation of the Ezra story written by different hands; see my discussion in *Rebuilding Identity*, 248–57.

29. Robert Fruin, "Is Ezra een historisch persoon?," *NTT* 18 (1929): 121–38; Martin Noth, *Überlieferungsgeschichtliche Studien: Die sammelnden und bearbeitenden Geschichtswerke im Alten Testament* (3d ed.; Darmstadt: Wissenschaftliche Buchgesellschaft, 1967), 125–26, 145–47; Arvid S. Kapelrud, *The Question of Authorship in the Ezra-Narrative: A Lexical Investigation* (Skrifter utgitt av det Norske Videnskaps-Akademi i Oslo 1; Oslo: Dybwad, 1944); Ulrich Kellermann, *Nehemia: Quellen, Überlieferung und Geschichte* (BZAW 102; Berlin: de Gruyter, 1967), 56–59; idem, "Erwägungen zum Problem der Esradatierung," *ZAW* 80 (1968): 55–87; Wilhelm Th. in der Smitten, *Esra: Quellen, Überlieferung und Geschichte* (SSN 15; Assen: Van Gorcum, 1973), 54–56; Antonius H. J. Gunneweg, *Esra* (KAT 19/1; Gütersloh: Gütersloher Verlagshaus, 1985), 121–23; Reinhard G. Kratz, *Die Komposition der erzählenden Bücher des Alten Testaments: Grundwissen der Bibelkritik* (UTB 2157; Göttingen: Vandenhoeck & Ruprecht, 2000), 77–79.

30. Whether the passage draws on the wording of Ezra 8:31b is difficult to say. The latter may itself represent an addition between 8:31a and 8:32–34. If so, it may have been written by the same hand responsible for 8:22. "We left the river Ahava on the twelfth day of the first month, to go to Jerusalem. The hand of our God was upon us, and he delivered us from the hand of the enemy and from ambushes along the way. We came to Jerusalem and remained there three days. On the fourth day...." That Ezra 8:22 was composed with Neh 2:9b in view is supported by Juha Pakkala's work on the Ezra account. Pakkala's approach to the formation of Ezra's account differs radically from my own. He attempts to show that it was an originally separate work rather than being formed for the book of Ezra–Nehemiah. But Pakkala recognizes that there is no way around the conclusion that Ezra 8:22 responds to Neh 2:9b. He also agrees that Ezra 8:22 does not have implications for the whole of Ezra 7–8 since this verse most likely was inserted between vv. 21 and 23 by an author who knew Nehemiah's account. See Juha Pakkala, *Ezra the Scribe: The Development of Ezra 7–10 and Nehemiah 8* (BZAW 347; Berlin: de Gruyter, 2004) 61, and in personal correspondence, January 19, 2010.

discussion of whether the Ezra memoir constitutes a late fictional work that seeks to place Nehemiah's account in a new historical and literary context.[31]

While the dependency of Ezra 8:22 on Neh 2:9b may not bear directly on the question of the dependency of Ezra's account on Nehemiah's, it does have significant implications for the question of the dependency of 1 Esdras on Ezra-Nehemiah. Insofar as Ezra 8:22 was composed with Neh 2:9b in view, there is only one way that 1 Esdras could still be older than Ezra-Nehemiah, namely, if the author of Ezra 8:22 knew Nehemiah's account as a *separately transmitted source* or in the context of *a separate book*.[32] Few scholars would deny that Nehemiah's account was composed and originally transmitted independently of its present literary context in the book of Ezra-Nehemiah. In *Rebuilding Identity*, I attempt to show that Nehemiah's account represents the point of departure for the formation of Ezra-Nehemiah. Yet I also seek to demonstrate that this account began at a very early stage to be transmitted with the same texts whose formation it had elicited. Not everyone will accept my conclusions. However, one may agree that the intertextuality between Ezra 8:22 and Neh 2:9b "works" better if these two passages stood in close proximity to each other, rather than in completely separate books. First, it would be much easier to explain the redactional character of Ezra 8:22. The author who inserted it would have been attempting to highlight the fundamentally different approaches of these two leaders. Second, and more importantly, the reader could more readily appreciate the nuanced play in Ezra's statement with respect to "request" and "seek" (לשאול and לבקש). As argued above, this statement needs to be in the same book as Nehemiah's account in order to function according to its intended narrative purpose: it presents Ezra's attitude and actions as the context in which the reader should interpret Nehemiah's subsequent statement that the king sent troops with him to Jerusalem. The formulation of Ezra 8:22 encourages the

---

31. The importance of this point is that one must not fear that the question of whether Ezra 8:22 depends on Neh 2:9b has any ramifications for the authenticity of the Ezra memoir. Nevertheless, the argument here does not require that one view Ezra 8:22 as an addition. The point of mentioning this possibility here is to show that one can agree that Ezra 8:22 has Neh 2:9b in view and still accept the authenticity of the "Ezra memoir."

32. In my "Seeking – Finding – Writing," in *Unity and Disunity in Ezra-Nehemiah: Redaction, Rhetoric and Reader* (ed. Mark J. Boda and Paul L. Redditt; Hebrew Bible Monographs 17; Sheffield: Sheffield Phoenix, 2008), 277–305, I respond to the suggestion of James VanderKam, David Kraemer, and others that Ezra and Nehemiah originally constituted separate books. See D. Kraemer, "On the Relationship of the Books of Ezra and Nehemiah," *JSOT* 59 (1993): 73-92; B. Becking, "Continuity and Community: The Belief System of the Book of Ezra," in *The Crisis of Israelite Religion: Transformation of Religious Tradition in Exilic and Post-Exilic Times* (ed. B. Becking and M. C. A. Korpel; OTS 42; Leiden: Brill, 1999), 256–75; J. C. VanderKam, "Ezra-Nehemiah or Ezra and Nehemiah?," in his *From Revelation to Canon: Studies in the Hebrew Bible and Second Temple Literature* (JSJSup 62; Leiden: Brill, 2000), 60–80, as well as the other contributions to Boda and Redditt's *Unity and Disunity in Ezra-Nehemiah* volume.

reader to conclude that the king sent troops with Nehemiah because Nehemiah *sought* these troops from him and hence lacked Ezra's faith in *seeking* the deity.

The reading of the evidence offered here is supported by an additional clue in 1 Esd 5:2. There Darius is said to have sent a thousand cavalry to escort Zerubbabel and the *aliyah* he organizes. This act of beneficence is reported in a passage from the story of the youths, which reinterprets the information found in Ezra 3 (such as the details regarding building materials from Lebanon) according to the format of Artaxerxes' decree and Ezra's response in Ezra 7–8.³³ Here we have another case in which someone appears to have composed an account portraying an Achaemenid ruler granting a Judean courtier *all that he asks for*.³⁴ Yet in keeping with Ezra's ethos in 8:22, Zerubbabel *does not ask* for a military convoy. Instead, Darius sends it on his own initiative. Moreover, he does not send just a few officers and cavalry, as Artaxerxes sends with Nehemiah; rather he commissions no less than a thousand cavalry—a *chiliarchy*, the largest equestrian unit available.³⁵

This text presents the imperial court as treating Zerubbabel much better than it treated Nehemiah. As such, it may be compared to other texts, such as the competition with Nehemiah that informs much of Ezra 7–8 and especially the inclusion of the story of the youths in 1 Esd 3–5.³⁶ The latter promotes the role of Zerubbabel by assigning more than two additional chapters to the account of his accomplishments. Past studies of 1 Esdras tend to treat the omission of Nehemiah's account as a separate issue from the inclusion of the substantial new material related to Zerubbabel. Yet as Zipora Talshir argues, the two issues should be seen as directly related: the promotion of Zerubbabel by means of this new material corresponds to a demotion of Nehemiah's activities.³⁷

---

33. The statement itself sticks out and may have been secondarily inserted.

34. τότε ὁ βασιλεὺς εἶπεν αὐτῷ αἴτησαι ὃ θέλεις πλείω τῶν γεγραμμένων καὶ δώσομέν σοι ὃν τρόπον εὑρέθης σοφώτερος καὶ ἐχόμενός μου καθήσῃ καὶ συγγενής μου κληθήσῃ, 4:42; cf. the discussion of "request" above.

35. 1 Esd 2:25 supports the contention that the authors of 1 Esdras knew Neh 2:9b. They changed their *Vorlage* to refer to "cavalry and a mass of troops" (ἵππου καὶ ὄχλου παρατάξεως), likely in order to prepare for the positive change of events in 5:2, where imperial cavalry are now commissioned to protect those who are building the temple.

36. For the general tendency in Ezra-Nehemiah and 1 Esdras to relativize the accomplishments of Nehemiah and his relationship to the imperial court, see *Rebuilding Identity*, 39–43, 63–65, 86–93, 321–39.

37. See Talshir, *1 Esdras: From Origin to Translation*, 55, and her discussion on 46–57. I am, however, not convinced by Talshir's larger claims (58): The story of the youths "was the catalyst for the formation of I Esdras—its raison d'être. I Esdras was created in order to interpolate the Story of the Youths into the story of the Restoration, and the whole book has no real existence without it.' I would argue instead that 1 Esdras was created as a response to Nehemiah's account. It elevates the status of Zerubbabel in the process of demoting Nehemiah and deleting his account. The inclusion of the story of the youths should be seen in

This evidence from 1 Esd 5:2 suggests, first, that we have not overinterpreted the evidence of Ezra 8:22. Nehemiah's statement about an escort of soldiers and cavalry seems to have provoked a response and polemics in more than one place. Second, it supports the challenge to the way Böhler interprets the evidence of 1 Esdras. That the authors of this work present Jerusalem as already rebuilt and repopulated during the time of Zerubbabel seems indeed to be a conscious attempt to obviate any occasion for Nehemiah's building project. This positive revisionism corresponds to the negative *damnatio memoriae* constituted by the authors of 1 Esdras *expunging* Nehemiah's account from the history of the restoration.

1 Esdras and the Battle over the Memory of Nehemiah

If the authors of 1 Esdras cut Nehemiah's account out of the history of the restoration, what might have been their motivation? A full response to this question must take account of the overtly pro-priestly and pro-temple character of 1 Esdras. This work does not emphasize both "temple and Torah obedience," as Böhler argues.[38] Admittedly, 1 Esdras concludes with the reading of the Torah, which contrasts with the introductory passages describing Josiah's elaborate celebration of Passover at the temple in Jerusalem. However, in comparing the final passage to its parallel in Neh 8, we immediately notice how 1 Esdras is much more priestly in orientation. Thus Neh 8:1 refers to Ezra as "the scribe," while 1 Esd 9:39 designates him "the chief priest and reader" (τῷ ἀρχιερεῖ καὶ ἀναγνώστῃ). The same applies to Ezra 8:4 and 1 Esd 9:42.[39] That 1 Esdras calls him "chief priest" is likely an attempt to place him in the role of the high priest Eliashib, who, according to Nehemiah's account, was corrupt. Similarly, the choice not to use the conventional Greek term for "scribe" suggests that the authors were seeking to distance themselves from a Second Temple group of "scribes" and what this group may have represented. The passages in Neh 8–10, which emphasize Torah study (even at the expense of the temple cult), notably have not been transmitted in 1 Esdras. As such, this work manifests a pronounced pro-priestly orientation and consciously does not embrace the emphasis on laity and Torah study driving the composition of Neh 8–10.

Nehemiah's account would have posed serious problems for the priestly circles:

---

connection with this promotion of Zerubbabel over Nehemiah; the story is, however, not the primary reason for the composition of 1 Esdras.

38. Böhler, *Die heilige Stadt*, 48.

39. As in the case of Ezra 4 (see n. 6 above), internal redactions within Ezra–Nehemiah anticipate the developments in 1 Esdras. As I show in *Rebuilding Identity*, 319–21, the verses in Neh 8 that others have assigned to secondary strata for independent reasons present Ezra as not just a scribe but also a priest.

1) It presents Jerusalem as a whole in a condition of ruins. Before Nehemiah's arrival, the Judeans lived in "trouble and disgrace" (1:3 and 2:17). Apparently, nothing had been done to bring about change since the Babylonian destruction (see 1:1–3).

2) The account fails to acknowledge the munificence of the Persian court with regard to Jerusalem's temple, priesthood, and cult. It presents the dismal situation in Judah being remedied not only by rebuilding the wall but also by the various social and religious reforms that Nehemiah, as a layperson, had introduced.

3) When he inquires about the inhabitants of the province in 1:2–3, Nehemiah refers to them as "the Judeans, the escapees/remnant who have been left from the captivity there in the province" (vv. 2–3). He fails to acknowledge, with Ezra 1–8, the presence of a large population that had made *aliyah* from Babylon in order to build the temple.

4) His work is very pro-Judean, at the expense of a broader Israelite perspective. Not only does it constantly address "Judeans" and refer to "Judah," but it also maintains that Judeans should only speak the language "Judahite" and marry only Judeans (see 13:23–27). Sanballat and Tobiah, with whom priests were intermarried, would have likely thought of themselves as Israelites; also, priestly literature (Num 32 and Josh 22) written in Jerusalem explicitly identifies and includes communities that remained faithful to the Torah in the Transjordan among the people of Israel.

5) His account portrays the decentralization of the city: holiness spreads out from the temple, at the center, to the periphery, symbolized by the municipal wall (see Neh 12:27–43; 13:18–22).

6) The account defends the need for a strong, fortified Judah that does not make alliances with its neighbors (6:1–9); such isolationism was not in keeping with the ideals of many aristocratic priests, as we know not least from the Nehemiah memoir itself. The militarization of the province, which the memoir advocates, threatened the good relations with imperial courts, which were crucial to the prosperity of the Jerusalem priesthood throughout the Hellenistic period.

7) Nehemiah also accuses these neighbors of planning war and violence against Judah. These same neighbors were allies and relatives of the Jerusalem priesthood and Judahite aristocracy, and remained so into the Hellenistic period; as stated above, they probably thought of themselves as Israelites in some fashion.

8) Later readers would have understood Nehemiah's comment in 5:15 about the abusive policies of his gubernatorial predecessors as also including Zerubbabel; as we can see in talmudic traditions, his audacity in this regard continued to provoke disapprobation for many centuries.

9) Throughout his account, Nehemiah refers to the temple only in passing (see 2:8 and 6:10–11) and mentions the priests with other groups rather than in a position of prominence (e.g., 2:16).

10) Nehemiah dares to accuse the Jerusalem priesthood of radical corruption. In ch. 13 he points his finger at the high priest's family, who had intermarried with Judah's archenemy, Sanballat (13:28–29). He also claims that the priest Eliashib, whom later readers would likely have identified with the high priest of the same name (cf. 3:1; 13:28–29), had provided Tobiah, to whom he was "close" or a relative, with a *pied-à-terre* in the temple (see vv. 4–9 and 28–29).

Because of these unholy alliances, Nehemiah, as a layperson, must interfere in the internal affairs of the temple and "purify" the temple chambers (13:9) as well as the priesthood. In the final lines of his account, he claims to have established the duties of the priest and Levites and provided for the wood offering and for the first fruits (vv. 30–31), just as he had made sure that the Levites had received their portions after they had been long neglected, and reorganized the temple personnel (vv. 10–14). By portraying these activities, his account implicitly subordinates the high priesthood and the temple to the jurisdiction of the פחה, an office that his account depicts in a form to be emulated (comparable, I would argue, to a *Fürstenspiegel*).

One could list more reasons, but these ten should suffice to dispel any doubt that Nehemiah's account would have caused great consternation among the Jerusalem priesthood. In *Rebuilding Identity*, I argue that the first response from priestly circles was the composition of Ezra 1–6 and 7–8, which place Nehemiah's building project and his account in a new historical and literary context. The reader of Ezra–Nehemiah knows that long before the imperial court merely *allowed* Nehemiah a leave of absence for his building project, it had *commanded* Zerubbabel and Ezra to make large-scale *aliyot* for the purpose of building and beautifying *the temple*.[40] In this "history of the restoration," which presents Nehemiah's account as one source among others, Nehemiah's criticism of Eliashib and the priesthood is allowed to stand. Yet his censure is recontextualized by the depiction of a productive diarchic relationship between Zerubbabel and Jeshua as they built the temple—long before Eliashib committed his crimes against Judah.

For others, this recontextualization was apparently not enough. A history of the restoration that gave so much bad press to the early representatives of the high priesthood was dangerous and subversive. Hence, they turned from positive amplification to negative deletion. Some in these priestly circles deemed Nehemiah's account still worthy of transmission and therefore they undertook only a partial editing. Thus when recounting Nehemiah's activities, the aristocratic priest Josephus (*Ant.* 11.5.8), or his pro-priestly source, expurgates

---

40. The validity of this statement can be judged not least by the weight of the material in Ezra 7–8: the narrative in these chapters is sustained by the mission to the temple. While Ezra refers at length to the temple vessels, he never mentions that he also transported Torah scrolls. Similarly the Artaxerxes rescript devotes much more space to the temple cult than to laws and judges.

anything that might perturb priestly circles. Even the criticism of the Jerusalem priests in 13:10-14 is reread to depict Nehemiah making sure that *the people would pay tithes to both the priests* and the Levites so that they would not have to leave Jerusalem. The setting of this action (Eliashib's provision of Tobiah with a temple chamber in 13:4-9) is passed over in silence.[41] Others, however, kept the name of Nehemiah, which apparently bore some symbolic authority, yet assigned a totally different role to it. Thus the legend transmitted in 2 Macc 1:18-36 transforms Nehemiah into a champion of the temple cult, which anticipates the identification of Nehemiah with Zerubbabel in later Jewish sources (see, e.g., *b. Sanh.* 38a).[42]

In this battle over Nehemiah's memory, the authors of 1 Esdras took the most radical step and attempted to consign his account to complete oblivion. We may compare this *damnatio memoriae* to Ben Sira's "Praise of the Fathers," which extols the work of Nehemiah (49:13) while excluding Ezra from its history of the restoration.[43] In 1 Esdras the erasure of the memory of Nehemiah's work corresponds to an amplification of the Zerubbabel story with the story of the youths. In this way, 1 Esdras focuses all attention first on Zerubbabel, who builds the temple, and then on Ezra, who transports abundant imperial resources to the temple.[44] Inasmuch as Ezra is designated "the chief priest" (1 Esd 9:40, 49), the authors effectively avoid the issues posed by the historical high priest, Eliashib. While Nehemiah's account is excised from 1 Esdras, his name is transmitted (1 Esd 5:8 and 40). Significantly the only thing for which he is commemorated in this work, aside from returning from Babylon in a mass *aliyah*, is joining

---

41. Although Josephus is careful to report each change in the office of the high priest he simply states in *Ant.* 11.5.5 that Eliashib took office. Although he has no qualms about transmitting stories of priestly intrigues and fratricide later in his history, these stories are well suited to his polemics against the Samaritans, not the Jerusalem priesthood.

42. See my discussion in *Rebuilding Identity*, 324.

43. See P. Höffken, "Warum schweeg Jesus Sirach über Esra?," *ZAW* 87 (1975): 184-202, and Christopher T. Begg, "Ben Sirach's Non-Mention of Ezra," *BN* 42 (1988): 14-18. Joseph Blenkinsopp writes: "We can readily understand the inclusion of Nehemiah, the intransigent opponent of Tobiah the Ammonite, in light of Jesus ben Sirach's attachment to the Oniad priestly house and its contemporary representative Simon II, and in the context of the bitter Oniad-Tobiad rivalry under Ptolemaic and Seleucid rule. We may also suppose that Ezra's singleminded theocratic ideal was uncongenial to the author, who took political realities, and the possibility and desirability of political autonomy, seriously. ... In this respect [Ben Sira] may be seen to anticipate the Hasmonean ideology which looked to Nehemiah as the real founder of the commonwealth and the ideal of political-religious leadership. The Hasmoneans, who traced their ancestry through the priest Jojarib of the first return (1 Chron. 9:10; Neh. 11:10; 12:6, 19; cf. 1 Chron. 24 7), seem to have cherished the memory of Nehemiah" (*Ezra-Nehemiah* [OTL; Philadelphia: Westminster, 1988], 55-56).

44. The transformation of Nehemiah into a champion of the temple cult in 2 Macc 1:18-36 and the identification of Nehemiah with Zerubbabel in later Jewish sources should be studied in connection with this shift from Nehemiah to Zerubbabel in 1 Esdras.

"Attharias" in commanding priests, who had been excluded from cultic service, to wait until a high priest appeared wearing Urim and Thummim.⁴⁵ Such deference to the high priest is remarkable given the way he goes head to head with Eliashib in his own account.⁴⁶

That 1 Esdras does not transmit much of the rest of Neh 1–13 is arguably related to the emphases in this material, which, like Nehemiah's memoir, would certainly have posed problems for priestly circles. We have already observed that the only passage from chs. 1–13 transmitted in 1 Esdras, namely 8:1–12, appears to have been altered so that Ezra is consistently identified as "the chief priest." The immediately following passages (8:13–9:37) do not refer to the temple where one would expect them to do so, nor do they assign a leading role to the priesthood, which is remarkable for an account of the sacred festivities of Tishrei.⁴⁷ Thus, 8:13–18 describes the celebration of Sukkoth throughout Jerusalem but fails to mention any sacrifices (in contrast to Ezra 3 and the pentateuchal ordinances). Moreover, this account begins with both lay leaders and priests gathering around "Ezra the scribe" to study Torah; nothing is said about the activities of the high priest during this holiest of all times in the cultic calendar. Furthermore, ch. 9 begins with the people reading Torah on their own and Levites (not priests) rising to offer a prayer (not a sacrifice). The extraordinarily lengthy prayer, which reviews all the high points of Israelite history, refers repeatedly to the Torah yet has nothing whatsoever to say about the temple. This omission is all the more astonishing in a book that devotes so much space to the reconstruction and aggrandizement of the temple. Instead of trying to save some of the material in chs. 9–12, the authors of 1 Esdras, after rewording 8:1–12, seem to have simply given up on the rest. They stop in midsentence—remarkably,

---

45. See Lisbeth S. Fried, "Did Second Temple High Priests Possess Urim and Thummim?," *JHS* 7, no. 3 (2007). "Attharias" here is the personified form of התרשתא (see Ezra 2:63). In 1 Esd 9:49 (Neh 8:9), Attharias is again the name of a leader. I would argue that Nehemiah is secondary in Neh 8:9 but was added earlier than the revisions made by the authors of 1 Esdras. This sequence would make the best sense of the way 1 Esdras personifies the title and then distinguishes him ("Attharias") from Nehemiah. In so doing, the authors of 1 Esdras can completely remove Nehemiah from Neh 8:9, which clearly identifies the two (נחמיה הוא התרשתא).

46. The case of Josephus is fascinating from the perspective of my theory. On the one hand, he follows the pro-priestly 1 Esdras, which makes perfect sense given his priestly background. On the other hand, he reintroduces the Nehemiah account into the history of the restoration. Yet, with respect to the latter, he omits, as noted above, all texts that were most offensive to priestly sympathies and transforms others in keeping with these sympathies.

47. I argue this point in various ways in several articles: "Seeking – Finding – Writing"; "A New Model for the Composition of Ezra–Nehemiah," in *Judah and the Judeans in the Fourth Century B.C.E.* (ed. Rainer Albertz, Gary Knoppers, and Oded Lipschits; Winona Lake, Ind.: Eisenbrauns, 2007), 333–48; "Writing the Restoration: Ezra as Meritocratic Icon in the Post-Destruction Period," in "Scribes before and after 587 BCE: A Conversation," ed. Mark Leuchter, special issue, *JHS* 7, no. 10 (2007): 19–29.

right before the description of the priests and lay leaders gathering around Ezra the scribe to study Torah (8:13).

All this evidence lends support to my approach to 1 Esdras. This works constitutes another response to Nehemiah's account. Whereas Ezra–Nehemiah and Josephus seek to relativize and recontextualize Nehemiah's account, 1 Esdras takes the more radical step of completely eliminating it from the historical record of the restoration.

Articles Investigating the Nature of 1 Esdras

THE IMAGE OF THE KING(S) IN 1 ESDRAS

Sebastian Grätz

The main aim of this article is to show that the portrayals of the particular kings, starting with Josiah and ending with the reign of a certain Artaxerxes, serve to establish and to elaborate the conception of the entire book of 1 Esdras.[1] The depiction of the Persian kings is shaped in accordance with the portrayal of Josiah in a way that is not observable in the canonical book of Ezra–Nehemiah.

It is well known that 1 Esdras starts abruptly with the reign of Josiah and his celebration of the Passover as is reported in 2 Chr 35. This abruptness is emphasized by the omission in 1 Esdras of the beginning of Josiah's reign (2 Chr 34) so that the integrity of the beginning of the book has been questioned.[2] However, A. van der Kooij, among others, has argued against the position of a damaged beginning of 1 Esdras by focusing on 1 Esd 1:21–22, which exist only in 1 Esdras and are without counterpart in 2 Chr 35. Van der Kooij has pointed out that by referring to 2 Kgs 22 (2 Chr 34), these two verses serve to highlight the difference between the pious king Josiah on the one hand and the impious people on the other. At the same time, a reference to the end of 2 Chr 34 is avoided because of the positive description of the people in this passage; thus, van der Kooij assumes that 1 Esd 1 is actually the original beginning of the book.[3] According to this assumption, it is possible to weaken the argument of K.-F. Pohlmann, who holds that from a grammatical point of view the beginning in 1 Esd 1:1 (καὶ

---

1. The numbering of verses and quotations is according to the edition of Robert Hanhart, *Esdrae liber I* (2d ed.; Septuaginta Vetus Testamentum Graecum 8/1; Göttingen: Vandenhoeck & Ruprecht, 1991).

2. See, e.g., Karl-Friedrich Pohlmann, *Studien zum dritten Esra: Ein Beitrag zur Frage nach dem ursprünglichen Schluss des chronistischen Geschichtswerkes* (FRLANT 104; Göttingen: Vandenhoeck & Ruprecht, 1970), 32.

3. See Arie van der Kooij, "Zur Frage des Anfangs des 1. Esrabuches," *ZAW* 103 (1991): 239–52, esp. 246–50; see also H. G. M. Williamson, *Israel in the Books of Chronicles* (Cambridge: Cambridge University Press, 1977), 19; Kristin De Troyer, "Zerubbabel and Ezra: A Revived and Revised Solomon and Josiah? A Survey of Current 1 Esdras Research," *Currents in Biblical Research* 1 (2002): 30–60, esp. 42.

ἤγαγεν Ιωσιας τὸ πασχα ἐν Ιερουσαλημ) cannot be a beginning of an independent story:[4] according to the grammar of R. Meyer, the narrative tense *wayyiqtol* serves very well as the beginning of a Hebrew sentence, a section of a narrative, or an entire book.[5] The beginnings of Leviticus and Numbers are also formulated with a *wayyiqtol*, which in each case is also reflected in the LXX (καὶ ἀνεκάλεσεν, καὶ ἐλάλησεν). Hence, it seems very likely that at the beginning of 1 Esdras, nothing is actually lost. Since the author of 1 Esdras must have assumed that King Josiah as well as the dating of the Passover (according to Exod 12:6 and Deut 16:2) were known to his readers, the question arises as to why this book starts with this account. Z. Talshir presumes rightly: "The particular reference to Josiah's reign must indicate the author's special attitude to that king."[6] Talshir's observation seems to be an appropriate starting point for an investigation of the image of the king/kings in 1 Esdras.

1. Josiah

First Esdras 1 mainly presents the text of its *Vorlage*, 2 Chr 35:1–36:21, in its own translation,[7] whereas—as mentioned above—both in 1 Esd 1:21-22 and, differently, in LXX 2 Chr 35:19a-d, a short section about Josiah as a pious accomplisher of the law is inserted. Apart from that, 1 Esdras presents a translation of its Hebrew *Vorlage* in 2 Chronicles, disregarding chapter 34 with its report of several important features of Josiah's reign: the eradication of the altars of the foreign gods, the discovery of the "book of the law of the Lord," the advice of Huldah, and finally the covenant. Instead, the author has chosen to start his account with Josiah's initiation of the Passover, which is described as an enduring institution on a solid organizational foundation, and thus exceeds the Passover of Hezekiah, as S. Japhet has pointed out.[8] The Passover of Josiah serves as a paradigm for every celebration of the Passover still to come. Thus, 1 Esdras starts consciously with the archetype of the central Israelite feast, which is inaugurated by King Josiah. The following table displays the composition of 1 Esd 1:

---

4. See Pohlmann, *Studien zum dritten Esra*, 32.
5. See R. Meyer, *Hebräische Grammatik: Mit einem bibliographischen Nachwort von U. Rüterswörden* (Berlin: de Gruyter, 1992), §100.3b.
6. Zipora Talshir, *1 Esdras: From Origin to Translation* (SBLSCS 47; Atlanta: Society of Biblical Literature, 1999), 19.
7. See Robert Hanhart, *Text und Textgeschichte des 1. Esrabuches* (MSU 12; Göttingen: Vandenhoeck & Ruprecht, 1974), 17.
8. See Sara Japhet, *2 Chronik* (HTKAT; Freiburg: Herder, 2003), 482; see already idem, *I and II Chronicles* (OTL; Louisville: Westminster John Knox, 1993), 1044–59.

vv. 1–6 (2 Chr 35:1–6):	καὶ ἤγαγεν Ιωσιας τὸ πασχα ... Josiah initiates the celebration of Passover and commands the priests.
vv. 7–9 (35:7–9):	καὶ ἐδωρήσατο Ιωσιας τῷ λαῷ ... Josiah and well-known persons give donations for the celebration (key word: δωρέω < רום *hip'il*).
v. 10 (35:10):	Summary and transition to the sacrifice according to the "book of Moses" (missing in 2 Chr 35:10).
vv. 11–15 (35:11–15):	Performance of the Passover by the responsible staff[9]—the ministry of the gatekeepers.
v. 16 (35:16):	Conclusion: Celebration of the Passover; κατὰ τὴν ἐπιταγὴν τοῦ βασιλέως Ιωσιου.
vv. 17–20 (35:17–19):	Passover and the Feast of Unleavened Bread; retrospection on the times of Samuel, dating to the eighteenth year of Josiah (+ additions in 1 Esd 1:21–22 // LXX 2 Chr 35 19a–d).

The beginning and end of the chapter clearly display the outstanding role of Josiah as initiator and exemplary financier of the Passover, although—due to the postexilic perspective of the text—the cultic acts, that is, the sacrifices, are carried out by the appropriate persons. The case that will now be developed is that the role of Josiah in 1 Esd 1 (developed from 2 Chr 35) served as a model for 1 Esdras' portrayal of foreign (Persian) rulers in postexilic times. In this way the literary Josiah can be seen as a pathfinder in view of cultic restoration in postexilic times.

The first observation concerns the comparable accounts of the Passover in 1 Esd 1 and 7:

1 Esd 1:1:	καὶ ἤγαγεν Ιωσιας τὸ πασχα ἐν Ιερουσαλημ τῷ κυρίῳ αὐτοῦ καὶ ἔθυσεν τὸ πασχα τῇ τεσσαρεσκαιδεκάτῃ ἡμέρᾳ τοῦ μηνὸς τοῦ πρώτου
1 Esd 7:10:	καὶ ἠγάγοσαν οἱ υἱοὶ Ισραηλ τῶν ἐκ τῆς αἰχμαλωσίας τὸ πασχα ἐν τῇ τεσσαρεσκαιδεκάτῃ τοῦ πρώτου μηνός<

Whereas 1 Esd 1:18 refers to the celebration of the Passover at the time of Samuel, chapter 7 seems to go back to the Passover of Josiah reported in the first chapter of the book: here the returnees celebrate the first Passover after building

---

9. 1 Esd 1:10 reports that the Passover was "roasted" (ὀπτάω) as well as "cooked" (ἕψω), which is an allusion to Exod 12:8 as well as Deut 16:7.

the second temple.[10] Furthermore, in 1 Esdras nothing is reported about the celebration of the Passover between the time of Josiah and the account in chapter 7. As the comparable diction in both accounts shows, one important concern of chapter 7 is the seamless transition from the time of Josiah to the first celebration of Passover at the newly built temple in Jerusalem, although there is an important and noticeable difference: the absence of the king in 1 Esd 7. Here, instead of the indigenous monarch who enabled the celebration, the foreign king helps out, as 1 Esd 7:15 stresses: ὅτι μετέστρεψεν τὴν βουλὴν τοῦ βασιλέως Ἀσσυρίων ἐπ᾽ αὐτοὺς κατισχῦσαι τὰς χεῖρας αὐτῶν ἐπὶ τὰ ἔργα κυρίου θεοῦ Ισραηλ ("Because he [i.e., God] has turned the counsel of the king of Assyria to them in order to strengthen their hands toward the labors of the Lord, the God of Israel"). The odd reference to the king of the Assyrians[11] comes from the *Vorlage* in Ezra 6:22 but surely focuses on the Persian king Darius who is mentioned several times in Ezra 4–6 // 1 Esd 3–6. His first appearance in 1 Esdras is in 1 Esd 2:25 (// Ezra 4:24).[12] I will now examine the portrayal of Darius in 1 Esdras a little closer.

2. Darius

After the introduction of Darius in 2:25, 1 Esdras proceeds with the account of the three young guardsmen/youths,[13] which plays an important role in the

---

10. In contrast, the canonical version in Ezra 6 lacks this storyline within the book simply because the reign of Josiah is herein not reported.

11. Only the *versio arabica* offers with "king of Persia" a *lectio facilior*. See Joseph Blenkinsopp, *Ezra-Nehemiah* (OTL; Philadelphia: Westminster, 1988), 133, who supposes that the "king of Assyria" is taken from 2 Chr 30:6 in order to allude to the reign of Hezekiah. Antonius H. J. Gunneweg, *Esra* (KAT 19/1; Gütersloh: Gütersloher Verlagshaus, 1985), 116–17, points out that the first occurrence of an Assyrian king in 1 Chr 5:26 is also motivated by YHWH's action (עור hiphil).

12. It is not necessary to discuss the historical question concerning the identification of the King Darius mentioned in 1 Esdras. Corresponding to the canonical version in 1 Esdras, Darius follows Cyrus, which would suggest that Darius I is meant. In both versions, the so-called correspondence of Artaxerxes (1 Esd 2:15–25; Ezra 4:6–24) disrupts the historical order.

13. On the disputed issue of whether this story is an interpolation, see (among others): Charles C. Torrey, *Ezra Studies* (Chicago: University of Chicago Press, 1910; repr., New York: Ktav, 1970), 18–61; Dieter Böhler, *Die heilige Stadt in Esdras α und Esra-Nehemia: Zwei Konzeptionen der Wiederherstellung Israel* (OBO 158; Freiburg: Universitätsverlag; Göttingen: Vandenhoeck & Ruprecht, 1997), 69–72; Talshir, *1 Esdras: From Origin to Translation*, 42–109, who assumes that the story of the three youths is the *raison d'être* of the entire 1 Esdras. Her assumption that 1 Esdras never existed without this story seems to be plausible. It is obvious, moreover, that neither 1 Esd 5:1–6 nor 5:7–45 would be an appropriate continuation of 2:25, if the story of the three youths was a simple insertion in the sequel of 1 Esdras. On the other hand, Talshir underestimates the beginning of the text with Josiah's Passover, which she regards as "not a good choice" (107). In this paper I try to demonstrate that the opposite is correct.

portrayal not only of Zerubbabel but also of King Darius. In the following I intend to show how the story of the three youths functions to highlight the role of Darius within 1 Esdras in excess of the canonical version.

The story, which is set at the court of King Darius, deals first with three guardsmen who are competing to name the most important or mightiest (ὑπερισχύω) thing on earth and second (4:42–63) with the king's rewarding the winner. In between the first and second parts (4:13), the third speaker is identified as Zerubbabel.[14] A short third section (5:1–6), not part of the original story of the three guards, is used to connect the story of the guards with 1 Esdras' starting point in 2:25.[15] Whereas the first part of the story resembles the Hellenistic tradition of wisdom and court stories, as in the Letter of Aristeas (§§181–194), the second part is devoted to the portrayal of the king as a generous donor for the benefit of the temple in Jerusalem. Darius permits and finances the construction of the sanctuary, the livelihood of the priests, Levites, and gatekeepers, and also the preliminary offerings at the cultic site. Besides this, Darius bestows a tax exemption for all of Judah (4:47–56). Having heard about these generous benefits, the young man who succeeds in the contest (that is, Zerubbabel) utters a prayer that functions as a cataphora to the prayer of Ezra in 1 Esd 8:25 (Ezra 7:27):

4:60:	εὐλογητὸς εἶ ὃς ἔδωκάς μοι σοφίαν καὶ σοὶ ὁμολογῶ δέσποτα τῶν πατέρων
8:25:	εὐλογητὸς μόνος ὁ κύριος ὁ δοὺς ταῦτα εἰς τὴν καρδίαν τοῦ βασιλέως δοξάσαι τὸν οἶκον αὐτοῦ τὸν ἐν Ιερουσαλημ

---

14. The identification is probably secondary; see Karl-Friedrich Pohlmann, *3. Esra-Buch* (JSHRZ 1/5; Gütersloh: Gütersloher Verlagshaus, 1980), 359.

15. Subsequent to the story of the three youths, 1 Esdras features the list of the returnees (1 Esd 5:7–45, cf. Ezra 2:1–70) and the beginning of the rebuilding of the temple (1 Esd 5:46–70, cf. Ezra 3:1–4:5). It thus accords with the canonical version. Consequently the temple-building freeze is reported twice: 1 Esd 2:25; 5:70. 1 Esd 5:70 thereby consciously amplifies the content of Ezra 4:5 ("and they bribed officials to frustrate their plan throughout the reign of King Cyrus of Persia and until the reign of King Darius of Persia") by adding καὶ εἴχθησαν τῆς οἰκοδομῆς ἔτη δύο ἕως τῆς Δαρείου βασιλείας. Afterwards, in 1 Esd 6:1, the cardinal number δύο is related to the second year of Darius (ἐν δὲ τῷ δευτέρῳ ἔτει τῆς τοῦ Δαρείου βασιλείας). This means, firstly, that in contrast to the canonical version, 1 Esdras mentions the exact time span of the building freeze and, secondly, that Darius is clearly regarded as direct successor of Cyrus. It seems obvious that the amplification in 1 Esd 5:70 serves to alleviate the logical difficulties in the order of chapters in the canonical book of Ezra. Furthermore, the time specification telescopes the events to a very limited period of time: the reign of Cyrus lasts for only two years after the building freeze and in the second year of his direct successor Darius, the temple was already built (I am grateful to PD Dr R. Heckl, Leipzig, for this information).

Ezra's prayer immediately follows the famous Rescript of Artaxerxes (1 Esd 8:9–24 // Ezra 7:12–26)[16] in which the king guarantees generous benefits and donations to the temple and the people of Judah.[17] In both cases the prayer thanks God for the benefits of the foreign king who was acting according to God's will. In 1 Esdras this motif serves as a literary device to interlock the different parts of the *Vorlage*, Ezra 1–6; 7–10. Turning back to the portrayal of Josiah, it is noteworthy that in the accounts of Chronicles and 1 Esdras, Josiah also enables the celebration of the extraordinary Passover by providing the people with the required means. God's guidance (δίδωμι) causes the foreign kings to act in the same way as Josiah by enabling the celebration of Passover or providing the temple cult with the needed means. The role of the particular king is defined by his positive attitude toward the temple and his fostering of an appropriate divine service in Jerusalem. In this way it is not surprising that the focus of the reign of Darius is not the completion of the temple but the celebration of Passover. Of course, unlike Josiah, Darius as a foreign king does not celebrate Passover himself, but his reign functions as a patronage under which the postexilic community is able to celebrate Passover as in the exemplary time of Josiah.

So, the story of the three youths serves also to highlight the role of Darius as a generous donor for the benefit of the temple in Jerusalem in a way that is not featured in the canonical book of Ezra. Indeed, the canonical version also offers an account of Darius as benefactor within the sequence of letters in Ezra 5–6 (6:6–12 // 1 Esd 6:26–33), but the story of the three youths enables the author of 1 Esdras to create a storyline from the permission to rebuild the temple up to its completion and the celebration of the Passover. Because of the absence of the story of the three youths in the book of Ezra, the role of Darius is less important: in Ezra 5:1, Haggai, Zechariah, Zerubbabel, and Jeshua start rebuilding the sanctuary without permission from Darius because the edict of Cyrus (Ezra 1:2–4) seems still to be in force. Ezra 6, though, shows the need for a renewed order of Darius *afterwards*. In 1 Esdras the insertion of the story of the three youths causes a twofold *Wiederaufnahme* of the edict of Cyrus in 4:42–46 (within the

---

16. See below.
17. All in all, the elaborated image of the generous king seems to be a Hellenistic feature. A prominent example is provided by Josephus, *Ant.* 12.138–44, a letter (whether fictitious or not) of Antiochus III. In this letter the king appears as a generous donor for the benefit of the temple and the town of Jerusalem. He allows the authorities to purchase wood from the Lebanon (141, cf. 1 Esd 4:48) and bestows the sanctuary and its cultic personnel with gifts and the exemption of taxes (140–42, cf. 1 Esd 4:50–57). Finally, the Jewish *ethnos* is allowed to "live according to the paternal laws" (πολιτεύειν κατὰ τοὺς πατρίους νόμους, 142). For a detailed discussion with further examples, see Sebastian Grätz, *Das Edikt des Artaxerxes: Eine Untersuchung zum religionspolitischen und historischen Umfeld von Esr 7,12–26* (BZAW 337; Berlin: de Gruyter, 2004), 111–94.

story of the three youths); 6:16–25 (// Ezra 5:13–6:5), and, more importantly, also a rearrangement of the narrative. This is shown briefly below in regard to the portrayal of Cyrus.

3. Cyrus

In 1 Esd 2:1–14 (// Ezra 1:1–11) Cyrus is portrayed as a pious ruler who has received from God the tasks of rebuilding the temple and setting the Judean people free. He is introduced by his famous edict, in which he commands the rebuilding of the temple. It is noteworthy that in the book of Ezra (1:2), the foreign king enunciates the name of the god of Israel, which is avoided in the books of Daniel and Esther; that is, the Hebrew phrase (יהוה אלהי שמים) is translated in 1 Esd 2:3 by ὁ κύριος τοῦ Ἰσραηλ κύριος ὁ ὕψιστος—not by κύριος ὁ θεὸς τοῦ οὐρανοῦ, as the translation of 2 Esdras offers and the Hebrew text suggests. The term κύριος ὁ ὕψιστος occurs only twice in 1 Esdras, here and in 9:46. When Ezra opens the book of the law, he utters the same wording: ὁ κύριος τοῦ Ἰσραηλ κύριος ὁ ὕψιστος.[18] In light of the fact that it is not really suggested by the *Vorlage*, it seems not to be accidental that we encounter the same wording in the very beginning and the end of the account of the postexilic restoration. Therefore, again, one can assume that the author of 1 Esdras has consciously created storylines to tie together the Persian kings and the postexilic Judean restoration in a more elaborate and reflective way than the canonical version does.

In order to enable the rebuilding of the sanctuary, Cyrus takes action in two ways: First, he organizes a fundraising campaign[19] within the places where the Judeans live (1 Esd 2:6, 8 // Ezra 1:4, 6).[20] Second, he returns the temple vessels that the Babylonians had carried away (1 Esd 2:9–13 // Ezra 1:7–11). The first point seems to be particularly interesting because it is not the king himself who acts as benefactor in favor of the temple but the local people—whether Babylonians or Judeans. Here we surely have an allusion to the behavior of the Egyptians who gave their precious things—as a kind of compensation—to the departing Israelites, as is reported several times in the book of Exodus (3:21–22; 11:2; 12:35). The beginning of the account of the postexilic restoration is

---

18. Here the Hebrew text has: יהוה האלהים הגדיל.
19. In 2 Chr 35:8, as well as in Ezra 1:4, 6, to denote "voluntary contribution" the term נדב/נדבה, *hithpael*, is used (e.g., Ezra 2:68; 6:4; 7:13, 15–16). The voluntary contribution, whether by the king or by the people, is also closely tied with the cultic offering (Lev 22–23) and belongs to the sphere of (cultic) donations. Hence, 1 Esdras translates נדב adequately with δωρέω and δίδωμι, respectively. See B. Laum, *Stiftungen in der griechischen und römischen Antike: Ein Beitrag zur antiken Kulturgeschichte* (2 vols.; Leipzig: Teubner, 1914; repr., Aalen: Scientia, 1964), 121–22.
20. See Gunneweg, *Esra*, 43–44.

modeled on the events of the exodus, with the important exception that Cyrus in no way acts the part of Pharaoh. Instead, he initiates the collection of donations among the population. At any rate, in the book of Ezra (6:4) and also in 1 Esdras (6:24), Cyrus himself is known as a benefactor of the temple. So it should be taken into account that for Ezra 1 it seems more important to elaborate the events of the exodus in the opposite direction than to display Cyrus in the same manner as the other Persian kings in the book of Ezra.

Looking at the reign of Cyrus in comparison with the canonical book of Ezra, 1 Esdras displays a special feature in the insertion of the story of the three youths (4:1–5:63). Because of that, the events in the times of Xerxes and Artaxerxes (together with the correspondence in Ezra 4:6–24) are already reported in 1 Esd 2:15–25, immediately following the beginning of the restoration under Cyrus in 2:1–14. Thus, the entire rebuilding of the temple takes place in the time of Darius, who is first mentioned in 1 Esd 2:25.[21] This first mention in the present text of 1 Esdras is the catchword for the insertion of the story of the three youths. Because Zerubbabel is linked here with the reign of Darius, it is quite logical that the beginning of the rebuilding of the temple under the supervision of Zerubbabel would also take place then.[22] Therefore, Cyrus' edict in 1 Esd 2 is interpreted as a vow (1 Esd 4:44–45) whose fulfillment, however, is inhibited by the opponents in 2:15–25. In this way, 1 Esdras provides the reader with an apology for Cyrus, whose honorable plan for the rebuilding of the temple (1 Esd 2:17: ναὸν ὑποβάλλονται) is blocked by certain opponents in the reign of Artaxerxes, as reported in 1 Esd 2:15–25. This chronological order seems odd, but in the canonical version the transition from the second year of the return of the Judeans to Jerusalem to the reign of Artaxerxes, and thereafter to the second year of Darius, with the same *dramatis personae* as in the beginning, is not very plausible from a historical point of view either.[23]

---

21. See also above, n. 14. Böhler, *Die heilige Stadt*, 119–42, is correct when he states that Ezra 4:12 mentions the temple, in contrast to 1 Esd 2:17. The conception of 1 Esdras is, indeed, to locate the rebuilding of the temple solely under the reign of Darius. It is not possible here to go into the related discussion of the original position of the correspondence in Ezra 4:1–25 (1 Esd 2:15–25). But the discrepancies between Ezra 4:1–5 (building the temple); 4:6–23 (building the city); and Ezra 4:24 (building the temple) are obvious.

22. Ezra 3, in contrast, is manifestly problematic: the seventh month in 3:1 has no point of reference in the context, and the appearance of Zerubbabel and Joshua hints at the time of Darius (Ezra 4:24–5:6), who already should have been mentioned in 3:1. See Pohlmann, *3. Esra-Buch*, 382–83.

23. In the book of Ezra there is no hint that Darius II could be meant. Zerubbabel and Joshua act in the reign of a certain Darius, before and after the insertion of the correspondence in Ezra 4, together with Judeans who still remember the first temple (Ezra 3:12). This feature is corroborated by Hag 2:3. In 1 Esdras the time of Darius II is clearly excluded (see above, n. 14).

4. Artaxerxes

The king or the kings named Artaxerxes appear basically on two occasions, in 1 Esd 2:15–25 and 8:1–64. As 1 Esd 2:22–24 points out, Artaxerxes is responsible for the interruption of the labors in Jerusalem and at the sanctuary. In this way he acts in the opposite manner to Cyrus and Darius, although this action is described as a consequence of the intrigue by certain opponents of the Judeans. The next short, and perhaps secondary, reference to Artaxerxes occurs in 1 Esd 7:4, where he is mentioned together with Cyrus and Darius.[24] After that he appears in 1 Esd 8:1 as the well-known benefactor who enables the mission of Ezra. The Hebrew text distinguishes between the Artaxerxes of the interruption and the Artaxerxes of Ezra's mission: Ezra 4:6–23: ארתחששתא; Ezra 7:1–8:36: ארתחשסתא.[25] In the second spelling we have a *samek* instead of a *sin*, but as in LXX Ezra, in the Greek rendering of 1 Esdras this distinction is blurred (Ἀρταξέρξης). In 1 Esd 8:9–24 (// Ezra 7:12–26), the famous letter of Artaxerxes to Ezra, the priest and "reader" (ἀναγνώστης), with its superb donations for the benefit of the temple and the "the law of the God" (viz., the "Torah"),[26] is cited. So, the negative image of the first Artaxerxes is allayed by the second bearer of this name—if the author of 1 Esdras was aware of any distinction at all between these kings. More important, however, is the intended point of Artaxerxes' promises: as is well-known, 1 Esdras presents the equivalent of Neh 8:1–13 (// 1 Esd 9:37–55) directly after the divorce of the so-called mixed marriages in 1 Esd 8:65–9:36 (// Ezra 9–10).[27] It is disputed whether this order represents the original progression of the narrative, but it should be borne in mind that the literary transition from 1 Esd 9:36 to 9:37 is not very satisfactory. The problematic v. 37 may have been left at its present position when the list of returnees (which in the book of Nehemiah precedes the events reported in Neh 8) was deleted.[28] The focal and concluding point of 1 Esdras is the reading of the law in

---

24. See Pohlmann, *3. Esra-Buch*, 411.
25. See Böhler, *Die heilige Stadt*, 133.
26. In Ezra 7:12–26 the Aramaic term *dāt* (דת) is used, whereas the context (7:6, 10) uses the Hebrew *tôrāh* (תורה). This distinction is avoided or leveled in 1 Esdras by the common translation with νόμου.
27. It is remarkable that 1 Esd 9:36 (πάντες οὗτοι συνῴκισαν γυναῖκας ἀλλογενεῖς καὶ ἀπέλυσαν αὐτὰς σὺν τέκνοις) does not parallel Ezra 10:44, where the problem of the "mixed marriages" is not explicitly solved. It is doubtful, however, that the Masoretic Text should be emended according to 1 Esdras. See, e.g., Gunneweg, *Esra*, 184.
28. 1 Esd 9:37 parallels the end of the list of returnees in both cases of the canonical version—Ezra 2:70 and Neh 7:72. This list, however, is displayed in 1 Esd 5:7–45 with a distinct ending. It seems that the authors of 1 Esdras and the canonical version shared the same *Vorlage*: after Neh 7:71, the Masoretic tradition inserts a *petucha*, whereas BHS displays a lacuna after v. 72. The author of 1 Esdras, thus, would have begun his context with the

9:37–55. Now, it is probable that this ending is not accidental, although v. 55 seems to end abruptly.[29] On the one hand, it should be noted that the Hebrew text names Ezra a "scribe" and a "priest" (Ezra 7:6, 11, 12; Neh 8:1–2), whereas 1 Esdras preferentially calls him ἀναγνώστης, which denotes somebody who reads something loudly (1 Esd 8:8, 9, 19; 9:42, 49). This function of Ezra as a reader fits the events in 1 Esd 9:37–55 perfectly: Ezra here reads (ἀναγιγνώσκω) from the book of the law of Moses (1 Esd 9:41). This function of Ezra in 1 Esd 9:37–55 may also have already been determined by the ending of Artaxerxes' letter, because here Ezra is depicted as a teacher of the law of God, namely, the Torah. This is shown in the use of the verb διδάσκω (8:23 imp. active; 9:55: διδάσκω, ind. passive). On the other hand, 1 Esd 9:37–55 also calls Ezra "high priest" (ἀρχιρεύς) several times. This twofold designation of Ezra fits the image of the high priest that was also known by Hecataios of Abdera: the high priest is responsible for announcing the divine will to the assembly.[30] In the same context Hecataios states that the high priest serves to substitute for the (missing) king. So, it is not accidental that Ezra at the very ending of 1 Esdras also becomes a political figure—as Josiah is at the beginning of the book. The book thus ends with Jewish autonomy under the religious and political leadership of Ezra, as it starts with the political (and partly religious) leadership of Josiah. The postexilic restoration is completed when the high priest Ezra implements the Torah of Moses as the indigenous law of the Jewish people.[31] Thus, the instructions of Artaxerxes given in his letter are accomplished with the reading and teaching of the law of Moses. The rendering of the verb διδάσκω fits the end of the book exactly. The instructions of the Persian king lead directly to the final concern of 1 Esdras: the teaching and implementing of the Torah. Hence the letter of Artaxerxes can be understood as a release into political and religious autonomy.

---

equivalent of Neh 7:72 and by deleting the list of the returnees that he displays already in ch. 5. Böhler, *Die heilige Stadt*, 86–92, however, assumes that 1 Esd 9:37a is not a translation of Neh 7:72a but a particular phrase which was created for the context of 1 Esdras.

29. See also Arie van der Kooij, "On the Ending of the Book of 1 Esdras," in *LXX: VII Congress of the International Organization for Septuagint and Cognate Studies* (ed. C. E. Cox; SCSt 31; Atlanta: Scholar Press, 1991), 37–49: "Instead of regarding the last two words to be an independent sentence it stands more to reason to consider them as belonging to the ὅτι-clause, that is to say to understand this clause as structured by double καί" (44–45). In this respect also the following argument may be added: the verb ἐπισυνάγω (9:55b), in most cases a translation of אסף, קהל, יעד, or קבץ, has a definite theological meaning. It is used for the assemblage of the people of Israel returning from the Diaspora (LXX Ps 105:47; LXX Ps 146:2; 2 Macc 1:27; 2:7, 18). Thus, the passive "they were assembled" seems to be an appropriate continuation of the beginning of 9:55 (ἐνεφυσιώθησαν ἐν τοῖς ῥήμασιν οἷς ἐδιδάχθησαν).

30. Diod. Sic. 40:5–6.

31. See Sebastian Grätz, "Gottesgesetz und Königsgesetz: Esr 7 und die Autorisierung der Tora," *ZTK* 106 (2009): 1–19, esp. 10–12.

5. Conclusion

First Esdras begins consciously with Josiah's celebration of the Passover as the acme of the preexilic temple cult in Jerusalem. Josiah is portrayed as a pious donor and benefactor of the cult when he provides the people with sacrificial animals and commands the cultic staff to make the offerings (1 Esd 1:16). Indeed, we find the same content also in 2 Chr 35, but 1 Esdras starts consciously with that account and adds to chapter 1—as mentioned above—the two additional verses, vv. 21–22. Thus, it may be sufficient to suppose that the report of the first Passover in postexilic times (1 Esd 7:10), using a very similar wording, is the intended goal of 1 Esd 1. It is noteworthy that the foreign kings are also portrayed in a manner comparable with Josiah: Darius acts primarily as a benefactor in favor of the sanctuary. The main difference can be seen in his absence from the temple services since he is a foreigner. Nevertheless, he sets the financial and political framework in which an appropriate temple service is possible. A second storyline through 1 Esd 4:60 // 8:25, interlocking with the first, covers the narrative of Ezra that begins with Ezra's mission and the letter of Artaxerxes in 1 Esd 8 and ends with the reading of the Torah in 1 Esd 9:55. The evaluation of the texts shows that 1 Esdras, by labeling Ezra as ἀναγνώστης and by mandating him to teach (διδάσκω) the "law of God," clearly stresses the beginning and the end of this storyline. At the beginning, the Persian king enables the mission of Ezra, as did Darius with Zerubbabel, and at the end Ezra carries out the mandate of Artaxerxes, which leads the Jewish community into a kind of autonomy under the leadership of Ezra. With the completion of the temple, the celebration of Passover, and the reading of the Torah, the time of restoration is accomplished. Thus, 1 Esdras places the restoration in postexilic times in the direct context of the celebration of the Passover by King Josiah, an event that can be identified as the cultic highlight of preexilic times. The postexilic era, the era of the author, is surely to be acclaimed in equal measure. The most important difference between these two eras is the loss of the indigenous king in Judah. This institution is (temporarily) replaced by the Persian kings, who behaved in the same manner as Josiah did by enabling and fostering the religious needs of the Judeans until the restoration is completed. Viewed against the background of the books of Daniel, Esther, and Maccabees this attitude of the author seems to be naïve, but in contrasting the Persian kings with Josiah he has also created a kind of *Fürstenspiegel*, which could be read as literature written to evaluate foreign rulers against the benchmark set by Josiah and his foreign successors.

Darius' Court and the Guardsmen's Debate: Hellenistic Greek Elements in 1 Esdras

Paul B. Harvey Jr.

The scholarly consensus seems to be unanimous in considering the narrative of the bodyguards debating before Darius the extraordinary, defining, if not entirely unique, element of 1 Esd 3:1–4:41.[1] Investigation of certain aspects of that narrative may assist us in placing the debates offered by the bodyguards before the great king and his court within the contexts of Greek history, historiography, and rhetoric. I discuss here, first, the terminology and titles employed to identify the members of the court. That discussion may inform us better of the author's (or translator's) knowledge of the administrative structures of Hellenistic kingdoms. I then offer a consideration of the nature of the debates and suggest that the debates—in form and style—may best be understood as a Hellenized, probably Alexandrine, Jew's attempt to incorporate Greek literary and pedagogical traditions to enhance his narrative.

1. Hellenistic Court Terminology in 1 Esdras 3:7–14

1.1. To Be a Kinsman

In 3:7, we read that the winner of the debate will be called "kinsman" (συγγενής, *suggenes* = "of the same family descent") of the king. That style of honorific title is typical of ancient Mesopotamian and Mediterranean courts and, for that matter, early modern European courts. *Suggenes* has a particular resonance, I suggest, in this text. As J. H. Moulton and George Milligan long since noted, *suggenes* was introduced by the Ptolemies (specifically by Ptolemy II Philadelphus, who ruled 283–246 B.C.E.) as the highest level of titles bestowed upon

---

[1] "As has been pointed by all students of I Esdras, the story of the bodyguards is unique." Jacob M. Myers, *I and II Esdras: A New Translation with Introduction and Commentary* (AB 42; Garden City, N.Y.: Doubleday, 1974), 53; Zipora Talshir, *1 Esdras: A Text Critical Commentary* (SBLSCS 50; Atlanta: Society of Biblical Literature, 2001), 125–27.

courtiers: the formal title was συγγενής Βασιλέως Πτολεμαίου = "kinsman of king Ptolemy."[2] We may add something pertinent to what will come later: the Ptolemaic court had, from the late second century B.C.E., six levels of honorific titles for courtiers. That division is not attested explicitly for other Hellenistic Greek monarchies (notably, the Seleucids).[3]

1.2. THE PLACE OF JUDGMENT

At 3:14, Darius seats himself ἐν τῷ χρηματιστηρίῳ, for which "in the judgment hall" is a good translation. Χρηματιστήριον, *chrematisterion*, is so rare as not to be listed in Liddell, Scott, and Jones' *Greek-English Lexicon* or any of its supplements. Nor does it appear in Lust, Eynikel, and Hauspie's *Greek-English Lexicon of the Septuagint* (1991-1996). The word is apparently a *hapax legomenon*—found only here.[4] But we can discern its sense. The verb χρηματίζω and other derivatives of τὸ χρῆμα—standard for "property/money"—connote dealing in money in some fashion. Thus, in Ptolemaic Egypt ὁ ἐπὶ τῶν τόπων χρηματιστής, "the financial officer for the locales," is the regional/circuit judge who resolves tax disputes and other monetary transactions with the government.[5] *Chrematisterion* as "judgment hall" is therefore appropriate: here Darius will decide which guardsman is worthy to be *suggenes*.

1.3. DARIUS' COURT

Darius banquets (3:1, 2) with "all the nobles of Media and Persia, and all the satraps and generals and governors" (compare Dan 5:28). Darius judges (3:14), attended by "all the nobles of Media and Persia, and all the satraps and generals and governors *and* prefects" (so the NRSV renders). "Prefects" is probably nowhere near the mark, but the source of that translation can be identified (see below).

Darius' retinue is of interest. Darius banquets with what Hellenistic Greek terminology would identify as his *synhedrion*, his advisory council.[6] The reader

---

2. J. H. Moulton and George Milligan, *Vocabulary of the Greek New Testament* (London: Hodder, 1930), 595; P. M. Fraser, *Ptolemaic Alexandria* (3 vols.; Oxford: Clarendon, 1972), 2:189 n. 81. See also Myers, *I and II Esdras*, 45 n. h. Συγγενής and φίλος, "kinsman" and "friend," are common in the vocabulary of Hellenistic diplomacy. For example: *SIG* 502 (228–225 B.C.E.); 559, lines 20 and 50 (Megalopolis and Magnesia on the Maeander; 207–206 B.C.E.).

3. Fraser, *Ptolemaic Alexandria*, 1:101–2; 2:189 n. 81.

4. Compare, in 3:6: ἄρμα χρυσοχάλινον, "chariot with golden bridles (?)." As Myers, *I and II Esdras*, 45 n. *f-f*, points out, χρυσοχάλινος appears solely here and at 2 Macc 10:29.

5. So in Ptolemy Philadelphus' Revenue Law 15.4 and many other papyrological texts. See B. P. Grenfell, ed., *Revenue Laws of Ptolemy Philadelphus: Edited from a Greek Papyrus in the Bodleian Library with a Translation, Commentary and Appendices* (introduction by the Rev. J. P. Mahaffy; Oxford: Clarendon, 1896), 7, no. 15.4, col. 15, line 4, and 83–84.

6. The Ptolemaic *synhedrion*: Fraser, *Ptolemaic Alexandria*, 2:188 n. 77.

can well appreciate Talshir's remark, in her commentary on 1 Esdras: "he [the presumed translator of an Aramaic *Vorlage*] supplies random titles that he knows from the contemporary official vocabulary."[7] I agree as to contemporary official vocabulary, and I agree that the list of officials in 1 Esd 3 is perhaps modeled on similar lists of royal (Persian) officials in the book of Daniel (esp. Dan 7:7), but I suggest the list is not random. It appears to be a list (in rank order) of Hellenistic honorific titles mixed with administrative officers.

1.4. THE OFFICIALS OF 1 ESDRAS 3 7, 14

"Nobles" (NRSV), "magnates" (Myers) = μεγιστᾶνες, *megistanes*. The word μεγιστάν is manifestly derived from the Greek adjective *megas, megale, mega* = "great." Compare another, more common derivative: *megistos* = "greatest." *Megistan* is very well attested in secular as well as in religious texts from the mid-fourth century B.C.E. on.[8] *Megistan* is a Koine neologism. It has no precise connotation beyond, simply, "big man."

In a Persian context, we expect satraps, of course, but we may note that satrapies and satraps survived into the Hellenistic age as administrative divisions of the Seleucid empire, especially in Anatolia and Syria.[9]

"Generals" = στρατηγοί, *strategoi*. The στρατηγός, *strategos*, is, of course, the commander of a *stratos*, an army. At all times, *strategos* could mean a military commander, as in the annually elected board of ten *strategoi* in classical Athens, where each *strategos* was the commander (at least in principle) of his tribe's military contingent. But the term also had political and military overtones. The most politically astute (or influential) of the Athenian board of *strategoi* was, effectively, the city-state's political spokesperson for his year of office (often iterated). Pericles is a prime example.[10]

In the fourth century B.C.E., the term *strategos* continued to be widely used for military-administrative officers but especially for local administrative officers with an inflated military title, as in Hellenistic Greece, Macedon, Thrace, and the

---

7. Talshir, *1 Esdras: A Text Critical Commentary*, 132.
8. LSJ 1089.
9. Hermann Bengtson, *Die Strategie in der hellenistichen Zeit* (3 vols.; rev. ed.; Munich: Beck, 1964), 2:12–29—satrapies as part of the Seleucid administrative system; Arnold H. M. Jones, *The Greek City from Alexander to Justinian* (Oxford: Oxford University Press, 1940), 21–22, 306 n. 6; idem, *Cities of the Eastern Roman Provinces* (2d ed.; Oxford: Clarendon, 1971), 263–64.
10. Classical *strategoi*: Aristotle, *Ath. Pol.* 61, with J. M. Moore, *Aristotle and Xenophon on Democracy and Oligarchy* (Berkeley: University of California Press, 1975), 300–302, and P. J. Rhodes, *A Commentary on the Athenaion Politeia* (Oxford: Oxford University Press, 1981), 676–82. See also Arnold H. M. Jones, *Athenian Democracy* (Oxford: Blackwell, 1966), 124–28; R. K. Sinclair, *Democracy and Participation in Athens* (Cambridge: Cambridge University Press, 1988), 17–18.

great cities of western Asia Minor.¹¹ The title *strategos* was particularly common in Ptolemaic Egypt. While some Ptolemaic *strategoi* did indeed have some military responsibilities—for example, the Ptolemaic administrator/governor of sometime-Ptolemaic possessions around the Hellespont and Thrace had a flotilla of warships at his disposal¹²—*strategoi* were most familiar in their regional administrative role in Egypt. Papyri make very clear that the *strategos* was the official in charge of the basic Ptolemaic unit of administration: forty nomes, each governed by a *strategos*; each nome included two or more *toparchai*; each toparchy was subdivided into villages. The Egyptian *strategoi* answered to the Ptolemy. The *strategos* apparently often had police under his jurisdiction and so could therefore claim some military responsibility commensurate with his title. (The well-attested office of the *nomarchos*, incidentally, was subservient to the *strategos*; the nomarch was, so to speak, the administrative assistant to the *strategos* for irrigation control and tax collection.¹³)

Next in the list are the "governors" (NRSV) or "district magistrates" (Myers) = τοπάρχαι, *toparchai*. Myers' "district magistrates" captures well the rank and function of the toparch; in many a Hellenistic monarchy, the toparch was a lower-level administrator of a specific geographical area. As such, the term (and office) was retained by the Romans—for a while—for (native) regional dynasts in previously Seleucid areas.¹⁴

Again, however, we know best of toparchs from their appearance in Ptolemaic papyri: the toparch administers the *topos*, which was a subdivision of the *nomos* governed by, as noted, the *strategos*. First Esdras, thus, has the rank order of *strategoi* and *toparchai* correct.

Finally, in 3:14, we have an additional rank: ὕπατοι, *hypatoi*. Myers renders with the odd-looking "consuls," and that rendering is both strange and wrong.

---

11. For a sample of the epigraphic evidence: *SIG* 561–62. The basic discussion is Bengtson, *Die Strategie*. See also A. Jones, *Greek City*, 83; idem, *Cities of the Eastern Roman Provinces*, 10–11, 111, 291. Note Bengtson, *Die Strategie*, 2:270, on Herodian *strategoi* in Jerusalem and the "*strategos* of the temple."

12. For example: *SIG* 502 (228–225 B.C.E.): Hippomedon, *strategos* of King Ptolemy in charge of the Hellespont and Ptolemaic possessions in Thrace.

13. For a brief summary of Ptolemaic administrative organization of Egypt: A. Jones, *Greek City*, 18–20. On the administration of the nomes, an old standard offers a concise summary: Edwyn Bevan, *The House of Ptolemy: A History of Egypt under the Ptolemaic Dynasty* (London: Methuen, 1927), 139–44. For examples of *strategoi* for individual Ptolemaic nomes, see Fraser, *Ptolemaic Alexandria*, 2:190 n. 82, nos. 1–2. A vivid illustration of the relationship of the *toparch* to the *strategos* appears in P.Tebt. 289 (A. S. Hunt and C. C. Edgar, *Select Papyri* [3 vols.; LCL; Cambridge, Mass.: Harvard University Press, 1934], 2:570–71, no. 419): the *strategos* threatens the *toparch* of Tebtunis for not submitting in timely fashion a list of payments.

14. Tarkondimotos of Cilicia, *toparch* in ca. 51 B.C.E.: R. Cagnat, *Inscriptiones graecae ad res romanas pertinentes* (4 vols. in 3; Paris: Leroux, 1906–1927), 3:901, 64.

Hypatos, of course, is simply a Greek superlative adjective: "highest." So it is employed in LXX Dan 3:2 to render "high officer." But ὕπατος, *hypatos*, is not attested as a formal administrative rank in any Hellenistic Greek monarchical or political context—with one exception. *Hypatos* was how Greeks, beginning in the second century B.C.E., translated the Roman office of consul. Thus, *hypatos* rendering the Roman consul appears in dozens of Greek inscriptions and (quite properly) in 1 Macc 15:16: "Lucius *hypatos*" writes to the Ptolemaic king.[15] Hence, I would guess, Myers' translation. The NRSV renders with an office title: "prefects." That translation is, in fact, a transliteration of how the Latin translation of 1 Esdras, transmitted with the Vulgate, rendered *hypatoi*. That translator—not Jerome, who knew nothing of our 1 Esdras and thought 2 Esdras noncanonical and unworthy of reading (*in Vigilantium* 6 [407 C.E.])—knew that *hypatos* = consul could not be correct, so he rendered with a formal, but midlevel, administrative and military title, *praefectus*.[16]

I stress that *hypatos* was not an attested officer in Hellenistic courts or officialdom. The word in 1 Esdras seems to be used in a fashion similar to *megistan* = "big man." I propose an amplification of Talshir's observation that our author/redactor used known "contemporary official vocabulary." I have already noted that, in descending order, *strategos* ("general") ranks above *toparches* ("district magistracy") and that these officers were familiar figures in Ptolemaic Egypt. What, then, of the *suggenes* ("kinsman"), *megistan* ("bigman"), and, finally, the *hypatos*? I have already observed that *suggenes* is the proper term for the highest honorific title at the Ptolemaic court. I also noted that the Ptolemaic court had six (descending) levels of courtiers. I suggest that we have all six levels in the list of five officers at 1 Esd 3 14 plus the *suggenes*: *suggenes*, *megistan*, satraps, *hypatos*, with administrative officers—*strategos* and *toparchos*—correctly ranked in the middle.[17]

---

15. ὕπατος (in older texts: στρατηγὸς ὕπατος) = consul: Robert K. Sherk, *Roman Documents from the Greek East: Senatus Consulta and Epistulae to the Age of Augustus* (Baltimore: Johns Hopkins University Press, 1969), 16 and nos. 10 and 14 Hugh J. Mason, *Greek Terms for Roman Institutions: A Lexicon and Analysis* (Toronto: Hakkert, 1974), 95–96, 165–71. 1 Macc 15:16: the consul is probably Lucius Caecilius Metellus, consul in 142 B.C.E., *not* (as in *The New Oxford Annotated Apocrypha*, 225 n.) the consul of 139, whose name was Gnaeus (not Lucius) Calpurnius Piso. See, in brief, T. Robert S. Broughton, *Magistrates of the Roman Republic* (3 vols.; Cleveland: American Philological Association, 1951–1986), 1:476 n. 1; see also Jonathan A. Goldstein. *I Maccabees* (AB 41; Garden City, N.Y.: Doubleday, 1976), 492.

16. R. Weber et al., eds., *Biblia Sacra iuxta vulgatam versionem* (5th ed.; Stuttgart: Deutsche Bibelgesellschaft, 2007), 1515: 3 Esd 3:14: ".. omnes magistratus Persarum et Medorum et purpuratos et praetores et praefectos." This is genuine translation, but the translator did not know what to do with *megistanes*; thus, simply *magistratus* = "magistrates"; *praetor* has ancient precedent to render *strategos*.

17. Ptolemaic ranks in the third century were less systematic than in the second century; from the late second century B.C.E., there were six Ptolemaic degrees of rank, of which ranks

1.5. A PTOLEMAIC CONTEXT?

I propose that, in the narrative of Darius and the guardsmen, we see an author/editor/redactor familiar with some aspects of the Ptolemaic vocabulary of rule. He knows that there are six levels but does not know the correct titles for every rank and does not know that *suggenes*, "kinsman," was often a designation in addition to another title or rank: the head of the Ptolemaic chancellery (the ἐπιστολογράφος), for example, could be a *suggenes*, as could a *strategos*.[18]

2. THE GUARDSMEN'S DEBATE

The nature of the debate at 1 Esd 3:1–4:41 is exceptional and perhaps more complex in composition than has been recognized. I suggest that we have examples in that debate of two Greek literary forms woven together.

2.1. THE HERODOTEAN PRECEDENT

A debate in the presence of the Persian great king, and Darius in particular, evokes immediately Herodotus' *Hist.* 3.80–82—the relevant passage is not lengthy—where the Greek historian narrates that after Darius' seizure of power in ca. 522 B.C.E., Darius and his advisers debated under what form of government (*politeia*) the Persians should live. The debate is in the form of the rhetorical genre of deliberative/persuasive formal *logoi*, "speeches."

First, the Persian nobleman Otanes argues against monarchy as neither "sweet nor good." Monarchy, in fact, is unrestrained autocracy. Herodotus' language here is similar to ancient Greek descriptions of archaic and classical "tyranny." Otanes in his speech explicitly contrasts *isonomia*, government of laws, not men, with *monarchia* and *tyrannis*. He proposes that the Persians should live in *isonomia*. Neither the noun *demokratia* nor any corresponding verbal phrase is used, but in proposing open debate and magistracies selected by lot, Otanes' *isonomia* would have been very familiar to fifth-century Hellenic democracies. Indeed, later in his history (6.43.3), when Herodotus affirms the reality of this debate, he refers to Otanes' argument by using the verb *demokratein* = "to rule popularly."

Darius' second friend and advisor, Megabyzos, commends oligarchy. He denounces monarchy as well as "the rule of many"; he speaks of the latter in

---

four and five were not our author's *strategoi* and *toparchai* (although they might be, in function): their court rank was τῶν πρώτων φίλων = "of the first friends"; τῶν φίλων = "of the friends." See Fraser, *Ptolemaic Alexandria*, 1:102–4, on Ptolemaic court titles and ranks.

18. *OGIS* 139, 14; 168, 49; Fraser, *Ptolemaic Alexandria*, 1:101–2; 2:189 n. 81. The *epistolographos* of the Seleucid court was εἷς τῶν φίλων = "one of the friends": Polybius 30.25.16, with Frank W. Walbank, *A Historical Commentary on Polybius* (3 vols.; Oxford: Clarendon, 1957–79), 3:452–53.

terms familiar to late fifth-century opponents of democracy.[19] Megabyzos proposes the rule of a "few best men" to govern the Persian empire in enlightened, informed fashion for the common good.

Darius himself forcefully argues for what early modern European political theorists and historians would style "enlightened despotism." Monarchy provides a restraint on oligarchic factional politics (Roman emperors eventually appreciated that principle); democracy leads to charismatic, irresponsible leadership of the uninformed masses; the distanced, well-advised, well-informed ruler can legislate most effectively.

We need not seek firm proof that Herodotus owed his rhetorical construct of political debate to some unknown (and, to me, implausible) Persian informant or written source.[20] Some have suggested a more probable context: the influence of Athenian sophists, notably that of Protagoras of Abdera, who, at least according to Plato (*Meno* 91e and, e.g., *Prot.* 322), was interested in political governance and social contract. But the extant fragments of Protagoras' writings do not support this assumption, although it may be significant that Herodotus and Protagoras were sometime residents in Athens' colonial foundation of 443 B.C.E., Thurii, in southern Italy.[21] Nonetheless, the Herodotean debate is, as many have observed, reflective of late fifth- and fourth-century Hellenic discourse on the proper and effective forms of *politeiai* (Plato and Isokrates, for example).

---

19. See especially the so-called "Old Oligarch's" *Athenaion Politeia*, ascribed to Xenophon but surely composed by a young sophist at the end of the fifth century: *Xenophon* (ed. and trans. G. W. Bowersock; LCL; Cambridge, Mass.: Harvard University Press, 1968), 7:459–507, and Moore, *Aristotle and Xenophon*, 19–61.

20. For example: W. W. How and J. Wells, *A Commentary on Herodotus* (2 vols.; Oxford: Clarendon, 1922), 1:277, 2:80, hypothesized that "Herodotus was probably following the account of a Hellenized Persian." Martin Ostwald, *Nomos and the Beginnings of Athenian Democracy* (Oxford: Clarendon, 1969), 107, 178–79, argues for the reality of the debate. On *isonomia*, see Ostwald, *Nomos*, 96–102, 120, esp. 107–13: in Otanes' debate, monarchy and tyranny are interchangeable, in contrast to *isonomia*. As Ostwald notes, H. Erbse, "Anmerkungen zu Herodot," *Glotta* 39 (1961): 215–30, esp. 228–30, forcefully argued for the Herodotean originality of the debate.

21. Martin Ostwald, *From Popular Sovereignty to the Sovereignty of Law* (Berkeley: University of California Press, 1986), 343; Erbse, "Anmerkungen zu Herodot," 226. On Protagoras in Athenian context, see Mark Munn, *The School of History: Athens in the Age of Socrates* (Berkeley: University of California Press, 2000), 78–80. See also Thomas Cole, *Democritus and the Sources of Greek Anthropology* (Cleveland: American Philological Association, 1967), 8, 50–51, on "the [Platonic] Protagoras myth." For the *fragmenta* of Protagoras' writings, see Michael J. O'Brien, "Protagoras," in Rosamond Kent Sprague, ed., *The Older Sophists* (Columbia: University of South Carolina Press, 1972), 3–28, no. 80; trans. of H. Diels and W. Kranz, *Die Fragmente der Vorsokratiker* (7th ed.; Berlin: Weidmann, 1951–54).

2.2. THE HERODOTEAN *NACHLEBEN*: CASSIUS DIO

The Herodotean debate had a long afterlife. A debate on forms of government at a critical moment—specifically, the consolidation of power after a period of anarchy or political strife—became something of a Greek historiographic trope. For example (and notably), the Greek Roman senator from Bithynia, Cassius Dio Cocceianus, who wrote in his native Greek a lengthy *Romaika*—a Roman history from the origins to approximately his own day (ca. 230 C.E.)—offered an elegant example of Herodotean *imitatio* (*mimesis*). In book 52 of his history, Cassius Dio presents a debate on the forms a "restored" government of Rome should take. The debate takes place, in 29 B.C.E., in front of the triumphant (over Mark Antony and Cleopatra, in 31 B.C.E.) Octavian, the later Caesar Augustus. First, M. Vipsanius Agrippa, Augustus' capable military commander and lifelong friend and assistant, argues against monarchy and (at great length) for *isonomia*. While use of that word evokes Otanes' argument for democratic rule, Dio's Agrippa urges not democracy but a return to an idealized form of the Roman *res publica*: *isonomia* here means government of an informed, wise aristocracy—that is, a reformed (and rather idealistic) oligarchic form of government as set out centuries earlier in Cicero's *De republica* and *De legibus*.[22] Second, the late Roman republican magnate Gaius Maecenas, patron of literature and adviser to Augustus, more concisely urges monarchy and does so in deliciously Machiavellian terms: you have the power; use it wisely and justly or resign power and face probable destruction. Octavian reflects, in terms very similar to Darius in Herodotus; he then affirms that he will rule as the well-advised autocrat (Cassius Dio 52.1–41).[23]

2.3. THE HERODOTEAN *NACHLEBEN*: PHILOSTRATUS

Cassius Dio appears to have written his "debate before Augustus" (52.1–41) ca. 214/15 C.E. and he may well have delivered the debate as a public speech (a declamation).[24] Dio's contemporary, the Greek sophist Philostratus, offers another example of a Herodotean debate, at a critical political point, on forms of government. In Philostratus' *Life of Apollonius of Tyana* (a late first-century C.E. sage; the *Life* dates to ca. 238 C.E. or perhaps earlier), Vespasian, after leaving Jerusalem, while (it seems) in Alexandria, before going to Italy, invites advice on how to rule. Once again, "advice" is offered in the form of the rhetorical genre of

---

22. See, for example, Elizabeth Rawson, *Cicero: A Portrait* (rev. ed.; Ithaca, N.Y.: Cornell University Press, 1983), 148–60.

23. The debates in Cassius Dio 52 are discussed in political and literary context by Fergus Millar, *A Study of Cassius Dio* (Oxford: Clarendon, 1964), 74–75, 102–18, and by Meyer Reinhold, *From Republic to Principate: An Historical Commentary on Cassius Dio's Roman History Books 49–52* (Atlanta: American Philological Association, 1988), 165–210.

24. Millar, *Cassius Dio*, 19.

deliberative/persuasive formal speeches (*logoi*). The Stoic philosopher Euphrates of Tyre (an historical personality known from Pliny the Younger's *Letters*[25]) argues against monarchy and for democracy (*eleutheria*: "freedom"; *ho tou demou kratos*: "the power of the people"). The next speaker, the rhetorician and Stoic-Cynic philosopher Dio Cocceianus (Chrysostomus) of Prusa in Bithynia (possibly, but not demonstrably, an ancestor of Cassius Dio the historian) prefers aristocracy but urges people's choice: surely, if wisely informed, the people will choose monarchy in the person of the strong, wise ruler (i.e., Vespasian).[26] Apollonius, in turn, argues for a law-abiding, consultative monarch who will be as a patron to his clients, the governed, and will rule as "a just and wise herdsman." Vespasian deliberates, then accepts Apollonius' vision of himself as an enlightened monarch (*Vit. Apoll.* 5.32–37).

2.3. A GREEK RHETORICAL TRADITION: *PROGYMNASMATA*

I suggest, then, that the structure of the debate before the king in 1 Esd 3–4 should be considered within the context of the Herodotean debate on forms of government before a presumptive monarch. Note that in the examples I have discussed, monarchy is either rejected (by Herodotus' Otanes, Cassius Dio's Agrippa, and Philostratus' Euphrates), or praised (by Herodotus' Darius, Cassius Dio's Maecenas, and Philostratus' Dio and Apollonius), as in 1 Esd 4:1–12. But the debates in 1 Esd 3–4 are not uniformly on the lofty matter of political power. Two of the debates are on the rather banal topics of the power of wine and women, one is on the familiar topic of the power of the monarch, and the last treats a commonplace of Greek discourse, truth.[27] Among other scholars, Tamara Cohn Eskenazi hypothesizes that the debates in 1 Esd 3–4 originated in a secular form praising the strength of kings, wine, and women, with perhaps the addition of the praise of *aletheia* (truth).[28] I could not agree more: the topics, rhetorical style, and (even) the length of these debates are familiar from two secular Greek sources. First, the traditions of the Greek symposium included competitive performances (in music and discussion/debate, for example) and

---

25. Euphrates: Pliny, *Ep.* 1.102, with A. N. Sherwin White, *The Letters of Pliny: A Historical and Social Commentary* (Oxford: Clarendon, 1966), 108–9; see also Cassius Dio 69.8.3.

26. Dio Chrysostom: Christopher P. Jones, *The Roman World of Dio Chrysostom* (Cambridge, Mass.: Harvard University Press, 1978), 14–15 (the debate). See also Albrecht Dihle, *Greek and Latin Literature of the Roman Empire from Augustus to Justinian* (trans. Manfred Malzahn; London: Routledge, 1989), Dio Chrysostom: 228–30; Philostratus: 341–45.

27. Protagoras (see above, n. 21), for example, reportedly composed a rhetorical treatise on truth: Plato, *Theaet.* 161C; *Crat.* 391C.

28. Tamara Cohn Eskenazi, "1 Esdras," in the *New Oxford Annotated Apocrypha* (ed. Bruce N. Metzger and Roland E. Murphy; 3d ed.; Oxford: Oxford University Press, 1991), 279–300 (284).

poetic praise of, in particular, οἶνος καὶ ἀλήθεια, "wine and truth."[29] The closest parallels, however, in ancient literature to the guardsmen's topics of debate are the *progymnasmata*: student compositions on topics assigned by the classical rhetorician school master. These "elementary exercises" are attested as early as the late fourth century B.C.E., and what we read in 1 Esd 3–4 corresponds to the categories for such exercises specified by the Greek rhetorician Hermogenes of Tarsus (late second century C.E.): confirmation (*kataskeue*), encomium (*enkomion*), and, especially, comparison (*synkresis*). Examples of precisely the topics we encounter in 1 Esdras may be found in C. Walz's great nineteenth-century (1832–1836) edition of the *Rhetores Graeci* and (selectively) in the fine translations of rhetorical treatises on *progymnasmata* by Kennedy and Gibson:[30] praise and denunciation of women (a common ancient topos in many a genre); praise and denunciation of strong drink; approval and otherwise of monarchy; disapproval of tyranny and democracy; the noble qualities of truth (*aletheia*). These exercises are, on average, about the length of the "debates" in 1 Esd 3–4.[31]

---

29. See, for example, the Herodotean narrative (*Hist.* 6.129–30) of suitors competing in music, talk, and dance at a banquet given by the tyrant of Sicyon. The passage is aptly noted by Talshir, *1 Esdras: A Text Critical Commentary*, 127 n. 1. See also Wolfgang Rösler, "Wine and Truth in the Greek Symposion," in *In Vino Veritas* (ed. Oswyn Murray and Manuela Tecuşan; London: British School at Rome, 1995), 106–12. Note the fragments of "drinking (symposion) songs" by Alcaeus of Mytilene: D. L. Page, ed., *Lyrica Graeca Selecta* (OCT; Oxford: Oxford University Press, 1968), frags. 153, 173.

30. The SBL series Writings from the Greco-Roman World offers two excellent translations of relevant texts: George Kennedy introduced, annotated, and translated various *progymnasmata* and rhetorical treatises in *Progymnasmata: Greek Textbooks of Prose Composition and Rhetoric* (SBLWGRW 10; Atlanta: Society of Biblical Literature, 2003), esp. 221–24, "On thesis"; Craig A. Gibson offers an exemplary edition (Greek text and facing translation) in *Libanius' Progymnasmata: Model Exercises in Greek Prose and Rhetoric* (SBLWGRW 29; Atlanta: Society of Biblical Literature, 2008), esp. 509–26, "The exercise in thesis."

31. For example: Gibson, *Libanius' Progymnasmata*, rhetorical exercises on the topics of women: 17, 23, 25, 27, 29, 33, 35, 41, 475, 511; tyranny: 179, 187; wine: 441. On truth, see above, n. 27.

On Greek rhetorical education, note especially the discussion of *progymnasmata* and list of topics suitable for an *encomion* in H. I. Marrou, *A History of Education in Antiquity* (trans. George Lamb; New York: Sheed & Ward; repr. Madison: University of Wisconsin Press, 1956), 194–205. I cite here the University of Wisconsin Press edition of 1981, with pagination different from the 1956 edition. See also D. A. Russell, *Greek Declamation* (Cambridge: Cambridge University Press, 1983), 4, 9–12, 140: exercises in composition are common on papyri from the third century B.C.E. and constitute a type of imaginative literature. For an excellent description of the rhetorical practice, see Raffaella Cribore, *Gymnastics of the Mind: Greek Education in Hellenistic and Roman Egypt* (Princeton: Princeton University Press, 2001), 220–30. See also Laura Miguélez Carvero, *Poems in Context: Greek Poetry in the Thebaid, 200–600 AD* (Berlin: de Gruyter, 2008), 266–370.

The Greek pedagogical practice of assigning declamatory exercises had a rich history at Rome, as may be seen in the surviving works of the elder Seneca and Quintilian: S. F. Bonner,

I suggest that we meet in 1 Esd 3–4 a literary form going back to Herodotus but modified for classroom use. That is, the Herodotean debate (before and including the monarch) set a historiographic precedent, as illustrated here by Cassius Dio and Philostratus. Greek declamatory exercises[32] on the virtues of truth, wine, and so forth as defended before a monarch were edited and incorporated into 1 Esdras as a "Herodotean" debate (thus imparting pedigree and plausibility): an oral contest, the literary purpose of which was, of course, to assert Darius' public ratification of the authority of the winner of the debate, Zerubbabel, to return to Jerusalem.

Where might our editor/author/redactor have encountered the Herodotean tradition and Greek rhetorical *progymnasmata*? In almost any eastern Mediterranean city with a Hellenic cultural establishment, including *gymnasia* with their typical schools of rhetoric—Athens, Ephesus, Tarsus, Antioch, and, above all and to return to the geographical focus of the first half of this discussion, Alexandria.[33]

3. CONCLUSION

The author of 1 Esd 3–4, then, was acquainted with Hellenistic Greek court terminology and was aware that the Ptolemaic court from the early third century B.C.E. was composed of rank orders, but our author's knowledge of the specific titles of each rank was not exact. Our author also knows something of the content of Greek rhetorical training as practiced in *gymnasia* from the late fourth century B.C.E. forward and as expressed in brief rhetorical exercises, the *progymnasmata*. As with other Hellenistic Greek writers, including authors of historical works,[34] the author of 1 Esdras was thus capable of incorporating into his work variations of common Greek rhetorical exercises, within a Greek

---

Roman Declamation in the Late Republic and Early Empire (London: University of Liverpool Press, 1949), 51–70.

32. Note that these exercises, the *progymnasmata*, do not survive apart from stray Greek papyri fragments of school exercises (see above, Russell, *Greek Declamation*, and Carvero, *Poems in Context*, in n. 30) and in the exemplary collections and didactic instructions of the ancient rhetorical writers. See Kennedy, *Progymnasmata*, ix–xvi; Gibson, *Libanius' Progymnasmata*, xvii–xxv.

33. On *gymnasia* in Hellenistic Egypt, see M. I. Rostovtseff, *The Social and Economic History of the Hellenistic World* (3 vols.; Oxford: Clarendon, 1942), 1058–60, and esp. 1583–90 nn. 23–24 and 1395 n. 121. See also A. Jones, *Greek City*, 220–25, 284–85, 351–53 nn. 20–22. 25–29, 365 n. 35, on the organization and diffusion in the Hellenistic-Roman period of the *gymnasion*.

34. Josephus, notably: see Louis H. Feldman, "Josephus' *Moses* and Plutarch's *Lycurgus*," in *Flavius Josephus and Flavian Rome* (ed. J. Edmondson, S. Mason, and J. Rives; Oxford: Oxford University Press, 2005), 237–41; and J. H. Neyrey, "Josephus' *Vita* and the Encomium: A Native Model of Personality," *JSJ* 25 (1994): 177–206.

historiographic tradition going back to Herodotus (ca. 420 B.C.E.). To recognize that tradition is not to assume that our author necessarily knew Herodotus at firsthand. Likewise, to argue for a strong Hellenistic Greek context and foundation for 1 Esd 3:1–4:41 is not to deny or ignore the obvious "Semitisms" in the Greek of this passage.[35] Rather, thus did Jewish tradition, Hellenistic literary and rhetorical culture, and Hellenistic court politics and society inform the narrative of the foundation of Yehud and the reconstruction of the temple in Jerusalem.

---

35. As noted, for example, in Myers, *I and II Esdras*, 44–55.

I am quite aware that my argument here is at variance with the views of Zipora Talshir, who has forcefully argued for a Semitic *Vorlage* of 1 Esdras: "The *raison d'être* of 1 Esd is the Story of the Three Youths. The book was created in order to incorporate this story, originally written in Aramaic, in the narrative of the Return"; Talshir, *1 Esdras: A Text Critical Commentary*, ix. See also Z. Talshir and D. Talshir, "The Story of the Three Youths (I Esdras 3–4): Towards the Question of the Language of its Vorlage," *Textus* 18 (1995): 135–55. In my view, the story of the three youths is a rhetorical addition to the narrative by the author/redactor/translator of 1 Esdras; the function of that addition was to provide context for the Persian royal authorization for Zerubbabel's return to Jerusalem.

CYCLICAL TIME AND CATALOGUES:
THE CONSTRUCTION OF MEANING IN 1 ESDRAS

Sylvie Honigman

The collective memory of Judean society in late Persian and Hellenistic times conveyed a story of destruction, deportation, return, and rebuilding. While narratives of this sort are universally traumatic, each society generates its own questions about the meaning and implications of these founding events for present-day concerns, and the questions articulated reflect the specific ideology shared by the society as a whole or by its elite strata. In effect, narratives about founding events of the past primarily operate as a source of legitimacy, as a charter myth.[1] In ancient societies in which ideal models of society are projected into the past and charges of "innovation" carry with them connotations of trespass and impiety, processes of reconstruction and rebuilding are potentially unsettling unless they can be perceived as forms of restoration of the ancient order. Issues relating to the legitimacy of the rebuilt temple and the society that—allegedly or not—emerged from the return were extensively dealt with in the so-called postexilic Judean literature.

The Masoretic Text of Ezra–Nehemiah (henceforth EN) and LXX 1 Esdras are prime evidence of this Judean search for a definition of a collective identity. As is well known, these two texts tell roughly the same story, with a few notable differences. Thus in the Masoretic Text a source narrating Nehemiah's deeds is intertwined with the source(s) relating to the figure of Ezra, whereas Nehemiah's character is entirely absent from 1 Esdras. Conversely, a tale featuring three bodyguards at Darius' court is inserted in the extant version of 1 Esdras but is not found in EN. Despite these differences in content, the two works seem to address a similar set of issues Insofar as these issues can be reconstructed, the two works constitute invaluable guides to the questions that Judean society, or at least specific circles within Judean society, coped with.

---

1. On the concept of charter myth, see Sylvie Honigman, *The Septuagint and Homeric Scholarship in Alexandria: Study in the Narrative of the Letter of Aristeas* (London: Routledge, 2003), Chapter 3.

One basic question, which apparently dominated the traditions handed down in oral or written forms, can be readily identified through reading EN and 1 Esdras. This question concerns the association in the tradition between Darius' name and the completion of the temple-building project. According to the worldview shared by Judean and other ancient Near Eastern societies, the temple should have been built by the founder of the Achaemenid dynasty, Cyrus the Great, and not by Darius. In effect, the "restoration"[2] of social, human order under the founder of the new dynasty should have coincided with the restoration of the cosmic order that accompanied the resumed activity of the temple beginning with its proper inauguration. In EN and 1 Esdras this worldview is precisely articulated in Cyrus' "acknowledgement" (Ezra 1:1–4; 1 Esd 2:1–7) that he had become King of Kings by the will of the Lord who lives in Jerusalem. The normal counterpart for, and therefore evidence of, this claim should have been Cyrus' rebuilding the temple of the Lord. Yet, since the king failed to do so, how could the claim to this privileged link between the founder of the Achaemenid dynasty and the Lord of Jerusalem be sustained? And how could the human order of both the Achaemenid Empire and Judean society possibly be accounted for without this link? This unbearable chronological gap between the restoration of the human order and that of the temple was an acute call for explanation.

This crucial problem is one of the basic issues that both EN and 1 Esdras deal with. However, their answers are different. More accurately, the difference between the two works lies in the means used by their respective final editors to design their answer. As this paper will contend, while EN's narrative is founded on a linear conception of time,[3] 1 Esdras, in its final edition, follows a cyclical construct of time. Many of the differences that have been pointed out between

---

2. In ancient Mesopotamian societies, usurpers consistently presented overthrown kings as impious rulers neglecting their duties toward local chief deities; the usurpers claimed that they had been chosen by the wrathful deities to rebuild their temples and restore their cults. This means of legitimization was still resorted to by Alexander the Great upon his conquest of Babylon. See A. Kuhrt and S. Sherwin-White, "Xerxes' Destructions of Babylonian Temples," *Achaemenid History* 2 (1987): 69–78.

3. The construction of time in EN has been studied by Sara Japhet in a series of important papers. See her "Composition and Chronology in the Book of Ezra–Nehemiah," in *Second Temple Studies 2* (ed. T. C. Eskenazi and K. H. Richards; JSOTSup 175; Sheffield: Sheffield Academic Press, 1994), 189–216; "Periodization between History and Ideology: The Neo-Babylonian Period in Biblical Historiography," in *Judah and the Judeans in the Neo-Babylonian Period* (ed. Oded Lipschits and Joseph Blenkinsopp; Winona Lake, Ind.: Eisenbrauns, 2003), 75–89; "Periodization between History and Ideology II: Chronology and Ideology in Ezra–Nehemiah," in *Judah and the Judeans in the Persian Period* (ed. Oded Lipschits and Manfred Oeming; Winona Lake, Ind.: Eisenbrauns, 2006), 491–508; essays reprinted in idem, *From the Rivers of Babylon to the Highlands of Judah: Collected Studies on the Restoration Period* (Winona Lake, Ind.: Eisenbrauns, 2006), nos. 12, 18, and 21, respectively. In these papers Japhet explores the link between chronology, composition, and periodization in EN.

the two works arguably result from this basic distinction. As for the many repetitions, contradictions, and chronological inconsistencies of 1 Esdras that have been deemed by modern scholarship to betray disconcerting editorial carelessness, they are in fact explained by this cyclical narrative structure. Repetitions in a cyclical construct of time are not only deliberate but constitute the basic means through which meaning is created. As for the contradictions and chronological inconsistencies, they can be accounted for if we accept that the editor restricted his interventions in his sources to the bare minimum required to extract meaning from them.

The first step of the present discussion will be to delineate the threefold structure of the narrative in 1 Esdras as well as to identify the various literary components that are used to create meaningful echoes throughout the three successive narrative cycles. The second step will be devoted to the static sections, in particular the descriptions of ceremonies and catalogues. Altogether the static sections far outnumber the narrative sections that mark progression in time and action. It will be argued that they play a crucial role in constructing meaning. I contend that the author aimed at providing coherent answers to burning issues of legitimacy for the internal needs of Judean society.

1. THE CYCLICAL STRUCTURE OF 1 ESDRAS

1.1. IDENTIFYING THE THREE NARRATIVE SEQUENCES

As is well known, a tale is inserted in the middle of the extant narrative of 1 Esdras (1 Esd 3:1–5:6).[4] While the work is pieced together from heterogeneous literary sources throughout, the contrast of tone between the tale and the rest of the narrative is blatant. The tale conspicuously belongs to a distinct literary genre. Remarkably, however, it does not form a narrative cycle of its own. This lack of coincidence between form and content is evidence that the extant version of 1 Esdras, far from being the outcome of unskilled literary patchwork,[5] went through a complex editorial process. The three successive narrative cycles are ordered around distinct pairs of characters.

[*Preliminary section*]. The narrative of 1 Esdras begins with the Levites depositing the holy Ark in Solomon's temple in the reign of King Josiah and with the founding celebration of the Passover festival ("No Passover like it had

---

4. The verse numbering of 1 Esdras follows the NRSV translation. All quotations from biblical texts follow the NRSV translation unless otherwise stated. Changes in the use of capital letters have been introduced for the sake of consistency and will not be pointed out.

5. Zipora Talshir has contended that 1 Esdras is "a section deliberately cut out from Chr-Ezra-Neh, to form a framework for the Story of the Youths," as she calls the tale. See her *1 Esdras: From Origin to Translation* (SBLSCS 47; Atlanta: Society of Biblical Literature, 1999), 6.

been kept in Israel since the times of the prophet Samuel"; 1:20). The distinct tasks incumbent upon priests, Levites, temple servants, temple singers, and gate-keepers are recorded, as are the priests' vestments and the priests' and Levites' grouping in ancestral houses (1:1–22). Next we are told how the temple and the city are destroyed and how the Judean kings, people, and holy vessels are taken away by Nebuchadnezzar. Nebuchadnezzar's removal of the holy vessels is mentioned three times in association with three successive Judean kings, Jehoiakim (1:39–42), Jehoiachin (1:43–46a), and Zedekiah (1:46b–57), while the prophet Jeremiah lived through all the disasters since Josiah's death (1:23–58).

1. From the beginning of ch. 2 the movement out of Judah is reversed. First, in fulfillment of Jeremiah's prophecy and in order to rebuild the house of the LORD in Jerusalem, King Cyrus authorizes the return (under Sheshbazzar's lead) of both the people and the holy vessels taken by Nebuchadnezzar (2:1–16). However, enemies succeed in halting the building project until the second year of Darius' reign (2:17–30).

2A. There now follows a tale that explains why and how Darius authorized the wise bodyguard, identified as Zerubbabel by a later editorial hand (4:13 and 5:5–6), to lead the people and the holy vessels taken by Nebuchadnezzar and bring them back to Judea to rebuild the house of the LORD in Jerusalem (3:1–5:6). This time the full catalogue of the returnees is provided. The genuine members of the community, the "holy ones," are listed first and then those "set apart," the "unholy"[6] (5:7–35, 36–43, 45–46). The founding ceremony of the

---

6. The semantic field of holiness adopted here to refer to the full-fledged members of the community and those excluded from it because of dubious genealogical credentials is inspired by a series of recent papers that read the episode of the "dismissed" wives related in Ezra 9–10 and 1 Esd 8:91–99 as a ritual and not an ethnic issue. In particular, Bob Becking, "Temples across the Border and the Communal Boundaries within Yahwistic Yehud," *Transeu* 35 (2008): 39–54 (with further bibliography), and Arnaud Sérandour, "Les femmes étrangères dans les livres grec et hébraïque d'Esdras: Répudiation ou exclusion du culte?" *Transeu* 35 (2008): 155–63, with diverging emphases. In Ezra 9:1–2, the "people of Israel, the priests, and the Levites" are denounced for not "*separat[ing]* themselves from the peoples of the lands with their abominations." As a result "the *holy seed* has mixed itself with the peoples of the land." As Sérandour points out, separation is distinct from repudiation. The wives are not repudiated, as this is usually understood, but they are set apart from the community for ritual matters. Bob Becking, in turn, comments, "Ezra 9:1–5 implies ... an extension of the concept of holiness from the priests and Levites to the community in its, be it restricted, entirety" ("Temples across the Border," 42). The genealogical concerns at stake in the catalogues of people inserted in 1 Esdras and Ezra–Nehemiah should be read in a similar light. As will be seen below, genealogical purity is a prerequisite for participation in rebuilding the temple and in communal rites. In other words, it is a precondition for ritual cleanness. As Sérandour points out, the Greek verb *chōrizein*, "to set apart, separate, divide, exclude," is used in two passages related to the catalogues in 1 Esdras ("Femmes étrangères," 158–59). In 1 Esd 5:39–40, the verb refers to the families who were unable to prove their priestly genealogy and therefore were "set apart," "excluded" from serving as priests and forbidden "to share in the

altar is depicted in 5:47–50, followed by the resumption of the sacrifices (5:50–53). Next the narrative proceeds to the collection of building materials, leading to the description of the ceremony of laying the foundation stone (5:54–65). At this point the enemies succeed in stopping the work of building until the second year of Darius' reign (5:66–73).

2B. There is a new beginning in ch. 6. Like the first beginning, which occurs in the first year of King Cyrus' reign, the cue for each is given by prophets—Jeremiah under Cyrus and now Haggai and Zechariah under Darius (2:1; 6:1–2). While the narrative thus far focuses mainly on royal authorization, the involvement of the prophets in the action is used to stress divine authorization. At the same time, the narrative returns to the circumstances under which Darius authorizes Zerubbabel and Jeshua to build the temple. This time the enemies, who write to the king, fail to stop the work of building (6:3–22). We now learn about Darius' measures in favor of the temple and the returnees not in a narrative mode, as in the tale (4:47–57), but in the form of an official letter (6:23–34). Finally, the temple is completed in the sixth year of Darius' reign (7:1–6). The ceremony of the dedication of the temple is described (7:7–9), as well as the founding celebration of the Passover festival, which echoes the festival celebrated under Josiah (7:10–15). Here the narrative leaves Darius and Zerubbabel and Jeshua.

3. When we return to the scene in ch. 8, King Artaxerxes, in his seventh year, authorizes Ezra to take the people and the holy vessels, gold and silver vessels, to Jerusalem (readers are prompted to ask themselves whether these holy vessels are those taken by Nebuchadnezzar, even though they apparently are not), in order, now that the house of the LORD is built, to implement the *Law* of the LORD, that is, the social order. A few clauses of Artaxerxes' edict complement the privileges bestowed by Darius (8:18–22, 67). The catalogue of the returnees is given again, but only the "holy ones" are mentioned (8:28–49). The catalogue of people is accompanied by a short catalogue of holy vessels (8:55–57), which are listed again as they are deposited in the temple chambers (8:62). Here the motif of the unholy ones is treated separately and extensively (8:68–9:36). A distinct and much longer catalogue is offered of those who are eventually purified by separating from their unholy wives (9:18–36). Finally the celebration of the founding ceremony of the reading of the Law is described (9:37–55). This was probably followed by the founding celebration of the Festival of Booths, now lost.

---

holy things." In the Ezra cycle, the verb refers to the twelve leaders of the priests "set apart" by Ezra to take care of the holy vessels handed out by Artaxerxes (1 Esd 8:54). Ezra further makes an explicit equation between the twelve priests and the vessels in the following words: "You are holy to the LORD, and the vessels are holy" (v. 58). The nomenclature of holiness that will be adopted in the present paper to refer to the two categories of people separated from each other in the catalogues of people is based on the combined perusal of Ezra 9:1–2 and 1 Esd 8:54, 58.

As this summary shows, the cyclical structure of the narrative emphasizes the cyclical recurrence of a definite set of items. Its comprehensive morphology would include in its first stage a King, Prophets, a Leader of the Returnees, the Holy Vessels, the Returnees, and the Return, each clan to its place of habitation. The second stage of the basic sequence pattern includes a disrupting factor, followed by the successful conclusion of a form of restoration of the cosmic order, embodied in altar, temple, or Law, and then a founding celebration of a festival.

This basic structure recurs three times in varying incomplete versions. While the recurrent components allow for the overall coherence of the work, each sequence has individualizing features. First, the *pair of actors* is different each time: Cyrus and Sheshbazzar in cycle 1; Darius and Zerubbabel/Jeshua (the two are functionally linked together) in cycle 2; and Artaxerxes and Ezra in cycle 3. Each sequence is further individualized through distinct *time markers*. While the Cyrus sequence takes place in the first year, the Darius sequence is associated with the second year for the beginning of the works (sequence 2A) and with the sixth year for their completion (sequence 2B). Artaxerxes, in turn, is linked to the number seven. While each reign delineates a cyclical unit of time, the ascending order of the reigning years mentioned, one, two, six, and seven, creates an illusion of progression in linear time. Thus, the Artaxerxes sequence is not only told after Darius', it also comes later in linear time.

The illusion of linear progression is strengthened further by the progressive stages of rebuilding. Of the three sequences, the Darius one alone is complete. The Cyrus sequence lacks a founding ceremony and festival. As a result, the sequence of action associated with Cyrus' first year is close to that associated with Darius' second year (see 2A above). They both relate to the early stage of the narrative, which takes place before temple building. However, while Cyrus' first year merely refers to the return of the holy vessels and the people, Darius' second year is also marked by the founding ceremony of the altar, the resumption of sacrifices, and the ceremony of laying the foundation stone.[7] Likewise, the sequence of actions associated with Artaxerxes' seventh year is close to that associated with Darius' sixth year, which refers to the ceremony of the dedication of the temple (2B). The Artaxerxes sequence logically lacks a prophet, since the temple is already built at this point of the narrative. Conversely, the deposition of the holy vessels in the temple is depicted in this last sequence alone (1 Esd 8:17, 54–60, 62–64). Thus, while years one and two are associated with the beginning of the action, years six and seven are associated with its completion. The function of this division into two narrative parts, linking years one and two on the one hand and years six and seven on the other, is analyzed below. Needless to say, the distribution of the various stages of the action (reception of

---

7. In EN, these episodes occur in Cyrus' reign.

the holy vessels from the Persian king, founding ceremonies of the altar and the temple, building and dedication of the temple, and deposition of the holy vessels) through the three sequences contributes decisively to the overall coherence of the narrative.

Incidentally, the cyclical organization of the narrative in 1 Esdras and its linear organization in EN explain the different treatment of dates by the two editors. In a cyclical organization, recurring references to Darius' "second year" in all possible variations (building interrupted until the second year of Darius; building renewed in the second year of Darius; events taking place in the second year after the exiles' return) add inner coherence to Darius' narrative sequence. In contrast, these varying references are incompatible with a linear organization of time and become chronological contradictions.[8] This explains their careful smoothing out by the editor of EN.

1.2. THE FUNCTION OF THE CYCLICAL STRUCTURE OF THE NARRATIVE

This cyclical construct of history offers definite advantages. To begin with, as just shown, it is remarkably efficient for smoothing out contradictions—not, to be sure, the technical inconsistencies picked up by our modern, linear construct of time (and also by the EN editor) but contradictions meaningful to Judean collective identity. The contents of 1 Esdras and EN suggest that in Hellenistic times, various characters were associated with the story of the return in Judean collective memory, and this multiplicity of names could have been confusing. While in EN the figure of Sheshbazzar is inserted clumsily, to be replaced immediately with that of Zerubbabel (Ezra 1:8, 11; 2:2), in 1 Esdras the three figures of Sheshbazzar, Zerubbabel, and Ezra are given balanced treatment, and instead of confusion, the cyclical organization leads to meaningful reinforcement.

This balanced treatment of the three characters may be compared, to some extent, with a narrative device commonly used by Greek historians. The latter, when examining the stories of the foundation of cities, were often confronted with versions featuring different characters as city founders. In some cases, modern scholars believe, these diverging versions reflected competing claims to social prestige as well as political power in the city. In other cases these different versions may have corresponded with different ritual contexts.[9] In yet other

---

8. A typical example is provided by the correspondence between the "enemies" and Artaxerxes inserted at the end of the Cyrus cycle—or rather, at the beginning of the Darius cycle (1 Esd 2:16–30). This correspondence is obviously misplaced and must have been copied as part of a longer literary section. The only date found in this passage refers to the second year of King Darius (v. 30).

9. Various ritual settings seem to be responsible for the preservation of three distinct stories relating the end of the Pisistratid tyranny in fifth-century Athens. See R. Thomas, *Oral Tradition and Written Record in Classical Athens* (Cambridge: Cambridge University Press, 1989).

cases they may have resulted from the historian's compilation of several literary sources. In all such cases, most ancient Greek historians would not select one story at the expense of others but would rather organize all available versions in sequential order. This device allowed them to account for all the founding characters that were remembered by local traditions while at the same time restoring order and harmony among them.[10] This procedure was also used to combine mythical variants.[11]

Most importantly, the cyclical construct erases chronological gaps. The three sequences of the return story are preceded by a single sequence, common to all three, that tells of an earlier founding Passover festival celebration performed under Josiah in Solomon's temple. The inclusion of Josiah's celebration as a precedent turns the founding celebrations of the return sequences into repetitions of this original ceremony. The inclusion of Josiah's celebration with the following ones forms a common pattern of cyclical repetition that creates continuity between the original building of the temple and the freshly restored one. Thus, the cyclical construct of time is a powerful means to bolster the legitimacy of the rebuilt temple. At the same time, the preliminary sequence, telling of the destruction of the temple and the deportation of the people and holy vessels, stands as a common etiological story for all three return sequences. The return occurred precisely because there had been a deportation. What happened in between is not only irrelevant but symbolically disruptive and is therefore passed over in silence.

Finally, the combined effect of the substitution of one etiological story for another within a pattern of cyclical repetition redirects, as it were, the unsettling questions arising from the chronological gap between the foundation of the Persian dynasty and the rebuilding of the temple of the LORD in Jerusalem. The events that occurred under Darius become a comforting repetition of earlier events, and the elapsed time between Cyrus' reign and Darius' simply vanishes, as does the time that elapsed between Josiah's celebration of the Passover and Zerubbabel and Jeshua's. This does away with the need for an etiological story to explain this chronological gap, and so, as pointed out, etiological queries are redirected to the story of the destruction and deportation. The etiological issue probably best illustrates the difference between cyclical and linear constructs of time. In EN, the etiological story is provided by the hostile intervention of the enemies of the returnees. While the intervention of the enemies is kept to a bare

---

10. The sources are collected in A. J. Graham, "The Colonial Expansion of Greece," in *The Cambridge Ancient History* (ed. J. Boardman and N. G. L. Hammond; 2d ed.; Cambridge: Cambridge University Press, 1982), III.3:83–162, and idem, "The Western Greeks," in ibid., 163–95. On diverging versions, see R. Osborne, *Greece in the Making, 1200–479 BC* (London: Routledge, 1996), 5–7.

11. Thus Herodotus (*Hist.* 4.110) used this device to accommodate the three distinct geographical origins that various mythical versions ascribed to the Amazons.

minimum in 1 Esdras (5:72–73), the functional importance of this episode in EN is emphasized through its narrative duplication (Ezra 4:1–6 and 7–24) and the insertion of the correspondence between the enemies and "King Artaxerxes" at this narrative point (vv. 7–24).

Interestingly, the tale inserted in 1 Esd 3:1–5:6 appears to have an underlying linear construct of time. However, unlike the learned literary elaboration of EN, the tale is not interested in accurate chronological reckoning. Accordingly, while EN is concerned with the question of why the building was delayed until Darius' reign, the etiological story of this tale, namely the debate of the three bodyguards before Darius, shifts the question to what prompted Darius to give the authorization to finally build the temple (1 Esd 4:42–63).

1.3. WAS THERE A FOURTH, NEHEMIAH SEQUENCE? 1 ESDRAS, EZRA–NEHEMIAH, AND 2 MACCABEES 1:18–36

The end of 1 Esdras is now lost. The extant text abruptly ends in mid-sentence at 9:55. Therefore there is at least a possibility that a fourth sequence, which would have revolved around the figure of Nehemiah, may have been lost. The structure of the four reigning years, one, two, six, and seven, examined above warrants a negative answer. The rationale for raising the question of a fourth cycle nevertheless derives not so much from the long section dedicated to the figure of Nehemiah in EN but from the treatment of this figure in 2 Macc 1:18–36. In this section, Nehemiah is presented as the leader in a story of the return that offers striking similarities to the story pattern delineated above (section 1.1). In 2 Macc 1:20, the king of Persia is not named, and this namelessness fosters suspicions that the names of the three Persian kings associated with the leaders of the returnees in the three narrative sequences of 1 Esdras—Cyrus, Darius, and Artaxerxes—are generic and do not derive from genuine historical data. In 2 Macc 1, Nehemiah is said to have celebrated the Festival of Booths and further founded the Festival of the Fire (v. 18). The miraculous fire celebrated in this festival plays a role functionally similar to that of the holy vessels in 1 Esdras, that is, it is a sign that guarantees continuity between the original temple and the restored building (2 Macc 1:19–23; see below on the notion of sign). The founding ceremony of kindling the altar with this fire was performed by priests under the dual control of Nehemiah and Jonathan, a pair that is reminiscent of Zerubbabel and Jeshua. The altar in the Nehemiah story (2 Macc 1:32) features prominently in 1 Esdras and EN as well and is granted equal status with the temple itself. Like in the Ezra sequence of 1 Esdras (as well as in EN), the "king of Persia" is involved in the ratification of the miracle that founds the new Festival of the Fire (2 Macc 1:33–35).[12]

---

12. At the same time a few items are slightly modified in accordance with new (?) concerns. Thus the motive of the clans of returnees going each to its place of residence is

Thus the comparison between the story variants found in 2 Macc 1:18–36 and 1 Esdras (as well as the tale variant inserted in 1 Esd 4:42–5:6) raises intriguing questions about the genesis of the story pattern underlying the three narrative sequences of 1 Esdras. A possible interplay between oral tradition and scholarly literary production that would explain the circulation of a fourth cyclical sequence identified with Nehemiah cannot be excluded. This issue, in turn, may affect our understanding of the relation between 1 Esdras and EN and support the view that these two works drew on common traditions independently.[13] However, too many questions remain open at this point to reach any definite conclusion.

2. The Function of the Static Sections in 1 Esdras: Descriptions and Catalogues

The cyclical repetition of the basic components in all three return sequences is 1 Esdras' basic means of emphasizing continuity. The comparison between 1 Esdras, EN, and 2 Macc 1:18–36 confirms that the issue of the continuity between Solomon's temple and the rebuilt edifice was a basic concern for the learned circles of Judean society in early Second Temple times. Continuity in society was also crucial. While the importance of the kings and leaders of the returnees was obvious without the need for further elaboration, attention is drawn to the rest of the basic items through a series of literary devices other than cyclical repetition. These consist of static, descriptive sections that suspend the continuous narrative. As mentioned earlier, these static sections, taken together, compose the main part of 1 Esdras' text. Three main literary devices are resorted to:[14] 1) descriptive units relating to festivals and ceremonies; 2) catalogues—of

---

substituted with a reference to the gathering of the scattered ones (2 Macc 1:27, 29), which seems to shift the stress to the Diaspora communities. Also, while the narratives of 1 Esdras and Ezra–Nehemiah dwell on the vestments and musical tools of the priests and Levites in describing the celebration of the festivals, 2 Macc 1 focuses on Jonathan's prayer (2 Macc 1:24–29).

13. One such tradition may be a simple building story. Compare Lisbeth S. Fried, "The Land Lay Desolate: Conquest and Restoration in the Ancient Near East," in Lipschits and Blenkinsopp, *Judah and the Judeans in the Neo-Babylonian Period*, 21–54.

14. The concern of the Judean society of Second Temple times for continuity is further reflected in the intriguing references to the twelve tribes that appear not only in 1 Esdras and Ezra–Nehemiah but also elsewhere in the Judean literature of Hellenistic times. Thus the returnees are said to be led by twelve leaders (1 Esd 5:8; Ezra 2:2, corrupt). Likewise, the Letter of Aristeas, a work written in Greek by an Alexandrian Judean, probably in the second half of the second century B.C.E., preserves the claim that the seventy-two elders sent by the high priest of Jerusalem to Alexandria in order to translate the Torah into Greek were composed of six scholars from each of the twelve tribes (*Let. Aris.* 46–50). It is also possible that the memory of the twelve tribes was symbolically maintained in the ritual practice of sacrifices. In

returnees and holy vessels; 3) official letters and royal edicts. Since the royal letters present specific problems of their own,[15] the following discussion will be restricted to the descriptions of festivals and catalogues.

2.1. DESCRIPTIONS OF CEREMONIES

The various ceremonies described in 1 Esdras (as well as EN and 2 Macc 1) mark the restoration of cosmic order. All the ceremonies described are founding ones, including the ceremony of the Passover festival celebrated under Josiah (1 Esd 1:1–22, esp. 20–21). Incidentally, this stress on the founding character of Josiah's Passover constitutes the main literary device that enables the editor of 1 Esdras to insert Josiah into the cycle of repetitions. In EN's linear construct of time, the foundation of the altar "in its place," which is distinguished from the rebuilding of the temple, allows for the cosmic order to be restored immediately upon the arrival of the returnees, even though the dedication of the temple is delayed.

Three ceremonies of foundation and dedication are described altogether, that of the altar (1 Esd 5:47–50), the ceremony of laying the foundation stone (5:54–65), and the ceremony of the dedication of the temple (7:7–9). Each time, the ceremony is followed by the renewed celebration of a festival "according to Moses." The ritual and symbolic meaning of the resumption of the sacrifices is best understood in the description of the founding ceremony of the altar:

> 50 And they offered sacrifices at the proper times and burnt offerings to the LORD morning and evening. 51 They kept the Festival of Booths, as it is commanded in the Law, and offered the proper sacrifices every day 52 and thereafter the regular offerings and sacrifices on Sabbaths and at new months and at all the consecrated feasts. (1 Esd 5:50–52)

Thus the resumption of regular sacrifices signifies the restoration of the ritual calendar, that is, of time. From its undifferentiated state since the destruction of Solomon's temple by Nebuchadnezzar, time is restored to its orderly divisions, as it was established in creation: day and night ("morning and evening"), sacred and secular (Sabbaths, new months, and feasts, as opposed to "every day"), days, weeks, months, and yearly seasons. Time is henceforth governed again by the rhythm of sacrifices ("at proper times"; "regular offerings").

The two dedication ceremonies of the altar and the temple are duly followed by the founding resumption of the two main festivals: that of Booths (following the altar's refounding, 5:51), and that of Passover and Unleavened Bread (following the temple dedication, 7:10–15). These two founding events are associated with Jeshua and Zerubbabel, as they probably were in the collective memory of

---

effect the twelve tribes are mentioned in a sacrificial context in both 1 Esdras and Ezra-Nehemiah (1 Esd 7:8 = Ezra 6:17; see also 1 Esd 8:66 = Ezra 8:35).

15. I hope to deal with them in a separate paper.

Judeans, and not distributed through the first two cyclical narratives. Nonetheless, they undoubtedly operate as precedents for all following founding festival celebrations. Ezra's reading of the Law in the third narrative sequence draws its legitimacy and founding character from this twofold precedent, as does the founding celebration of the Festival of the Fire led by Nehemiah in 2 Macc 1:18–36.

The descriptions of the various ceremonies further display several recurrent elements that echo Josiah's ceremony in Solomon's temple and Zerubbabel and Jeshua's celebrations and, through this, establish continuity: priestly vestments, music, and purity requirements are mentioned in each case. Continuity is also ascertained, however, through witnessing. Both in EN and in 1 Esdras the ceremony of laying the foundation stone is said to have been accompanied by outcries and weeping together with music and merriment. In both works the weeping is related to the old men, priests, and heads of the ancestral houses, who had known Solomon's temple (1 Esd 5:63 = Ezra 3:12).[16]

2.2. CATALOGUES OF HOLY VESSELS

In antiquity, as theorists of Greek rhetoric make plain, evidence was primarily based on sight.[17] The catalogues of objects and people in 1 Esdras appeal to the visual sense even more clearly than the descriptions of ceremonies.

Objects are signs. When looking at a specific object, the viewer is reminded of the story associated with this object. This function has been well studied in the ancient Greek cultural area. Thus Herodotus is prompted to tell us the story of Gyges and Midas, the son of Gordias, because these men were the first barbarians to dedicate ex-votos at Delphi (*Hist.* 1.14), which the historian actually saw there. For similar reasons, the pharaohs whose stories Herodotus tells are those who left buildings behind them as signs of their past existence. Likewise, objects deposited in sanctuaries as ex-votos are concrete signs. A catalogue of ex-votos dedicated to Athena Lindia was proudly displayed on a stele erected in the goddess's sanctuary at Lindos, in Rhodes, in 96 B.C.E. The prestigious names gathered in the catalogue were signs that outstanding heroes, kings, and embassies from cities paid visits to the sanctuary in order to honor the goddess, and their cumulative list was in turn a sign of the fame and importance of the sanctuary.[18]

---

16. *Pace* Fried, "The Land Lay Desolate," 43–46, who argues for a ritualized lamentation ceremony.

17. See in particular C. Calame's suggestive remarks, in "Quand dire c'est faire voir: L'évidence dans la rhétorique antique," *Études de Lettres* 4 (1991): 3–22.

18. Edition, English translation, and commentary may be found in C. Higbie, *The Lindian Chronicle and the Greek Creation of Their Past* (Oxford: Oxford University Press, 2003). N. Massar, "La 'Chronique de Lindos': Un catalogue à la gloire du sanctuaire d'Athéna Lindia," *Kernos* 19 (2000): 239–43, offers an important discussion of the catalogue.

The holy vessels mentioned in 1 Esdras are those that were taken by Nebuchadnezzar when Solomon's temple was destroyed, and these selfsame vessels are those that are now brought back by the returnees and deposited in the newly built temple. These holy vessels stand as concrete signs for all three events: destruction, deportation, and return. They are signs guaranteeing the continuity between the destroyed temple and the new building.[19] In order that the holy vessels may function as signs, the story of their restitution is told in detail (2:10–12, 15), and they are dwelt upon in the form of a short catalogue (vv. 13–14), their shapes and precious materials diligently recorded and numbered. While all other numbers are round, the twenty-nine silver censers (v. 13), as well as the total number of a few thousand and "sixty-nine" (v. 14), reassure the readers that the numbering is accurate, as befits their holiness (a similar procedure is found in Ezra 1:9).

A second catalogue of holy vessels is inserted in the Ezra sequence (1 Esd 8:55–57). Like the first time, the vessels are handed out by the Persian king to the leader of the returnees (8:55), and their very display in the form of a catalogue further suggests—indeed establishes—the equivalence between the two sets. Indeed, the readers were prepared to accept this assimilation beforehand. In ch. 1, as pointed out in the summary, Nebuchadnezzar's removal of the holy vessels is told three times, each time in association with a different Judean king. This triplet in the section operating as an etiology for the three following cyclical sequences may not be coincidental. Readers are implicitly induced to expect the threefold return of the holy vessels. It took three attempts to remove all the vessels from the temple, and it took three attempts to take them back, to the very last one.

The duplication of the catalogue of vessels seems to participate in the construction of meaning. The clue lies in the close association between holy vessels and returnees, which is emphasized by the parallel listing of returnees and holy vessels in catalogues. The second catalogue of the holy vessels seems to respond to queries about the status of Ezra's journey from Mesopotamia to Judea, and these queries, in turn, had further bearing on the status of the ceremony of reading the Torah initiated by Ezra. The sacred status of the Torah reading, which is expressed in 1 Esdras through its narrative and functional similarity with the Festivals of Booths and Passover, was apparently deemed to depend on the identification of Ezra's arrival at Jerusalem as a full-fledged return.

As common perception probably had it, a return necessarily implied three items: a complete sampling of society (as opposed to an undifferentiated throng of people), holy vessels linked to Solomon's temple, and royal authorization. The two catalogues of holy vessels and of returnees inserted in the Ezra narrative

---

19. On this symbolic function of the vessels, see Peter R. Ackroyd, "The Temple Vessels: A Continuity Theme," in *Studies in the Religious Tradition of the Old Testament* (ed. Peter R. Ackroyd; London: SCM, 1987), 45–60.

sequence precisely guarantee the status of Ezra's journey, thereby legitimating Ezra's own status and therefore the ceremony of Torah reading first instituted under his lead.

2.3. THE TWO CATALOGUES OF RETURNEES AND UNHOLY ONES[20]

By displaying men as well as temple vessels, the catalogues in 1 Esdras and EN function as signs of the symbolic connection between the community and its temple. Like the holy vessels, the returnees brought back by the leaders mandated by the Persian kings are those who had been taken by Nebuchadnezzar (1 Esd 5:7; Ezra 2:1). As in deportation, their common fate demands that one cannot be restored without the other. Since the temple founds a cosmic order on which society is based, society cannot properly operate, or even exist as a society, without its temple. Conversely, the temple needs a society to exist, lest it be a head without a body.

This interdependence of temple and society should not surprise us. The state of cognitive perception reflected in this worldview has long been familiar to students of Archaic and Classical Greece. In the Homeric epics man is not an autonomous agent—what modern nomenclature would call an individual—but is interconnected with cosmic forces. A recent study of Plato's *Critias* and *Timaeus* by Johansen has shown that a similar analysis still applies to Plato's cosmogony in the fourth century B.C.E.[21] As Johansen argues, Plato's depiction of the ideal city in the *Republic* is complemented by Timaeus' account of the genesis and nature of the universe and nature of man in the dialogue named after him. In Plato's view, his depiction of the just life must be rooted in the natural order of things as a token of credibility.[22] Likewise, men were perceived as integrated into larger social units to form an organic society. In the Homeric epics these social units do not comprise men alone. The Greek *oikos* (household) consists of the head of the household, his wife and legitimate children, concubines and illegitimate children, male and female slaves, flocks and cattle, house, furniture, tools, and fields.[23] This perception of society as embedded (or

---

20. For this nomenclature, see above, n. 6.
21. T. K. Johansen, *Plato's Natural Philosophy: A Study of the* Timaeus–Critias (Cambridge: Cambridge University Press, 2004), Chapter 1.
22. Ibid.
23. C. Leduc ("Marriage in Ancient Greece," in *A History of Women in the West* [ed. P. Schmitt Pantel; 2 vols.; Cambridge, Mass.: Harvard University Press, 1992], 1:35–95, 240–41) points out that the household (*oikos*), the "coherent assemblage of 'well-built' parts," is designated by the father's name, while the word *oikos* designates both the main beam holding the house together and the household. The wife's womb, in turn, is equated with the central hearth (*eschara*), and the man's legitimate sons with the ashes of the hearth. "There is a clear homology between people and things. The father, who bears the same name as the household, is, like the *oikos*, a 'whole.' He keeps the various components of the reproductive group

organic) is still reflected in the lack of distinction between social units and administrative divisions that characterizes Greek *poleis* in classical times. Thus, the Athenian *demes* and tribes were primarily social and not "objective" administrative units. This remained the case at least as late as the fourth century B.C.E.[24]

The catalogues of returnees in 1 Esd 5:7-46 (= Ezra 2 = Neh 7, under Jeshua and Zerubbabel's lead) and 1 Esd 8:28-49 (= Ezra 8:1-20, under Ezra's lead) are, in essence, descriptions of society and function as signs of its restoration alongside that of the temple. The composition of the catalogues, their internal organization and order, reflect the composition of society, its social categories and hierarchies. As mentioned earlier, the returnees are led by twelve leaders representing the Israelite tribes. In the same way as the resumption of the sacrifices enables time to be differentiated again into its proper divisions and categories, men do not return as a shapeless, undifferentiated mass of human beings but are properly ordered according to ancestral houses. Clans of lay people are listed and counted first (1 Esd 5:9-23). The priests, Levites, temple servants, and descendants of Solomon's servants are listed next, in descending hierarchical order (vv. 24-35). The catalogues' all-embracing picture of society is dramatized in the second list of returnees led by Ezra. While the version extant in 1 Esdras (8:42-49) seems corrupt or abbreviated, the intention of this dramatization may be clearly retrieved from EN's version (Ezra 8:15-20). In this passage Ezra is depicted as engaging in an active search for Levites. Ezra's conviction that he cannot undertake his return without Levites certifies that the catalogue is a reliable and exhaustive inventory of society.

Thanks to their certified comprehensiveness, the catalogues offer a clear delineation of social boundaries, separating members from nonmembers. Thus society becomes a community. The inclusion of categories of outsiders at the end of the first catalogue (1 Esd 5 = Ezra 2) guarantees in hindsight both the very existence of these boundaries and their nature. In other words, these outsiders help define the essence of the community. Thus male and female slaves and cattle are listed separately (1 Esd 5:42-43; Ezra 2:65-67). More significantly, a section at the end of the catalogues gathers the names of those, sons of Israel and priests, whose genealogy is uncertain (1 Esd 5:36-40 = Ezra 2:59-63). It is

---

together. The mother on her wedding day comes to sit beside the hearth. Children, if legitimate, were 'born twice': five days after delivery the newborn was placed on the ashes of the hearth, and the father then lifted the child into an upright position ..." (40-41).

24. This perception has been studied many times. For a convenient overview and further bibliography, see C. Farrar, *The Origins of Democratic Thinking* (Cambridge: Cambridge University Press, 1988), Chapter 2. On Athenian *demes* and tribes, see R. Osborne, Demos: *The Discovery of Classical Attika* (Cambridge: Cambridge University Press, 1985); R. Parker, *Athenian Religion: A History* (Oxford: Oxford University Press, 1996); on the Greek *polis* as an organic social unit, see P. B Manville, "Toward a New Paradigm of Athenian Citizenship," in *Athenian Identity and Civic Ideology* (ed. A. L. Boegehold and A. C. Scafuro; Baltimore: Johns Hopkins University Press, 1994), 21-33.

explicitly stated that these doubtful priests were excluded from serving as priests. The inclusion of this category of unholy families retrospectively defines the community as the gathering of the holy ones.

Space, like time, was not perceived as objective in many ancient societies. The quality of a territory was defined through its inhabitants. To ancient Greek authors, Greece comprises all the territories inhabited by Greeks throughout the Mediterranean, and Arabia was the space inhabited by Arabs.[25] No territorial continuity is assumed in these definitions. Unsurprisingly, geographical lore was often transmitted in the form of mythical genealogies, blurring the distinction between territory and men.[26] As late as Hellenistic times, as N. Massar has shown, the catalogue of donors to Athena's sanctuary listed in the Lindian Chronicle easily translates into geography.[27] Commentators have long since noted that the catalogues of returnees in EN and 1 Esdras record part of the clans according to their place of living and not according to their patronymics.[28] However, inasmuch as each clan in the catalogues is associated with a place of living, the entire list functions as a geographical description of the territory where the community lives or the territory claimed by the community.

If the catalogues of returnees are meaningful through their inner organization, their two points of insertion carry further meaning both in 1 Esdras and EN. In both cases and in both texts the catalogues are associated with an important ritual performance. In the Zerubbabel–Jeshua sequence and its EN counterpart, the catalogues are inserted immediately before the building of the altar, the renewal of the sacrifices, and the ceremony of laying the foundation stone that cues the beginning of the temple building. Clearly, only the members of the community included in the list are entitled to participate in the rites. In the Ezra sequence, the list is split in two. The catalogue of those who returned

---

25. On Greece, see lastly L. Mitchell, *Panhellenism and the Barbarian in Archaic and Classical Greece* (Swansea: Classical Press of Wales, 2007); on Arabs, P. Briant, *États et pasteurs au Moyen-Orient ancien* (Paris: Ed. Maison des sciences de l'homme, 1982); Sylvie Honigman, "Les divers sens de l'ethnique *Arabs* dans les sources documentaires grecques d'Égypte," *Ancient Society* 32 (2002): 43–72; on a similar definition of space and territory applied to Judea, John W. Wright, "Remapping Yehud: The Borders of Yehud and the Genealogies of Chronicles," in Lipschits and Oeming, *Judah and the Judaeans in the Persian Period*, 67–89.

26. C. Calame, "Spartan Genealogies: The Mythical Representation of a Spatial Organisation," in *Interpretations of Greek Mythology* (ed. J. Bremmer; London: Croom Helm, 1987), 153–86, offers an illuminating analysis of this phenomenon through a case study of the Spartan royal genealogy. As Calame shows, the extant version of the myth can be precisely dated through a careful analysis of the spatial lore displayed in it, since the latter was subject to continuous updating.

27. Massar, "Chronique de Lindos," 233–37.

28. H. G. M. Williamson, *Ezra, Nehemiah* (WBC 16; Waco, Tex.: Word, 1985), translation, notes and commentary to Ezra 2:1–70.

under Ezra's leadership is composed of the holy families alone. The careful distinction between the holy and the unholy is subsequently dramatized by the members of the community of the returnees separating from their wives and the rest of the peoples of the land.[29] This episode, like its functional parallel in Neh 7, immediately precedes the founding ceremony of reading the Law. Thus the symbolic equation between sacrifices and Torah reading is made explicit through their symmetrical position in the Zerubbabel and the Ezra sequences, respectively. Incidentally, this equivalence is further pointed to by Ezra's explicit reference to the link between genealogical stock and material wealth in the context of his founding the reading of the Law:

> Do not seek ever to have peace with [the peoples of the land], so that you may be strong and eat the good things of the land and leave it for an inheritance to your children forever. (1 Esd 8:85)

Holiness is needed in order to take part in the sacrifices and in the reading of the Law, and both ritual performances in turn bring blessings and wealth.

2.4. THE CLAIMS FOR CONTINUITY IN HISTORICAL PERSPECTIVE

The genealogical claim appears to be the supreme argument in a scaled historical polemic. The catalogues of holy vessels and community members, as well as the descriptions of ceremonies, were additional, lower-ranking symbolic weapons in the service of the same cause. By purporting to demonstrate a link between the community of returnees and Solomon's temple, as well as with a specific territory, the catalogues support one claim to continuity and legitimacy against an alternative one. The efficacy of the catalogues and ceremonies is best illustrated by the episode of the enemies' request to share in rebuilding the temple (1 Esd 5:66–71 = Ezra 4:1–3). The enemies' justification sounds as follows:

> For we obey your Lord just as you do and we have been sacrificing to him ever since the days of King Esar-haddon of the Assyrians, who brought us here. (1 Esd 5:69; cf. Ezra 4:2)

Not only do these "enemies" have no royal mandate to boast of, as the leaders of the returnees make clear in their reply (v. 3), their legitimacy, as they admit, is based on chance continuity. Inasmuch as they were not brought to the returnees' territory by Nebuchadnezzar but by a meaningless Assyrian king, they have no link whatsoever with the original temple edifice, unlike the returnees, whose elders were eyewitnesses (1 Esd 5:63 = Ezra 3:12). The "enemies" have no association whatsoever with the holy vessels, unlike the returnees, who can display the parallel catalogues of vessels and people as evidence. Next, they have

---

29. For this reading, see Sérandour, "Femmes étrangères."

been sacrificing in the wrong place, while the returnees are rebuilding the altar "in its place" (1 Esd 5:50; Ezra 2:2). Therefore their sacrifices are worthless and unable to perform the proper divisions in the indistinct stream of continuous time. The claim that the sacrifices of the returnees had the symbolic power to institute these divisions is made in the very same verse that refers to the altar being erected "in its place" (1 Esd 5:50 + 51–52; Ezra 3:2 + 3–5). Finally, the "enemies" have no prophets to warrant their claim to equal status. The returnees' ritually privileged status, in short, is predicated on their link with Solomon's temple, from which the links with the "Law of Moses" and royal and divine (prophetic) authorization follow.

Conclusion

As is shown in this essay, the cyclical structure of the narrative establishes links and equations between past and present: between three of the founding figures who were recorded by the collective memory of the Judeans in Hellenistic times—Sheshbazzar, the paired Zerubbabel and Jeshua, and Ezra (Nehemiah, for some reason, was omitted); between Solomon's temple and the rebuilt temple, through the holy vessels and the founding ceremonies; between the society of old and the society that rebuilt the temple, through the catalogues of people and their close association with the catalogues of holy vessels; and between rites of sacrifices and the rite of reading the Torah, through the structural repetition of narrative sequences displaying a catalogue of the people whose genealogical pedigree is certified and a following founding ceremony. The assertion of the close connection between the Judeans of Hellenistic times and Solomon's temple further vindicates the Judeans' (exclusive) right to their land, as rejecting the request of the enemies to build the temple together with them shows. The cyclical structure of the narrative was a perfect means to root the present firmly into the founding events of the past.

1 ESDRAS:
ITS GENRE, LITERARY FORM, AND GOALS

Sara Japhet

A superficial review of the history of research into 1 Esdras reveals that the interest in the book shown by biblical scholars has been directed mainly to two matters: the literary relationship between 1 Esdras on the one hand and Chronicles and Ezra–Nehemiah on the other; as well as the textual relationships between 1 Esdras and its parallel chapters. By contrast, very little attention has been paid to the work itself. The majority of scholars have not attended to either the purpose of the book or the goals of its author. These issues constitute the topic of the present study.

I

The most pressing question is the purpose of 1 Esdras: Why was it composed? What is its message? Some answers to this question have been given in the past and they do contain kernels of truth, but there is room to change or supplement them.[1] The point of departure for our study is the literary genre of

---

1. Thus, for example, Wilhelm Rudolph suggests (following Bertholdt) that 1 Esdras deals with three restorations of Jewish worship and religious organization—by Josiah, by Zerubbabel, and by Ezra (*Esra und Nehemia samt 3 Esra* [HAT 20; Tübingen: Mohr Siebeck, 1949], xiv). Jacob M. Myers (*I and II Esdras* [AB 42; Garden City, N.Y.: Doubleday, 1974], 3–15) concludes his section about "purpose and date" with the statement that "no definite conclusion as to the date and purpose of 1 Esdras is possible at this time" (14). Another direction altogether is followed by Dieter Böhler (*Die heilige Stadt in Esdras α und Esra-Nehemia: Zwei Konzeptionen der Wiederherstellung Israels* [OBO 158; Freiburg: Universitätsverlag; Göttingen: Vandenhoeck & Ruprecht, 1997], 78–142), who tries to prove that 1 Esdras (without ch. 1, taken from Chronicles, with which he does not deal, and without the story of the three guardsmen, which he regards as a later interpolation) is the original and authentic history of the period of the restoration. The secondary and nonhistorical revision is that of Ezra–Nehemiah, which aims to include the story of Nehemiah and to shift the center of gravity from Zerubbabel to Nehemiah. According to Talshir, the motivation of 1 Esdras is to include

1 Esdras—that is, it is a history. I claim that 1 Esdras belongs to the group of works defined as "rewritten Bible." However, "rewritten Bible" is not a literary genre but a literary technique. Thus, whereas in terms of literary technique 1 Esdras is a "rewritten Bible" involving the rewriting, restructuring, and supplementing of existing biblical texts, in terms of genre, it is a history—an account of the history of a certain period within the broader history of Israel. Therefore, the purpose of the book should not be looked for in its literary features. It is not a midrash whose aim is to write "imaginary tales about biblical figures,"[2] and it was not written in order to insert new passages into an existing literary work.[3] Its goal is to create a new historical picture of a certain phase in the history of Israel. Our views of the historical reliability or value of the work, be what they may, should not affect our understanding of the author's goal as a historian.

The period that 1 Esdras presents is the restoration. The author of 1 Esdras was apparently not satisfied with the picture of this period portrayed by his predecessors and wished to correct it—while nevertheless making abundant use of his predecessors' work. The self-evident questions are therefore: How does 1 Esdras present the period of the restoration? What were the foci of the author's interests and emphases? What was the point in history that determined his historical perspective, and what were his goals?[4]

II

First Esdras presents the period of the restoration around three foci, in three different phases:

1) The end of the Judean kingdom: the history of the last kings, the conquest of the land by the Babylonians, the destruction of the temple and Jerusalem, and the exile of the people (1 Esd 1).

---

the story of the three guardsmen in the history of the restoration: "The Story of the Youths was the catalyst for the formation of 1 Esd ... 1 Esd was created in order to interpolate the Story of the Youths into the story of the Restoration, and the whole book has no real existence without it" (Zipora Talshir, *1 Esdras: From Origin to Translation* [SBLSCS 47; Atlanta: Society of Biblical Literature 1999], 58).

2. Talshir, *1 Esdras: From Origin to Translation*, 109.
3. Ibid., 58.
4. See also Sara Japhet, "Postexilic Historiography: How and Why," in *Israel Constructs Its History: Deuteronomic Historiography in Recent Research* (ed. Albert de Pury, Thomas Römer, and Jean-Daniel Macchi; JSOTSup 306; Sheffield: Sheffield Academic Press, 1996), 169–71 (= idem, *From the Rivers of Babylon to the Highlands of Judah: Collected Studies on the Restoration Period* [Winona Lake, Ind.: Eisenbrauns, 2006], 327–29); idem, "1 Esdras," in *The Oxford Bible Commentary* (ed. John Barton and John Muddiman; Oxford: Oxford University Press, 2001), 753–54.

2) The return from exile and the rebuilding of the temple and the city (1 Esd 2-7).
3) The firm establishment of religious norms and practices in the Judean community (1 Esd 8-9).

Although these historical periods are of different chronological lengths and are separated from one another by quite lengthy intervals, they are depicted in 1 Esdras as a historical continuum.[5] The picture created by 1 Esdras—in each of the three periods and in their conjunction—is the expression of the author's overall view of the history of Israel and of his particular time and interests.

The first feature of 1 Esdras—and perhaps the most striking—is the concept of historical continuity. First Esdras presents an immediate continuity between the destruction of Judah, at the end of the first commonwealth, and the restoration, at the beginning of the second.[6] The direct transition from 2 Chr 36 to Cyrus' declaration in Ezra 1, from destruction to rehabilitation, presents the return to Zion and the rebuilding of the temple and Jerusalem as a continuous historical process.

---

5. According to the available data from biblical and extrabiblical sources, the first period lasted thirty-five and a half years. It began with the eighteenth year of Josiah's reign, ended with the downfall of Zedekiah, and comprised thirteen years under Josiah's rule, three months under Jehoahaz, eleven years under Jehoiakim, three months under Jehoiachin, and eleven years under Zedekiah. The second period was of twenty-two years—from the first year of Cyrus to the sixth year of Darius (538–517 or 516 B.C.E.); and the length of the third period was a year and a half: from the beginning of Ezra's mission in the seventh year of Artaxerxes (Ezra 7:9; 1 Esd 8:6) until the seventh month of the next year (Neh 7:72; 1 Esd 9:37). The interval between the first and the second periods, that is, the period of the Babylonian rule of the land of Judah, is described in 1 Esd 1:55 (following 2 Chr 36:21) as having lasted seventy years; according to extrabiblical data, its duration was forty-eight years (586–538 B.C.E.). The interval between the sixth year of Darius and the seventh year of Artaxerxes I was fifty-eight years (516–458 B.C.E.); if the name Artaxerxes referred to Artaxerxes II rather than to Artaxerxes I, then its length was 118 years (516–398 B.C.E.).

6. This major feature of 1 Esdras has been overlooked or downplayed in biblical research in different ways. The most common way is through the self-evident result of the supposition that 1 Esdras is a fragment of the supposed "Chronistic history," which describes the history of Israel from its beginning until the time of the author. According to this view, the direct transition from the Babylonian conquest to Cyrus' declaration has no particular meaning (see, for example, Talshir [*1 Esdras: From Origin to Translation*, 107], who covers this important feature by a short, casual remark: "The link between Chr and Ezra is not the personal contribution of the author of 1 Esd"). The rejection in modern scholarship of this formerly predominant view led Böhler to leave out ch. 1 of 1 Esdras (parallel to 2 Chr 35-36) and to begin his study with the chapters of 1 Esdras parallel to Ezra (*Die heilige Stadt*, 15-16). This decision results in a complete disregard of 1 Esdras's point of departure—one of the most important characteristics of the historical account.

The author's decision to describe the restoration against the background of the destruction of the kingdom determines the precise point in history at which he begins his story. As indicated by the beginning of the work, the author of 1 Esdras was not interested in King Josiah himself, certainly not in the religious reforms that he introduced. Therefore the book does not open with the first chapter of Josiah's reign (2 Chr 34), which deals with the repair of the temple, the finding of "the Book," and the comprehensive religious reforms that followed. First Esdras begins with the second part of Josiah's reign, the celebration of the Passover in his eighteenth year (2 Chr 35; 1 Esd 1).[7] This event is the climax of Josiah's reign and the beginning of its decline, emphatically expressed by Josiah's untimely death. The interest of 1 Esdras in the kingdom's demise also explains why the only two verses that 1 Esdras adds to the story taken from 2 Chronicles—verses that justify in advance the approaching catastrophe—are inserted into the story immediately after the description of the Passover celebration: "And the deeds of Josiah, with a heart full of piety, were upright before his Lord. His deeds were recorded in former times, [together with the deeds] of those who sinned and acted impiously toward the Lord more than any people and kingdom and intentionally grieved him. And the words of the Lord against Israel were fulfilled" (1 Esd 1:21–22).[8] Notwithstanding Josiah's righteousness, the kingdom of Judah was doomed. From this point 1 Esdras moves to the end of Josiah's reign, to the history of the last four Judean kings—Jehoahaz, Jehoiakim,

---

7. It is therefore difficult to accept Rudolph's claim (*Esra-Nehemia*, see n. 1, above) that the topic of 1 Esdras is the description of three events in which God's worship is restored and reorganized, the first among them being Josiah's reform. This view is contradicted by the book itself.

8. All references to verse numbers in this article are according to Hanhart's edition: Robert Hanhart, *Esdrae Liber I* (Septuaginta Vetus Testamentum Graecum 8/1; Göttingen: Vandenhoeck & Ruprecht, 1974). The translation from 1 Esdras is based on the Greek source; the text is difficult and seems to be somewhat corrupt. The passage rephrases 2 Kgs 23:25–27:

"Before him there was no king who turned back to the Lord with all his heart and with all his soul and with all his might, according to all the Law of Moses, nor did any like him arise after him. Still, the Lord did not turn from the fierceness of his great wrath by which his anger was kindled against Judah because of all the provocations with which Manasseh had provoked him. The Lord said: 'I will remove Judah also out of my sight as I have removed Israel, and I will reject this city that I have chosen, Jerusalem, and the house of which I said, "My name shall be there."'"

These verses were omitted in the Chronicler's account of Josiah's reign and formed no part of 1 Esdras's immediate source. The theological view of the passage, that the deeds of earlier generations affect the fate of later ones, is in sheer contrast to the Chronicler's own view of God's providence (see Sara Japhet, *The Ideology of the Book of Chronicles and Its Place in Biblical Thought* [BEATAJ 9; Frankfurt am Main: Lang, 1989], 150–65. (In the new edition of this book [Winona Lake, Ind.: Eisenbrauns, 2009], 117–29). The passage was reintroduced into the account of Josiah's reign in the Septuagint translation of 2 Chr 35:19.

Jehoiachin, and Zedekiah—and to the Babylonian conquest and its results: the end of the Davidic dynasty, the destruction of Jerusalem and the burning of the temple, and the exile of the remaining population (1 Esd 1:23–55). Immediately following this stage, the story moves to Cyrus' declaration and to the process of restoration.

The conjunction of the end of the first commonwealth with the beginning of Israel's revival, initiated by Cyrus' declaration, is not a complete innovation of 1 Esdras. It is hinted at already in two passages at the end of 2 Chr 36: first, the short reference there to the end of servitude, "They became servants to him and to his sons until the establishment of the kingdom of Persia" (2 Chr 36:20); and second, the Chronicler's inclusion of the first two verses of Cyrus' declaration (36:22–23). This ending of 2 Chronicles greatly diminishes the impact and weight of the catastrophe, as it loses the dimension of an absolute finality. Indeed, the downplaying of the significance of exile and destruction in the history of Israel conforms well to the Chronicler's general view of Israel's history,[9] even though according to him the revival and salvation of Israel is a prospect to be fulfilled in the future. For 1 Esdras, by contrast, the very continuation of the historical account from the end of Chronicles to Ezra 1 expresses the view that the turning about of Israel's fortunes has actually been achieved; the reality of the restoration period is the wished-for salvation of Israel.

First Esdras also expresses historical continuity by presenting the rebuilt temple in the restoration period as a direct continuation of the first. According to 1 Esdras, the period in which the temple lay in ruins was merely a short *intermezzo*, during which the people of Israel suffered a deserved punishment for their transgressions but after which the temple was quickly rebuilt and restored to its glory. This idea, too, is not an innovation of 1 Esdras. It is clearly expressed by Haggai "Who is left among you that saw this house in its former glory? How does it look to you now?" (Hag 2:3). It is also emphasized by the eloquent response of the elders of Judah to the inquiry of Tattenai, the governor of the province Beyond the River. To the governor's question, "Who gave you a decree to build this house?" (Ezra 5:3, and with a slight variation, v. 9), they respond: "We are rebuilding the house that was built many years ago, which a great king of Israel built and finished. But because our ancestors had angered the God of heaven he gave them into the hands of King Nebuchadnezzar ... who destroyed this house ... However, King Cyrus of Babylon ... made a decree that this house should be rebuilt" (Ezra 5:11–13).

There is some tension between this view and the phrasing of Cyrus' declaration, which implies that the house is a new undertaking: "The Lord the God of heaven ... charged me to build him a house at Jerusalem in Judah" (Ezra 1:2). The same sense of newness may be inferred also from Ezra 3:10, "The builders

---

9. See Japhet, *Ideology of the Book of Chronicles*, 364–73 (284–92 in the new edition).

laid the foundation of the temple of the Lord," and from the description of the joy at the founding of the temple, which contrasts the "first house" and "this house" (3:12). Since all these statements are repeated literally in 1 Esdras, with only very slight variations (1 Esd 2:4; 5:56, 59, 60), the tension between the two views is expressed within 1 Esdras itself—as in Ezra-Nehemiah.[10]

The tight continuity between the destruction and the return is further expressed in 1 Esdras by its transferring of Jerusalem's rebuilding to the beginning of the restoration period, that is, to the time of Zerubbabel. The catastrophe in 1 Esdras—following 2 Chr 36—includes five components: 1) massacring the people of Jerusalem (2 Chr 36:17; 1 Esd 1:53); 2) carrying off the temple's vessels and the treasures of the king and his officials (2 Chr 36:18; 1 Esd 1:54); 3) burning the temple (2 Chr 36:19a; 1 Esd 1:55a); 4) breaking down the walls of Jerusalem and burning its palaces (2 Chr 36:19b; 1 Esd 1:55b–56a); and 5) exiling the rest of Jerusalem's inhabitants to Babylon (2 Chr 36:20; 1 Esd 1:56b).

In the book of Ezra, at the first stage of the restoration, during the reigns of Cyrus and Darius, only three of these components are attended to: the temple is rebuilt, the temple's vessels are given back, and the exiles return to their homeland.[11] There is naturally no mention of the people killed, and so the only absent component is the restoration of Jerusalem: Ezra-Nehemiah does not include rebuilding Jerusalem and its walls in the first period of the restoration but leaves these projects to a later generation under the leadership of Nehemiah, as described in detail in Neh 1–6.[12]

---

10. See also the rephrasing of Tattenai's letter to Darius in 1 Esdras. Ezra 5:8 reads: "May it be known to the king that we went to the province of Judah, to the house of the great God. It is built of hewn stones and timber is laid in the walls." In contrast, 1 Esd 6:8–9 reads: "Let all be known to the king our lord, that going to the land of Judah and coming to the city of Jerusalem, we found the elders of the Judeans of the exile in the city of Jerusalem building a *great new house* to the Lord, of costly hewn stones, and timber set in the walls. And that work is done with speed, and the work proceeds successfully at their hands and is being completed with all splendor and attention." This phrasing portrays a difference between Tattenai's view that the house is new and the elders' account of its long history.

11. The focus of the first section of Ezra-Nehemiah (Ezra 1–6) is on building the temple, but this literary unit also includes the return of the temple's vessels (Ezra 1:7–11; 5:14–15) and the return and settlement of the exiles (Ezra 1:11b; 2:1–70).

12. According to the account in the book of Nehemiah, the walls of Jerusalem are restored in the twenty-first year of Artaxerxes, which—according to extrabiblical sources—was 444 B.C.E.; that is, seventy-two years after the dedication of the temple in the sixth year of Darius (Ezra 6:15). According to the periodization of Ezra-Nehemiah, Nehemiah's mission falls in the second generation of the restoration. See Sara Japhet, "Periodization between History and Ideology II: Chronology and Ideology in Ezra-Nehemiah," in *Judah and the Judeans in the Persian Period* (ed. Oded Lipschits and Manfred Oeming; Winona Lake, Ind.: Eisenbrauns, 2006), 496–502 (= *From the Rivers of Babylon*, 420–26).

This presentation of the events is "corrected" in 1 Esdras in two ways: on the one hand, the author transfers the building of the city and its walls to the time of Zerubbabel, that is, to the first period of the restoration; and on the other hand, he completely suppresses the story and projects of Nehemiah. According to 1 Esdras, rebuilding the temple and the city are carried out together; they are begun at the time of Cyrus and completed at the time of Darius. Both the decrees of the Persian emperors and the contrivances of Judah's enemies are directed from the very outset not only toward rebuilding the temple but also toward restoring the city. This position is expressed first of all by moving the letter of accusation (directed against rebuilding the city) and its aftermath from its place in Ezra 4:6–24 to the beginning of the 1 Esdras story, that is, immediately after the account of the initial return (i.e., to 1 Esd 2:15–25). Moreover, whereas the letter of accusation as recorded in Ezra 4 mentions only the city, 1 Esdras also mentions the temple (2:17, 18, 25).

First Esdras also refers to rebuilding Jerusalem in passages peculiar to it. Thus, we see it in Zerubbabel's reference to Darius' vows: "Remember the vow that you made ... to build Jerusalem ... and to return all the vessels. ... And you vowed to build the temple" (4:43–45); and several times in Darius' letter to Zerubbabel, for example, "to build Jerusalem ... that they should build the city with him" (4:47–48); "twenty talents are to be given yearly for the building of the temple, until it is built" (4:51); and "until the time when the house is completed and Jerusalem built" (4:55). It appears finally in the blessing of the people: "They blessed the God of their fathers, for he gave them rest and release to go up and build Jerusalem and the temple upon which his name is called, and they celebrated for seven days, with music and joy" (4:62–63).

In 1 Esdras, in the first period of the restoration Judah returns in every way to its former state of physical well-being, and the consequences of the destruction are fully reversed: Jerusalem and the temple are rebuilt, the vessels are returned, and the exiles are settled back in their original localities.

III

Another major feature of 1 Esdras' account is its elaboration of the figure of Zerubbabel the son of Shealtiel. I dealt with this matter quite extensively in an article written in 1983, and it was further emphasized in the study of Z. Talshir.[13] First Esdras develops the tendency, the seeds of which are found already in

---

13. See Sara Japhet, "Sheshbazzar and Zerubbabel against the Background of the Historical and Religious Tendencies of Ezra–Nehemiah, II," *ZAW* 95 (1983): 218–29 (= *From the Rivers of Babylon*, 85–95). Talshir discussed this issue first in her doctoral thesis ("First Esdras: Origins and Translation" [in Hebrew] [Ph.D. diss., Hebrew University of Jerusalem]) and then in the book based on the thesis (*1 Esdras: From Origin to Translation*, 46–57). She did not mention the above article and it seems that she was not aware of it.

Ezra–Nehemiah, to elaborate and glorify Zerubbabel's figure and achievements. This tendency receives a literary expression in the insertion of the story of the "three guardsmen" and by a series of notes in which the name and titles of Zerubbabel have been added to existing texts.[14]

The addition of the story of the three guardsmen and its adjacent passages (1 Esd 3:1–5:6) creates a major change in the quantitative proportions of 1 Esdras and places Zerubbabel at the center of the historical account. Zerubbabel is presented in full glory, not merely as a wise man whose wisdom is universally recognized but as a man who gives up the glorious future that awaits him as the viceroy of Darius and who prefers to put himself at the service of his people. Zerubbabel uses the unreserved favor of Darius as a lever to promote the revival and restoration of the people and the land of Judah. He is successful in everything that he undertakes and witnesses the rebuilding of the temple and Jerusalem.

By the short notes and passages in 1 Esdras that are added to the text taken from Ezra–Nehemiah, the author corrects and supplements what he must have regarded as omissions in the original account. Perhaps the most obvious omission is the purposeful absence in Ezra–Nehemiah of any hint that Zerubbabel is of Davidic origin.[15] In 1 Esdras' introduction to the list of returnees, Zerubbabel's genealogy is presented in detail: "Zorobabel the son of Salatiel, of the house of David, of the family of Fares, of the tribe of Judah" (1 Esd 5:5).[16] In another place in 1 Esdras, Zerubbabel is labeled in the footsteps of Haggai, "the servant of the Lord" (1 Esd 6:26; Hag 2:23). Zerubbabel is also defined in 1 Esdras as governor (פחה, 1 Esd 6:26 and 28)—a title that appears in the book of Haggai but is purposely avoided in Ezra–Nehemiah.[17]

---

14. Although the story of the three guardsmen with its adjacent passages is a secondary interpolation into 1 Esdras, it should be remembered that the interpolator was none other than the author of 1 Esdras himself. The same is also true for the occasional notes in which the name of Zerubbabel is added to the text (see Talshir, *1 Esdras: From Origin to Translation*, 42–54). They are indeed "additions," but they were introduced by the author of 1 Esdras himself. On this story, see also Charles C. Torrey, "The Story of the Three Youths," *AJSL* 23 (1907): 183–87; idem, "A Revised View of First Esdras," in *Louis Ginzberg Jubilee Volume* (2 vols.; New York: American Academy for Jewish Research, 1945), 1:395–410; Abraham Schalit, "The Date and Place of the Story about the Three Bodyguards of the King in the Apocryphal Book of Ezra" [in Hebrew], *BJPES* 13 (1947): 119–28; Wilhelm Th. in der Smitten, "Zur Pagenerzählung im 3 Esra (3 Esr. III 1–V 6)," *VT* 22 (1972): 492–95. See also the commentaries on 1 Esdras.

15. See Sara Japhet, "Sheshbazzar and Zerubbabel against the Background of the Historical and Religious Tendencies of Ezra–Nehemiah, I," *ZAW* 94 (1982): 71–80 (= *From the Rivers of Babylon*, 57–66).

16. On the textual problem in this verse and its explanation, see Myers, *I and II Esdras*, 66; Talshir, *1 Esdras: From Origin to Translation*, 249–50.

17. Japhet, "Sheshbazzar and Zerubbabel, I," 80–86 (= *From the Rivers of Babylon*, 66–69).

Finally, Zerubbabel is included in 1 Esdras as a participant in events from which he is absent in the account of Ezra–Nehemiah. He is added to Sheshbazzar, who together with him receives the temple's vessels from Cyrus (1 Esd 1:17; cf. Ezra 5:14), and he is mentioned explicitly as the governor of Judah in the letter of Darius to Tattenai, the governor of Beyond the River (1 Esd 6:26; cf. Ezra 6:7). Although Zerubbabel's name is not included in 1 Esdras' depiction of the temple's dedication, it seems that according to the view presented there, Zerubbabel begins the temple-building process and witnesses its completion. According to 1 Esdras, the prophecy of Zechariah, "The hands of Zerubbabel have laid the foundation of this house; his hands shall also complete it" (Zech 4:9), has indeed been fulfilled.

IV

The last part of the history described in 1 Esdras is dedicated to the figure and activity of Ezra the scribe. Although all the material found in this section is taken over from Ezra–Nehemiah, with no additions and only slight variations, the period at large is differently portrayed. The first expression of the new formulation is the selection of the material. First Esdras incorporates the full story of Ezra that is in Ezra–Nehemiah (Ezra 7–10) but includes only the small portion of the book of Nehemiah in which the protagonist is also Ezra (Neh 8:1–13aα). Accordingly, Nehemiah's entire enterprise finds no expression in 1 Esdras. This literary feature is explained by quite a few scholars as a representation of the "original composition" and consequently is accorded little significance when evaluating the tendencies in 1 Esdras. However, the realization that the author of 1 Esdras knew the book of Nehemiah and included it among his sources[18] should result in a fully reversed evaluation of this feature. The omission of the story of Nehemiah should be regarded as one of the important changes introduced in 1 Esdras' historical account. How should it be explained?

Rudolph is of the opinion that the activity of Nehemiah is omitted because little interest is shown in 1 Esdras of the political aspects of Judah's restoration and it concentrates exclusively on religious affairs; this explains both its omission of Nehemiah's activities and its emphasis on Ezra.[19] Talshir explains that after 1 Esdras transfers the main achievements of Nehemiah to Zerubbabel,

---

18. First Esdras transferred various features from the Nehemiah story and figure to Zerubbabel. See in particular Talshir, *1 Esdras: From Origin to Translation*, 47–52; and in another direction, Ulrich Kellermann, *Nehemia: Quellen, Überlieferung und Geschichte* (BZAW 102; Berlin: de Gruyter, 1967), 130–44. See also Richard J. Coggins and Michael A. Knibb, *The First and Second Books of Esdras* (CBC; Cambridge: Cambridge University Press, 1979), 37, and further below.

19. Rudolph, *Esra-Nehemia*, xiv. See also below, n. 21.

Nehemiah himself becomes superfluous.[20] I suggest that 1 Esdras omits the book of Nehemiah as part of its overall purpose, the reformulation of the historical picture.[21]

The first thing to note is that the figure of Nehemiah is not completely ignored in 1 Esdras.[22] Nehemiah is mentioned in 1 Esdras twice, the first time as one of the leaders of the return in the time of Zerubbabel (1 Esd 5:8; Ezra 2:2). One may argue that this is nothing but a mechanical repetition of an existing list of names or, alternatively, that the person referred to was not conceived of as Nehemiah the son of Hachaliah, the protagonist of the book of Nehemiah, but as another person by the same name. Such arguments cannot be raised against the second mention of Nehemiah, however, which is peculiar to 1 Esdras. The text of Ezra 2:63, which states that "the governor (*Tirshata*) told them that they were not to partake of the most holy food until there should be a priest to consult Urim and Thummim," is represented in 1 Esd 5:40 as "and Neemias and Hattharias told them not to partake of the consecrated [food] until a high priest arises (lit.: 'stands up'), dressed with insight and truth." It is commonly accepted that Hattharias is a misrepresentation of the title *Tirshata*, taken to be a proper name, and that the original reading was: "Nehemiah the *Tirshata* told them," etc.[23] The attribution of the title *Tirshata* to Nehemiah could have been taken only from the book of Nehemiah, where Nehemiah is twice identified by this title: "Nehemiah the *Tirshata*, the son of Hachaliah" (Neh 10:2); "Nehemiah who was the *Tirshata*" (Neh 8:9). Of these two references, Neh 10:2 is not repeated in 1 Esdras, but Neh 8:9 is, with the omission of the name of Nehemiah. The representation of this verse in 1 Esd 9:49 is: "And Hattharates said to Ezra," etc.

All these changes amount to a well-devised process of editing. Following the book of Nehemiah, in 1 Esdras "the *Tirshata*" is identified with Nehemiah, but he is moved from the time of Artaxerxes to the time of Cyrus and Darius and is

---

20. Talshir (*1 Esdras: From Origin to Translation*, 55–57) explains this matter, too, in literary terms: "the common tendency of aggadic homilies to build up one character by borrowing traits from another."

21. This is in fact the line followed by Rudolph (see n. 19, above), but his specific argument is unconvincing. Although the source of Nehemiah's authority was his office as governor, his actions were far wider than the narrow political aspect of this office. Nehemiah took active part in the maintenance and promotion of the religious institutions in Judah and in upholding the religious norms of the community. We may mention the observance of the Sabbath (Neh 10:32; 13:15–27); the struggle against mixed marriages (10:31; 13:23–28); the care for the temple's purity and maintenance (10:33–40; 12:44–47; 13:4–13, 29–31); and more. Moreover, the chapters omitted from 1 Esdras in addition to Nehemiah's memoirs contained many passages pertaining to the religious organization, such as the lists of priests and Levites (12:1–26) and more.

22. See also Böhler, *Die heilige Stadt*, 110–15, 179–95, but in the opposite direction. See also Wilhelm Th. in der Smitten, "Der *Tirshata* in Esra-Nehemia," *VT* 21 (1971): 618–20.

23. See, e.g., S. A. Cook, "I Esdras," *APOT* 1:37; Coggins and Knibb, *First and Second Books of Esdras*, 41; and many more.

presented as a contemporary of Zerubbabel, rather than as a contemporary of Ezra. The name Nehemiah is added in 1 Esd 5:40 but omitted in 1 Esd 9:49. This editing procedure implies that the person Nehemiah mentioned among the leaders of the return in the time of Zerubbabel (1 Esd 5:8) was conceived by 1 Esdras' author to be Nehemiah the son of Hachaliah.

The view that Nehemiah was a contemporary of Zerubbabel may have been triggered by a statement in the book of Nehemiah itself. The book Ezra–Nehemiah has a specific chronological view according to which the period of the restoration consists of two consecutive generations.[24] This view is expressed in Ezra–Nehemiah, among other ways, by the explicit statement "In the days of Zerubbabel and in the days of Nehemiah all Israel gave the holy portions for the singers and the gatekeepers" (Neh 12:47). First Esdras' author could easily have understood the phrase "in the days of Zerubbabel and in the days of Nehemiah" to refer to a single period in which Zerubbabel and Nehemiah acted together.

The inevitable conclusion from all these data is that the person Nehemiah does figure in 1 Esdras but is relegated to the period of Zerubbabel and presented as a person of secondary significance. The book of Nehemiah, however, which places Nehemiah at the time of Artaxerxes and describes him as a powerful and successful leader, is omitted. In this way, the third period in the history of the restoration is presented in 1 Esdras as having had only one leader, Ezra.[25]

The presentation of Ezra in 1 Esdras is also marked by an important change in his titles. Differently from the book of Ezra, he is designated here as "high priest"—a title that is never accorded to him in the book of Ezra. In Ezra–Nehemiah, Ezra has several titles: "the scribe" (Neh 8:1, 4, 13; 12:36); "a scribe skilled in the law of Moses" (Ezra 7:6); "a scribe of the commandments of the Lord and his statutes for Israel" (Ezra 7:11); "the priest" (Ezra 10:10, 16; Neh 8:2); "the priest the scribe" (Ezra 7:11; Neh 8 9; 12:26); and in the Aramaic portion of the book: "the priest Ezra, the scribe of the law of the God of heaven" (Ezra 7:12, 21).[26] This set of titles undergoes several changes in 1 Esdras, of which the most significant are: 1) a diminishing use of the title scribe, which appears in 1 Esdras only once or twice as γραμματευς;[27] 2) the use of a peculiar title, exclusive to this book: "the priest who reads [the Torah]," αναγνοστες, as a

---

24. See Japhet, "Periodization, II," 496–502 (= *From the Rivers of Babylon*, 420–26).

25. This procedure completely forfeits the efforts made by the book of Ezra–Nehemiah to present Ezra and Nehemiah as contemporaries and counters the general view of Ezra–Nehemiah that in each sub-period of the Restoration Period the people were led by two leaders. See Japhet, "Periodization, II."

26. Ezra is also called by his name alone, with no title, in Ezra 7:1, 6, 10, 25; 10:1, 2, 5, 6; Neh 8:5, 6.

27. The title appears in 1 Esd 8:3, parallel to Ezra 7:6 and in some of the manuscripts also in 1 Esd 8:25, which has no parallel in Ezra 7:27. See Zipora Talshir, *1 Esdras: A Text Critical Commentary* (SBLSCS 50; Atlanta: Society of Biblical Literature, 2001), 409.

representation of several titles in Ezra–Nehemiah;[28] 3) the change of "priest" to "high priest," with the title peculiar to 1 Esdras: αρχιερευς (see below).

These changes belong to different categories. The use of the Greek αναγνοστες to represent the Hebrew "scribe" and the Aramaic ספר דתא could have been introduced by either the author of 1 Esdras or the Greek translator. One of the pertinent considerations is the fact that the term "scribe" (γραμματευς) does appear in 1 Esd 8:3, a fact that suggests that the Greek translator was familiar with this common rendition of the title "scribe" and did not use it because he did not find it in his *Vorlage*; namely, that it was already changed in the Semitic text of 1 Esdras. This assessment, however, seems inconclusive. Such is not the case regarding the change from "priest" to "high priest," where the origin of the change at the earlier stage of composition rather than at the secondary stage of translation is much more plausible. In Ezra–Nehemiah, Ezra is not termed "high priest" even once. Although his genealogy is artificially connected to the list of the high priests of the first temple, which reaches as far back as "Aaron the chief priest" (Ezra 7:5), there is nothing in the whole of Ezra–Nehemiah to imply that Ezra ever served in this capacity. In Ezra–Nehemiah only one priest is explicitly described as "high priest"—Eliashib, the high priest in the time of Nehemiah (Neh 3:1, 20; 13:28), who is also designated "priest" alone (Neh 13:4) or simply called by his name (Neh 13:7).[29] With the omission of the book of Nehemiah in 1 Esdras, Eliashib disappears; his title is transferred to Ezra and is used there three times: "Ezra the high priest" (1 Esd 9:40) replacing "Ezra the priest" of Neh 8:2; "The high priest and the reader [of the law] (αναγνοστες)" (1 Esd 9:49) replacing "Ezra the priest, the scribe" of Neh 8:9; and "Ezra the high priest and the reader [of the law]" (1 Esd 9:39) replacing "Ezra the scribe" in Neh 8:1.

One should also note the peculiar definition of Ezra's garment, referred to twice in Ezra 9. Over against the neutral description of Ezra 9:3, "When I heard this I tore my garment and my mantle" (similarly in v. 5), 1 Esdras reads: "Upon hearing these things I rent my clothes and the holy garments" (1 Esd 8:68, similarly v. 70). The "holy garments," among them the mantle, were the specific garments of the high priest (Exod 28:4) and were clearly distinguished from those of other priests: "The holy vestments for the priest Aaron and the vestments of his sons" (Exod 35:18). Even by his specific attire Ezra is distinguished in 1 Esdras as a high priest.[30]

---

28. It represents the Aramaic title ספר דתא (Ezra 7:12, 21; 1 Esd 8:9, 19); the title "scribe," סופר (Neh 8:1, 4, 9; 1 Esd 9:39, 42, 49), and the title/description סופר דברי מצות ה' וחוקיו (Ezra 7:11; 1 Esd 8:8).

29. On the intentional suppression of the title "high priest" in references to Joshua, the son of Jozadak, see Japhet, "Sheshbazzar and Zerubbabel, I," 82–86 (= *From the Rivers of Babylon*, 68–72).

30. These two elements—the title "high priest" and a nuanced description of his garments—appear together in 1 Esd 5:40. While Ezra 2:63 reads, "until there should be a priest to consult Urim and Thummim," the parallel 1 Esd 5:40 reads, "until a high priest arises dressed

V

All these relatively minor changes in the text of the received sources provide a new picture of the period of the restoration. In the first part of the period as defined in 1 Esdras, Judah is governed by the Davidic kings, but their reign ends with a major catastrophe. The second period, under the leadership of Zerubbabel and the auspices of the Persian rulers, sees the physical rehabilitation of the land of Judah and the city of Jerusalem. The climax of the historical process, however, is reached in the third period with the firm establishment of religious affairs under the leadership of Ezra. Ezra's efforts are directed mainly to a rigorous solution of the problem of mixed marriages, to the public reading of the Torah, and to implementing the authority of the Law in the Judean community. The political power in this period, as much as in the preceding one, belongs to the Persian rulers, who give Ezra an extensive and generous bill of rights, but the leader of the people of Judah was the high priest Ezra.

With the culmination of the historical process, the author of 1 Esdras arrives at his goal: the actual situation in Judah in his own time. This was the time when the political power in the land of Judah belonged to the Hellenistic rulers, the foreign masters of the province, but when the hegemony over the people of Judah was invested in the hands of the high priests. First Esdras presents the historical development that led to the author's own time. It legitimizes the political reality then current and sanctions the ideology that supported this reality.

VI

The historical picture as presented in 1 Esdras has a very interesting analogy in another text, which on the face of the matter may seem to present a different picture of history and in some of its features even a contrasting one. The text I am referring to is the historical review included in Ben Sira's "Praise of the Fathers" (Ben Sira 44:1–50:24[28]). This poetic composition is a comprehensive review of the history of Israel, through praises and glorification of the great heroes of the past.[31] The review begins with Enoch and ends with the high priest Simeon the son of Johanan. From among the kings of Judah, Ben Sira mentions

---

with the insight and the truth." It seems that here, too, 1 Esdras alludes to Ezra, whose appearance was expected to solve all the pending problems.

31. There are no biblical parallels to this literary genre, but it is attested in the Hellenistic literature. See John J. Collins, "Ecclesiasticus, or the Wisdom of Jesus Son of Sirach," in Barton and Muddiman, *Oxford Bible Commentary*, 694; Reinhold Bohlen, *Die Ehrung der Eltern bei Ben Sira* (Trier: Paulinus Verlag, 1991); Thomas R. Lee, *Studies in the Form of Sirach 44–50* (Atlanta: Scholars Press, 1986).

only four righteous kings: David and Solomon, the founders of the dynasty (47:2–11, 12–23), and Hezekiah and Josiah toward its end (48:17–25; 49:1–3). After a short reference to the destruction of the kingdom (49:4–6) and to the prophets (49:7–10), Ben Sira presents in very concise terms the period of the restoration, represented by three persons: Zerubbabel, Joshua the son of Jehozadak, and Nehemiah (49:11–13). After a short transition passage, the composition arrives at the climax of the poem and the culmination of history. The figure who is accorded the longest praise and the most enthusiastic and eloquent eulogy is the high priest Simeon: "Highly esteemed among his brothers and the glory of his people" (50:1). Ben Sira devotes to the high priest Simeon the longest poem (50:1–36), the most extravagant praise, and the most detailed and eloquent description, exceeding even those accorded to Aaron, the venerable founder of the priesthood (45:9–30).[32]

Three matters in Ben Sira's description of the restoration period attract the attention of the reader: the brevity of the passage devoted to this period; the total absence of Ezra;[33] and the position of the contemporary priest, Simeon. All three are different aspects of the same phenomenon. The purpose of the description is to present the actual leadership of the author's time, the leadership of the acting high priest, as the climax of the restoration and as the final target of the history of Israel. The praise of the acting high priest is composed of two unequal parts: first, the description of his role in the physical well-being of Judah, a continuation of the acts of Zerubbabel, Joshua, and Nehemiah (50:1–4); and then, in the major part of the praise, the depiction of the splendor of his appearance, his majestic conduct of the temple's services, and his leadership of the people in religious worship. He is the person in whom the eternal covenant, the covenant of Phineas, has been realized and concretized (50:24).

What we see in the poem of Ben Sira is the continuation of the line begun by 1 Esdras, although differently conceived and formulated. Also in 1 Esdras, the final stage in the restoration of Judah, and the climax of the historical process, is the leadership and activity of a high priest. However, in 1 Esdras it is Ezra the scribe, "the high priest and the reader [of the law]," who is the offspring of "Aaron the chief priest" (1 Esd 8:1–2; Ezra 7:1–5). The omission of his contemporary, Nehemiah, emphasizes Ezra's leadership role. This is also what Ben

---

32. For a detailed study of the passage about Simeon, see Otto Mulder, *Simon the High Priest in Sirach 50: An Exegetical Study of the Significance of Simon the High Priest as the Climax to the Praise of the Fathers in Ben Sira's Concept of the History of Israel* (JSJSup 78; Leiden: Brill, 2003).

33. The omission of the name and activity of Ezra in the "Praise of the Fathers" is described by Collins as "most striking," with "no apparent ideological reason for the omission" ("Ecclesiasticus," 696). Some scholars suggested reasons for the omission; e.g., Moses Segal, *The Complete Book of Ben Sira* [in Hebrew] (3d ed.; Jerusalem: Mosad Bialik, 1972), 339; or Christopher T. Begg, "Ben Sirach's Non-Mention of Ezra," *BN* 42 (1988): 14–18.

Sira does. For him too, the climax of the historical process is the leadership of the high priest of his own time, but for him, this person is not Ezra the Scribe but Simeon the Righteous. In both cases the exclusivity of the elevated leader is preserved by the suppression of rivals. According to Ben Sira, a straight line of promise leads from Aaron and Phineas at the one end to Simeon the high priest at the other end, and on this line there is no place for any other high priest. In the book of Ben Sira the high priest Simeon is the one who occupies the position established by Aaron, as does Ezra the high priest in 1 Esdras.

This analogy—notwithstanding the difference between the two compositions in contents, genre, and literary formulation—sheds light on the goals and methods of 1 Esdras. The historical continuum in the history of Israel leads to the author's own time, to the period of Hellenistic rule in the land of Judah. This historical continuum serves as the means of legitimization for the exclusive rule of the high priests. The course of the history of Israel under God's providence leads from the period of the kingdom—which turned out to be a failure—through the restoration of Judah and the return of exiles in the time of Zerubbabel, to the ultimate leader, the high priest Ezra.

The Rendering of 2 Chronicles 35–36 in 1 Esdras

Ralph W. Klein

It has been more than forty years since my dissertation on the text-critical implications of 1 Esdras was accepted at Harvard.[1] In the meantime, I have spent little time on 1 Esdras, except to write brief notes for several study Bibles. It was therefore a pleasure to accept the invitation of Liz Fried to the first meeting of this new consultation and to return to the arena of my earliest scholarly work. In the course of writing this essay, I gave great attention to the two books by Zipora Talshir on this subject, *1 Esdras: From Origin to Translation* (1999)[2] and *1 Esdras: A Text Critical Commentary* (2001),[3] both of which I had reviewed for the *Journal of Near Eastern Studies*.

First Esdras 1 is clearly based on the Hebrew text of 2 Chr 35–36, although in a form somewhat different from the Masoretic Text. It remains difficult today, as it was forty years ago, to be sure about retroversions from 1 Esdras back into Hebrew. The translator does not always stick to formal equivalences and sometimes demonstrates inconsistencies, the most notorious of which is his frequent use of κύριος both for the Tetragrammaton *and* for various forms of Elohim.

1. Statistical Comparison of MT, 1 Esdras,
and the Paraleipomena

In preparing this essay I worked up the translation of 2 Chr 35–36 for the second volume of my Hermeneia commentary on Chronicles and created more than two hundred text-critical notes for these chapters. The following approximate statistics do not tell the whole story, but they may help us to understand the amount of variation between 1 Esdras and the MT.

---

1. Ralph W. Klein, "Studies in the Greek Texts of the Chronicler" (Ph.D. diss., Harvard University, 1966).
2. Zipora Talshir, *1 Esdras: From Origin to Translation* (SBLSCS 47; Atlanta: Society of Biblical Literature, 1999).
3. Zipora Talshir, *1 Esdras: A Text Critical Commentary* (SBLSCS 50; Atlanta: Society of Biblical Literature, 2001).

- 1 Esdras differs from the MT in 2 Chr 35–36 111 times (seventy times representing differences in the *Vorlage* and forty-one times representing changes due to the translator).
- 1 Esdras and Paraleipomena agree together against the MT's forty-two times (thirty-six times representing differences in the *Vorlage* and six times representing changes due to the translator).
- The Paraleipomena differ from the MT and 1 Esdras combined twenty-eight times (eighteen times representing differences in the *Vorlage* and ten times representing changes due to the translator).

In addition, there are two times where the MT and 1 Esdras differ, and Paraleipomena conflates the variants; and one time where the MT and Paraleipomena differ, and 1 Esdras conflates the variants. About twenty-five cases were deemed too unclear to be included in these statistics.

The bulk of this essay examines a number of cases in which the variations in 1 Esdras lead to significant changes in meaning.

2. The Death of Josiah

The variant readings in 1 Esdras dealing with the death of Josiah are worthy of special attention. The Chronicler adds two verses to the *Vorlage* from Kings, and they read as follows (2 Chr 35:21–22):

> 35:21 He [Neco] sent messengers to him [Josiah], saying, "What have I to do with you, king of Judah? I am not (coming) against you today, but against the house with which I am at war, and God has commanded me to hurry. Cease opposing God who is with me lest he destroy you." 22 But Josiah would not turn his face away from him, but he disguised himself in order to fight him. He did not listen to the words of Neco from the mouth of God, but came to fight with him in the valley of Megiddo.

In my translation for the Hermeneia commentary I have fifteen text-critical notes on these two verses. Only the most significant can be discussed here.

2 Chr 35:21:

לא עליך אתה היום

I am not against *you* (אתה) today (MT); or, I am not coming (אתה) against you today (*Par.*)

1 Esd 1:25:
οὐχὶ πρὸς σὲ ἐξαπέσταλμαι ὑπὸ κυρίου τοῦ θεοῦ

Not against you have I been sent by the Lord God.

Talshir translates this back into Hebrew as:

לא עליך שלחני יהוה אלהים

Whether the Greek rendering in 1 Esdras is the translator's paraphrase of a difficult text or whether it is a passive translation of an alternate Hebrew *Vorlage*, as Talshir suggests,[4] the text of 1 Esdras provides additional theological rationale for two later clauses in 2 Chr 35:21, namely, "God has commanded me to hurry" and "cease opposing God who is with me."[5] First Esdras therefore reinforces what is said about divine empowerment of Israel's enemies, but 1 Esdras also interprets. The rendering in 1 Esdras makes clear that the God sending Neco is the God of Israel and not Pharaoh's god, as Japhet proposes.[6]

The Hebrew expression כי אל בית מלחמתי in 2 Chr 35:21 was as difficult for translators in antiquity as it is for us. My translation of the MT is paraphrastic: "but against the house with which I am at war." The Paraleipomena translate this clause πόλεμον ποιῆσαι ("to make war"), which Leslie C. Allen proposes represents the simple omission of כי אל בית as incomprehensible and a loose translation of מלחמתי.[7] First Esdras renders this expression by ἐπὶ γὰρ τοῦ Εὐφράτου ὁ πόλεμός μού ἐστιν (כי על פרת מלחמתי), "For on the Euphrates is my war"). Does 1 Esdras represent a different Hebrew text or an interpretative paraphrase of the MT?

A major theological difference comes in the rendering of the second sentence in v. 22. According to MT, "He [Josiah] did not listen to the words of Neco from the mouth of God," presumably the God of Israel. In vv. 23–24 the death of Josiah is apparently retribution for not listening to Israel's God. A reader might well ask, "Did God make himself known through a Gentile king?" First Esdras solves that dilemma with its translation of v. 22: "He did not heed the words of Jeremiah the prophet from the mouth of God" (1 Esd 1:26). Talshir cites a parallel from *Lamentations Rabbah*: "Nevertheless Josiah ... hearkened not unto the words of Neco from the mouth of God—this alludes to Jeremiah who said to Josiah, I have this tradition from my teacher Isaiah, And I will spur Egypt against Egypt, but he would not listen to him."[8] First Esdras and *Lamentations Rabbah* represent a common exegetical tradition. Whether this interpretation was brought in by the translator of 1 Esdras or whether it was already represented in his Hebrew *Vorlage* is difficult to determine.

---

4. Talshir, *1 Esdras: A Text Critical Commentary*, 47.
5. Divine empowerment of an Israelite enemy is also attested in 2 Kgs 18:25 Sennacherib said to Hezekiah: "Moreover, is it without YHWH that I have come up against this place to destroy it? YHWH said to me, Go up against this land, and destroy it."
6. Sara Japhet, *I and II Chronicles* (OTL; Louisville: Westminster John Knox, 1993), 1056.
7. Leslie C. Allen, *The Greek Chronicles, Part I: The Translator's Craft* (VTSup 25; Leiden: Brill, 1974), 118–19.
8. Talshir, *1 Esdras: A Text Critical Commentary*, 50 n. 2.

One more difference in regard to the death of Josiah merits attention. According to 2 Kgs 23:29, Neco killed Josiah at Megiddo when he saw him. In 2 Chr 35:23–24 the account is both longer and different: when the archers shot at King Josiah, the king said to his servants, "Take me away for I am severely wounded." His servants took him away from the chariot, and they made him ride in his second chariot. They brought him to Jerusalem, where he died. Instead of archers shooting at the king (וירו הירים, 2 Chr 35:23), 1 Esd 1:27 states that the leaders came down toward him (καὶ κατέβησαν οἱ ἄρχοντες), representing a divergent and secondary Hebrew text, וירדו החרים or וירדו השרים, and in 1 Esd 1:28 the king cries out, "I am very weak," ἠσθένησα γὰρ λίαν. After his servants remove him from the battle line or chariot,[9] Josiah climbs up[10] into the second chariot and, arriving in Jerusalem, he dies. This alternate account results from a miswriting of several Hebrew words and a choice of "weak" instead of "wounded" as a translation for the Hebrew word חלה. The net result is that in 1 Esdras, Josiah is not explicitly wounded by Neco, and in fact he is gathered to his grave in peace, as Huldah had prophesied (2 Kgs 22:20 // 2 Chr 34:28).

3. Two Supplementary Verses in 1 Esdras 1:21–22

1 Esd 1:21:
καὶ ὠρθώθη τὰ ἔργα Ιωσιου ἐνώπιον τοῦ κυρίου αὐτοῦ ἐν καρδίᾳ πλήρει εὐσεβείας. 22 καὶ τὰ κατ' αὐτόν δὲ ἀναγέγραπται ἐν τοῖς ἔμπροσθεν χρόνοις περὶ τῶν ἡμαρτηκότων καὶ ἠσεβηκότων εἰς τὸν κύριον παρὰ πᾶν ἔθνος καὶ βασιλείαν καὶ ἃ ἐλύπησαν αὐτὸν ἐν αἰσθήσει καὶ οἱ λόγοι τοῦ κυρίου ἀνέστησαν ἐπὶ Ισραηλ.

Talshir's translation:[11]

> 1:21 The work of Josiah was well-established (the deeds of Josiah were upright) before (in the eyes of) his Lord with a heart full of piety (with a whole heart and with piety). 22 And the things that came to pass in his days have been written in former times concerning those who sinned and acted impiously against the Lord beyond every nation and kingdom and how they grieved (vexed) him intentionally (with their evil), so that the words of the Lord against Israel were fulfilled.

Talshir's retroversion of these verses into Hebrew:

---

9. ἀπὸ τῆς παρατάξεως probably renders מן המערכה. MT: מן המרכבה.

10. Is this a paraphrase of וירכיבהו ("they made him ride") or does it represent an alternate Vorlage, ויעל? In either case Josiah does not seem to be near death.

11. Talshir, *1 Esdras: A Text Critical Commentary*, 36. The words in parentheses reflect her alternate Hebrew retroversions that are indicated in the Hebrew text below by footnotes.

1:21 ותבון[12] מלאכת[3] יאשיהו לפני[14] אלוהיו בלב מלא יראה[15]
22 ודבריו הנם כתובים על הימים הראשנים על החוטאיכ והפושעים ביהוה מכל גוי וממלכה ואשר העציבוהו[16] בדעת[17] ודברי יהוה קמו על ישראל

Arie van der Kooij renders the verses as follows:[18]

> 1:21 And Josiah's deeds were deemed right before his Lord because his heart was filled with piety. 22 The events of his reign have been recorded in former times concerning those who sinned and acted impiously toward the Lord beyond any nation or kingdom, and how they grieved him [Josiah] in his (moral) consciousness. Therefore the (judgmental) words of the Lord were fulfilled against Israel.

The most significant difference between 1 Esdras and 2 Chr 35–36 is the addition in 1 Esd 1 of these two verses, vv. 21–22. These verses are inserted between the translation in 1 Esdras of 2 Chr 35:19 and 35:20, at nearly the same spot that the LXX of Chronicles, the Paraleipomena, inserts a translation for the equivalent of 2 Kgs 23:24–27. The crucial point is how 1 Esd 1:22 is to be understood. Scholars debate the identity of the people who sinned and acted wickedly, and whether they grieved the Lord deeply or whether by their sinning they grieved Josiah deeply.

3.1. WHY WERE INSERTIONS MADE AT THIS POINT IN BOTH THE PARALEIPOMENA AND IN 1 ESDRAS?

I believe the insertions were made at this point because readers of Chronicles were not satisfied with the transition between the highly laudatory account of Josiah's Passover in 2 Chr 35:1–19 and the immediately following account of his death at the hands of Neco, resulting from his sin in 2 Chr 35:20–26.

3.2. IS THE WORDING OF THE INSERTION IN 1 ESDRAS RELATED TO THE CONTENT OF THE INSERTION IN THE PARALEIPOMENA?

In his book on the textual history of 1 Esdras, Robert Hanhart argues that 1 Esd 1:21–22 differs both in form and content from 2 Kgs 23:24–27, but he finds in the mention of the records about Josiah in 1 Esd 1:22 an echo of 2 Kgs 23:28:

---

12. Or: ויישרו.
13. Or: מעשי.
14. Or: בעיני.
15. Or: בלבב שלם ובירא.
16. Or: הכעיסוהו.
17. Or: ברעתם.
18. Arie van der Kooij, "Zur Frage des Anfangs des 1. Esrabuches," *ZAW* 103 (1991): 242–48. I have translated Van der Kooij's German rendition into English.

"Now the rest of the acts of Josiah, and all that he did, are they not written in the Book of the Annals of the Kings of Judah?"[19] Jacob M. Myers,[20] following C. C. Torrey, however, finds a relationship between 1 Esd 1:21–22 and *2 Par.* 35:19^{a-d}, although most scholars disagree (e.g., Hanhart, Williamson, van der Kooij, Talshir). After all, *2 Par.* 35:19^{a-d} // 2 Kgs 23:24–27 describe how Josiah put away mediums, etc., and how there was no king comparable to Josiah previously or since. And yes, it goes on, because of the sins of Manasseh, God had decided to destroy Judah, Jerusalem, and the temple. There is nothing in the Paraleipomena supplement and its Kings source comparable to the wording of 1 Esd 1:22. Torrey and Myers think that 1 Esd 1:21–22 is corrupt in Greek but that in its Hebrew form it is part of the original text of the Chronicler, and Myers holds that this material was intentionally dropped in Chronicles MT because it appeared to put Josiah in the same category as the most evil kings, which he certainly was not. Myers errs, in my judgment, in concluding that vv. 21–22 portray a negative image of Josiah.

3.3. WHAT DOES VERSE 22 MEAN AND TO WHAT EARLIER WRITING DOES IT REFER?

Robert Hanhart finds in 1 Esd 1:22 a reminiscence of 1 Kgs 13, the prophecy of Josiah's attack on the altar at Bethel, and its fulfillment in 2 Kgs 23:14–20. Zipora Talshir holds a similar position, but her argument can only be understood on the basis of her English translation and her retroversion of these verses into their supposedly original Hebrew (see the citations of Talshir's work above).

Talshir notes that v. 21, with its praise of the work of Josiah, travels the same road as 2 Kgs 23:25, but in details the two verses differ completely. When she turns to v. 22, she asks why Josiah's history is included among the deeds of the impious and who these impious folk are. She believes, with Fritzsche,[21] Hanhart, and many others, that 1 Esd 1:22 refers to 2 Kgs 23:15–20, which mentions a prophecy about Josiah in the days of Jeroboam. This prophecy is contained in 1 Kgs 13:2: "O altar, altar, thus says YHWH: 'A son shall be born to the house of David, Josiah by name, and he shall sacrifice on the altar at Bethel the priests of the high places, and human bones shall be burned on you.'" That prophecy is confirmed in 1 Kgs 13:32, namely, the saying that the old prophet cried by the word of YHWH against the altar in Bethel and against the high places in Samaria. First Esdras 1:22, according to Talshir, notes that the prophecy foretelling the role of Josiah has now come to pass, as written in the account of the impious King Jeroboam.

---

19. Robert Hanhart, *Text und Textgeschichte des 1. Esrabuches* (MSU 12; Göttingen: Vandenhoeck & Ruprecht, 1974), 13.

20. Jacob M. Myers, *I and II Esdras: A New Translation with Introduction and Commentary* (AB 42; Garden City, N.Y.: Doubleday, 1974), 28.

21. Otto F. Fritzsche. *Kurzgefasstes exegetisches Handbuch zu den Apokryphen des Alten Testament*, vol. 1 (Leipzig: Weidmann, 1851), *apud* Talshir.

Talshir states her position clearly: "The meaning of the passage [v. 22] would then be as follows: Josiah's actions were foretold long ago, in the early days, in the book that told the history of the sinners against the Lord (the sins of Jeroboam)."[22] In Talshir's reading, therefore, v. 22 does not refer to those who sinned in Josiah's time, but rather it says that Josiah's time was predicted in the book known today as 1 Kings that told the history of the sinners against YHWH in the time of Jeroboam. Talshir translates the first clause of the Greek text of v. 22 into English as "the things that came to pass in his days," but her Hebrew retroversion would have to be translated somewhat differently: "His deeds, behold they are written in[23] former times concerning those who sinned and acted impiously." The phrase "concerning those who sinned and acted impiously" is a very awkward way of saying that the prophecies about Josiah (now fulfilled) were written earlier in the books of Kings and in their sharp critique of Jeroboam I.

One also wonders why the supplements in 1 Esdras and in the Paraleipomena would both have made additions at this particular spot. The present reason for this insertion, as stated above in my response to the first question, results from the fact that the account of Josiah's God-pleasing Passover is followed immediately in Chronicles by the brief account of his rejecting the word of God, which led to his death. The supplemental verses in the Paraleipomena do give an etiology for YHWH's continuing anger by mentioning the sins of Manasseh, but the supplement in 1 Esdras, according to Talshir's exegesis, makes the contrast between the Josiah of the Passover celebration and his death immediately following even more exasperating since Josiah is also being hailed as the fulfillment of prophecy made three centuries earlier.

Wilhelm Rudolph has also argued that 1 Esd 1:22 refers to 1 Kgs 13:2 and 32,[24] but we must note that the words of the Lord in 1 Esd 1:22 refer to the people of Israel and not to Josiah as in 1 Kgs 13, and the words that come to pass in v. 22 are also directed to Israel, not Josiah.[25]

3.4. VERSE 22 AND THE ORIGINAL BEGINNING OF 1 ESDRAS

The question about the meaning of v. 22 has been related to the discussion of whether the beginning of 1 Esdras once included more of the text we know as 1 and 2 Chronicles. Karl-Friedrich Pohlmann argued, like many before him, that 1 Esdras is a fragment of a larger work and must begin with at least the beginning of the reign of Josiah in 2 Chr 34, but he surmised that it probably

---

22. Talshir, *1 Esdras: From Origin to Translation*, 17.
23. She suggests על as a translation for ἐν. Her citation of על for ἐν in 1:31, 40, however, is not completely persuasive.
24. Wilhelm Rudolph, *Chronikbücher* (HAT 21; Tübingen: Mohr Siebeck, 1955), 331.
25. Van der Kooij, "Zur Frage des Anfangs," 246.

included all of the books of Chronicles, beginning with 1 Chr 1:1.[26] Lurking behind Pohlmann's position is the old question of whether Chronicles–Ezra–Nehemiah once formed a united work, a fragment of which is preserved in 1 Esdras, a position I now reject.

H. G. M. Williamson, in his published dissertation, *Israel in the Books of Chronicles*,[27] concluded that vv. 21–22 were integral to 1 Esdras but were never included in the Hebrew text of Chronicles. These verses were occasioned by the untimely death of pious Josiah (recounted in 2 Chr 35:20–26), who faced immediate retribution because he had disobeyed the words of Neco, whose words came in turn from the mouth of God, and also by the wider problem of the exile itself. That is, v. 21 emphatically asserts the piety of Josiah while v. 22 states that the sins of others in Josiah's day were nevertheless sufficient to condemn Israel. Williamson feels that the words of v. 22 "echo precisely" the judgment on Manasseh cited in 2 Chr 33:9 (cf. 2 Kgs 21:9), namely, "Manasseh misled Judah and the inhabitants of Jerusalem, so that they did more evil than the nations whom YHWH had destroyed before the people of Israel." The reference to Manasseh in 1 Esd 1:22 is not explicit, and Williamson argues that this can only result from the fact that the narrative of 1 Esdras begins sometime after the reign of Manasseh. Otherwise the allusion to Manasseh by the author of 1 Esdras would not be veiled. Second Chronicles 33, therefore, belongs to "writings in former times" and not to the hypothetical earlier chapter of 1 Esdras. Williamson proposes that the narrative of 1 Esdras once began only with the accession of Josiah (2 Chr 34:1) and not with the beginning of the books of Chronicles (contra Pohlmann).

In his article published in *ZAW* in 1991,[28] van der Kooij argues that 1 Esd 1:21–22 does not refer to Manasseh at all nor to the pre-Israelite nations that are explicitly mentioned in 2 Chr 33:9 (2 Kgs 21:9), and therefore he rejects the allusion to 2 Kgs 21:9 // 2 Chr 33:9 that Williamson had proposed. The impiety of Israel in Josiah's time, represented by a perfect participle from the root ἀσεβέω in v. 22, contrasts explicitly with the piety, εὐσεβεία, of Josiah in v. 21.[29] Josiah is not among the sinners of his day (contra Torrey and Myers). Van der Kooij also differs on who was grieved by the actions of these sinners. While NRSV and Talshir, for example, find the Lord as the antecedent of the word αὐτὸν, van der Kooij believes this pronoun refers to Josiah. The sinful behavior of the people grieved Josiah.

---

26. Karl-Friedrich Pohlmann, *Studien zum dritten Esra: Ein Beitrag zur Frage nach dem ursprünglichen Schluss des chronistischen Geschichtswerkes* (FRLANT 104; Göttingen: Vandenhoeck & Ruprecht, 1970), 32–33.

27. H. G. M. Williamson, *Israel in the Books of Chronicles* (Cambridge: Cambridge University Press, 1977), 16–21.

28. Van der Kooij, "Zur Frage des Anfangs," 246.

29. Van der Kooij, "Zur Frage des Anfangs," 248.

The decision in this case is complicated by the Greek word αἴσθησις, which is usually translated as "insight" or "experience" or (Talshir) "perception." Talshir retroverts this word into Hebrew with either בדעת, "with knowledge," that is, they provoked the Lord intentionally, or she suggests a reading בדעתם as a corruption of ברעתם, "with their evil."[30] Van der Kooij, on the other hand, argues that αἴσθησις here refers to Josiah's "sittliche Empfindung" or "sittliche Verständnis"—moral consciousness or ethical understanding. He cites passages from Prov 1:7 and 1:22 where αἴσθησις is the translation for דעת.[31] In both cases the LXX of Proverbs makes a relationship between εὐσεβεια/ἀσεβείς and αἴσθησις. First Esdras 1:22 talks about Josiah's αἴσθησις and 1:21 also about his εὐσεβεία.

Van der Kooij himself thinks that v. 22 alludes to the words of Huldah in 2 Kgs 22:11–20 // 2 Chr 34:19–28. The mention of "those who sinned and acted wickedly toward the Lord beyond any other people or kingdom" is matched by 2 Kgs 22:17 // 2 Chr 34:25, where Huldah notes that they, that is, the people and not the king, "have abandoned me and made offerings to other gods." The reference to their grieving Josiah in his moral consciousness or understanding (ἐν αἰσθήσει) is matched by 2 Kgs 22:11b, 19b // 2 Chr 34:19b, 27b, where Josiah tears his clothes and weeps before YHWH. Similarly Ezra, in 1 Esd 8:68–69, acts dramatically when he learns about the mixed-marriage crisis—he tears his garments, pulls out his hair, mourns, and sits quietly and grief stricken. The reference in 1 Esd 1:22 to the words of the Lord being fulfilled upon Israel is matched by 2 Kgs 22:16, 17b // 2 Chr 34:24a, 28b, where Huldah announces threats of disaster on Jerusalem and its inhabitants. These threats came true in the events of 2 Kgs 25. Hence 1 Esdras, in mentioning what had been written down about Josiah in earlier times, refers to the Huldah passage from 2 Kgs 22 // 2 Chr 34. For van der Kooij, the links to 1 Esd 1:47 and 8:68–69 incline him to think that the addition of vv 21–22 is related to the composition of 1 Esdras itself.[32]

More importantly, if the words of Huldah in 2 Chr 34 were recorded in earlier times, then it appears likely that the present beginning of 1 Esdras, with its translation of 2 Chr 35:1, is the original beginning of the work. Van der Kooij also finds a significant conflict between his understanding of the meaning of 1 Esd 1:22 and 2 Chr 34:33: "Josiah took away all the abominations from all the territory that belonged to the people of Israel, and made all who were in Israel worship YHWH their God. All his days they did not turn away from following

---

30. Talshir, *1 Esdras: A Text Critical Commentary*, 42–43.
31. Van der Kooij, "Zur Frage des Anfangs," 244.
32. Van der Kooij has to admit that Huldah in 2 Kgs 22 // 2 Chr 34 does not accuse Israel of sinning in a superlative way beyond every nation and kingdom, but he finds something similar within 1 Esdras, as with Ezra above, namely, in 1 Esd 1:47 (its translation of 2 Chr 36:14): "Even the leaders of the people and of the priests committed many acts of sacrilege and lawlessness beyond all the unclean deeds of all the nations."

YHWH the God of their ancestors." That is, the Chronicler says that Josiah had transformed the sinners of his time into people with perfect obedience, but 1 Esd 1:22 states that the people of Josiah's time persisted in sinning and acting impiously. This conflict prohibits, in his view, any edition of 1 Esdras that included 2 Chr 34.

In 2 Chr 35:20 the Chronicler refers to Josiah's work on the temple, that is, he alludes to 2 Chr 34. But in the translation of this verse in 1 Esd 1:23 we read only, "After all this activity of Josiah, it happened that Pharaoh, king of Egypt, came to make war." Thus there is no explicit reference in 1 Esd 1:23 to the temple. That might be dismissed as due to the somewhat paraphrastic nature of the translation in 1 Esdras, except that the reference to the temple (בית) is also absent from the regular Greek translation of Chronicles, the Paraleipomena.[33] In any case, the absence of the word "temple" in this verse in 1 Esdras supports van der Kooij's hypothesis that 1 Esdras did not once contain a translation of 2 Chr 34, which describes Josiah's purification of the temple.

Van der Kooij next seeks a parallel to the notion that the sins of the people caused grief to Josiah or that he grieved over their sins. He turns to the Hebrew text of Sirach, which may be translated as follows: "For he grieved over our betrayals and destroyed the abominable idols. He kept his heart fixed on God and in times of lawlessness he practiced virtue" (Sir 49:2–3).[34] Both Sirach and 1 Esdras, therefore, rate Josiah highly and the people of his time negatively.

Finally, van der Kooij concludes, against Torrey and Myers, that vv. 21–22 would not have fit in the context of 2 Chr 35, and so there was never a corresponding Hebrew text there that later fell out.

3.5. THE ORIGINAL LANGUAGE OF THE INSERTION IN 1 ESDRAS 1:21–22

Williamson holds that vv. 21–22 are integral to the book we call 1 Esdras but that they were never included in the Hebrew text of Chronicles.[35] Robert Hanhart, however, finds behind the supplemental texts in 2 Par. 35:19[a–d] and 1 Esd 1:21–22 divergent Hebrew *Vorlagen* that result from alternate attempts to harmonize the books of Kings and Chronicles.[36] Zipora Talshir, as we have seen, translates the Greek of vv. 21–22 back into the "original" Hebrew. Talshir concludes that the expansion could not have been written originally in Greek, although she concedes that reconstructing the *Vorlage* is a difficult chore and much remains uncertain. It is not self-evident to me that this expansion could not originally

---

33. *Par.* omits a translation for אחרי כל זאת אשר הכין יאשיהו את הבית, "After all this which Josiah had established—the house." Note also the awkward location of the word "house" in Hebrew. 2 Kgs 23:29 does not have this clause.

34. Patrick W. Skehan and Alexander A. Di Lella, *The Wisdom of Ben Sira* (AB 39; New York: Doubleday, 1987), 540.

35. Williamson, *Israel in the Books of Chronicles*, 20.

36. Hanhart, *Text und Textgeschichte*, 13.

have been written in Greek. Does the pun in Greek not suggest that this is a Greek composition and not a translation of a Hebrew *Vorlage*? I have in mind Josiah's piety, εὐσεβείας, in v. 21 and the impiety of the people in v. 22, rendered by ἠσεβηκότων (root = ἀσεβέω). Talshir's retroversion of these words into Hebrew shows no punning at all. The first word is retroverted by her as יראה, "fear," and the second by a participial form of פשע.[37]

5. CONCLUSION

So what can we say about the rendering of 2 Chr 35–36 in 1 Esdras? The translator used a Hebrew text that was not identical with the MT, since there are more than one hundred cases where 1 Esdras alone or 1 Esdras with the Paraleipomena presuppose a different *Vorlage*.

In its description of Josiah's death, 1 Esdras asserts that the oracle from Israel's God that Josiah disobeyed was delivered by Jeremiah, not by Neco. It also suggests that Josiah was not wounded by Neco and hence was gathered to his grave in peace as Huldah had prophesied. The two additional verses, 1 Esd 1:21–22, whether added in Hebrew or, more likely, in Greek, indicate that readers of Chronicles were also not satisfied at the transition between the laudatory account of Josiah's Passover and the immediately following account of the king's death at the hands of Neco. This supplement states that Josiah was not among the sinners of his day but was grieved by their sinful behavior (see also Sirach). Van der Kooij has shown that the present beginning of 1 Esdras is also its original beginning. The modifications in the manner of Josiah's death and the comments on Josiah's piety that distinguished him from his contemporaries in 1 Esdras may have suggested this beginning point.

---

37. Talshir, *1 Esdras: A Text Critical Commentary*, 38.

1 ESDRAS AS REWRITTEN BIBLE?

H. G. M. Williamson

Scholars continue to debate the nature of 1 Esdras.[1] There are three main possibilities. It could be the end of a translation into Greek of an earlier form of the books of Chronicles, Ezra, and Nehemiah than that with which we are familiar from their present canonical form;[2] it could be the fragment of an originally longer work that drew on those same books, they, however, having already reached more or less their present form;[3] or it could be a complete work in itself, again based on the finished form of the canonical works.[4]

Scholars who adopt the first view do not need to consider further the question of literary genre. It is true that they generally take the view that the story of the three guardsmen was added later to this translation, so that the ques-

---

1. For surveys of past research, see Karl-Friedrich Pohlmann, *Studien zum dritten Esra: Ein Beitrag zur Frage nach dem ursprünglichen Schluss des chronistischen Geschichtswerkes* (FRLANT 104; Göttingen: Vandenhoeck & Ruprecht, 1970), and Kristin De Troyer, "Zerubbabel and Ezra: A Revived and Revised Solomon and Josiah? A Survey of Current 1 Esdras Research," *Currents in Biblical Research* 1 (2002): 30–60.
2. This view has been maintained in relatively recent times in particular by Pohlmann, *Studien zum dritten Esra*; Adrian Schenker, "La relation d'Esdras A' au texte massorétique d'Esdras-Néhémie," in *Tradition of the Text: Studies Offered to Dominique Barthélemy in Celebration of his 70th Birthday* (ed. Gerard J. Norton and Stephen Pisano; OBO 109; Freiburg: Universitätsverlag; Göttingen: Vandenhoeck & Ruprecht, 1991), 218–48; Dieter Böhler, *Die heilige Stadt in Esdras α und Esra-Nehemia: Zwei Konzeptionen der Wiederherstellung Israels* (OBO 158; Freiburg: Universitätsverlag; Göttingen: Vandenhoeck & Ruprecht, 1997); idem, "On the Relationship between Textual and Literary Criticism: The Two Recensions of the Book of Ezra: Ezra-Neh (MT) and 1 Esdras (LXX)," in *The Earliest Text of the Hebrew Bible: The Relationship between the Masoretic Text and the Hebrew Base of the Septuagint Reconsidered* (ed. Adrian Schenker; SBLSCS 52; Atlanta: Society of Biblical Literature, 2003), 35–50; see too the related position of Frank Moore Cross, "A Reconstruction of the Judean Restoration," *JBL* 94 (1975): 4–18.
3. So, prominently, for instance, Zipora Talshir, *1 Esdras: From Origin to Translation* (SBLSCS 47; Atlanta: Society of Biblical Literature, 1999).
4. Especially influential in this regard have been the two studies of Arie van der Kooij: "Zur Frage des Anfangs des 1. Esrabuches," *ZAW* 103 (1991): 239–52, and "On the Ending of the Book of 1 Esdras," in *LXX: VII Congress of the International Organization for Septuagint and Cognate Studies* (ed. C. E. Cox; SCSt 31; Atlanta: Scholars Press, 1991), 37–49.

tion might arise at this secondary level, but the basic position is clear and familiar.

For those who adopt either the second or third position, however, the question is more acute. Why should anyone have written this work in the first place, and why did he do it in this particular form? In a previous study I sought to defend this second general approach by gathering and evaluating the main arguments that I considered strongest in showing that 1 Esdras was dependent on more or less the present canonical form of these books.[5] (The question of whether the work is complete as it stands or whether it is fragmentary is important, of course, but less easily decided, and I do not wish to pursue that aspect of the problem further here.) I commented at the end, however, that my far-from-original conclusion served only to open up other questions that do not seem to be so generally asked, and I speculated that perhaps the work might have been an example of "rewritten Bible." I did not have the space there to explore this suggestion further, and in any case recent years have seen quite some discussion of the proposed genre itself. It therefore seems appropriate in the present context to take up this question in rather more detail.

It is just on fifty years since my colleague Geza Vermes first introduced the term rewritten Bible.[6] In a subsequent and more extensive study he has suggested that it can be applied to a seemingly diverse group of texts which have in common that they work through a section of the Bible, embedding that text within their presentation and simultaneously offering additional material and interpretative comments. They are thus distinct from the early commentaries, in which text and interpretation are sharply distinguished, but united by their adherence to the re-presentation of a biblical text of some extent. His own later definition is "a narrative that follows Scripture but includes a substantial amount of supplements and interpretative developments."[7] He thinks that the biblical books of Chronicles are a prototype,[8] and Josephus' *Antiquities* are the fullest

---

5. H. G. M. Williamson, "The Problem with First Esdras," in *After the Exile: Essays in Honour of Rex Mason* (ed. John Barton and David J. Reimer; Macon, Ga.: Mercer University Press, 1996), 201–16.

6. Geza Vermes, *Scripture and Tradition in Judaism: Haggadic Studies* (StPB 4; Leiden: Brill, 1961), esp. 126.

7. Geza Vermes, "Biblical Midrash," in E. Schürer, *The History of the Jewish People in the Age of Jesus Christ (175 B.C.–A.D. 135)* (rev. and ed. Geza Vermes, Fergus Millar, and Martin Goodman; 3 vols.; Edinburgh: T&T Clark, 1986), 3.1:308–41 (cf. 326).

8. There is a recent full discussion of Chronicles as rewritten Bible in Gary N. Knoppers, *1 Chronicles 1–9: A New Translation with Introduction and Commentary* (AB 12; New York: Doubleday, 2004), 129–34. He argues cogently that Chronicles is not an example of rewritten Bible in itself, though he acknowledges that it includes a number of features that it has in common with the later category. For some initial response to Knoppers, see G. J. Brooke, "The Books of Chronicles and the Scrolls from Qumran," in *Reflection and Refraction: Studies in*

example. Other texts that he includes are the *Genesis Apocryphon* (from which his original essay started out), Pseudo-Philo, and *Jubilees*.⁹

Since Vermes wrote, many examples have been suggested, mainly among the Dead Sea Scrolls published in the intervening decades. At the same time, however, questions have arisen as to whether the genre categorization is justified in the first place.¹⁰ Most scholars who have discussed the issue agree with the general definition even while refining it in certain respects. Among the earlier cohort, Nickelsburg is positive and generous to a fault in the range of texts he includes.¹¹ More reflectively, Alexander considers in detail whether there was such a genre and if so how it should be defined. His answer is "an emphatic Yes," and he lists nine principal characteristics from his survey of a representative sampling of examples (see further below).¹² But the publication of more suggested examples among the Dead Sea Scrolls has led to a greater focus on the variety of material that is here included, and this has led some to suggest that perhaps the label has outlived its usefulness. There are those who would thus prefer to speak of a category of texts rather than a genre.¹³

Biblical Historiography in Honour of A. Graeme Auld (ed. R. Rezetko, T. H. Lim and W. B. Aucker; VTSup 113; Leiden: Brill, 2007), 35–48.

9. The value of Vermes' suggestion is obvious from its subsequent widespread adoption. Purely by way of example, one may compare the titles of the following works on some of the major texts from which he started out: C. A. Evans, "The Genesis Apocryphon and the Rewritten Bible," *RevQ* 13 (1988): 153–65; Louis H. Feldman, *Studies in Josephus' Rewritten Bible* (JSJSup 58; Leiden: Brill, 1998); B. N. Fisk, *Do You Not Remember? Scripture, Story and Exegesis in the Rewritten Bible of Pseudo-Philo* (JSPSup 37; Sheffield: Sheffield Academic Press, 2001), who, without comment, includes 1 Esdras in his list of examples of the corpus on p. 14; Michael H. Segal, *The Book of Jubilees: Rewritten Bible, Redaction, Ideology and Theology* (JSJSup 117; Leiden: Brill, 2007); see too B. Halpern-Amaru, *Rewriting the Bible: Land and Covenant in Postbiblical Jewish Literature* (Valley Forge, Pa.: Trinity, 1994).

10. For a recent survey, see E. Koskenniemi and P. Lindqvist, "Rewritten Bible, Rewritten Stories: Methodological Aspects," in *Rewritten Bible Reconsidered: Proceedings of the Conference in Karkku, Finland, August 24–26, 2006* (ed. A. Laato and J. van Ruiten; Studies in Rewritten Bible 1; Turku: Åbo Akademi University; Winona Lake, Ind.: Eisenbrauns, 2008), 11–39.

11. George W. E. Nickelsburg, "The Bible Rewritten and Expanded," in *Jewish Writings of the Second Temple Period: Apocrypha, Pseudepigrapha, Qumran Sectarian Writings, Philo, Josephus* (ed. Michael E. Stone; Assen: Van Gorcum, 1984), 89–156.

12. P. S. Alexander, "Retelling the Old Testament," in *It Is Written: Scripture Citing Scripture; Essays in Honour of Barnabas Lindars, SSF* (ed. D. A. Carson and H. G. M. Williamson; Cambridge: Cambridge University Press, 1988), 99–121.

13. Cf. D. J. Harrington, "The Bible Rewritten (Narratives)," in *Early Judaism and Its Modern Interpreters* (ed. Robert A. Kraft and George W. E. Nickelsburg; Philadelphia: Fortress, 1986), 239–47 (243); G. J. Brooke, "Rewritten Bible," *EDSS* 2:777–81; idem, "The Rewritten Law, Prophets and Psalms: Issues for Understanding the Text of the Bible," in *The Bible as Book: The Hebrew Bible and the Judaean Desert Discoveries* (ed. E. D. Herbert and Emanuel Tov; London: The British Library; New Castle, Del.: Oak Knoll, 2002), 31–40;

Some of the subsequent refinements seem technically correct. In particular, several scholars have pointed out that the word Bible is anachronistic for the period under discussion, both because there is uncertainty as to whether one may properly speak of "a fixed collection of books in a particular textual form"[14] and because the phrase implies that the new text will be less authoritative than the original, something that cannot be taken for granted at least for every Jewish community at the time. For these reasons, the phrase "rewritten Scripture" or similar is now generally preferred.[15] While I entirely agree with that, I have retained the older phrase here simply for the reason of familiarity.

More importantly, however, the accumulation of texts under the general rubric of rewritten Bible has led to the point where commentators are beginning to be as much interested in what differs among them as in what unites them as a single group. In her helpful recent student guide, for instance, White Crawford follows Brooke in speaking of a spectrum (Brooke: "sliding scale") of texts that start, effectively, as a biblical recension (the pre-Samaritan pentateuchal texts) and work all the way through to the classic texts from which Vermes started.[16] Clearly such an approach gathers under a single classification texts that certainly differ considerably in style from one another. To that extent, a degree of skepticism may be justified[17] and the looser term "category of text" might seem more suitable. But this need not deflect us a priori from our question. On the one hand, the similarity in genre among the original core texts remains,[18] and

---

Sidnie White Crawford, *Rewriting Scripture in Second Temple Times* (Studies in the Dead Sea Scrolls and Related Literature; Grand Rapids, Mich.: Eerdmans, 2008).

14. Brooke, "Rewritten Law," 31.

15. The strongest argument against the whole use of the term has been advanced by J. G. Campbell, "'Rewritten Bible' and 'Parabiblical Texts': A Terminological and Ideological Critique," in *New Directions in Qumran Studies: Proceedings of the Bristol Colloquium on the Dead Sea Scrolls, 8-10 September 2003* (ed. J. G. Campbell, W. J. Lyons and L. K. Pietersen; LSTS 52; London: T&T Clark, 2005), 43-68. While I accept above that use of the word Bible is, strictly speaking, anachronistic, his objections to "rewritten" seem far less cogent. Even though, as he indicates, *Jubilees* was not seen as rewritten but as authoritative in itself, he nevertheless accepts that it was, in fact, "rewritten."

16. D. D. Swanson, "How Scriptural is Re-Written Bible?," *RevQ* 83 (2004): 407-27, thus prefers to speak of a "continuum."

17. See, for instance, C. Martone, "Biblical or Not Biblical? Some Doubts and Questions," *RevQ* 83 (2004): 387-94.

18. This has been emphasized in particular by M. J. Bernstein, "'Rewritten Bible': A Generic Category Which Has Outlived Its Usefulness?," *Textus* 22 (2005): 169-96. He makes some excellent points in defense of a narrower definition of the genre, more in line with Vermes, but adding the *Temple Scroll*, published since. He suggests that many of the texts from Qumran that some have added to the category since should more appropriately be labeled and studied separately as parabiblical literature. He also insists that "rewritten Bible" describes a genre, not a process; on this, see the completely contrary position of Daniel K. Falk (who also includes an extensive and helpful survey of the whole debate), *The Parabiblical*

whatever label we give them, the question remains reasonable whether and to what extent another text resembles them. On the other hand, the observation that there may be greater diversity within a general group than was originally appreciated can be a help as we look to see whether other texts might belong.[19] Indeed, they sharpen the inquiry: not only does it belong? but if it does, where does it fit on the spectrum?

First Esdras certainly deserves to be investigated from this point of view. It clearly follows a biblical text, and it equally clearly includes material additional to the biblical text. The fact that it is in Greek is no obstacle. On the one hand, the *Genesis Apocryphon* is in Aramaic, so that composition in a language other than the parent text is allowable. On the other hand, it is not certain whether 1 Esdras was originally written in Greek in any case. The argument has been advanced, and seems to be widely held, for a Semitic *Vorlage*, and this would reflect one of the main languages of the relevant biblical text.[20]

As I have already noted, Alexander's analysis of the genre concludes with a list of what he deduced were nine distinguishing characteristics. Brooke is in broad agreement but reduces the number to four. It will be simplest to work through Alexander's longer list, noting Brooke's small qualifications where appropriate, and to gauge the extent to which 1 Esdras measures up against them.

(1) Alexander's first point is that rewritten Bible texts are "narratives, which follow a sequential chronological order." In more recent years, some other scholars have rather confused Alexander's clarity by trying to expand the criterion to include legal and other texts, such as the *Temple Scroll*. Whether that

---

Texts: Strategies for Extending the Scriptures in the Dead Sea Scrolls (Companion to the Qumran Scrolls 8; LSTS 63; London: T&T Clark, 2007), 3–17. In addition, it should be noted that some strong complementary considerations have been advanced by Michael H. Segal to indicate that there was a sharper awareness in antiquity than some have allowed between Bible and rewritten Bible; cf. "Between Bible and Rewritten Bible," in *Biblical Interpretation at Qumran* (ed. M. Henze; Studies in the Dead Sea Scrolls and Related Literature; Grand Rapids, Mich.: Eerdmans, 2005), 10–28.

19. The variety of texts is stressed especially by S. D. Fraade, "Rewritten Bible and Rabbinic Midrash as Commentary," in *Current Trends in the Study of Midrash* (ed. C. Bakhos; JSJSup 106; Leiden: Brill, 2006), 59–79. However, like many others he embraces a wider group of texts than Bernstein (see previous note), for instance, would allow.

20. See especially Talshir, *1 Esdras: From Origin to Translation*, 94–105, who there discusses the language of the three bodyguards and of the verses whereby that was bound editorially to the wider narrative. If that was in Aramaic (or Hebrew), as she argues, then clearly the remainder must also have been originally. See too Z. and D. Talshir, "The Story of the Three Youths (I Esdras 3–4): Towards the Question of the Language of Its Vorlage," *Textus* 18 (1995): 135–55, and Zipora Talshir, "The Original Language of the Story of the Three Youths (1 Esdras 3–4)" [in Hebrew], in *Sha'arei Talmon: Studies in the Bible, Qumran, and the Ancient Near East Presented to Shemaryahu Talmon* (ed. Michael Fishbane and Emanuel Tov; Winona Lake, Ind.: Eisenbrauns, 1992), 63*–75*.

is justified need not concern us here, as clearly 1 Esdras fits Alexander's point well. Indeed, as we shall discuss shortly, one of the most significant differences between 1 Esdras and its canonical *Vorlage* is precisely that it has sought to improve the confused chronological sequence in Ezra 1–6. The fact that it has not been entirely successful in this endeavor is neither surprising nor damning for the hypothesis.

(2) Rewritten Bibles are "free-standing compositions which replicate the form of the biblical books on which they are based." Alexander amplifies this with reference to the way in which the biblical text is integrated into the retelling rather than being highlighted (as is the case in rabbinic midrash) in the form of lemmata or by the use of citation formulae. So far as 1 Esdras is concerned, this last, negative point is clearly appropriate. So far as the opening, more positive aspect is concerned, it might be suggested that the biblical text is presented merely as translation rather than as rewritten.[21] Here, however, there are other considerations to be borne in mind that Alexander does not highlight but of the first of which his earlier discussion in the article shows that he is well aware. First, when the *Genesis Apocryphon* reaches its version of Gen 14 (from XXI, 23 on), it too becomes a fairly close rendering of the Hebrew *Vorlage*. Indeed, there are plenty of instances in which it is an even closer rendering than some of the pentateuchal Targumim. Such close adherence to the biblical text is not an automatic disqualification in our genre categorization. Second, as we shall see later, there are quite a number of deviations (mostly of only modest proportions) between MT and 1 Esdras, and while some of these are admittedly to be studied solely from the point of view of textual criticism, others certainly are to be grouped as testifying to a particular line of interpretation. The issue, therefore, is one of degree, not of principle. Third, were we to include the Qumran pentateuchal texts from which White Crawford and Brooke start out, 1 Esdras might not seem so anomalous here either, and if they are right to look to Chronicles as an early prototype, we could there also cite extensive passages in which the author follows his *Vorlage* equally closely. So 1 Esdras does not necessarily differ in type from rewritten Bible on this account, but clearly there is here an important element of distinctiveness to be borne in mind when we return later to considerations of spectrum.

(3) Alexander's third point is that rewritten Bibles were not intended to replace or supersede the Bible. While he admits that the special circumstances of the composition of Josephus' *Antiquities* perhaps put it in a different category, he is clear that for the remainder they presuppose a knowledge of the biblical version, *Jubilees*, indeed, explicitly acknowledging it. While subsequent discussion has agreed with this, some refinement has been added by the additional

---

21. Without reference to 1 Esdras, Bernstein, "Rewritten Bible," 175, for instance, excludes translations from his category. He does not, however, discuss whether this encompasses works that *include* translation, such as the *Genesis Apocryphon*.

observation that some, at least, of the texts were expected to be, and did in fact become, authoritative in their own right in at least some communities. So far as 1 Esdras is concerned, our evidence is too slender to say a great deal, but nothing would seem to contradict this criterion in either its limited or its more expanded form. On the one hand, I am not aware of any evidence that anyone ever thought that 1 Esdras should replace the canonical form of the narrative, and on the other, its final position in the so-called Apocrypha is an indication of the high value placed upon it in some later communities. Josephus also chose to use it as the base of his narrative for this period in *Antiquities*, showing his high regard for it. It would thus seem that it attained an appropriate status in some Jewish and Christian circles.

(4) Rewritten Bible texts "cover a substantial portion of the Bible." While this is clearly a somewhat ill-defined criterion, Alexander's development of it indicates that it is intended to exclude those texts that expand on a single episode. While rewritten Bible may include legendary material, the latter is integrated into the biblical history rather than being the focus of attention in itself. First Esdras clearly meets this requirement. Although it includes one long and at least one short expansion, the underlying narrative is derived from the Bible, to which it returns each time, and that biblical material is extensive, coming from three canonical books. (It remains disputed whether the text we have is complete or is only fragmentary.)

(5) "Rewritten Bible texts follow the Bible serially, in proper order, but they are highly selective in what they represent." Furthermore "A proper balance between the 'literal' and the 'non-literal' sections is probably of fundamental importance to the genre." This is a most important part of our discussion and needs to be broken down into its constituent elements.

First, there is no doubt that 1 Esdras basically follows the canonical narrative, and I take it that this is what Alexander has in mind when he says "in proper order." It is not some sort of anthology or selection from here and there. Furthermore, it is also selective in the sense that it does not include the material now found in Neh 1–7 as well as briefer elements such as Ezra 4:5. It is recognizably the same basic story as found in 2 Chr 35–36, Ezra, and Neh 8.

Second, however, there is an important deviation from the biblical order with regard to the setting of Zerubbabel's activity and some associated material. Put rather crudely, it may be said that the exchange of correspondence with (Xerxes and) Artaxerxes in Ezra 4:6–24 has been moved (with some simplification of its introduction) to follow the equivalent of Ezra 1 (at 1 Esd 2:16–30). This is then followed immediately by the inclusion of the story of the three bodyguards, which is not present in the canonical text. One of these three is identified as Zerubbabel, and so it leads naturally enough into the resumption of the biblical text at Ezra 2 (dated now to the reign of Darius, of course), which is then followed in order (with the exception of 4:6–24, already discussed). It may well be that these differences are all part of the same package. If our author was keen for reasons of his own to include the story of the three bodyguards, one of whom, for him, was Zerubbabel, then it was obvious that he was going to have to reorder Ezra 2–4 to some extent. But as is well known, Ezra 4 is itself chronologically confusing, so that his movement of most of it to an earlier point, resulting effectively in a swapping around of two elements in the narrative that he inherited, could well have been a related move, consequential to his need to move the date of Zerubbabel's journey to Jerusalem. While the text that results seems to differ a good deal from the Ezra 1–4 with which we are familiar, this should not be treated as more than one major exegetical move.

In terms specifically of the order of the material, all that the author has done is to date Zerubbabel to the reign of Darius and thus to move Ezra 2:1–4:5 to follow 4:24. This results automatically in his implying that there was an Artaxerxes between Cyrus and Darius, and there are also some other minor variations in wording necessary to make the new order fit. These are consequential changes, however, and should not be allocated to some separate category. Now, it might be inferred from Alexander's rubric that such a change in order rules this work out from consideration as rewritten Bible, but such an inference would be premature, in my opinion. In fact, Alexander himself accepts an occasional small reordering of material in the course of retelling a biblical narrative without that worrying him unduly.[22] Furthermore, Bernstein has added several examples from the *Genesis Apocryphon* in which the biblical order is changed "to improve the flow of the story in some way" and to make it "more logical or easier to understand,"[23] while Segal points to some significant examples of reordering in *Jubilees*.[24] Other such examples have been attended to in some of the more recent additions to the category. Brooke, for instance, discusses the situation in 4QJosh[a], in which the building of the altar comes in the equivalent of Josh 5 rather than Josh 8 in MT.[25] (It is not necessary here to debate priority.) Furthermore, in all the texts that White Crawford sets out in the first two of the various stages of her spectrum (pentateuchal texts and reworked Pentateuch), it is precisely the repositioning of biblical material, usually for harmonizing purposes, that is the focus of her discussion. And finally in the *Temple Scroll*, the repositioning of some biblical material is even more marked.[26] (It could be added that

---

22. See, e.g., Alexander, "Retelling the Old Testament," 115.

23. M. J. Bernstein, "Re-Arrangement, Anticipation and Harmonization as Exegetical Features in the Genesis Apocryphon," *DSD* 3 (1996): 37–57 (38).

24. Segal, "Between Bible and Rewritten Bible," 19, and idem, *Book of Jubilees*, 3–4, 121–22, etc.; for the somewhat different use of out-of-sequence "secondary" biblical material in Pseudo-Philo, see Fisk, *Do You Not Remember?*

25. Brooke, "Rewritten Bible," 32.

26. For a summary introduction, see Yigael Yadin, *The Temple Scroll* (4 vols.; Jerusalem: Israel Exploration Society, 1983), 1:71–88; for more detail, see D. D. Swanson, *The Temple Scroll and the Bible: The Methodology of 11QT* (STDJ 14; Leiden: Brill, 1995).

there are a few significant examples of changes to the order of his *Vorlage* by the Chronicler as well, e.g., in 1 Chr 14 and 2 Chr 1.) I conclude that the change in order, motivated at least in part by the desire to include the story of the three bodyguards, is striking but not exceptional or decisive in terms of genre analysis.

Third, the question of balance between "literal" and "non-literal" is again imprecise. Clearly, the story of the guardsmen as well as a few other short elements come into what is meant by "non-literal," but by comparison with Alexander's core texts the balance is less exact. Here too, however, several of the additional texts that are now generally reckoned to come into this category would tend in the opposite direction, so that this again cannot be a decisive factor. It seems that in this respect 1 Esdras comes between reworked Pentateuch texts and Alexander's core texts—within the fold, therefore, but not quite as Alexander defined it.

(6) Alexander's next criterion is that rewritten Bible texts aim to produce an interpretative reading of Scripture. Following Vermes, he finds them doctrinally "more advanced" than the original narrative.[27] They are like an indirect commentary in silent, but intense, dialogue with the original. Despite the close manner in which 1 Esdras mostly follows its parent text, this nevertheless seems to be a fair way of describing what it is doing throughout. Obviously a full analysis of this point would require a running discussion of the complete text, which cannot be undertaken here, but some highlights may be mentioned. In the following, the assumption is made that we have the complete, or virtually the complete, text. Were this not to be the case, some modifications would obviously be required, but the main point would still stand.

We note first that, following the widespread agreement that Chronicles and Ezra–Nehemiah were not an original unity, 1 Esdras is the first text we have that explicitly links by narrative the fall of Jerusalem to the Babylonians and the account of the postexilic restoration. While there is room for discussion of the historical aspects of this presentation, there can be no doubt of its major interpretative significance for questions of social and religious self-identity. The more continuity is stressed between pre- and postexilic periods in this particular manner, the more the voice of the Babylonian *golah* becomes determinative and the more the break of the Neo-Babylonian period is lessened

This is in line, secondly, with a trait to which Böhler has drawn particular attention, namely, the way in which in quite a number of small ways 1 Esdras indicates its presupposition that "(1) the city of Jerusalem is rebuilt at the time of Zerubbabel and Ezra, (2) that the returning exiles can at once settle down in it, and (3) that the temple is furnished with a walled precinct, gates and active gatekeepers."[28] Böhler's position is that this was changed by the redactor of Ezra

---

27. Vermes, "Biblical Midrash," 305.
28. Böhler, "On the Relationship," 44–45. In this article, he briefly presents the position at 1 Esd 5:45, 46; 6:8; 7:9; 8:78, 88; 9:1. In his earlier monograph, these and other passages are

and Nehemiah as a consequence of his inclusion of the Nehemiah material because the statements seem to anticipate his major accomplishments. If, on other grounds, we find ourselves unable to share his understanding of the order of composition, then it follows that these changes must be due to the author of 1 Esdras, and they may be seen as a related part in his attempt to minimize the effect of the exile.

This may by extension be linked with a third important element, namely, the fact that, at least in its present shape, 1 Esdras begins and ends with a presentation of the community gathered at the temple for a festival. If the beginning represents effectively a portrait of Israel in its ideal state, with all the people gathered together in worship according to the prescriptions of the law, the remainder of the work, having shown how quickly that ideal was marred, traces the path to full restoration. Within this, therefore, although physical restoration is obviously an element, the main focus is on the community, and it may be suggested that the overall shape of the work makes it into something of an ideal portrayal; it leaves the later reader with an aspiration toward which to move and an encouragement that God is able to order things so.[29]

Fourth, the particular prominence of Zerubbabel in this work cannot be overlooked. The most obvious evidence for this is the inclusion of the story of the three bodyguards in 3:1–5:3,[30] but that is not all. In addition to his chronological rearrangement, already noted, whereby Zerubbabel does not come to Jerusalem until the reign of Darius, he also becomes thereby the person more

---

discussed at greater length. It may be noted in passing here with regard to the other text that he cites, in particular, that of course 1 Esdras's omission at 2:23 of an equivalent for Ezra 4:21's comment by Artaxerxes, עד־מני טעמא יתשם, was inevitable once he had relocated this material to a reign between Cyrus and Darius. Other possible considerations are mentioned by Zipora Talshir, *1 Esdras: A Text Critical Commentary* (SBLSCS 50; Atlanta: Society of Biblical Literature, 2001), 120.

29. We may compare the recent summary of A. Siedlecki: "the text begins in Jerusalem and ends in Jerusalem, with the effect that the story comes full circle, conveying the idea of stable containment, in contrast to the more linear movement of Ezra–Nehemiah, which reports several movements from Mesopotamia to Jerusalem, the success of which is characterized by interruptions and setbacks"; "Contextualizations of Ezra–Nehemiah," in *Unity and Disunity in Ezra–Nehemiah: Redaction, Rhetoric and Reader* (ed. Mark J. Boda and Paul L. Redditt; Hebrew Bible Monographs 17; Sheffield: Sheffield Phoenix, 2008), 263–76 (274).

30. According to Talshir, *1 Esdras: From Origin to Translation*, the whole of 1 Esdras was written precisely in order to give a context for the preservation of this story. While we may readily agree that there is no need to downplay its significance, still less to relegate it to the status of a later addition, the various other emphases in the work sketched out above suggest that there is more to 1 Esdras than this story alone. Note should also be taken here, however, of the attempt by T. J. Sandoval to detect evidence of the story's influence on later parts of the book: "The Strength of Women and Truth: The Tale of the Three Bodyguards and Ezra's Prayer in First Esdras," *JSJ* 58 (2007): 211–27.

responsible than any other for the first significant steps in the path to restoration. This is clear already from the highly suggestive language of Zerubbabel's request to the king in 4:43–46 (almost certainly composed by our author himself),[31] and it continues thereafter by minor additions through the remaining chapters, which describe Zerubbabel's work.[32] And of course, the fact that this all concluded with a Passover celebration, just as in the opening scene under Josiah, will have been taken to mean that, although there remained more yet to be done, nevertheless a significant landmark had been reached. We may note here also the interesting suggestion of De Troyer[33] that some of the changes are due to a desire to establish a parallel between Zerubbabel and Solomon. This may also be linked with the obvious wisdom shown by Zerubbabel in the story of the three bodyguards.

The reason for this heightened attention to Zerubbabel is less easily discerned, and we may suspect that it has something to do with debates about the nature of political and religious leadership that were in play at the time of composition. Since this date is uncertain, with a number of suggestions currently on the table, we may simply note for the moment that the major addition of the story of the three bodyguards should not be overlooked. Whatever his previous position in court, Zerubbabel rises to prominence and becomes the leader of the restoration not because of military or political acumen but because of his wisdom and understanding of religious truth. Such a portrayal could well have contributed to debates in connection with several of the possible settings that have been proposed for the work, but our lack of a firm date or setting for the original composition of 1 Esdras means that it would not be profitable to speculate further about this here.

Finally, without going into particular detail, it is worth just mentioning that 1 Esdras is not lacking in those small matters of interpretation that are such an obvious feature of other examples of rewritten Bible. To give one small but revealing example, elsewhere in his essay, for instance, Alexander shows a particular interest in geographical matters, and here we may note similarly that 1 Esdras regularly renders the name of the Persian satrapy Beyond the River as "Coele Syria and Phoenicia," a designation firmly rooted in Hellenistic usage.[34]

---

31. For further details, see my short commentary on 1 Esdras in *The Eerdmans Commentary on the Bible* (ed. J. D. G. Dunn and J. W. Rogerson; Grand Rapids, Mich.: Eerdmans, 2003), 851–58 (854).

32. Cf. Sara Japhet, "Sheshbazzar and Zerubbabel against the Background of the Historical and Religious Tendencies of Ezra–Nehemiah, II," *ZAW* 95 (1983): 218–29.

33. De Troyer, "Zerubbabel and Ezra," 51–52. Later she suggests further that the start and finish of the work with Josiah and Ezra is a means of interpreting Ezra as standing "in the line of Josiah, and not as a counterpart to Nehemiah" (54–55).

34. Jacob M. Myers, *I and II Esdras: A New Translation with Introduction and Commentary* (AB 42; Garden City, N.Y.: Doubleday, 1974), 12.

I conclude, therefore, that 1 Esdras matches this sixth criterion particularly well.

(7) By contrast with a commentary, rewritten Bible texts can impose only a single interpretation on the original. (Whether this criterion is so appropriate to some of the more recent additions to the category, such as the *Temple Scroll*, may be debated but is not relevant in the present context.) So far as 1 Esdras is concerned, I believe that my remarks in the previous section have already shown that this criterion is well met. Although inevitably in a narrative there is scope for a variety of smaller points to be made, I have indicated how the major changes, along with the choice of starting and finishing points, are interrelated and so may well be said to be determined by an overarching interpretative standpoint.

(8) The narrative form of text (which is the only sort that Alexander considers) precludes making clear the exegetical reasoning; although it includes attempts to solve problems in the original, including by midrashic means, it cannot make those workings explicit as in the rabbinic midrashim themselves. This criterion is obviously true of 1 Esdras without the need for further comment.

(9) "Rewritten Bible texts make use of non-biblical tradition and draw on non-biblical sources, whether oral or written." This is often legendary and could not be derived directly from the biblical text. The material is synthesized with the biblical text in order to "unify the tradition on a biblical base." This too seems a very apt description with regard to 1 Esdras, even though it has only one such addition, the story of the three bodyguards. All who have studied this material are in agreement that it existed prior to its incorporation into 1 Esdras (indeed, there is good evidence to think that it had already gone through one major literary development before it reached our author, with regard to both the order of the first three responses and the addition of the extra speech about truth[35]). What is more, it has been well integrated, as we have seen, into its new context, with the biblical text nevertheless remaining at the narrative base. It is also worth observing that although there were not many examples in Alexander's texts of an addition so extensive in length (see his point 5, above, with its talk of balanced proportion), this has been paralleled now by those who include the *Temple Scroll* within the category, where sizable additions to the biblical paraphrase may be found. This is also true, of course, of the books of Chronicles, which we have seen are often cited as a prototype.

Following this simple strategy of plotting 1 Esdras against the criteria that Alexander lays down for the identification of an example of rewritten Bible, I conclude that it comes very close to fulfilling them all, although in one or two instances we find that the alignment is slightly skewed. Most of this is mitigated

---

35. I have summarized the principal arguments for these conclusions in my commentary, "1 Esdras," 854 (above, n. 31).

by reference to other examples of the category that scholars have proposed more recently. In my opinion, the most significant differences are that 1 Esdras follows the biblical text more closely for much of its course than any of the examples with which Alexander worked and that it includes only one substantial nonbiblical addition. And these, it must be admitted, are significant elements in the classification of the genre.

I should therefore make two suggestions in closing. The first is that if we are prepared to work with the kind of wider category that Brooke has encouraged, dealing not so much with a genre of literature as with a type or category of interpretative text, then it seems to me that 1 Esdras may be included. It has its distinctive elements, but that is probably true of any text within the category, precisely because the avenue for interpretation in the presentation of rewritten narrative is so varied. This suggestion allows us to appreciate more what the author was trying to achieve by his selection, reordering and presentation than any other. As was emphasized above (see especially categories 6 and 7), we should see in the work a reflection of the point of view, which was becoming increasingly prevalent, of the victory of the Babylonian community and its ideology; their way of reading the previous history of the people was now becoming increasingly dominant, so that the narrative joining of Chronicles and Ezra–Nehemiah seemed natural and the focus at the start and the end of the work (at least as it has reached us) on the community in some sort of idealized state helped underline where continuity lay in terms of the present community's sense of identity. We need no longer look for some ulterior "purpose" behind the composition but regard it rather as a vivid witness to the development of a shared history by a previously fragmented population. And second, if others are not prepared to accept the first suggestion, they face the obligation to propose something better. Of all the suggestions that I have read with regard to 1 Esdras so far, I have not yet found any that match the material with which we are presented so well.

BIBLIOGRAPHY

Ackroyd, Peter R. "The Temple Vessels: A Continuity Theme." Pages 45–60 in *Studies in the Religious Tradition of the Old Testament*. Edited by Peter R. Ackroyd. London: SCM, 1987.
Albertz, Rainer. *Die Exilszeit 6. Jahrhundert v. Chr.* Biblische Enzyklopedie 7. Stuttgart: Kohlhammer, 2001.
Alexander, Philip S. "Retelling the Old Testament." Pages 99–121 in *It Is Written: Scripture Citing Scripture; Essays in Honour of Barnabas Lindars, SSF*. Edited by D. A. Carson and H. G. M. Williamson. Cambridge: Cambridge University Press, 1988.
Allen, Leslie C. *The Greek Chronicles, Part I: The Translator's Craft*. VTSup 25. Leiden: Brill, 1974.
———. *The Greek Chronicles, Part II: Textual Criticism*. VT Sup 27. Leiden: Brill, 1974.
Amara, Dalia. "The Old Greek Version of the Book of Daniel." [In Hebrew.] Ph.D. diss., Ben-Gurion University of the Negev, 2006.
Auld, A. Graeme. *Kings without Privilege*. Edinburgh: T&T Clark, 1994.
Barrera, Julio C. Trebolle. *Centena in libros Samuelis et Regum: Variantes textuales y composición literaria en los libros de Samuel y Reyes*. Textos y estudios "Cardenal Cisneros" 47. Madrid: Consejo Superior de Investigaciones Científicas Instituto de Filología, 1989.
Barstad, Hans M. *The Myth of the Empty Land: A Study in the History and Archaeology of Judah during the 'Exilic' Period*. Symbolae Osloenses Fasciculus Suppletorius 28. Oslo: Scandinavian University Press, 1996.
Bartlett, John R. *Edom and the Edomites*. JSOTSup 77. Sheffield: Sheffield Academic, 1989.
Barton, John, and John Muddiman, eds. *The Oxford Bible Commentary*. Oxford: Oxford University Press, 2001.
Batten, Loring W. *A Critical and Exegetical Commentary on the Books of Ezra and Nehemiah*. ICC. Edinburgh: T&T Clark, 1913.
Bayer, Edmund. *Das dritte Buch Esdras und sein Verhältnis zu den Büchern Esra-Nehemia*. BibS(F) 16/1. Freiburg: Herder, 1911.
Becking, Bob. "Continuity and Community: The Belief System of the Book of Ezra." Pages 256–75 in *The Crisis of Israelite Religion: Transformation of Religious Tradition in Exilic and Post-Exilic Times*. Edited by Bob Becking and M. C. A. Korpel. OTS 42. Leiden: Brill, 1999.

———. "Ezra on the Move: Trends and Perspectives on the Character and His Book." Pages 154–79 in *Perspectives in the Study of the Old Testament and Early Judaism: A Symposium in Honour of Adam S. van der Woude on the Occasion of His 70th Birthday*. Edited by F. García Martínez and E. Noort. VTSup 73. Leiden: Brill, 1998.

———. "Temples across the Border and the Communal Boundaries within Yahwistic Yehud." *Transeu* 35 (2008): 39–54.

Bedford, Peter R. *Temple Restoration in Early Achaemenid Judah*. JSJSup 65. Leiden: Brill, 2001.

Beentjes, Pancratius C. *"Die Freude war gross in Jerusalem" (2Chr 30,26): Eine Einführung in die Chronikbücher*. SEThV 3. Münster: LIT-Verlag, 2008.

Begg, Christopher T. "Ben Sirach's Non-Mention of Ezra." *BN* 42 (1988): 14–18.

Bengtson, Hermann. *Die Strategie in der hellenistichen Zeit*. 3 vols. Rev. ed. Munich: Beck, 1964.

Bernstein, Moshe J. "Re-Arrangement, Anticipation and Harmonization as Exegetical Features in the Genesis Apocryphon." *DSD* 3 (1996): 37–57.

———. "'Rewritten Bible': A Generic Category Which Has Outlived Its Usefulness?" *Textus* 22 (2005): 169–96.

Bevan, Edwyn. *The House of Ptolemy: A History of Egypt under the Ptolemaic Dynasty*. London: Methuen, 1927.

Bewer, Julius A. *Der Text des Buches Esra*. FRLANT 31. Göttingen: Vandenhoeck & Ruprecht, 1922.

Blenkinsopp, Joseph. *Ezra–Nehemiah*. OTL. Philadelphia: Westminster; London: SCM, 1988.

Boardman, John, and Nicholas G. L. Hammond, eds. *The Cambridge Ancient History*. 14 vols. 2d ed. Cambridge: Cambridge University Press, 1982.

Boda, Mark J., and Jamie R. Novotny, eds. *From the Foundations to the Crenellations: Essays on Temple Building in the Ancient Near East and Hebrew Bible*. AOAT 366. Münster: Ugarit-Verlag, 2010.

Boda, Mark J., and Paul L. Redditt, eds. *Unity and Disunity in Ezra–Nehemiah: Redaction, Rhetoric and Reader*. Hebrew Bible Monographs 17. Sheffield: Sheffield Phoenix, 2008.

Bogaert, Pierre-Maurice. "La Porte Orientale, place de rassemblement du peuple, et l'extension de l'oeuvre du Chroniste." *Transeu* 17 (1999): 9–16.

Bohlen, Reinhold. *Die Ehrung der Eltern bei Ben Sira*. Trier: Paulinus Verlag, 1991.

Böhler, Dieter. *Die heilige Stadt in Esdras α und Esra-Nehemia: Zwei Konzeptionen der Wiederherstellung Israels*. OBO 158. Freiburg: Universitätsverlag; Göttingen: Vandenhoeck & Ruprecht, 1997.

———. "On the Relationship between Textual and Literary Criticism: The Two Recensions of the Book of Ezra; Ezra-Neh (MT) and 1 Esdras (LXX)." Pages 35–50 in *The Earliest Text of the Hebrew Bible: The Relationship between the Masoretic Text and the Hebrew Base of the Septuagint Reconsidered*. Edited by Adrian Schenker. SBLSCS 52. Atlanta: Society of Biblical Literature; Leiden: Brill, 2003.

———. Review of Zipora Talshir, *I Esdras: A Text Critical Commentary*. *Bib* 84 (2003): 280–84.

Bonner, Stanley F. *Roman Declamation in the Late Republic and Early Empire*. London: University of Liverpool Press, 1949.

Brand, Peter James. *The Monuments of Seti I: Epigraphic, Historical and Art Historical Analysis*. Probleme der Agyptologie 16. Leiden: Brill, 2000.
Briant, Pierre. *États et pasteurs au Moyen-Orient ancien*. Cambridge: Cambridge University Press; Paris: Maison des sciences de l'homme, 1982.
Brooke, Alen E., Norman McLean, and Henry J. Thackeray. *The Old Testament in Greek According to the Text of Codex Vaticanus, IV.1: I Esdras, Ezra–Nehemiah*. London: Cambridge University Press, 1935.
Brooke, George J. "The Books of Chronicles and the Scrolls from Qumran." Pages 35–48 in *Reflection and Refraction Studies in Biblical Historiography in Honour of A. Graeme Auld*. Edited by Robert Rezetko, T. H. Lim, and W. B. Aucker. VTSup 113. Leiden: Brill, 2007.
———. "Rewritten Bible." Pages 777–81 in vol. 2 of *The Encyclopedia of the Dead Sea Scrolls*. Edited by Lawrence H. Schiffman and James C. VanderKam. 2 vols. Oxford: Oxford University Press, 2000.
———. "The Rewritten Law, Prophets and Psalms: Issues for Understanding the Text of the Bible." Pages 31–40 in *The Bible as Book: The Hebrew Bible and the Judaean Desert Discoveries*. Edited by E. D. Herbert and Emanuel Tov. London: British Library; New Castle, Del.: Oak Knoll, 2002.
Broughton, T. Robert S. *Magistrates of the Roman Republic*. 3 vols. Cleveland: American Philological Association, 1951–86.
Brown II, A. Philip. *Hope amidst Ruin: A Literary and Theological Analysis of Ezra*. Greenville, S.C.: Bob Jones University Press, 2009.
Cagnat, René. *Inscriptiones graecae ad res romanas pertinentes*. 4 vols. in 3. Paris: Leroux, 1906–27.
Calame, Claude. "Quand dire c'est faire voir: L'évidence dans la rhétorique antique." *Études de Lettres* 4 (1991): 3–22.
———. "Spartan Genealogies: The Mythical Representation of a Spatial Organisation." Pages 153–86 in *Interpretations of Greek Mythology*. Edited by J. Bremmer. London: Croom Helm, 1987.
Campbell, Jonathan G. "'Rewritten Bible' and 'Parabiblical Texts': A Terminological and Ideological Critique." Pages 43–68 in *New Directions in Qumran Studies: Proceedings of the Bristol Colloquium on the Dead Sea Scrolls, 8–10 September 2003*. Edited by J. G. Campbell, W. J. Lyons, and L. K. Pietersen. LSTS 52. London: T&T Clark, 2005.
Canessa, André. "De l'Originalité d'Esdras A." Pages 487–90 in *KATA TOUS O' Selon Les Septante: Hommage a Marguertie Harl*. Edited by G. Dorival and O. Munnich. Paris: Cerf, 1995.
Carr, David M. "A Response." In "Revisiting the Composition of Ezra–Nehemiah: In Conversation with Jacob Wright's *Rebuilding Identity: The Nehemiah Memoir and Its Earliest Readers*." Edited by Gary Knoppers. Special issue, *JHS* 12 (2007).
Carvero, Laura Miguélez. *Poems in Context: Greek Poetry in the Thebaid, 200–600 AD*. Berlin: de Gruyter, 2008.
Clines, David J. A. *Ezra, Nehemiah, Esther*. NCB. London: Marshall, Morgan & Scott; Grand Rapids, Mich.: Eerdmans, 1984.
Coggins, Richard J. "The First Book of Esdras." Pages 4–75 in Coggins and Knibb, *The First and Second Books of Esdras*.

Coggins, Richard J., and Michael A. Knibb, eds. *The First and Second Books of Esdras*. CBC. Cambridge: Cambridge University Press, 1979.
Cohen, Margaret. "Leave Nehemiah Alone: Nehemiah's 'Tales' and Fifth-Century BCE Historiography." Pages 55–74 in Boda and Redditt, *Unity and Disunity in Ezra-Nehemiah*.
Cole, Thomas. *Democritus and the Sources of Greek Anthropology*. Cleveland: American Philological Association, 1967.
Collins, John J. *Daniel*. Hermeneia. Minneapolis: Fortress, 1993.
———. "Ecclesiasticus, or the Wisdom of Jesus Son of Sirach." Pages 667–98 in Barton and Muddiman, *The Oxford Bible Commentary*.
Cook, Stanley A. "I Esdras." Pages 1–58 in vol. 1 of *The Apocrypha and the Pseudepigrapha of the Old Testament*. Edited by R. H. Charles. 2 vols. Oxford: Clarendon, 1913.
Cowley, Arthur. *Aramaic Papyri of the Fifth Century B.C.* Oxford: Clarendon, 1923.
Cribore, Raffaella. *Gymnastics of the Mind: Greek Education in Hellenistic and Roman Egypt*. Princeton: Princeton University Press, 2001.
Cross, Frank Moore. "The Contribution of the Discoveries at Qumran to the Study of the Biblical Text." *IEJ* 16 (1966): 81–95.
———. "A New Qumran Biblical Fragment Related to the Original Hebrew Underlying the Septuagint." *BASOR* 132 (1953): 15–26.
———. "Problems of Method in the Textual Criticism of the Hebrew Bible." Pages 31–54 in *The Critical Study of Sacred Texts*. Edited by W. D. O'Flaherty. Berkeley, Calif.: Graduate Theological Union, 1979.
———. "A Reconstruction of the Judean Restoration." *JBL* 94 (1975): 4–18.
Dam, Cornelius van. *The Urim and Thummim: A Means of Revelation in Ancient Israel*. Winona Lake, Ind.: Eisenbrauns, 1997.
Davies, Gordon F. *Ezra and Nehemiah*. Berit Olam. Studies in Hebrew Narrative and Poetry. Collegeville, Minn.: The Liturgical Press, 1999.
De Troyer, Kristin. "Zerubbabel and Ezra: A Revived and Revised Solomon and Josiah? A Survey of Current 1 Esdras Research." *Currents in Biblical Research* 1 (2002): 30–60.
———. *Rewriting the Sacred Text: What the Old Greek Texts Tell Us about the Literary Growth of the Bible*. Text-Critical Studies. Atlanta: Society of Biblical Literature, 2003.
Dihle, Albrecht. *Greek and Latin Literature of the Roman Empire from Augustus to Justinian*. Translated by Manfred Malzahn. London: Routledge, 1989.
Edelman, Diana. *The Origins of the "Second" Temple*. London: Equinox, 2005.
Edmonds, John M., trans. *The Greek Bucolic Poets (Theocritus, Bion, and Moschus)*. LCL 28. Cambridge, Mass.: Harvard University Press; London: William Heinemann, 1912.
Ellis, Richard S. *Foundation Deposits*. New Haven: Yale University Press, 1968.
Erbse, Harmut. "Anmerkungen zu Herodot." *Glotta* 39 (1961): 215–30.
Eron, Lewis J. "'That Women Have Mastery over Both King and Beggar' (TJud. 15.5): The Relationship of the Fear of Sexuality to the Status of Women in Apocrypha and Pseudepigrapha; 1 Esdras (3 Ezra) 3–4, Ben Sira and the Testament of Judah." *JSP* 9 (1991): 43–66.

Eskenazi, Tamara C. "1 Esdras." Pages 279–300 in the *New Oxford Annotated Apocrypha*. Edited by Bruce N. Metzger and Roland E. Murphy. 3d ed. Oxford: Oxford University Press, 1991.

———. "The Chronicler and the Composition of 1 Esdras." *CBQ* 48 (1986): 39–61.

———. *In an Age of Prose: A Literary Approach to Ezra–Nehemiah*. SBLMS 36. Atlanta: Scholars Press, 1988.

Evans, Craig A. "The Genesis Apocryphon and the Rewritten Bible." *RevQ* 13 (1988): 153–65.

Falk, Daniel K. *The Parabiblical Texts: Strategies for Extending the Scriptures in the Dead Sea Scrolls*. Companion to the Qumran Scrolls 8. LSTS 63. London: T&T Clark, 2007.

Farrar, Cynthia. *The Origins of Democratic Thinking*. Cambridge: Cambridge University Press, 1988.

Feldman, Louis H. "Josephus' *Moses* and Plutarch's *Lycurgus*." Pages [237–41] in *Flavius Josephus and Flavian Rome*. Edited by J. Edmondson, S. Mason, and J. Rives. Oxford: Oxford University Press, 2005.

———. *Studies in Josephus' Rewritten Bible*. JSJSup 58. Leiden: Brill, 1998.

Fensham, Frank C. *The Books of Ezra and Nehemiah*. NICOT. Grand Rapids, Mich.: Eerdmans, 1982.

Fishbane, Michael. *Biblical Interpretation in Ancient Israel*. Oxford: Clarendon, 1985.

Fisk, Bruce N. *Do You Not Remember? Scripture, Story and Exegesis in the Rewritten Bible of Pseudo-Philo*. JSPSup 37. Sheffield: Sheffield Academic, 2001.

Fraade, Steven D. "Rewritten Bible and Rabbinic Midrash as Commentary." Pages 59–79 in *Current Trends in the Study of Midrash*. Edited by C. Bakhos. JSJSup 106. Leiden: Brill, 2006.

Fraser, Peter M. *Ptolemaic Alexandria*. 3 vols. Oxford: Clarendon, 1972.

Fried, Lisbeth S. "The ʿam-hā ʾaretz in Ezra 4:4 and Persian Imperial Administration." Pages 123–45 in Lipschits and Oeming, *Judah and the Judeans in the Persian Period*.

———. "The Artaxerxes Correspondence of Ezra 4, Nehemiah's Wall, and Persian Provincial Administration." In *'Go Out and Study the Land' (Judges 18:2): Archaeological, Historical and Textual Studies in Honor of Hanan Eshel*. Edited by A. M. Maeir, J. Magness and L. H. Schiffman. JSJSup. Leiden: Brill, in press.

———. "*Deus ex Machina*: The Role of the Prophetic Voice in Ezra 5:1." In *Prophets and Prophecy in Ancient Israelite Historiography*. Edited by Mark J. Boda and L. M. Wray Beal. Winona Lake, Ind.: Eisenbrauns, in press.

———. "Did Second Temple High Priests Possess the Urim and Thummim?" *JHS* 7, no. 3 (2007).

———. "The House of the God Who Dwells in Jerusalem: Review Article of P. Bedford's *Temple Restoration in Early Achaemenid Judah*, 2001, and of J. Schaper's *Priester und Leviten im achaëmenidischen Juda*, 2000." *JAOS* 126 (2006): 1–14.

———. "The Land Lay Desolate: Conquest and Restoration in the Ancient Near East." Pages 21–54 in Lipschits and Blenkinsopp, *Judah and the Judeans in the Neo-Babylonian Period*.

———. "The Political Struggle of Fifth-Century Judah." *Transeu* 24 (2002): 61–73.

———. *The Priest and the Great King: Temple–Palace Relations in the Persian Empire*. BJSUCSD 10. Winona Lake, Ind.: Eisenbrauns, 2004.

———. "Who Wrote Ezra-Nehemiah and Why Did They?" Pages 75–97 in Boda and Redditt, *Unity and Disunity in Ezra-Nehemiah*.
Fritzsche, Otto F. *Kurzgefasstes exegetisches Handbuch zu den Apokryphen des Alten Testament*, vol. 1. Leipzig: Weidmann, 1851.
Fruin, Robert. "Is Ezra een historisch persoon?" *NTT* 18 (1929): 121–38.
Galling, Kurt. *Die Bücher der Chronik, Esra, Nehemia*. ATD 12. Göttingen: Vandenhoeck & Ruprecht, 1954.
———. *Studien zur Geschichte Israels im persischen Zeitalter*. Tübingen: Mohr, 1964.
Garbini, Giovanni. *Myth and History in the Bible*. JSOTSup 362. Sheffield: Sheffield Academic, 2003.
Gardner, Anne E. "The Purpose and Date of I Esdras." *JJS* 37 (1986): 18–27.
Gibson, Craig A. *Libanius' Progymnasmata: Model Exercises in Greek Prose and Rhetoric*. SBLWGRW 27. Atlanta: Society of Biblical Literature, 2008.
Glatt-Gilad, David. *Chronological Displacement in Biblical and Related Literatures*. SBLDS 139. Atlanta: Scholars Press, 1993.
Goldstein, Jonathan A. *I Maccabees*. AB 41. Garden City, N.Y.: Doubleday, 1976.
Gooding, David W. *Relics of Ancient Exegesis: A Study of the Miscellanies in 3 Reigns 2*. Cambridge: Cambridge University Press, 1976.
Grabbe, Lester L. *Ezra-Nehemiah*. OTR. London: Routledge, 1998.
———. *A History of the Jews and Judaism in the Second Temple Period, Volume 1: Yehud; A History of the Persian Province of Judah*. LSTS 47. London: T&T Clark, 2004.
———. *A History of the Jews and Judaism in the Second Temple Period, Volume 2: The Coming of the Greeks; The Early Hellenistic Period (335–175 BCE)*. LSTS 68. London: T&T Clark, 2008.
———. "Josephus and the Reconstruction of the Judean Restoration." *JBL* 106 (1987): 231–46.
———. "The Law of Moses in the Ezra Tradition." Pages 91–113 in *Persia and Torah*. Edited by James W. Watts. SBLSymS 17. Atlanta: Society of Biblical Literature, 2001.
———. Review of Zipora Talshir, *I Esdras: From Origin to Translation*. *JSS* 47 (2002): 343–45.
Graham, Alexander J. "The Colonial Expansion of Greece." Pages 83–162 in vol. 3.3 of Boardman and Hammond, eds., *The Cambridge Ancient History*.
———. "The Western Greeks." Pages 163–95 in vol. 3.2 of Boardman and Hammond, eds., *The Cambridge Ancient History*.
Grätz, Sebastian. *Das Edikt des Artaxerxes: Eine Untersuchung zum religionspolitischen und historischen Umfeld von Esra 7,12–26*. BZAW 337. Berlin: de Gruyter, 2004.
———. "Gottesgesetz und Königsgesetz: Esr 7 und die Autorisierung der Tora." *ZTK* 106 (2009): 1–19.
Grenfell, Bernard P., ed. *Revenue Laws of Ptolemy Philadelphus: Edited from a Greek Papyrus in the Bodleian Library with a Translation, Commentary and Appendices*. Introduction by the Rev. J. P. Mahaffy. Oxford: Clarendon, 1896.
Gunneweg, Antonius H. J. *Esra*. KAT 19/1. Gütersloh: Gütersloher Verlagshaus, 1985.
———. *Nehemia*. KAT 19/2. Gütersloh: Gütersloher Verlagshaus, 1987.
Guthe, Hermann. "Das dritte Buch Esra." Pages 1–23 in vol. 1 of *Die Apokryphen und Pseudepigraphen des Alten Testaments*. Translated and edited by E. Kautzsch. 2 vols. Tübingen: Mohr, 1900.

Halpern, Baruch. "A Historiographic Commentary on Ezra 1–6: Achronological Narrative and Dual Chronology in Israelite Historiography." Pages 81–141 in *The Hebrew Bible and Its Interpreters*. Edited by William H. Propp, Baruch Halpern, and David Noel Freedman. Biblical and Judaic Studies 1. Winona Lake, Ind.: Eisenbrauns, 1990.

Halpern-Amaru, Betsy. *Rewriting the Bible: Land and Covenant in Postbiblical Jewish Literature*. Valley Forge, Pa.: Trinity, 1994.

Hanhart, Robert. *Esdrae liber I*. Septuaginta Vetus Testamentum Graecum 8/1. Göttingen: Vandenhoeck & Ruprecht, 1974. 2d ed., 1991.

———. *Esdrae liber II*. Septuaginta Vetus Testamentum Graecum 8/2. Göttingen: Vandenhoeck & Ruprecht, 1993.

———. *Text und Textgeschichte des 1. Esrabuches*. MSU 12. Göttingen: Vandenhoeck & Ruprecht, 1974.

———. *Text und Textgeschichte des 2. Esrabuches*. MSU 25. Göttingen: Vandenhoeck & Ruprecht, 2003.

Haran, Menahem. "Book Scrolls at the Beginning of the Second Temple Period." *ErIsr* 16 (1982): 86–92.

———. "Book Scrolls in Israel in Pre-Exilic Times." *JJS* 32 (1982): 161–73.

———. "Book Size and the Device of Catch-Lines in the Biblical Canon." *JJS* 36 (1985): 1–11.

Harrington, Daniel J. "The Bible Rewritten (Narratives)." Pages 239–47 in *Early Judaism and Its Modern Interpreters*. Edited by Robert A. Kraft and George W. E. Nickelsburg. Philadelphia: Fortress, 1986.

Hartberger, Brigit. *"An den Wassern von Babylon …": Psalm 137 auf dem Hintergrund von Jeremia 51, der biblischen Edom-Traditionen und babylonischer Originalquellen*. BBB 63. Bonn: P. Hanstein, 1986.

Higbie, Carolyn. *The Lindian Chronicle and the Greek Creation of Their Past*. Oxford: Oxford University Press, 2003.

Hilhorst, Anthony. "The Speech on Truth in 1 Esdras 4,34–41." Pages 135–51 in *The Scriptures and the Scrolls: Studies in Honour of A. S. van der Woude on the Occasion of His 65th Birthday*. Edited by F. García Martínez, A. Hilhorst, and C. J. Labuschagne. Leiden: Brill, 1992.

Höffken, Peter. "Warum schwieg Jesus Sirach über Esra?" *ZAW* 87 (1975): 184–202.

Hölscher, Gustav. *Die Bücher Esra und Nehemia*. HAT 2. Tübingen: Mohr Siebeck, 1923.

Honigman, Sylvie. "Les divers sens de l'ethnique *Arabs* dans les sources documentaires grecques d'Égypte." *Ancient Society* 32 (2002): 43–72.

———. *The Septuagint and Homeric Scholarship in Alexandria: Study in the Narrative of the Letter of Aristeas*. London: Routledge, 2003.

How, Walter W., and Joseph Wells. *A Commentary on Herodotus*. 2 vols. Oxford: Clarendon, 1922.

Hunt, Arthur S., and Campbell C. Edgar, eds. *Select Papyri*. 3 vols. LCL. Cambridge, Mass.: Harvard University Press, 1934.

Hurowitz, Victor A. *I Have Built You an Exalted House: Temple Building in the Bible in Light of Mesopotamian and Northwest Semitic Writings*. JSOTSup 115. Sheffield: Sheffield Academic, 1992.

In der Smitten, Wilhelm Th. "Der *Tirshata* in Esra-Nehemia." *VT* 21 (1971): 618–20.

———. *Esra: Quellen, Ueberlieferung und Geschichte.* SSN 15. Assen: Van Gorcum, 1973.
———. "Zur Pagenerzählung im 3 Esra (3 Esr. III 1–V 6)." *VT* 22 (1972): 492–95.
Janzen, Gerald. *Studies in the Greek Text of Jeremiah.* HSM 6. Cambridge, Mass.: Harvard University Press, 1973.
Japhet, Sara. *I and II Chronicles.* OTL. Louisville: Westminster John Knox, 1993.
———. "I Esdras." Pages 751–70 in Barton and Muddiman, *The Oxford Bible Commentary.*
———. *2 Chronik.* HTKAT. Freiburg: Herder, 2003.
———. "The Book of Chronicles: A History." [In Hebrew.] *Shnaton* 14 (2004): 101–17.
———. "Composition and Chronology in the Book of Ezra–Nehemiah." Pages 189–216 in *Second Temple Studies 2.* Edited by Tamara C. Eskenazi and K. H. Richards. JSOTSup 175. Sheffield: Sheffield Academic, 1994. Repr., pages 245–67 in *From the Rivers of Babylon.*
———. *From the Rivers of Babylon to the Highlands of Judah: Collected Studies on the Restoration Period.* Winona Lake, Ind.: Eisenbrauns, 2006.
———. *The Ideology of the Book of Chronicles and Its Place in Biblical Thought.* BEATAJ 9. Frankfurt am Main: Lang, 1989. Repr., Winona Lake, Ind.: Eisenbrauns, 2009.
———. "People and Land in the Restoration Period." Pages 103–25 in *Das Land Israel in biblischer Zeit.* Edited by G. Strecker. GTA 25. Göttingen: Vandenhoeck & Ruprecht, 1983.
———. "Postexilic Historiography: How and Why." Pages 144–73 in *Israel Constructs Its History: Deuteronomic Historiography in Recent Research.* Edited by Albert de Pury, Thomas Römer, and Jean-Daniel Macchi. JSOTSup 306. Sheffield: Sheffield Academic, 1996.
———. "Sheshbazzar and Zerubbabel against the Background of the Historical and Religious Tendencies of Ezra–Nehemiah, I." *ZAW* 94 (1982): 66–98.
———. "Sheshbazzar and Zerubbabel against the Background of the Historical and Religious Tendencies of Ezra–Nehemiah, II." *ZAW* 95 (1983): 218–29.
———. "The Supposed Common Authorship of Chronicles and Ezra–Nehemiah Investigated Anew." *VT* 18 (1968): 330–71.
———. "Periodization between History and Ideology: The Neo-Babylonian Period in Biblical Historiography." Pages 75–89 in Lipschits and Blenkinsopp, *Judah and the Judeans in the Neo-Babylonian Period.*
———. "Periodization between History and Ideology II: Chronology and Ideology in Ezra–Nehemiah." Pages 491–508 in Lipschits and Oeming, *Judah and the Judeans in the Persian Period.*
———. "The Portrayal of the Restoration Period in 1 Esdras." [In Hebrew.] *Meghillot* 5–6 (2007): 109–28.
Johansen, Thomas K. *Plato's Natural Philosophy: A Study of the Timaeus-Critias.* Cambridge: Cambridge University Press, 2004.
Johnson, Sara R. *Historical Fictions and Hellenistic Jewish Identity: Third Maccabees in Its Cultural Context.* Hellenistic Culture and Society 43. Berkeley: University of California Press, 2004.
Jones, Arnold H. M. *Athenian Democracy.* Oxford: Blackwell, 1966.
———. *Cities of the Eastern Roman Provinces.* 2d ed. Oxford: Clarendon, 1971.
———. *The Greek City from Alexander to Constantine.* Oxford: Clarendon, 1940.

Jones, Christopher P. *The Roman World of Dio Chrysostom*. Cambridge, Mass.: Harvard University Press, 1978.
Kapelrud, Arvid S. *The Question of Authorship in the Ezra-Narrative: A Lexical Investigation*. Skrifter utgitt av det Norske Videnskaps-Akademi i Oslo. Oslo: J. Dybwad, 1944.
Kellermann, Ulrich. "Erwägungen zum Problem der Esradatierung." *ZAW* 80 (1968): 55–87.
———. *Nehemia: Quellen, Überlieferung und Geschichte*. BZAW 102. Berlin de Gruyter, 1967.
———. "Psalm 137." *ZAW* 90 (1978): 43–58.
Kennedy, George. *Progymnasmata: Greek Textbooks of Prose Composition and Rhetoric*. SBLWGRW 10. Atlanta: Society of Biblical Literature, 2003.
Klein, Ralph W. "Studies in the Greek Texts of the Chronicler." Ph.D. diss., Harvard University, 1966.
———. *1 Chronicles*. Hermeneia. Minneapolis: Augsburg Fortress, 2006.
Knauf, Ernst Axel. "Supplementa Ismaelitica." *BN* 45 (1988): 62–81.
Knoppers, Gary N. *1 Chronicles 1–9: A New Translation with Introduction and Commentary*. AB 12. New York: Doubleday, 2004.
———. "Beyond Jerusalem and Judah: The Commission of Artaxerxes to Ezra in the Province Beyond the River." Pages 78–87 in *Ephraim Stern Volume*. Edited by J. Aviram, A. Ben Tor, I. Eph'al, S. Gitin, and R. Reich. ErIsr 29. Jerusalem: Israel Exploration Society, 2009.
———. "Mt. Gerizim and Mt. Zion: A Study in the Early History of the Samaritans and the Jews." *SR* 34 (2005): 309–38.
Kooij, Arie van der. "On the Ending of the Book of 1 Esdras." Pages 37–49 in *LXX: VII Congress of the International Organization for Septuagint and Cognate Studies*. Edited by C. E. Cox. SCSt 31. Atlanta: Scholars Press, 1991.
———. "Zur Frage des Anfangs des 1. Esrabuches." *ZAW* 103 (1991): 239–52.
Koskenniemi, Erkki, and Pekka Lindqvist. "Rewritten Bible, Rewritten Stories: Methodological Aspects." Pages 11–39 in *Rewritten Bible Reconsidered: Proceedings of the Conference in Karkku, Finland, August 24–26, 2006*. Edited by A. Laato and J. van Ruiten. Studies in Rewritten Bible 1. Turku: Åbo Akademi University; Winona Lake, Ind.: Eisenbrauns, 2008.
Kraemer, David. "On the Relationship of the Books of Ezra and Nehemiah." *JSOT* 59 (1993): 73–92.
Kratz, Reinhard G. *Die Komposition der erzählenden Bücher des Alten Testaments: Grundwissen der Bibelkritik*. UTB 2157. Göttingen: Vandenhoeck & Ruprecht, 2000.
Kugel, James. *Traditions of the Bible: A Guide to the Bible as It Was at the Start of the Common Era*. Cambridge, Mass.: Harvard University Press, 1998.
Kuhrt, Amélie, and Susan Sherwin White. "Xerxes' Destructions of Babylonian Temples." *Achaemenid History* 2 (1987): 69–78.
Kunin, Seth D. "Israel and the Nations: A Structuralist Survey." *JSOT* 82 (1999): 19–43.
Laum, Bernhard. *Stiftungen in der griechischen und römischen Antike: Ein Beitrag zur antiken Kulturgeschichte*. 2 vols. Leipzig: Teubner, 1914. Repr., Aalen: Scientia, 1964.

Leduc, Claudine. "Marriage in Ancient Greece." Pages 35–95 in vol. 1 of *A History of Women in the West*. Edited by P. Schmitt Pantel. 2 vols. Cambridge, Mass.: Harvard University Press, 1992.

Lee, Thomas R. *Studies in the Form of Sirach 44–50*. Atlanta: Scholars Press, 1986.

Lemaire, André. *Nouvelles inscriptions araméennes d'Idumée*. Transeuphratène Supplément 9. Paris: Gabalda, 2002.

Levinson, Bernard M. *Deuteronomy and the Hermeneutics of Legal Innovation*. New York: Oxford University Press, 1997.

———. *Legal Revision and Religious Renewal in Ancient Israel*. New York: Cambridge University Press, 2008.

Liddell, Henry G., Robert Scott, and H. Stuart Jones. *A Greek–English Lexicon, with Supplement*. Edited by E. A. Barber et al. Oxford: Clarendon, 1968.

Lipschits, Oded. *The Fall and Rise of Jerusalem: Judah under Babylonian Rule*. Winona Lake, Ind.: Eisenbrauns, 2005.

Lipschits, Oded, and Joseph Blenkinsopp, eds. *Judah and the Judeans in the Neo-Babylonian Period*. Winona Lake, Ind.: Eisenbrauns, 2003.

Lipschits, Oded, and Manfred Oeming, eds. *Judah and the Judeans in the Persian Period*. Winona Lake, Ind.: Eisenbrauns, 2006.

Macchi, Jean-Daniel. "Le livre d'Esther: Écrire une histoire perse comme un Grec." Pages 197–226 in *Comment la Bible saisit-elle l'histoire?* Edited by D. Doré. Paris: Cerf, 2007.

Manville, Philip B. "Toward a New Paradigm of Athenian Citizenship." Pages 21–33 in *Athenian Identity and Civic Ideology*. Edited by A. L. Boegehold and A. C. Scafuro. Baltimore: Johns Hopkins University Press, 1994.

Marcus, David, ed. עזרא ונחמיה; *Ezra and Nehemiah*. Biblia Hebraica Quinta 20. Stuttgart: German Bible Society, 2006.

Marrou, Henri I.. *A History of Education in Antiquity*. Translated by George Lamb. New York: Sheed & Ward, 1956. Repr., Madison: University of Wisconsin Press, 1981.

Martone, Carrado. "Biblical or Not Biblical? Some Doubts and Questions." *RevQ* 83 (2004): 387–94.

Mason, Hugh J. *Greek Terms for Roman Institutions: A Lexicon and Analysis*. Toronto: Hakkert, 1974.

Massar, Natacha. "La 'Chronique de Lindos': Un catalogue à la gloire du sanctuaire d'Athéna Lindia." *Kernos* 19 (2000): 239–43.

McCarter, P. Kyle. *I Samuel*. AB 8. Garden City, N.Y.: Doubleday, 1980.

———. *Textual Criticism*. Philadelphia: Fortress, 1986.

McKenzie, Steven L. "The Chronicler as Redactor." Pages 70–90 in *The Chronicler as Author*. Edited by M. Patrick Graham and Steven L. McKenzie. JSOTSup 263. Sheffield: Sheffield Academic, 1999.

Metzger, Bruce M., and Roland E. Murphy, eds. *The New Oxford Annotated Apocrypha*. New York: Oxford University Press, 1991.

Meyer, Rudolf. *Hebräische Grammatik: Mit einem bibliographischen Nachwort von U. Rüterswörden*. Berlin: de Gruyter, 1992.

Millar, Fergus. *A Study of Cassius Dio*. Oxford: Clarendon, 1964.

Millard, Alan R. "Assyrian Royal Names in Biblical Hebrew." *JSS* 21 (1976): 1–14.

Mitchell, Lynette. *Panhellenism and the Barbarian in Archaic and Classical Greece*. Swansea: Classical Press of Wales, 2007.

Moore, John M. *Aristotle and Xenophon on Democracy and Oligarchy*. Berkeley: University of California Press, 1975.
Moulton, James H., and George Milligan. *Vocabulary of the Greek New Testament*. London: Hodder, 1930.
Mowinckel, Sigmund. *Studien zu dem Buche Ezra-Nehemia I–III*. Skrifter utgitt av Det Norske Videnskaps-Akademi i Oslo II. Historisk-Filosofisk Klasse, Ny Serie 3. Oslo: Universitätsforlaget, 1964–65.
Mulder, Otto. *Simon the High Priest in Sirach 50: An Exegetical Study of the Significance of Simon the High Priest as the Climax to the Praise of the Fathers in Ben Sira's Concept of the History of Israel*. JSJSup 78. Leiden: Brill, 2003.
Munn, Mark. *The School of History: Athens in the Age of Socrates*. Berkeley: University of California Press, 2000.
Myers, Jacob M. *I and II Esdras: A New Translation with Introduction and Commentary*. AB 42. Garden City, N.Y.: Doubleday, 1974.
———. *Ezra–Nehemiah*. AB 14. New York: Doubleday, 1965.
Neyrey, Jerome H. "Josephus' *Vita* and the Encomium: A Native Model of Personality." *JSJ* 25 (1994): 177–206.
Nickelsburg, George W. E. "The Bible Rewritten and Expanded." Pages 89–156 in *Jewish Writings of the Second Temple Period: Apocrypha, Pseudepigrapha, Qumran Sectarian Writings, Philo, Josephus*. Edited by Michael E. Stone. Assen: Van Gorcum, 1984.
Niehr, Herbert. *Aramäischer Aḥiqar*. JSHRZ 2/2. Gütersloh: Gütersloher Verlagshaus, 2007.
Noth, Martin. *Überlieferungsgeschichtliche Studien: Die sammelnden und bearbeitenden Geschichtswerke im Alten Testament*. Darmstadt: Wissenschaftliche Buchgesellschaft, 1967.
O'Brien, Michael J. "Protagoras." Pages 3–28 in Sprague, ed., *The Older Sophists*.
Osborne, R. *Demos: The Discovery of Classical Attika*. Cambridge: Cambridge University Press, 1985.
———. *Greece in the Making, 1200–479 BC*. London: Routledge, 1996.
Ostwald, Martin. *From Popular Sovereignty to the Sovereignty of Law*. Berkeley: University of California Press, 1986.
———. *Nomos and the Beginnings of Athenian Democracy*. Oxford: Clarendon, 1969.
Page, Denys L., ed. *Lyrica Graeca Selecta*. OCT. Oxford: Oxford University Press, 1968.
Pakkala, Juha. *Ezra the Scribe: The Development of Ezra 7–10 and Nehemiah 8*. BZAW 347. Berlin: de Gruyter, 2004.
Parker, Robert. *Athenian Religion: A History*. Oxford: Oxford University Press, 1996.
Pohlmann, Karl-Friedrich. *3. Esra-Buch*. JSHRZ 1/5. Gütersloh: Gütersloher Verlagshaus, 1980.
———. *Studien zum dritten Esra: Ein Beitrag zur Frage nach dem ursprünglichen Schluss des chronistischen Geschichtswerkes*. FRLANT 104. Göttingen: Vandenhoeck & Ruprecht, 1970.
Radner, Karen. *Die Macht des Namens: Altorientalische Strategien zur Selbsterhaltung*. Santag 8. Wiesbaden: Harrassowitz, 2005.
Rawson, Elizabeth. *Cicero: A Portrait*. Rev. ed. Ithaca, N.Y.: Cornell University Press, 1983.

Reinhold, Meyer. *From Republic to Principate: An Historical Commentary on Cassius Dio's Roman History Books 49–52*. Atlanta: American Philological Association, 1988.
Rhodes, Peter J. *A Commentary on the Athenaion Politeia*. Oxford: Clarendon, 1981.
Roehrig, Catharine, et al., eds. *Hatshepsut: From Queen to Pharaoh*. New Haven: Yale University Press, 2005.
Rösler, Wolfgang. "Wine and Truth in the Greek Symposion." Pages 106–12 in *In Vino Veritas*. Edited by Oswyn Murray and Manuela Tecuşan. London: British School at Rome, 1995.
Rostovtseff, Michael I. *The Social and Economic History of the Hellenistic World*. 3 vols. Oxford: Clarendon, 1942.
Rudolph, Wilhelm. *Chronikbücher*. HAT 21. Tübingen: Mohr Siebeck, 1955.
———. *Esra und Nehemia samt 3 Esra*. HAT 20. Tübingen: Mohr Siebeck, 1949.
Russell, Donald A. *Greek Declamation*. Cambridge: Cambridge University Press, 1983.
Sandoval, Timothy J. "The Strength of Women and Truth: The Tale of the Three Bodyguards and Ezra's Prayer in First Esdras." *JSJ* 58 (2007): 211–27.
Schalit, Abraham. "The Date and Place of the Story about the Three Bodyguards of the King in the Apocryphal Book of Ezra." [In Hebrew.] *BJPES* 13 (1947): 119–28.
Schenker, Adrian. "La relation d'Esdras A' au texte massorétique d'Esdras-Néhémie." Pages 218–48 in *Tradition of the Text: Studies Offered to Dominique Barthélemy in Celebration of His 70th Birthday*. Edited by Gerard J. Norton and Stephen Pisano. OBO 109. Freiburg: Universitätsverlag; Göttingen: Vandenhoeck & Ruprecht, 1991.
———. *Septante et texte massorétique dans l'histoire la plus ancienne du texte de 1 Rois 2–14*. CahRB 48. Paris: Gabalda, 2000.
Schmid, Konrad. *Buchgestalten des Jeremiabuches: Untersuchungen zur Redaktions- und Rezeptionsgeschichte von Jer 30–33 im Kontext des Buches*. WMANT 72. Neukirchen-Vluyn: Neukirchener Verlag, 1996.
Schunck, Klaus-Dietrich *Nehemia*. BK. Neukirchen-Vluyn: Neukirchener Verlag, 2009.
Schürer, Emil. "The Greek Ezra (Also Called III Ezra or I Esdras)." Pages 708–18 in idem, vol. 3 of *History of the Jewish People in the Age of Jesus Christ*.
———. *The History of the Jewish People in the Age of Jesus Christ (175 B.C.–A.D. 135)*. Revised and edited by Geza Vermes, Fergus Millar, and Martin Goodman. 3 vols. Edinburgh: T&T Clark, 1973–87.
Segal, Michael H. "Between Bible and Rewritten Bible." Pages 10–28 in *Biblical Interpretation at Qumran*. Edited by M. Henze. Studies in the Dead Sea Scrolls and Related Literature. Grand Rapids, Mich.: Eerdmans, 2005.
———. *The Book of Jubilees: Rewritten Bible, Redaction, Ideology and Theology*. JSJSup 117. Leiden: Brill, 2007.
Segal, Moses H. *The Complete Book of Ben Sira*. [In Hebrew.] 3d ed. Jerusalem: Mosad Bialik, 1972.
Sérandour, Arnaud. "Les femmes étrangères dans les livres grec et hébraïque d'Esdras: Répudiation ou exclusion du culte?" *Transeu* 36 (2008): 155–63.
Sherk, Robert K. *Roman Documents from the Greek East: Senatus Consulta and Epistulae to the Age of Augustus*. Baltimore: The Johns Hopkins University Press, 1969.
Sherwin White, Adrian N. *The Letters of Pliny: A Historical and Social Commentary*. Oxford: Clarendon, 1966.

Siedlecki, Armin. "Contextualizations of Ezra–Nehemiah." Pages 263–76 in Boda and Redditt, *Unity and Disunity in Ezra–Nehemiah*.
Sinclair, Robert K. *Democracy and Participation in Athens*. Cambridge: Cambridge University Press, 1988.
Skehan, Patrick W., and Alexander A. Di Lella. *The Wisdom of Ben Sira*. AB 39. New York: Doubleday, 1987.
Smith, Rogers M. *Stories of Peoplehood: The Politics and Morals of Political Membership*. New York: Cambridge University Press, 2003.
Smith-Christopher, Daniel L. "Between Ezra and Isaiah: Exclusion, Transformation, and Inclusion in Post-Exilic Biblical Theology." Pages 116–42 in *Ethnicity and the Bible*. Edited by M. G. Brett. BibInt 19. Leiden: Brill, 1996.
Sprague, Rosamond Kent, ed. *The Older Sophists*. Columbia: University of South Carolina Press, 1972. Translation of H. Diels and W. Kranz, *Die Fragmente der Vorsokratiker*. 7th ed. Berlin: Weidmann, 1951–54.
Steiner, Richard. "Bishlam's Archival Search Report in Nehemiah's Archive: Multiple Introductions and Reverse Chronological Order as Clues to the Origin of the Aramaic Letters in Ezra 4–6." *JBL* 125 (2006): 641–85.
———. "Why Bishlam (Ezra 4:7) Cannot Rest 'in Peace': On the Aramaic and Hebrew Sound Changes That Conspired to Blot out the Remembrance of Bel-Shalam the Archivist." *JBL* 126 (2007): 392–401.
Stolper, Matthew. "Persepolis Fortification Archive." Cited 15 March 2010. Online: http://oi.uchicago.edu/research/projects/pfa/.
Strootman, Rudolf. 'The Hellenistic Royal Court: Court Culture, Ceremonial and Ideology in Greece, Egypt and the Near East, 336–30 BCE." Ph.D. diss., Utrecht University, 2007.
Stulman, Louis. *The Other Text of Jeremiah*. Lanham, Md.: University Press of America, 1985.
Swanson, Dwight D. "How Scriptural is Re-Written Bible?" *RevQ* 83 (2004): 407–27.
———. *The Temple Scroll and the Bible: The Methodology of 11QT*. STDJ 14. Leiden: Brill, 1995.
Talmon, Shemaryahu. "The Judaean *'am ha'arez* in Historical Perspective." Pages 71–76 in *The Fourth World Congress of Jewish Studies, 1: Papers*. Jerusalem: World Union of Jewish Studies, 1967.
———. "The Textual Study of the Bible: A New Outlook." Pages 321–400 in *Qumran and the History of the Biblical Text*. Edited by Frank Moore Cross and Shemaryahu Talmon. Cambridge, Mass.: Harvard University Press, 1975.
Talshir, Zipora. *1 Esdras: From Origin to Translation*. SBLSCS 47. Atlanta: Society of Biblical Literature, 1999.
———. *1 Esdras: A Text Critical Commentary*. SBLSCS 50. Atlanta: Society of Biblical Literature, 2001.
———. *The Alternative Story of the Division of the Kingdom*. Jerusalem: Simor, 1993.
———. "Ezra–Nehemiah and First Esdras: Diagnosis of a Relationship between Two Recensions." *Bib* 81 (2000): 566–73.
———. "First Esdras: Origins and Translation." [In Hebrew.] Ph.D. diss., Hebrew University of Jerusalem, 1984.

———. "The Original Language of the Story of the Three Youths (1 Esdras 3–4)." [In Hebrew.] Pages 63*–75* in *Sha'arei Talmon: Studies in the Bible, Qumran, and the Ancient Near East Presented to Shemaryahu Talmon*. Edited by Michael Fishbane and Emanuel Tov. Winona Lake, Ind.: Eisenbrauns, 1992.

———. "The Reign of Solomon in the Making: Pseudo-Connections between 3 Kingdoms and Chronicles." *VT* 50 (2000): 233–49.

———. "Synchronic and Diachronic Approaches in the Study of the Hebrew Bible: Text Criticism within the Frame of Biblical Philology." *Textus* 23 (2007): 1–32.

———. "Synchronic Approaches with Diachronic Consequences in the Study of Parallel Redactions: First Esdras and 2 Chronicles 35–36; Ezra 1–10; Nehemiah 8." Pages 199–218 in *Yahwism after the Exile: Perspectives on Israelite Religion in the Persian Era*. Edited by Rainer Albertz and Bob Becking. Studies in Theology and Religion 5. Assen: Van Gorcum, 2003.

Talshir, Zipora, and David Talshir. "The Story of the Three Youths (I Esdras 3–4): Towards the Question of the Language of Its Vorlage." *Textus* 18 (1995): 135–55.

Thomas, Rosalind. *Oral Tradition and Written Record in Classical Athens*. Cambridge: Cambridge University Press, 1989.

Toorn, Karel van der. "In the Lion's Den: The Babylonian Background of a Biblical Motif." *CBQ* 60 (1998): 626–40.

Torrey, Charles C. *Ezra Studies*. Chicago: University of Chicago Press, 1910. Repr., New York: Ktav, 1970.

———. "A Revised View of First Esdras." Pages 395–410 in vol. 1 of *Louis Ginzberg Jubilee Volume*. 2 vols. New York: American Academy for Jewish Research, 1945.

———. "The Story of the Three Youths." *AJSL* 23 (1907): 183–87.

Tov, Emanuel. *Hebrew Bible, Greek Bible, and Qumran*. TSAJ 121. Tübingen: Mohr Siebeck, 2008.

———. "The Literary History of the Book of Jeremiah in the Light of Its Textual History." Pages 213–37 in *Empirical Models for Biblical Criticism*. Edited by Jeffrey H. Tigay. Philadelphia: University of Pennsylvania Press, 1985.

———. *Scribal Practices and Approaches Reflected in the Texts Found in the Judean Desert*. STDJ 54. Leiden: Brill, 2004.

———. *The Septuagint Translation of Jeremiah and Baruch: A Discussion of an Early Revision of Jeremiah 29–52 and Baruch 1:1–3:8*. HSM 8. Missoula, Mont.: Scholars Press, 1976.

———. "Some Aspects of the Textual and Literary History of the Book of Jeremiah." Pages 145–67 in *Le livre de Jérémie: Le prophète et son milieu, les oracles et leur transmission*. Edited by P.-M. Bogaert. BETL 54. Leuven: University of Leuven Press, 1981.

———. *Textual Criticism of the Hebrew Bible*. 2d rev. ed. Assen: Van Gorcum, 2001.

Ulrich, Eugene C. *The Dead Sea Scrolls and the Origin of the Bible: Studies in the Dead Sea Scrolls and Related Literature*. Grand Rapids, Mich.: Eerdmans, 1999.

———. "Multiple Literary Editions: Reflections Toward a Theory of the History of the Biblical Text." Pages 78–105 in *Current Research and Technological Developments of the Dead Sea Scrolls: Conference on the Texts from the Judean Desert, Jerusalem, 30 April 1995*. Edited by D. W. Parry and S. D. Ricks. STDJ 20. Leiden: Brill, 1996. Repr., pages 99–120 in *The Dead Sea Scrolls and the Origin of the Bible*.

———. *The Qumran Text of Samuel and Josephus.* HSM 19. Missoula, Mont.: Scholars Press, 1978.
VanderKam, James C. "Ezra-Nehemiah or Ezra and Nehemiah?" Pages 55-75 in *Priests, Prophets, and Scribes: Essays on the Formation and Heritage of Second Temple Judaism in Honour of Joseph Blenkinsopp.* Edited by Eugene C. Ulrich, John W. Wright, Robert P. Carroll, and Philip R. Davies. JSOTSup 149. Sheffield: JSOT Press, 1992. Repr. as pp. 60-80 in his *From Revelation to Canon: Studies in the Hebrew Bible and Second Temple Literature.* JSJSup 62. Leiden: Brill, 2000.
———. *From Joshua to Caiaphas: High Priests after the Exile.* Minneapolis: Fortress, 2004.
Varner, Eric R. *Mutilation and Transformation:* Damnatio Memoriae *and Roman Imperial Portaiture.* Monumenta Graeca et Romana. Leiden: Brill, 2004
Veijola, Timo. *Das 5. Buch Moses: Deuteronomium.* ATD 8/1. Göttingen: Vandenhoeck & Ruprecht, 2004.
Vermes, Geza. "Biblical Midrash." Pages 308-41 in vol. 3.1 of Schürer, *History of the Jewish People in the Age of Jesus Christ.*
———. *Scripture and Tradition in Judaism: Haggadic Studies.* StPB 4. Leiden: Brill, 1961.
Walbank, Frank W. *A Historical Commentary on Polybius.* 3 vols. Oxford: Clarendon, 1957-79.
Walde, Bernhard. *Die Esdrasbücher der Septuaginta: Ihr gegenseitiges Verhältnis untersucht.* BibS(F) 18/4. Freiburg: Herder, 1913.
Weber, Robertus, et al., eds. *Biblia Sacra iuxta vulgatam versionem.* 5th ed. Stuttgart: Deutsche Bibelgesellschaft, 2007.
White Crawford, Sidnie. *Rewriting Scripture in Second Temple Times.* Studies in the Dead Sea Scrolls and Related Literature. Grand Rapids, Mich.: Eerdmans, 2008.
Willi, Thomas. *Juda - Jehud - Israel: Studien zum Selbstverständnis des Judentums in persischer Zeit.* FAT 12. Tübingen: Mohr Siebeck, 1995.
Williamson, Hugh G. M. *1 and 2 Chronicles.* NCB. Grand Rapids, Mich: Eerdmans, 1982.
———. "1 Esdras." Pages 851-58 in *The Eerdmans Commentary on the Bible.* Edited by J. D. G. Dunn and J. W. Rogerson. Grand Rapids, Mich.: Eerdmans, 2003.
———. "The Composition of Ezra i-vi." *JTS* 34 (1983): 1-30.
———. *Ezra, Nehemiah.* WBC 16. Waco, Tex.: Word, 1985.
———. *Israel in the Books of Chronicles.* Cambridge: Cambridge University Press, 1977.
———. "The Problem with First Esdras." Pages 201-16 in *After the Exile: Essays in Honour of Rex Mason.* Edited by John Barton and David J. Reimer. Macon, Ga.: Mercer University Press, 1996. Repr., pages 294-305 in idem, *Studies in Persian Period History and Historiography.* FAT 38. Tübingen: Mohr Siebeck, 2004.
Wright, Jacob L. "A New Model for the Composition of Ezra-Nehemiah." Pages 333-48 in *Judah and the Judeans in the Fourth Century B.C.E.* Edited by Rainer Albertz, Gary Knoppers, and Oded Lipschits. Winona Lake, Ind.: Eisenbrauns, 2007.
———. *Rebuilding Identity: The Nehemiah Memoir and Its Earliest Readers.* BZAW 348. Berlin: de Gruyter, 2004.
———. "Seeking - Finding - Writing." Pages 277-305 in Boda and Redditt, *Unity and Disunity in Ezra-Nehemiah.*

———. "Writing the Restoration: Ezra as Meritocratic Icon in the Post-Destruction Period." In "Scribes before and after 587 BCE: A Conversation." Edited by Mark Leuchter. Special issue, *JHS* 7, no. 10 (2007): 19–29.

Wright, John W. "Remapping Yehud: The Borders of Yehud and the Genealogies of Chronicles." Pages 67–89 in Lipschitz and Oeming, *Judah and the Judaeans in the Persian Period*.

Yadin, Yigael. *The Temple Scroll*. 4 vols. Jerusalem: Israel Exploration Society, 1983.

Zimmermann, Frank. "The Story of the Three Guardsmen." *JQR* 54 (1963–64): 179–200.

Zucconi, Laura M. "From the Wilderness of Zin alongside Edom: Edomite Territory in the Eastern Negev during the Eighth–Sixth Centuries BCE." Pages 241–56 in *Milk and Honey: Essays on Ancient Israel and the Bible in Appreciation of the Judaic Studies Program at the University of California, San Diego*. Edited by S. Malena, D. Miano, and Frank Moore Cross. Winona Lake, Ind.: Eisenbrauns, 2007.

INDEX OF AUTHORS

Ackroyd, Peter R., 203
Albertz, Rainer, 65, 68, 124, 162
Alexander, Philip S., 7, 239, 241–45, 247–49
Allen, Leslie C., 227
Amara, Dalia, 121
Auld, A. Graeme, 113, 239

Barrera, Julio C., 12
Barstad, Hans. M., 68
Bartlett, John R., 68
Barton, John, 16, 31, 61, 110, 114, 131, 148, 210, 221, 238
Batten, Loring W., 18, 20, 25, 95
Bayer, Edmund, 147
Becking, Bob, 2, 15, 64–65, 124, 194
Bedford, Peter R., 91
Beentjes, Pancratius C., 69
Begg, Christopher T., 161, 222
Bengtson, Hermann, 181–82
Bernstein, Moshe J., 240–42, 244
Bevan, Edwyn, 182
Bewer, Julius A., 136
Blenkinsopp, Joseph, 15, 19–21, 26, 38, 53, 62–63, 71, 75, 88, 138, 161, 170, 192, 200
Boardman, John, 198
Boda, Mark J., 15–16, 64, 88, 95, 119, 156, 246
Bogaert, Pierre-Maurice, 14, 45

Bohlen, Reinhold, 221
Böhler, Dieter, 17–18, 25, 45–46, 49, 53–54, 58, 62–63, 65–66, 86–87, 100, 105, 107, 113, 119, 121–22, 124, 126–27, 132, 138–40, 148–50, 158, 174–76, 211, 218, 245
Bonner, Stanley F., 188
Brand, Peter James, 146
Briant, Pierre, 206
Brocke, Alan E., 19
Brooke, George J., 238–42, 244, 249
Broughton, T. Robert S., 183
Brown II, A. Philip, 63–64

Cagnat, René, 182
Calame, Claude, 202, 206
Campbell, Jonathan G., 240
Canessa, André, 70–71
Carr, David M., 148
Carvero, Laura Miguélez, 189
Clines, David J. A., 74
Coggins, Richard J., 134, 136, 217–18
Cohen, Margaret, 16
Cole, Thomas, 185
Collins, John J., 14, 221–22
Cook, Stanley A., 134, 136, 218
Cowley, Arthur, 19
Cribore, Raffaella, 188
Cross, Frank Moore, 12–13, 29, 68, 237

Dam, Cornelis van, 71
Davies, Gordon F., 75
De Troyer, Kristin, 3, 31, 61, 78, 83, 167, 237, 247
Di Lella, Alexander A., 234
Dihle, Albrecht, 187

Edelman, Diana, 126
Edgar, Campbell C., 182
Edmonds, John M., 67
Ellis, Richard S., 88
Erbse, Hartmut, 185
Eron, Lewis J., 70
Eskenazi, Tamara C., 11, 31, 62, 131–33, 137, 153, 187, 192
Evans, Craig A., 239

Falk, Daniel K., 132, 240
Farrar, Cynthia, 205
Feldman, Louis H., 189, 239
Fensham, Frank C., 74, 153
Fishbane, Michael, 29, 241
Fisk, Bruce N., 239, 244
Fraade, Steven D., 241
Fraser, Peter M., 180, 182, 184
Fried, Lisbeth S., 3, 20, 27, 45, 53, 64, 71, 88, 90, 119, 154, 162, 200, 202, 225
Fritzsche, Otto F., 230
Fruin, Robert, 155

Galling, Kurt, 21, 75
Garbini, Giovanni, 110, 113
Gardner, Anne E., 137
Gibson, Craig A., 188–89
Glatt-Gilad, David, 18
Goldstein, Jonathan A., 183
Gooding, David W., 117
Goodman, Martin, 140, 238
Grabbe, Lester L., 20, 22, 32, 61–62, 68, 109, 120
Graham, Alexander J., 198

Grätz, Sebastian, 5, 26, 172, 176
Grenfell, Bernard P., 180
Gunneweg, Antonius H. J., 27, 95, 107, 155, 170, 173, 175
Guthe, Hermann, 134

Halpern, Baruch, 27
Halpern-Amaru, Betsy, 239
Hammond, Nicholas G. L., 198
Hanhart, Robert, 19, 31–32, 46, 74, 94, 110, 116, 134, 136, 140, 167–68, 212, 229–30, 234
Haran, Menahem, 15
Harrington, Daniel J., 239
Hartberger, Brigit, 68
Higbie, Carolyn, 202
Hilhorst, Anthony, 66, 70
Höffken, Peter, 161
Hölscher, Gustav, 94
Honnigman, Sylvie, 5–6, 191, 206
How, Walter W., 185
Hunt, Arthur S., 182
Hurowitz, Victor A., 88

In der Smitten, Wilhelm Th., 64, 66–67, 74, 155, 216, 218

Janzen, Gerald, 14
Japhet, Sara, 6, 15, 27, 114, 118, 127–28, 145, 168, 192, 210, 212–16, 219–20, 227, 247
Johansen, Thomas K., 204
Johnson, Sara R., 67
Jones, Arnold H. M., 181
Jones, Christopher P., 187
Jones, H. Stuart, 180

Kapelrud, Arvid S., 155
Kellermann, Ulrich, 68, 155, 217
Kennedy, George, 188–89
Klein, Ralph W., 6, 11, 15, 17, 225
Knauf, Ernst Axel, 68

Knibb, Michael A., 134, 217–18
Knoppers, Gary N., 1, 13, 15–16, 26, 45, 148, 162, 238
Kooij, Arie van der, 62, 112, 167, 176, 229–35, 237
Koskenniemi, Erkki, 239
Kraemer, David, 156
Kratz, Reinhard G., 155
Kugel, James, 133
Kuhrt, Amélie, 192
Kunin, Seth D., 69

Laum, Bernhard, 173
Leduc, Claudine, 204
Lee, Thomas R., 221
Lemaire, André, 148
Levinson, Bernard M., 29
Liddell, Henry G., 180
Lindqvist, Pekka, 239
Lipschits, Oded, 53, 68, 88, 162, 192, 200, 206

Macchi, Jean-Daniel, 210
Manville, Philip B., 205
Marcus, David, 19
Marrou, Henri I., 188
Martone, Carrado, 240
Mason, Hugh J., 183
Massar, Natacha, 202, 206
McCarter, P. Kyle, 13, 25
McKenzie, Steven L., 69, 118
McLean, Norman, 19
Metzger, Bruce N., 187
Meyer, Rudolf, 168
Millar, Fergus, 140, 186, 238
Millard, Alan R., 22
Milligan, George, 179–80
Mitchell, Lynette, 205
Moore, John M., 181, 185
Moulton, James H., 179–80
Mowinckel, Sigmund, 31, 38–39, 95, 107, 181

Muddiman, John, 114, 210, 221
Mulder, Otto, 222
Munn, Mark, 185
Murphy, Roland E., 187
Myers, Jacob M., 11, 18, 22, 24, 62–63, 65, 74, 134, 179–83, 190, 209, 216, 230, 232, 234, 247

Neyrey, Jerome H., 189
Nickelsburg, George W., 239
Niehr, Herbert, 67
Noth, Martin, 155
Novotny, Jamie R., 88

O'Brien, Michael J., 185
Oeming, Manfred, 206
Osborne, R. Demos, 198, 205
Ostwald, Martin, 185

Page, Denys L., 188
Pakkala, Juha, 3, 11–12, 16, 93, 95–97, 99–101, 103, 105, 107, 118, 127, 155
Parker, Robert, 205
Pohlmann, Karl-Friedrich, 31, 34, 38–39, 61–62, 64–65, 75, 83, 131, 167–68, 171, 174–75, 231–32, 237

Radner, Karen, 146
Rawson, Elizabeth, 186
Redditt, Paul L., 16
Reinhold, Meyer, 186
Rhodes, Peter J., 181, 202
Roehrig, Catherine, 146
Rösler, Wolfgang, 188
Rostovtseff, Michael I., 189
Rudolph, Wilhelm, 27, 38, 212, 217–18
Russell, Donald A., 188–89

Sandoval, Timothy J., 66, 70, 246
Schalit, Abraham, 216

Schenker, Adrian, 2, 11–12, 16, 45, 62, 83–84, 94, 109, 113, 132, 151, 237
Schmid, Konrad, 14
Schunck, Klaus-Dietrich, 110
Schürer, Emil, 140, 238
Scott, Robert, 180
Segal, Michael H., 239, 241, 244
Segal, Moses, 222
Sérandour, Arnaud, 1, 194, 207
Sherk, Robert K., 183
Sherwin White, Adrian N., 187
Sherwin White, Susan, 192
Siedlecki, Armin, 246
Sinclair, Robert K., 181
Skehan, Patrick W., 234
Smith, Rogers M., 146
Smith-Christopher, Daniel L., 27
Sprague, Rosamond Kent, 185
Steiner, Richard, 19–21, 139
Stolper, Matthew, 153
Strootman, Rudolf, 67
Stulman, Louis, 14
Swanson, Dwight D., 240, 244

Talmon, Shemaryahu, 20, 29, 111, 241
Talshir, David, 190, 241
Talshir, Zipora, 4, 11, 16–17, 22, 24, 36, 49, 52–53, 62–63, 65–66, 68–71, 119, 126, 134–37, 139, 143, 147, 151, 157, 168, 170, 179, 181, 183, 188, 190, 193, 209–11, 215–19, 225, 227–28, 230–35, 237, 241, 246

Thackeray, Henry J., 19
Thomas, Rosalind, 197
Toorn, Karel van der, 67
Torrey, Charles C., 83, 137, 170, 216, 230, 232, 234
Tov, Emanuel, 12–14, 239, 241

Ulrich, Eugene C., 12–15, 138

VanderKam, James C., 4, 138, 156
Varner, Eric R., 145
Veijola, Timo, 106
Vermes, Geza, 7, 140, 238–40, 245

Walbank, Frank W., 184
Walde, Bernhard, 54, 147
Weber, Robertus, 183
Wells, Joseph, 185
White Crawford, Sidnie, 240, 242, 244
Willi, Thomas, 15, 20
Williamson, Hugh G. M., 7, 15–16, 19–21, 27, 31, 38–39, 61, 63, 74, 110, 112, 114–16, 118, 127–28, 131–32, 148, 167, 206, 230, 232, 234, 238–39
Wright, Jacob L., 5, 16, 27–28, 147–48, 208
Wright, John W., 15, 138, 206

Yadin, Yigael, 244

Zimmermann, Frank, 61, 64, 66, 70
Zucconi, Laura M., 68

INDEX OF ANCIENT SOURCES

HEBREW BIBLE
Genesis
2:24	134
4:40	134
14	242
31:47	25
41:2–3	56
41:5	56

Exodus
12:6	168
12:8	169
28:4	220
28:26	71
28:30	71
35:18	220

Leviticus
8:8	71
22–23	173

Numbers
27:21	71
32	159

Deuteronomy
7:24–25	146
16:2	168
16:7	169
33:8	71

Joshua
5	244
8	244
22	159

Judges
1	116
1:1	116
2:8	116
9:8–15	56

1 Samuel
1–2	13
8	52
10:22–27	52
11	52
12	52
12:24	52
16:14–23	52, 116
17–18	13
17	116
17:55–58	52
24	52
26	52
28:6	71
31	111

2 Samuel
12:1–6	56
21–24	123
23:8–39	123

1 Kings
2	116, 117
2:35	116
2:46	116
7:1–13	120
7:13–47	141
7:39–50 LXX	120
7:45	141

1 Kings (continued)

7:47	141
7:48–50	141
11–12	52
11	117
11:30–32	57
11:36	57
12	117
12:21	57
12:23	57
12:24	116
12:24 LXX	116
12:26–33	57
13	52, 230, 231
13:2	230, 231
13:32	230, 231
14	117
21–21	120
22	121

2 Kings

3	121
12:13	141
14:8	56
14:14	141
16:8	141
17:24–33	23
18:15	141
18:25	227
18:26	26
21:9	232
22	79, 167, 233
22:11–20	233
22:11	233
22:17	233
22:19	233
22:20	228
23:14–20	230
23:15–20	230
23:24–27	229, 230
23:25–27	212
23:25	230
23:28	229
23:29	228, 234
24:13	141
25	233
25:13	141
25:14–16	141

Isaiah

36:11	26

Jeremiah

10:11	25
25:13	120
25:14–32:14	120
46–51	120
46:1	120

Ezekiel

17:2–6	56
25:12–14	69
35:5–7	69

Obadiah

10–16	69

Haggai

1:1–11	141
1:1	73, 133
1:12	133
1:14	133
1:15	87
2:1	73
2:2	133
2:3	174, 213
2:10	73
2:21	133
2:23	133, 136, 216

Zechariah

1:1	73
1:7	73
3:8	136
4:6	133
4:7	133
4:9	87, 133, 217
4:10	133

Psalms		1:2	173, 213
105:47	176	1:3	112
137	69	1:4	173
146:2	176	1:6	173
		1:7–11	141, 173, 214
Proverbs		1:7–10	58
1:7	233	1:8	197
1:22	233	1:9	203
		1:11	197, 214
Lamentations		2–7	48
2:7–9	58	2–6	48, 55, 58
		2–4	244
Esther		2–3	151
4:17	115	2	32, 38, 48, 77, 117, 140, 142, 151, 205, 243
Daniel		2:1–4:5	117, 118, 122, 244
1–6	67	2:1–70	75, 79, 80, 171, 206, 214
2:4	26	2:1–67	133
3	113	2:1–2	122
3:2 LXX	183	2:1	204
3:24–44	115	2:2	85, 133, 197, 200, 218
3:45–49	115	2:16–30	118
3:52–90	115	2:59–63	205
5	33, 68	2:63	70, 71, 162, 218, 220
5:28	180	2:65–67	205
7	68	2:68–3:11	54
7:7	181	2:68	53, 54, 173
7:14	68	2:70–3:1	38, 40, 41
7:28	26	2:70	126, 151, 175
		3–6	64
Ezra		3	55–57, 77, 117, 142, 157, 162, 174
1–10	32		
1–8	159	3:1–5:6	143
1–7	148	3:1–4:5	32, 171
1–6	27, 28, 74, 84, 87, 92, 129, 139, 154, 160, 172, 214, 242	3:1–13	75, 79, 80
		3:1–6	48, 55
		3:1–3	75, 89, 90
1–4	244	3:1	138, 174
1	18, 32, 117, 118, 139, 140, 142, 174, 211, 213	3:2	63, 133, 208
		3:3–5	208
1:1–4:5	2	3:4	75
1:1–11	75, 79, 80, 173	3:5–6	75
1:1–4	19, 192	3:5	105
1:1–3	33	3:6	48, 75
1:1–2	88	3:7–13	55
1:2–4	172	3:7	75, 88

Ezra (*continued*)

3:8–10	53	4:8–10	20
3:8	74, 75, 89, 133, 142	4:8	18, 21–24, 96, 97
3:9	75, 98, 99, 106	4:9–10	21, 23, 24, 28, 97
3:10–13	75	4:9	21, 22
3:10	48, 53, 88, 213	4:10	22, 24, 26
3:11	48, 53, 54	4:11–22	25
3:12	52, 53, 56, 174, 202, 207, 214	4:11–16	24, 97
4–6	20, 170	4:11–13	17
4	18, 27, 63, 77, 85, 139, 149, 158, 174, 215, 244	4:11	21, 24
		4:12	125, 142, 174
4:1–25	174	4:14	125, 143
4:1–6	199	4:16	24
4:1–5	23, 117, 174	4:17–22	17, 76
4:1–3	48, 55, 75, 79, 80, 207	4:17	21, 22, 24, 26
4:1	18, 20, 28	4:18	19, 21, 25, 125
4:2–3	133	4:20	24, 26
4:2	22, 28, 76, 207	4:21–22	99
4:3	76	4:21	99, 138, 149, 246
4:4–6	75, 79, 80	4:22	138
4:4–5	48, 54, 76	4:23–24	55, 75, 79–81
4:4	20, 28	4:23	19, 21, 54, 76
4:5–24	55	4:24–5:6	174
4:5–10	18	4:24	48, 63, 64, 74, 76, 80, 84, 86, 139, 141, 170, 174, 244
4:5–6	58		
4:5	19, 23, 25, 28, 54, 57, 74, 76, 85, 171	4:42	157
		4:43–44	141
4:6–24	55, 117, 170, 174, 215, 243	5–10	2
		5–6	56, 115, 172
4:6–23	174, 175	5	63, 77, 139
4:6–16	76	5:1–6:24	48
4:6–11	1, 3, 17–19, 21, 25–27, 96	5:1–6:12	32
4:6–10	23	5:1–4	17
4:6–8	97, 98	5:1–2	64, 75, 79, 81, 141
4:6	18–21, 23, 25, 28, 48, 54, 56, 96, 98, 124, 138, 243	5:1	74, 76, 78, 81, 138, 172
		5:2	63, 76, 85, 133
4:7–24	32, 48, 54, 56, 118, 139, 140, 142, 199	5:3–6:22	133
		5:3–6:12	55
4:7–23	27	5:3–5	75, 76, 79
4:7–22	75, 79, 80	5:3	27, 213
4:7–11	20, 22, 28	5:5	19
4:7–10	23, 26, 123	5:6–17	75, 76, 80
4:7–8	20	5:8	148, 214
4:7	18–21, 23–25, 96, 97	5:9	213
4:8–6:18	21	5:11–13	213
4:8–11	20	5:12	55

5:13–6:5	173	7:13	173
5:14–15	141, 214	7:15–16	173
5:14	17, 135, 217	7:19	141
5:16	135	7:21–24	33
6	77, 170, 172	7:21	219, 220
6:1–12	75, 80	7:25	219
6:4	173, 174	7:26	26
6:6–12	28, 172	7:27–28	151
6:6–10	33	7:27	152, 171, 219
6:7	4, 136	7:28	152
6:8	4, 136	7:72–3:12	32
6:9	136	8	151, 154
6:11–12	89	8:1–20	205
6:13–22	32	8:1–14	33, 154
6:13–15	75, 80	8:1	151
6:14–17	48	8:4	158
6:14–15	139, 140	8:13–18	32
6:14	141	8:15–20	154, 155, 205
6:15	89, 214	8:15	33, 154
6:16–18	75, 80, 155	8:16	17
6:16	89	8:21–23	151
6:17	201	8:21	154, 155
6:18	89	8:22	151–58
6:19–22	75, 80, 155	8:23	154, 155
6:19	89	8:24–30	155
6:22	170	8:25–30	141
7–10	75, 103, 138, 151, 172, 217	8:31–34	154
7–8	32, 154, 155, 157, 160	8:31	155
7	129, 154	8:32–34	155
7:1–10:5	33	8:33	33, 141
7:1–8:36	175	8:35–36	152, 155
7:1–6	154	8:35	33, 201
7:1–5	222	9–10	32, 175, 194
7:1	219	9	220
7:5	220	9:1–5	194
7:6	4, 104, 151, 154, 175, 176, 219	9:1–2	194, 195
		9:1	33
7:7–9	95, 102, 106	9:3	220
7:7	151	9:4	103
7:8	96	9:5	220
7:9	96, 211	9:9	138, 139
7:10	175, 219	9:37	120
7:11	154, 176, 219, 220	10	103, 151
7:12–28	154	10:1	150, 219
7:12–26	172, 175	10:2	33, 219
7:12	25, 176, 219, 220	10:5	126, 219

Ezra (continued)		7:65	70
10:6	103, 150, 219	7:71	175
10:7	103, 138	7:72–8:1	17, 38–41
10:8	103	7:72	39, 125, 126, 175, 176, 211
10:9	138	8–10	158
10:10	94, 219	8	2, 14, 37–39, 42, 43, 102, 103, 113, 119, 151, 158, 175, 243
10:16	103, 219		
10:24	127		
10:44	125, 175	8:1–13	119, 175, 217
		8:1–12	37, 163
Nehemiah		8:1–2	176
1–13	149	8:1	42, 105, 158, 219, 220
1–8	58	8:2	105, 219, 220
1–7	14, 119, 151, 243	8:4	219, 220
1–6	35, 214	8:5–6	102
1–2	122	8:5	219
1:1–7:4	102	8:6	219
1:1–3	159	8:9–12	100, 101
1:2–3	159	8:9	100–102, 105, 162, 218–20
1:3	27, 138, 159		
2	154	8:10	100, 101
2:1–10	154	8:11	101, 102
2:1–6	151	8:13–9:37	163
2:3	138	8:13–18	38, 43, 163
2:7–9	151	8:13	163, 219
2:7–8	137, 151	9–13	14
2:8–9	151	9–12	163
2:8	150, 159	9–10	119
2:9–11	152	9	163
2:9	151, 152, 154–56	9:6	93
2:13	138	10:2	218
2:17	138, 159	10:31	218
2:19	27	10:32	218
3:1	160, 220	10:33–40	218
3:20	220	11	119
3:33	27	11:10	161
4:1–2	27	12:1	133
5	35	12:6	161
5:15	159	12:12–26	218
6:1–9	159	12:19	161
6:1	27	12:26	219
6:6	27	12:27–43	159
6:10–11	159	12:33	37
7–8	42	12:36	37, 219
7	38, 39, 119, 151, 205, 207	12:44–47	218
7:7	133	12:47	133, 219

ANCIENT SOURCES

13	129, 160	35–36	14, 17, 32, 38, 79, 113, 211, 225, 226, 229, 235, 243
13:4–14	147		
13:4–13	218		
13:4–9	160, 161	35	7, 167, 169, 177, 212, 234
13:4	220	35:1–36:21	168
13:7	220	35:1–19	32, 229
13:10–14	161	35:1–6	169
13:15–27	218	35:1	233
13:18–22	159	35:7–9	169
13:23–28	218	35:8	173
13:23–27	159	35:10	169
13:28–29	1160	35:11–15	169
13:28	220	35:16	169
13:29–31	218	35:17–19	169
13:30–31	160	35:19	168, 169, 212, 229
49:13	161	35:19 LXX	230, 234
		35:20–36:21	32
1 Chronicles		35:20–26	229, 232
1:1	232	35:20	229, 234
3:19–20	135	35:21–22	226
3:19	133	35:21	226, 227
5:26	170	35:22	227
9:10	161	35:23–24	227, 228
10	111	35:23	7, 228
11:10–47	123	36	33, 213, 214
11:10	123	36:14	233
11:11	123	36:17	214
14	245	36:18	214
24:7	161	36:19	214
		36:20	213, 214
2 Chronicles		36:21	33, 211
1	245	36:22–23	33, 112, 213
4	141	36:23	112
24:14	141		
30:6	170	APOCRYPHA	
33	232	1 Esdras	
33:9	232	1–7	66, 84, 87, 92
33:18–19	115	1–6	66
34	7, 167, 168, 212, 231, 233, 234	1	6, 34, 38, 43, 127, 169, 177, 209, 210
34:1	232	1:1–58	79
34:19–28	233	1:1–22	32, 194, 201
34:24	233	1:1–6	169
34:25	233	1:1	167, 168, 211, 212
34:28	228, 233	1:7–9	169
34:33	233	1:10	169

1 Esdras (*continued*)		2:4–6	46
1:11–15	169	2:4	214
1:16	169, 177	2:6	173
1:17–20	169	2:7–8	46
1:17	217	2:8	173
1:18	169	2:9–14	47
1:20–21	201	2:9–13	173
1:20	194	2:9	46
1:21–22	7, 33, 167–69, 177, 212, 228–30, 232–35	2:10–25	149
		2:10–14	58
1:21	7, 228, 230, 232, 233, 235	2:10–12	203
1:22	7, 229–35	2:10–11	46, 47
1:23–58	194	2:11	49
1:23–55	32, 213	2:13–14	203
1:23	234	2:13	203
1:25	226	2:14–15	55
1:26	227	2:14	47, 49, 203
1:27	228	2:15–26	63
1:28	228	2:15–25	32, 34, 35, 49, 50, 52, 117, 170, 174, 175, 215
1:31	231		
1:39–42	194	2:15–24	77–80
1:40	231	2:15–16	123
1:43–46	194	2:15	1, 3, 17–19, 21–25, 51, 63, 96–98, 124, 203
1:46–58	88		
1:46–57	194	2:16–30	139, 197, 243
1:47	233	2:16–18	17
1:53	214	2:16	24, 51, 124
1:54	214	2:17–30	194
1:55–56	214	2:17	49, 51, 58, 125, 174, 215
1:55	211, 214	2:18	142, 215
1:56	214	2:20	143
2–7	6, 56, 127, 128, 211	2:21–24	17
2–6	52	2:21	24
2	2, 18, 21, 27, 38, 42, 46–49, 51, 52, 55, 58, 115, 118, 174	2:22–24	175
		2:23	246
2:1–16	194	2:24	99
2:1–15	139, 140	2:25	47, 49, 51, 55, 74, 77–81, 86, 115, 157, 170, 171, 174, 215
2:1–14	32, 34, 35, 46, 47, 49, 77, 79, 80, 173, 174		
		2:28	138
2:1–7	192	2:30	3, 197
2:1–6	46	2:31	64
2:1–5	33	3–6	170
2:1–2	88	3–5	67, 157
2:1	49, 54, 195	3–4	32–35, 43, 46, 61, 116, 150, 187–89
2:2	47, 53		
2:3	173		

3	115, 181	4:61	47, 134
3:1–5:6	11, 32, 34, 46, 47, 134, 193, 194, 199, 216	4:62–63	134, 215
		4:63	47, 149
3:1–5:3	77–79, 81, 246	5–9	2, 38, 42
3:1–5:1	80	5–7	48, 49, 51, 52, 55, 56
3:1–4:41	179, 184, 190	5–6	58
3:1–4:5	63	5	47, 57, 116, 129, 205
3:1–3	33, 68	5:1–45	34
3:1	180	5:1–6	47, 122, 170, 171
3:2	180	5:1	47, 122
3:5	66	5:2–3	47
3:6	180	5:2	47, 151, 152, 157, 158
3:7	5, 179, 181	5:4–45	77–80
3:14	5, 180–83	5:4–42	49
3:21–22	173	5:4–5	122
4	78	5:4	2
4:1–5:63	174	5:5–6	134, 135, 194
4:1–12	187	5:5	47, 133, 135, 216
4:7–24	63	5:6	46, 47
4:13	134, 135, 171, 194	5:7–6:1	51
4:40	70	5:7–70	122
4:42–5:6	47, 200	5:7–46	63
4:42–63	134, 171, 199	5:7–45	32, 117, 170, 171, 175
4:42–46	172	5:7–42	47
4:42	66	5:7–35	194
4:43–46	247	5:7–8	122
4:43–45	215	5:7	204
4:43–44	135	5:8	161, 200, 218, 219
4:43	46	5:9–23	205
4:44–45	174	5:24–35	205
4:44	47	5:31–32	89
4:45–46	46	5:32–33	89
4:45	2, 68, 69	5:36–43	194
4:47–57	195	5:36–40	205
4:47–56	46, 171	5:38	47
4:47–49	47	5:39–40	194
4:47–48	4, 137, 215	5:40	70, 161, 218–20
4:48	172	5:41–45	35
4:50–57	172	5:42–43	205
4:50	2, 68, 148, 149	5:43–7:9	49, 50
4:51	215	5:43–6:1	50
4:54–56	47	5:43–70	52
4:55	215	5:43–62	51, 54
4:57	46, 135	5:43–45	49
4:59	68	5:43	49, 51–53
4:60	171, 177	5:44–45	81

1 Esdras (*continued*)		5:67–69	50
5:44	58	5:69–70	23, 47, 50, 54, 77–81
5:45–46	38, 40–42, 194	5:69	207
5:45	42, 150, 245	5:70–6:1	55, 56
5:46–70	32, 171	5:70	50–52, 54, 57, 58, 74, 77, 78, 84, 116, 171
5:46–62	34, 78–81		
5:46–53	35	5:71	84
5:46–52	77	5:72–73	199
5:46–48	49	6–7	115
5:46–47	89	6	32, 47, 195
5:46	150, 245	6:1–33	34, 50
5:47–50	195, 201	6:1–4	17
5:47	149, 150	6:1–2	35, 77, 79, 81, 195
5:48	133	6:1	3, 51, 54, 74, 77, 78, 84, 85, 171
5:49	49, 91		
5:50–53	195	6:2	133
5:50–52	201	6:3–22	195
5:50	208	6:3–21	35
5:51–52	105, 208	6:3–6	77, 79
5:51	105, 201	6:3	85
5:52–53	49	6:7–21	77, 79, 80
5:52	51	6:8–9	214
5:53–54	47, 53	6:8	148, 149, 245
5:53	47, 49, 53, 88	6:16–25	173
5:54–70	35	6:17	17
5:54–65	195, 201	6:18	4, 135, 136
5:54–62	51	6:20	135
5:54–55	49	6:22–7:15	35
5:54	74, 77, 78	6:22–33	77, 79, 80
5:55	51, 88	6:23–34	195
5:56–69	50	6:23–31	35
5:56	49, 51–53, 89, 98, 99, 133, 214	6:24	174
		6:26–33	172
5:57–62	50	6:26	216, 217
5:57	50, 89	6:27	4, 135, 136
5:59–62	50	6:28	216
5:59–60	49	6:29	4, 135, 136
5:59	51–53, 214	7	32, 169, 170
5:60	51–53, 56, 214	7:1–9	34
5:61–62	49	7:1–6	195
5:63–70	23, 34, 35, 51, 78	7:1–5	77, 79, 80
5:63–68	77–81	7:1–4	50
5:63	202, 207	7:3–5	140
5:66–73	195	7:4	50, 51, 140, 175
5:66–71	207	7:5	50, 89
5:66	51	7:6–9	50, 77, 80, 89

ANCIENT SOURCES 281

7:7–9	195, 201	8:63	33
7:8	201	8:65–9:36	32, 175
7:9	245	8:65–87	34
7:10–15	34, 62, 77, 80, 195, 201	8:66	33, 201
7:10	89, 169	8:67	195
7:13–15	66	8:68–9:36	195
7:15	170	8:68–69	233
8–9	6, 35, 127, 211	8:68	220
8	33, 177, 195	8:69	103
8:1–64	32, 175	8:70	220
8:1–27	34	8:78	245
8:1–2	222	8:81	138, 139
8:1	175	8:85	207
8:3	219, 220	8:88–9:36	34
8:4	4, 104, 151	8:88	150, 245
8:5–6	95	8:89	33, 70
8:6	211	8:91–99	194
8:8	176, 220	8:92	126
8:9–24	172, 175	9	38, 42
8:9	25, 176, 220	9:1	150, 245
8:17	196	9:2	103
8:18–22	195	9:3	103
8:19	176	9:4	103
8:23	176	9:7	94
8:24	26	9:15	103
8:25–27	151	9:18–36	195
8:25	171, 177, 219	9:24–25	127
8:27	152	9:27–55	37
8:28–64	34	9:36–55	119
8:28–49	195, 205	9:36	125, 175
8:28–48	34	9:37–38	39
8:28–40	33	9:37–55	32, 34, 126, 175, 176, 195
8:39	33		
8:42–49	205	9:37–38	17, 38–42
8:42	33	9:37	39, 42, 125–27, 175, 176, 211
8:43–44	17		
8:50–53	151	9:38	42
8:51–52	151, 152	9:39	6, 105, 158, 220
8:52	151, 152	9:40	105, 161, 220
8:54–60	196	9:41	176
8:54	195	9:42	158, 176, 220
8:55–57	195, 203	9:46	173
8:56	33	9:49–55	100–102
8:58	195	9:49	105, 161, 162, 176, 218–20
8:62–64	196		
8:62	33, 195	9:50	102

1 Esdras (*continued*)		NEW TESTAMENT	
9:52	101	Mark	
9:55	62, 176, 177, 199	1:15–45	24
11:2	173	2:1–12	24
12:35	173		
19	220	PSEUDEPIGRAPHA	
		Letter of Aristeas	
Esdras β		46–50	200
2.70–3.1	40	184–194	171
17.73–18.1	39–41		
		BABYLONIAN TALMUD	
Sirach		*Sanhedrin*	
44:1–50:28	221	38a	161
44:1–50:24	221		
44:1–15	146	QUMRAN	
45:9–30	222	*Genesis Apocryphon*	
47:2–11	222	XXI, 23	242
47:12–23	222		
49:2–3	234	JOSEPHUS	
49:7–10	222	*Antiquities*	
49:11–13	222	11.1–158	131
49:13	16	11.1.1–3 §§1–11	35
50:1–36	222	11.1.3 §§11	35
50:1–4	222	11.1.3 §§12–18	35
50:1	222	11.1.3 §13	35
50:24	222	11.2.1–2 §§20–30	35
		11.2.1 §§19–20	35
1 Maccabees		11.3.1–9 §§31–67	35
15:16	183	11.3.10 §§68–74	35
		11.4.1 §§75–78	35
2 Maccabees		11.4.2–4 §§79–88	35
1	199, 201	11.4.4 §§89–94	35
1:18–36	37, 161, 199, 200, 202	11.4.4 §93	35
1:18	199	11.4.5 §§95–96	35
1:19–23	199	11.4.6–8 §§97–110	35
1:20	199	11.4.8–9 §§111–19	35
1:24–29	200	11.5–6	121
1:27	176, 200	11.5–6 §80	121
1:29	200	11.5–6 §106	121
1:32	199	11.5–6 §158	121, 122
1:33–35	199	11.5–6 §§159–173	122
2:7	176	11.5–6 §§174–183	122
2:13	37	11.5–6 §183	121, 122
2:18	176	11.5.1–5 §§120–57	35
10:15–17	69	11.5.5	161
10:29	180	11.5.5 §158	35

11.5.8	160	Plato	
11.19–30	20	*Cratylus*	
11.19	23	391C	187
11.20	23		
11.21–30	140	*Meno*	
11.21	21–23	91e	185
11.26	22, 24		
11.93	4, 136	*Protagoras*	
12.138–44	172	322	185

GREEK/ROMAN/
CLASSICAL WORKS

Theaetetus
161C — 187

Athenaios
6.211d — 67

Pliny
Epistulae
1.102 — 187

Bion of Phlossa
2.1–8 — 67

Polybius
30.25.16 — 184

Cassius Dio
52 — 186
52.1–41 — 186
69.8.3 — 187

Tomas of Kempis
De Imitatione Christi
1.5.2 — 66

Diodorus Siculus
40.5–6 — 176

Vit. Apoll.
5.32–37 — 187

Herodotus
Histories
1.14 — 202
3.80–82 — 5, 184
4.110 — 198
6.43.3 — 184
6.129–30 — 67, 188

Ptolemy Philadelphus
Revenue Law
15.4 — 180

LIST OF CONTRIBUTORS

BOB BECKING is Senior Professor for Bible, Religion and Identity in the Faculty of Humanities at the University of Utrecht. Among his most recent publications are *From David to Gedaliah: The Book of Kings as Story and History* (Vandenhoeck & Ruprecht, 2007). He is co-editor of *From Babylon to Eternity: The Exile Remembered and Constructed in Text and Tradition* (Equinox, 2010), and *Out of Paradise: Eve and Adam and Their Interpreters* (Sheffield Phoenix, 2011).

KRISTIN DE TROYER is Professor of Hebrew Bible/Old Testament at the School of Divinity at the University of St. Andrews in Scotland. Among her many publications is the recently published Schoyen Old Greek Leviticus papyrus in *Papyrologica Florentina*, XL (Gonnelli, 2010). She also co-edited *Reading the Present in the Qumran Library: The Perception of the Contemporary by Means of Scriptural Interpretations* (Society of Biblical Literature, 2005).

LISBETH S. FRIED is Visiting Scholar in the Frankel Center for Judaic Studies and the Department of Near Eastern Studies at the University of Michigan. Her publications include *The Priest and the Great King: Temple Palace Relations in the Persian Empire* (Eisenbrauns, 2004), as well as numerous articles and reviews.

DEIRDRE N. FULTON is a graduate student at Pennsylvania State University in the Department of History and Religious Studies. Recently she has co-edited and published in *Exile and Restoration: Essays in Memory of Peter R. Ackroyd* (T&T Clark Continuum, 2009).

LESTER L. GRABBE is Professor of Hebrew Bible and Early Judaism at the University of Hull. His numerous publications include *A History of the Jews and Judaism in the Second Temple Period*, and *Ancient Israel: What Do We Know and How Do We Know It?* (T&T Clark International, 2006 and 2008).

SEBASTIAN GRAETZ is Professor for Old Testament at the University of Mainz. His main research is on the books of Ezra and Nehemiah, the Megillot, and the history of Ancient Israel in the Second Temple Period. His most recent book is *Das Edikt des Artaxerxes: Eine Untersuchung zum Religion-politischen und Historischen Umfeld von Esra 7,12-12* (De Gruyter, 2004).

PAUL B. HARVEY, JR. teaches classical languages and ancient history in the Departments of Classical and Ancient Mediterranean Studies and of History at the Pennsylvania State University. He has published studies on a range of classical Roman authors and has edited two volumes in the series *Decreta Regni Mediaevalis Hungariae*. He has contributed to and co-edited *Religion in Republican Italy* (Cambridge University Press, 2006), and *"Maxima Debetur Magistro Reverentia": Essays on Rome and the Roman Tradition in Honor of Russell T. Scott* (New Press, 2009).

SYLVIE HONIGMAN is Senior Lecturer in Ancient Greek History in the Department of History at Tel Aviv University. She published *The Septuagint and Homeric Scholarship in Alexandria: Study in the Narrative of the "Letter of Aristeas"* (Routledge, 2003).

SARA JAPHET is Yehezkel Kaufmann Professor of Bible at the Hebrew University of Jerusalem and currently a fellow at the Katz Center for advanced Judaic Studies in Philadelphia. She most recently authored *Collected Studies in Biblical Exegesis* (Mosad Bialik, 2008). She is also the editor of *Shnaton—An Annual for Biblical and Ancient Near Eastern Studies*.

RALPH W. KLEIN is Christ Seminary-Seminex Professor of Old Testament Emeritus at the Lutheran School of Theology at Chicago. In 2006 he published *1 Chronicles* in the Hermeneia Commentary Series; *2 Chronicles* is forthcoming in 2011.

GARY N. KNOPPERS is Edwin Erle Sparks Professor of Classics and Ancient Mediterranean Studies, Religious Studies, and Jewish Studies at the Pennsylvania State University. Recent co-edited publications include *The Pentateuch as Torah: New Models for Understanding Its Promulgation and Acceptance* (Eisenbrauns, 2007), and *Community Identity in Judean Historiography: Biblical and Comparative Perspectives* (Eisenbrauns, 2009).

JUHA PAKKALA, is Docent and University Lecturer at the University of Helsinki. He was recognized with a European Young Investigator Award in 2006. His monographs include *Intolerant Monolatry in the Deuteronomistic History* (Finnish Exegetical Society, 1999), and *Ezra the Scribe* (De Gruyter, 2004).

CONTRIBUTORS

ADRIAN SCHENKER is Professor Emeritus for Old Testament of the University of Fribourg, Switzerland. He is a member and coordinator of the Editorial Committee of the *Biblia Hebraica Quinta,* and has done research in the fields of biblical law, biblical theology, and especially the field of text history and text criticism of the Hebrew Bible. His most recent major publication is *Die früheste Textgeschichte der hebräischen Bibel* (Kohlhammer, 2011).

ZIPORA TALSHIR is Professor of Biblical Studies in the Department of Bible Archaeology and Near Eastern Studies, at Ben-Gurion University of the Negev, Israel. She is editor of the *Book of Chronicles* for the *Biblia Hebraica Quinta* and general editor of the Former Prophets for the Oxford Hebrew Bible. Her noteworthy publications include *I Esdras—From Origin to Translation* (Scholars Press, 1999), *I Esdras—A Text-Critical Commentary* (Society of Biblical Literature, 2001). She is co-editor of *The Literature of the Hebrew Bible—Introductions and Studies* (Yad Ben-Zvi, 2011).

JAMES VANDERKAM is the John A. O'Brien Professor of Hebrew Scriptures in the Department of Theology at the University of Notre Dame and General Editor of the *Journal of Biblical Literature.* He is the author of a number of books, including *From Joshua to Caiaphas: High Priests after the Exile* (Fortress, 2004), and *From Revelation to Canon: Studies in the Hebrew Bible and Second Temple Literature* (Brill, 2000).

HUGH G. M. WILLIAMSON is the Regius Professor of Hebrew at the University of Oxford, a Student of Christ Church, and a Fellow of the British Academy. His most recent major publication was a commentary on *Isaiah 1–5,* the first of three volumes in the International Critical Commentary series.

JACOB L. WRIGHT is Assistant Professor of Hebrew Bible at Candler School of Theology and serves as the Director of Graduate Studies in the Tam Institute of Jewish Studies of Emory University. His first book, *Rebuilding Identity: The Nehemiah Memoir and Its Earliest Readers* (De Gruyter, 2004), won the Sir John Templeton Award. His current research focuses on war, military organization, and political identities in the ancient Near East, Israel, and Greece.

www.ingramcontent.com/pod-product-compliance
Lightning Source LLC
Chambersburg PA
CBHW031707230426
43668CB00006B/141